CLASS

From Witchcraft to Christ

Set Free to Serve Christ

Spiritual Warfare

This omnibus edition first published 2001

ISBN 0 85476 950 1

Published by
KINGSWAY PUBLICATIONS
Lottbridge Drove, Eastbourne, BN23 6NT, England.
Email: books@kingsway.co.uk

Designed and produced for the publishers by
Bookprint Creative Services, P. O. Box 827, BN21 3YJ, England.
Printed in Great Britain.

Reproduced from the original typesetting
of the single-volume editions.

From Witchcraft to Christ

DOREEN IRVINE

KINGSWAY PUBLICATIONS
EASTBOURNE

Contents

AUTHOR'S NOTE

I have of necessity omitted many details of my former life, the people I was associated with at this time and other personal details.

I should also point out that the time and sequence of events described in my book covers a very wide period in my life and so it is advisable that they do not be read as a continuing sequence within an assumed time span. The reason for this was to present a readable account of part of my life and to avoid having to relate definite dates and situations with known persons living or dead.

Foreword

IN 1968, while conducting a church anniversary service in a city suburb, I was deeply moved and greatly encouraged to see in the congregation a woman I had not met since her deliverance from forty-seven demons three years previously. Once a prostitute, heroin addict, witch, satanist and a victim of abominable practices, here she was now radiant with the glory of the Lord and rejoicing in him. It wasn't by chance that we were singing

Long my imprisoned spirit lay
Fast bound in sin and nature's night;
Thine eye diffused a quickening ray,
I woke, the dungeon flamed with light.
My chains fell off, my heart was free,
I rose, went forth, and followed Thee.

How especially true this was of her! Yes, it was Doreen Irvine.

When I spoke with her after the service Doreen told me that her time was now spent in dealing with the kind of people with whom she had mixed in past years, and in speaking to groups seeking illumination and instruction in the ministry of deliverance. What impressed me most was that, three years before, the Holy Spirit had restrained me from continuing immediate contact with her. But now he confirmed for me that what he begins he continues and completes in his own perfect way and time.

When I recall the experiences through which the Lord took me in relation to Doreen's emancipation, I marvel at his authority, his mercy and his compassion. She gives her own vivid and vibrant account in this book.

It was in Bristol in June 1964 that our paths first crossed. Doreen's condition was that of unbelievable evil, for her life had been immersed in debauchery of a kind I had never before come across. For seven months I knew what it was to contest the terrible powers of evil in her ruined life. On the occasion of every session of exorcism, she had to be restrained by Christian men and women in prayerful support.

The New Testament came alive as we battled against demons of different character who contested the ground they had in her life. With extraordinary intelligence, utterly beyond the mere human, they acted and spoke through her. We were driven to the Bible to discover what we needed to know relative to this particular phenomenon of evil. I remember so well the Sunday night in February 1965 when the last of the forty-seven demons was expelled from her tormented and tortured being, so ending seven harrowing months of hell in a life-and-death struggle.

Doreen is a veritable trophy of God's grace. The power of God was demonstrated in her supernatural deliverance by the dynamic authority of the Lord Jesus Christ. All the credit and glory go to him. It was my awful privilege simply to be his agent. There are facts of an alarming nature which it would be unwise to divulge, but I have revealed some aspects of my involvement with Doreen in my book, *Aid Us in Our Strife* (Vol 2), which fills in much about which Doreen herself was unaware at the times of ministry.

In a personal note to me Doreen said:

All I know is that I am *free* for ever from demons. I

went to the doctors, and they are all amazed at my marvellous recovery. They cannot understand what has happened to me. I've been to London and been examined by top brain specialists there. My X-rays are normal since the demons have gone. Previous brain scans and X-rays of my cranium had revealed extensive brain damage, and I was classified as being in a serious and well-nigh hopeless state neurologically and physically. In the psychiatric category I was a very bad and perplexing patient. One thing they cannot get away from, and that is that I was a hopeless case. I was a very dangerous "schizophrenic" (so called) with only six months at the outside to live. It was such a marvel, and the source of much discussion among the doctors. No one there [London] or here [Bristol] can explain it. But I know that Jesus lives, and he is the One who has done it. Glory be to God! Once I was in darkness, thick and black, controlled by powers of evil within. Once I was bound, now I am *free*. It's been a long road to deliverance—a year in fact, since the first step was taken at the Colston Hall at that Eric Hutchings crusade meeting. But it's over, and I am out of darkness. Praise be to God!

Subsequent events from 1965 until 1994 have validated the reality of the work of God in this former queen of witches. She has been graciously used by the Lord in this and other lands to advocate his power to save and deliver from satanic bondage and hell.

During the thirty years since our first contact, I have had periodic fellowship with Doreen, and have marvelled at the way she has been enabled to witness clearly and courageously through good report and ill, to expose the works of the devil, and to honour him to whom she owes everything.

This book makes a vital contribution in warning those who indulge in the deep and dangerous things of Satan; it serves to open the eyes of Christians to the stark reality of the demonic in these critical times, and points positively to the means of grace for salvation and deliverance through our Lord Jesus Christ. It is my prayer that the Holy Spirit will use this new edition to magnify the name of our all-powerful Redeemer. "Thanks be to God who gives us the victory through our Lord Jesus Christ."

Arthur Neil
Torbay, 1994

CHAPTER ONE

Life's Early Morning

THAT Sunday morning in September 1939 began in the East End of London like any other Sunday. I was born there, and I knew its blend of sounds and way of life.

The voices of children at play in the streets mingled with the excited barking of dogs. Clad only in my knickers, I was having my weekly wash at the rough wooden table in the kitchen of our tenement home. The dirt from the grimy street seemed reluctant to leave my knees as my mother scrubbed them with a piece of rough flannel.

The radio in a corner of the bare room added a sort of accompaniment to the scrubbing operation. My mother paused as the solemn stroke of Big Ben rang from the radio set. I, at the age of seven, was more interested in the beckoning sound of play from the streets than in the droning sound from the radio.

"Oh, my God!" cried my mother suddenly, dropping the soap to the floor.

"What's up, Mum?" I asked.

"It's war, war. . . ."

Almost as she said the word – which I little understood – the hollow frightening wail of an air-raid alert rang out over the city. It was a sound I was to hear frequently in the months ahead.

By early summer of 1940 the air-raids had increased so greatly that we were evacuated to Uxbridge – not a great move in terms of geographical distance, for Uxbridge lies only sixteen miles from London. Here a true Cockney kid – a cheeky one – whose early years had been spent within the sound of Bow Bells, was to spend the rest of her childhood, with all the problems that came with it.

Uxbridge lies at the end of the Metropolitan Line and is now the home of many London commuters. Not a very large town, it is, however, busy with a steady flow of traffic mainly on the London Road. The beautiful surrounding countryside, in the neighbourhood of Windsor, is popular with Londoners seeking week-end recreation. Two rivers run through Uxbridge, also small streams and a canal, all giving rise to industries needing water.

On the edge of the town is a large moor, and it was near here that our new home stood: a new council house on a small estate. Other evacuee families lived nearby in their "home from home."

Our house was treated with no great respect by the tenants, who had come from an East-end slum. The front gate was ripped off for fire-wood. The garden, soon a wilderness, fronted a house that became increasingly untidy.

Home life centred in the kitchen which was dirty and scantily furnished. Dominating the room was a large, rough wooden table, on which I sat to have my weekly wash. The tablecloth was an old newspaper, patterned with news from the war fronts. In the centre of the table stood a huge brown teapot, very rarely empty, as someone was always making tea. A bottle of milk, watered down to make it go farther, had its place near the brown teapot.

There were only three chairs in the kitchen. No rugs or lino covered the bare boards of the floor. No curtains hung from the windows – just old sacks that also served as black-out blinds.

Very few meals were eaten at the table. My four young sisters and I had to sit on the floor or the back doorstep to eat whatever we had given us, which was not much – mostly

10

bread and lard. We drank tea from a jam jar. I had to hold my jam jar with the end of my dress as it was so hot.

"Why can't we have meat and roast potatoes and cake, Mum?" I asked one day. "My friend 'round the corner does."

"We can't afford things like that, so stop moaning and eat what you've got."

"Do yer need a lot of money, Mum, to buy meat, potatoes, and cake?" I persisted.

"Yes. So be a good girl and be satisfied with what you've got."

But my mum's answer didn't satisfy me any more than my diet did. My curiosity grew, and one day when school was over, I decided to find out more.

It was a warm spring day, and the trees and lawns were lovely. The blossoms looked so beautiful, in fact, that I wanted to climb up into the pink-laden branches.

Beyond the trees were well-built, expensive properties, where the "posh people" lived. This little girl, open-mouthed in wonder, somehow managed to peer through the windows of one or two of the nice houses.

It was like looking into another world: furniture so highly polished you could see your face in it, big, soft-looking chairs, coloured carpets, and lovely, lace tablecloths.

"I wonder what it's like to live in a house like that?" I asked myself. "I wonder what it's like upstairs. And fancy having such lovely trees growing in the garden!"

I remembered that my friend who lived 'round the corner had a real bed with white sheets – not at all like my bed, which wasn't a bed at all, only a makeshift pile of dirty coats on the floor, upstairs. Mum and dad had the only bed in the house, but it was without sheets too.

I giggled when I thought how the large brass knobs of the bed often fell to the floor with a loud clang. Sometimes that happened late at night, when dad stumbled in from his night out at the pub.

"Ah, well."

After one final, envious look at the houses and the lovely trees I made my way home.

No one asked me why I was home late from school, although I nearly lost my tea. Keeping the exploration a secret, I decided I would go again another day. This experience was the first discovery of beauty in the life of a sensitive, neglected little girl. It made me wonder about a lot of things.

I was the eldest of five girls and as "big sister" was often left to look after the rest of the family (even though I was still very young myself). Dad worked as a refuse collecter for the local council – at least when he was sober. My mum, thin and worried, often had to go out late at night into the blacked-out streets in search of him. In a strange way she always made excuses for his drinking habits and blamed them on the war.

With my keen sense of humour and vivid imagination I carried out my family responsibilities easily. My younger sisters loved me, even though I took a page from the tough book of life as I observed it and didn't think twice about giving them a sharp box around the ears when the situation demanded it. In fact, my own special brand of discipline became widely known.

No one minded – after all, it was my job to look after them. And after others too – lots of them – as neighbours also left their children in my tender care. The little ones looked up to me and respected me. Because I was bigger, had a good sense of humour, and was, in fact, a born leader, like a youthful Pied Piper of Uxbridge I was followed by a selection of grubby but smiling children.

And of course by my dog.

Animals played a lively part in my life. The back garden was full of them. My father kept chickens, although there were never any eggs to eat. Perhaps dad sold the eggs in the pub to obtain more money for drink.

"Him and his beer," I would say.

The garden also contained two rabbits, a couple of ferrets, many cats, and a goat. But the family dog – Bessie, a black Labrador – was my favourite and was known everywhere as "Doreen's dog." Bessie followed me everywhere I went.

With such company I needed wide, open spaces. Fortunately there were several places to have adventures: two recreation grounds, the river banks, and a playing field, where the grass was always green and springy. My form of democratic decision-making was quite unique in someone so young.

"Now kids," I would address the grubby throng around me, "where shall we go tonight – the swing rec or the playing field?"

"The swing rec, Dor, the swing rec!" the children would shout.

I reflected for a moment and said, "No, we'll go to the river," and they duly followed me. The swing rec, with a multitude of playing apparatus, was a great favourite. But it was bound to be fun wherever Dor went.

The fun often inclined to mischief, and my nimble mind invented many pranks to keep my charges happy – even if the grown-ups were less amused.

One of my tricks was to assemble the children at the bus stop. When the bus approached I would solemnly hold out my hand. The driver dutifully slowed down. When the bus stopped, we would all race away laughing. But the trick didn't fool the driver for long. He got wise to us. Instead of stopping he accelerated, and with a broad grin at us he hurtled past.

One night when I and the children were passing the public house, we saw "Old Joe's" horse and cart outside, as usual. Old Joe was the local "rag and bone" merchant and was well known for his drunkenness. I had a sudden inspiration: why not unharness the horse and put him back to front between the shafts and wait to see what happened?

The docile old horse was very obliging, as led by me we performed the tricky operation. An hour or so later out came Old Joe, drunk as usual – so drunk in fact, he noticed nothing wrong as he stumbled up onto the cart.

"Yee up! Get up, there!" shouted Old Joe.

Imagine our shrieks of delight as the old horse obeyed and the cart with Old Joe went hurtling backward instead of forward. Old Joe couldn't understand it at all and swore and shouted at the poor horse, while we were doubled up in fits of laughter.

Not all the tricks were so harmless however – like the petty thefts from the local shops. But these acts were prompted by my concern for the children, who were always hungry and never had sweets and other nice things to eat that some of the other children enjoyed. The only way to get them was to steal them.

My strategy was simple. Somehow I would obtain a penny or two, usually by begging from a passer-by, then walk into the sweet shop with the children. Whilst the shop-keeper's attention was taken up by me and my penny, the other children would be helping themselves to what they wanted.

The cake shop was another easy target where it was easy to grab a bun from the display in the window if you were quick – and I was quick. On one occasion we nearly got caught. My sister snatched a bun, only to find that five more came with it. As they fell to the ground, she stopped to pick them up instead of running away at once. It was a near thing.

Had my mother known about this stealing she would have been angry, but in the face of her own worries mother was often apathetic. Life was too much of a struggle to worry about morality – or God. God! It was just like another swear word to me.

There were plenty of swear words in our house. My father's drinking habits were getting far worse, and he was often violent. I saw the cut lips and bruises on my mother s face. She always had black eyes.

I would run into the back garden. "Oh, God!" I would say aloud. "Don't let anything awful happen, oh, God!"

That word again. How readily it came to my lips!

What would happen to us all if things continued this way?

But it was the look of sadness and resignation on my mother's face that was the worst of all. I tried to push my fears away by thinking, "Perhaps things will be all right in a little while. Perhaps things will be different tomorrow."

One morning I felt mum's hand gently shaking me.

"Wake up, Dolly, wake up!"

Mum always called me Dolly, as I was so small for my age.

I sat bolt upright on the pile of dirty coats that were my bed.

"What's up, Mum? What's up?"

"Nothing's wrong, Dolly. I just want you to take this little note to the shop on the moor."

Even though it was early in the day, I did not fail to see the look of concern on my mother's face.

"Ain't yer got no money, Mum?"

"That's right. Now you be a good girl and hurry back home."

Asking for credit was now the only way my mother could feed her young family. Yet her pride dictated that she send her daughter early in the morning, when no one else was around.

I dressed quickly and was off. It was a long way for my young legs, and the morning was cold and windy. As I hurried along the main road, I looked up at the tall trees and saw the branches bending in the strong wind. I felt a sense of mystery as I watched the dark trees.

I paused at the entrance to the small graveyard, which was a short-cut to the shop. Familiar in the broad light of day, it looked so eerie in the wild dawn. Although I was afraid, remembrance of my mum's face drove me to begin my cautious way along the graveyard path, glancing over my shoulder as I went along. I was afraid that at any moment one of the graves would open and swallow me.

At last the other side was reached. Here I had to cross a small wooden bridge. Having fished for tiddlers in the stream below, I knew the bridge well, but today, creaking in the wind, it looked so different. In fact, everything looked different – larger, more menacing, and strangely new.

The bright lights at the little shop cheered me up a bit. The shopkeeper read the note and smiled at me.

"You're up early today."

He gave me a few groceries, and I retraced my steps home.

"All right, Dolly?" asked my mum.

"Yes, Mum. I'm just cold."

Mum made some cocoa, and we sat by the fire chatting as Uxbridge itself awoke to another day in war-time England.

I never forgot that early morning experience in the early morning years of my life. So many questions spun around in my little head – questions which I had never asked before.

"Where did the wind come from? Who made the trees so tall, and how long do they live? Why was I born? And what is it like to die?"

There seemed to be no one to whom I could put such questions. Mum had enough on her mind. Besides, I wasn't sure that mum would know about such matters.

I had become aware of life. What did it all mean?

Memories of my early years are stamped indelibly on my mind. So much happened – sad things, comical things, puzzling things, but not many happy things.

However, life is for living and not for brooding. Instead of brooding, I stored things up inside me.

In the summer holidays the sun always seemed to shine. The days were long and warm, and most of them were spent out of doors. I roamed the streets, often having fun until late at night. And always with my little band of followers.

We must have looked a very sorry sight. My constant attire summer and winter was a thin cotton dress and a matted jumper which seemed to last for years. Socks were an unknown luxury, and we often had no shoes to wear.

But at this stage of my life appearances didn't worry me, although at times I was aware of these things. After all, I was very young. This was still life's early morning.

CHAPTER TWO

The Fishing Trip

ALTHOUGH my father was usually drunk and often aggressive, I loved him with all my heart.

"If only he wouldn't drink so much and make mum unhappy," I thought.

Every penny he earned was spent on drink. Even the ration and clothing coupons were sold at the pub for more drink. What was left for clothes, food, or fuel? Still, he was *my dad*, and he did have his sober moments, even if they were few and far between. These times were precious to me.

Let us look at one of these rare events, for I recall it very clearly.

It was a fine summer morning, a Saturday, when there was no school. My dad was up early for a change, having a shave in the dingy kitchen. He was cheerful too and singing at the top of his voice.

Suddenly he called out, "Doreen, are you awake?"

"Yes, Dad," I answered.

"Are you coming fishing with me today?"

"Yes, Dad."

I could hardly believe my ears and couldn't dress fast enough. Dad got out the rusty old fishing tackle, and very soon father and daughter set off happily down the road, hand in hand.

When we reached the river, I watched my dad proudly as he cast the line. Dad was a good fisherman. He began talking about fish and how fish should be caught. I listened — not that I understood all he was saying. But it didn't matter.

18

Most important for me was that I was out with my dad, with no grubby children around.

I enjoyed every moment of that fishing trip as we sat side by side, chatting and laughing and watching the red float in the water. It was a perfect day, like those cloudless, sunny mornings we remember from childhood.

The clean, sweet air smelt fresh, as the summer breeze swept my long brown hair across my face. I felt good to be alive. The tall trees looked beautifully green. The mossy river bank was soft, the green rushes stately and peaceful. All the unhappiness of the past weeks seemed to melt away in the golden sunshine.

Apart from the singing of the birds and the gentle ripple of the river nothing could be heard. No one would believe there was a war on. Everything was so peaceful and still that it seemed *my dad* and I were the only ones alive in the whole wide world.

Little did my father know what else I was thinking.

"Perhaps dad won't want to drink anymore. Perhaps he will take me fishing with him instead. Everything would be so wonderful!"

These were the happy thoughts and this was the bright hope that filled my young heart.

"Time to go home now, Doreen," said my dad.

The time had passed so quickly. When dad got home, he put the few fish he had caught into the bath, where he always deposited his catch. The bathroom was never used for its proper purpose.

One time dad caught a large eel. My sister and I watched in awe as he filled the bath with water and put in the big eel. I remember standing on an old wooden box and poking the funny eel with a long stick – through the small window, as dad always locked the bathroom door.

If my hopes had risen that unforgettable Saturday, they were soon to be dashed, for as soon as dad had put the fish into the bath, he went straight to the pub and stayed there until closing time.

There were times when I felt I could hate my dad for all the unpleasantness he caused. At other times a great sense of pity for him would sweep over me. It was then I would try to please him by cleaning his big boots, hoping he in turn would take me on his knee and tell me how much he loved me. But I never heard the words I dearly longed to hear. The conflicting emotions of love, hate, and pity for my father only made me more confused and insecure than ever.

"If only someone really loved me," I would think sadly.

Life only seemed to worsen. My father drank more heavily, and mum always looked worried.

As the war progressed with alarming severity, more air-raids were made, and other fears were then added to my life. Anti-aircraft guns stood at the top of Chandler's Hill, not very far from my home. In the daytime the air-raids and the sound of gunfire were not so bad, but at night they were terrifying. On more than one night I was left alone to look after my sisters, while mum as usual was out looking for my dad. I was beginning to think that mum was right, and it was the war that caused dad to drink so much.

My four sisters would be very frightened, crying and clinging to me as we sat on the dirty coats that served as our beds.

"It will be all right, you'll see. I won't let anything happen to yer. I'll look after yer," I would say, trying hard not to show how frightened I too was.

When at last they fell asleep, tears would run down my cheeks – tears I had held back for the sake of my sisters. I felt utterly miserable and all alone. The strange, eerie light from the searchlights across the night sky lit the otherwise dark and bare room.

I would stand at the dirty windows and look up into the starry sky and then down into the street below, hoping to see mum and dad returning home. Sometimes I would stand there hours on end. It was then I would try to pray.

"Oh, God, please help me, and if You don't think I'm worth it, please do something for my sisters and don't bother about me. I know I'm not always very good, but I do try. Please, God, let it be all right for all of us – mum and dad and everybody."

Nothing changed for the better, however, and because I felt my prayers went unanswered, I finally decided that there was no God and did not pray again.

My four sisters and I went to Sunday school every week, but it was only to get us out of the way for a while so that dad could have some "peace and quiet." Dad came home from the pub stone drunk every Sunday afternoon, and my sisters and I were only too glad to get out of his way.

The Sunday school mission hall was just around the corner at Waterloo Road. I hardly listened to a word. In fact, I was most unruly and difficult to manage.

More than once I was sent out for disrupting the meetings, putting my own words to the hymns and choruses, and generally making life very difficult for the poor teachers, even throwing stones at the windows after being turned out for bad behaviour. Someone would then come out to chase me away. They never caught me – I was too quick for them.

We rough Cockneys sat apart from the better-dressed children, nearly all of whom were the children and friends of the adults who tried to teach us. I nicknamed these children "the posh kids" and made fun of their Sunday-best clothes, straw hats, and white socks.

When Doreen and her band of followers marched into Sunday school, battle commenced. I was the ringleader, and the other Cockney kids merely followed my lead. In my estimation Sunday school was just another place in which to have a bit of fun. Little did the teachers realize that if I had a hard and unhappy time at home during the week, I took it out on the Sunday school, and they bore the brunt of it on Sundays.

Nevertheless, the Sunday school teachers were patient and took an interest in me and my sisters. For no matter how many times I had to be turned out, no matter how unruly I was, the door was always open for me the next Sunday.

These incidents may be a source of encouragement to readers who are Sunday school teachers or youth workers, for as you read on you will see that the seed sown many years before my conversion did bring forth fruit.

The teachers may have felt that they were struggling in vain with me, but I never forgot those days at Sunday school. Occasionally I did pay some attention to what they were trying to say, and many times my conscience would be pricked as they spoke of the sin in boys' and girls' hearts and of the Saviour's love and forgiveness.

I could never sing these words from the *Golden Bells Hymn Book:*

> *There is a city fair;*
> *Closed are its gates to sin.*
> *Naught that defileth, naught that defileth,*
> *Can ever enter in.*

The words conjured up a picture of a pair of golden gates with an angel on both sides holding flaming swords and barring the way from the golden streets and the place called heaven. I knew there was sin in my heart. I thought there was no chance of my getting into heaven. The Sunday school teacher had told me that no sin could ever enter that city so fair.

"No one who steals can enter heaven."

No one who steals.

"That's me," I thought. "I will never get in, because it's steal or starve."

So I gave up any idea of getting into heaven. Still I would go to the mission hall Sunday after Sunday, if only to get lemonade and cake, and sometimes apples, after the meetings had finished – gifts the teachers offered to us Cockney kids.

Besides, there were the Sunday school outings and parties to think about. I was not going to miss those. My sisters and I had little else to look forward to. Christmas came and went each year with neither me nor my little sisters ever getting a single toy – or indeed anything else. It was the same on our birthdays – not one card, not one present.

The outings and parties at the mission, then, were very important indeed to all of us. My sisters and I were always the first children to arrive, sometimes waiting for hours before the doors opened.

When the air-raids were severe and I was frightened, I thought of the lessons I had heard at Sunday school. I considered prayer but in the end rejected it, thinking that Christianity was after all just a silly fairy tale.

When I was ten years old, however, I decided to join the C.A.W.G. Messengers, a group similar to the Brownies. Here I learned many interesting things, like tying knots, the Morse code, first-aid, etc.

The captain took a great deal of interest in me, and I in turn liked her very much. She gave me a uniform, knowing I would never get the money from my parents.

On Sundays, then, I was unruly and badly behaved, but on Monday evenings, when the Messengers met, I was as good as gold. The captain could hardly believe the reports she heard of my Sunday escapades.

One day she asked if I would like to go camping with the Messengers during the summer holidays, explaining that she would pay for me herself. Would I like to go! Why, I had never heard of anything more wonderful. I ran home and asked mum if I could go. Mum agreed.

I could hardly wait for the day to come. One week before

camp was to start captain drew me to one side and gave me all the things I would be needing for camp: scented soap, a soft flannel and towel, a new hairbrush and comb, tooth brush, and toothpaste, together with two new pairs of socks and a pair of pyjamas. I could only stand and stare at the lovely things, for I never before had such articles.

Captain said, "Tell no one I have given them to you. Take them home now, and bring them along when you go to camp."

She wanted me to be no different from any other Messenger. I was filled with gratitude and joy beyond my wildest dreams. Every now and then I would unwrap the small parcel to see if all the items were still safe and, of course, to have another long look at them.

At last the great day came. I was up with the lark. It was a Saturday, unlike any other I had known. I was the first around the corner to wait for the transport – hours before it was due to arrive.

Eventually it came, and I scrambled into the huge van with the other Messengers. All "the gang", as I always called them, plus my little sisters, were there to wave me good-bye. It was a proud moment in my life.

The campsite was situated in the beautiful countryside near Woking. Although it was not far from Uxbridge, it seemed like hundreds of miles away to me, who had never been on a bus ride.

I have never forgotten that glorious week away from home. We had the greatest fun playing in the woods, picking flowers, and running in and out among the trees. Campfire was just wonderful as we sat around it in a circle every evening, singing choruses. The fragrance of pine needles and the smoke from the fire mingled with the delicious smell of baked potatoes in their jackets and lingered in the warm evening air.

Yes, everything was too wonderful for mere words: the

crackling of twigs in the campfire, the singing of the birds in the woods nearby, and the sun like a big red rubber ball glowing behind the tall fir trees.

It seemed that all creatures, from the birds to the grass-hoppers, knew of the joy and utter contentment in my heart. My heart was singing, and even my quota of duties were a pleasure.

Sleeping in a real pair of pyjamas and under clean blankets was a delightful change from what I was used to. Cleaning my teeth was completely new to me. A change too was the good food – and plenty of it – the fresh air and spare time to do just what I liked. Even washing was an adventure – with the nice scented soap, soft flannel, and a big, fluffy towel to dry on.

Those seven days away from home were the happiest in my young life.

We were taken to a chapel on Sunday, and I enjoyed that too. I noticed that when the preacher spoke of Jesus dying on the cross, he wept real tears. That did impress me and made me feel very guilty about my bad behaviour at the mission hall in Uxbridge.

I didn't want the week to end but to last forever and ever, as I told the captain. But the day came to leave, and all the Messengers were busy packing the equipment into the van, ready for the trip home.

I was very sad but thought, "Oh, well, there's still the journey home and the ride in the van to look forward to."

All too soon we were back in Uxbridge. It seemed to take hours to get to camp, yet the journey home lasted only a short time.

Back in Uxbridge on the grimy estate, a grubby crowd of children, "the gang," was there to welcome me home as I jumped down from the huge van. The ugliness of home life was more evident than before, contrasting with the camp I had enjoyed so much.

I did not know then that in a strange way the camp had prepared me to become a different kind of messenger. I did not know that I, who had been fishing by the river bank, would one day hear God call me to be a fisher of men.

CHAPTER THREE

My Mum

AFTER my short holiday at camp with the C.A.W.G. Messengers life went on much the same as before. The fights and arguments at home were unbearable at times. I wondered where and when it was going to end. What would happen to us all – my father, mother, and young sisters?

I could hardly be the school's best pupil when my mind was preoccupied with such questions. I had been attending day school at St. John's Primary in Uxbridge but was never able to learn very much. The teachers, who did not understand my problems, were always telling me off. School was one long nightmare. I constantly got into trouble for being late, etc. Even if I did try, nothing went right.

"It's all right for them," I thought. "It's easy just to sit there and tell me off all the time."

"Maybe it's because of my clothes," I decided.

I was beginning to realize I was different from some of the other children. My hair was always untidy, and the nurse kept sending me home because I had lice. "Nitty Nora" I called her. I hated her.

"It's not fair. She's always picking on me and my small sisters. Why do the teachers poke their nose where they're not wanted? Why can't they leave me alone?"

I was an object of ridicule to other boys and girls, who were better dressed and well cared for. The ridicule hurt me as I was very sensitive, despite my outward show of bravado. Yells of "Flea head!" and "Yellow teeth!" followed me wherever I went. The teachers were as bad as some of the children and made unkind remarks about my appearance.

"I can't 'elp it, can I? I hate yer and yer rotten old school," I would say.

Inevitably I played truant many times. Instead of going to school I went off to the park for the day. On these occasions I would lie on the grass, gazing up at the tall poplar trees and the clouds, daydreaming about faraway places like Africa and India – which proved I had listened to something at school – wondering what it would be like to travel to those distant lands across the sea.

I missed school for other reasons too. Mum often kept me at home to look after my baby sister Sylvia, or simply because I had no shoes to wear.

There was one subject in which I excelled: P.T. I could run like a hare, jump like a frog, and swim like a fish. These accomplishments earned me a little respect from some of the children at day school.

But even here I had problems, for long ago the elastic had parted from my very old knickers, which had to be held up by a very large safety pin. You can imagine the loud laughter of the girls when I had to remove my dress for P.T.

One day I went to the churchyard near the little shop on the moor, intending to play there. As I wandered around, I stumbled across a children's communal grave.

"Violet May" was one of the names on the headstone. The name appealed to me, and I began to speak to the dead child, fully believing she heard and understood. In my loneliness I built a fantasy around that grave. It gave me the feeling of having a bond with someone. It was as if Violet May represented the gentle father I had never known, the kindly school teacher I had never met.

On my way to and from school I would stop to kneel

at the side of the grave, always bringing flowers I had taken from other graves. I would tell my new friend all my problems and share my fears with her. No one knew about the unusual friendship, for I regarded the meetings as secret and the dead child as my own special and private friend.

Other times I would go on expeditions to the top of a very large hill on the edge of town, picking bluebells or gathering conkers as I went. During the war an American camp was situated at the top of the hill, and I would creep under the hedge and through the barbed wire to watch the soldiers. When they came near, I would beg for chewing gum and chocolate. The Americans were kind and always gave me something. Then I would run back home and share the gum and chocolate with my sisters.

My fears throughout the years about the possible collapse of our family were soon to be realized. All love between my mum and dad had long since disappeared. Fights and rows, shouting and swearing were occurring every evening and during the daytime as well.

But the reason was different now. The rows were not about money or drink but about a strange woman. Who was this strange woman? I was puzzled. It was not long before I found out.

Dad got to know a woman who had recently lost her husband (he died in a mental hospital). Dad got friendly with her – too friendly, as far as my mum was concerned. Mum was broken-hearted and went to pieces right before my eyes. I was at a loss what to do. She was always crying, and I was afraid to leave her alone.

"Don't cry, Mum. It will be all right, you'll see," I would say in a desperate effort to comfort her.

"He has found someone else," my mum would say. "He doesn't want me anymore."

"I'll kill her if I get my hands on her," I would say, "and I mean it."

Life looked blacker than ever for me. Dark storm clouds

were gathering overhead, threatening to burst any moment. My faithful friend Bessie, the black Labrador, sensed something was very wrong, and she looked sadly at her little mistress with her big brown eyes.

"Good old Bessie." I would stroke her black head. "You understand, don't yer, old girl."

One fateful evening I returned home from play only to find yet again that mum was not there. I sighed as I saw the fire was out and there was no more fuel. The house was freezing cold. I got busy and gave my sisters some bread and margarine and then sent them off to bed on their usual heap of dirty coats. They were soon fast asleep, and I was alone.

It was dark outside now, and the night light had gone out. I was afraid that both mum and dad had left us all forever. I buried my face in my hands and wept.

Suddenly I heard my father's voice and what seemed like a great crowd coming in through the front door. I tiptoed out on the landing to listen and heard something about the canal. At that I rushed downstairs.

There was my mum sitting on a chair, a grey blanket wrapped over her wet clothes. Several neighbours and an irate father looked on, he with a strange woman by his side. The foul smell of the canal met my nose.

"Yer rotten swine, yer can't wait to get rid of her, can yer?" I shouted, thinking my dad had pushed my mum into the canal.

"The silly fool chucked herself in," shouted my dad.

Then for the first time I noticed his wet clothes.

"Well, it's all yer fault – yer and yer fancy woman," I yelled.

"And I suppose yer her," I continued, turning to the woman at his side. "Get out of our house! Get out and stay out!"

The neighbours left one by one, and so did my father and his fancy woman, as I called her.

30

Later I heard the whole sad story. Apparently mum had seen dad with his woman friend and followed them. She caught up with them at the canal bridge. A terrible argument followed, and mum ended it by jumping from the bridge into the canal below. Dad then felt obliged to jump in and rescue her, for mum couldn't swim. She just wanted to die, poor mum.

I was filled with fear that my mum would try to do something else to end her life. I was afraid to let her out of my sight.

Next day, Sunday, mum said she was going to leave home. Then it was my turn to go to pieces.

"Please, Mum, don't leave us. Oh, please, Mum, don't go away!" I pleaded. "I love yer, and I would die if yer left us."

I cried so much that my mum promised not to go, but I wasn't fully convinced by her words. The Sunday school teachers somehow heard of the sad happenings and were very kind to me and my sisters that afternoon.

On Monday morning I went to school, but my mind was not on my work. I was glad when dinner time came and ran all the way home, my dog Bessie at my heels.

The house was empty – not a sign of anyone, not even my baby sister. Then I saw a note propped against the half-empty milk bottle.

"Dear Dolly, Mummy's gone away and she won't be coming home anymore. Be a good girl and look after the others for me. Don't cry. Love, Mum."

I felt as if all my life had been squeezed from my little body. I read the note again, slightly dazed. My first reaction was disbelief.

"It can't be true. It's all a horrible nightmare."

It seemed as if an eternity had passed. I called mum, but the house was empty. I don't know how long it was before I began to weep. This broken-hearted child was overcome with grief.

When at last my sobbing ceased, the great void in my heart filled with intense anger and bitterness.

"I will show the world just how I feel. I will get my own back somehow!"

Then I left the empty house, hoping I might find my beloved mum. I did find the baby, Sylvia, but not mum. No one knew, or even cared, where she was or when she left.

Taking my baby sister with me, I spent hours looking and asking for my mum. But it was all in vain, and I returned yet again to a cold and empty house. There was no food in the house, not even a crust of stale bread. My sisters and I were cold, frightened and very hungry.

When dad decided to come home at six o'clock and found his wife had left him, he was completely unconcerned.

"How can yer stand there and say nothing?" I blazed. "Yer drove my mum out – you and yer fancy woman friend!"

He ignored my outburst.

"Tomorrow you'll have a new mum to look after you."

"I don't want any new mum. I want my own mum," I cried.

My protest was of no use, for dad had made up his mind. After sending tearful Doreen to the shop for some chips to eat he went out to meet the other woman at the pub.

Next day, true to his word, dad brought in the new mum to take my mum's place. She brought with her two children of her own. That made me angrier than ever.

Then my sharp eyes noticed she was expecting a baby.

"Oh, I see now. Yer in the club," I said in true Cockney fashion. "That's why yer wanted to trap him. Well, I'm not calling yer mum. Yer not my mum, and yer never will be."

Dad thought his angry daughter would learn to accept the new situation, but he was wrong. Though a mere eleven years old, I had a very strong will. Even when his new woman made some toffee apples to win our affection, I refused to be bribed, telling her exactly what to do with her toffee apples.

The mutual hatred between us was never far below the surface. I dreamed of running away as my mother had done. But if I went too, who would look after my sisters? So I stayed and daily learned to hate anew.

CHAPTER FOUR

Black Arrow

S HE's your mother now," insisted my father.

But this young spitfire was unconvinced by the outward show of affection, if you could call it that.

The two young children she had brought with her were, in my opinion, spoiled brats, since they were allowed to do whatever they pleased.

The new woman who now ruled the household was younger than my real mother. I found a name for her – Black Arrow, because she had jet black hair and reminded me of a witch. Black Arrow seemed an appropriate name. It caused more trouble, but I flatly refused to call her anything else.

My father attempted to persuade his fiery daughter to accept the new woman, but his efforts were in vain.

He needed me to look after the increased number of children, for Black Arrow always accompanied my father on his constant trips to the pub. In contempt I called them "a couple of boozers". There were frequent arguments.

In comparison with life as I now experienced it, the time when my mother cared for us was precious. I continued to look for my real mother, sometimes walking for miles – no easy task with a crowd of children and a dog at my heels. I stared into shops and houses in the hope I would encounter that beloved face. Alas, I never saw her again.

In those unsettling war years and postwar years it was

not difficult to lose one's identity. My mother could have gone anywhere with anyone, and no one would have noticed. The neighbours were not in the least interested in my questions. They regarded me as a nuisance from a house full of nuisances.

Yes, the house was certainly full, and very noisy. At first there was outright hostility between me and the two new children brought by Black Arrow. It came to a head when the children's grandparents visited the house, bringing with them sweets and other gifts, but none for me or my sisters.

I watched my sisters gaze at the presents with envious eyes.

"Give some to the others, yer greedy little perishers," I demanded, as I grabbed the bags of sweets from the gobbling children. They were too astonished to object.

After a while the two new ones accepted me as the boss who often assumed the roles of father and mother combined. I began to realize that they were not to blame for the state of animosity. Indeed, they too were victims of circumstance. Thus we became reconciled, and I acquired additional followers – for the inevitable crowd of kids continued to follow me wherever I went, even when I went looking for my real mum.

On a few occasions, when I was alone, I would visit the graveyard and tell Violet May my troubles and sorrows. Perhaps my friend was in the sky somewhere and could see my mum.

One day I returned from school to discover Black Arrow hitting my young sister. I was furious. I picked up the bread knife and chased Black Arrow around the room.

"I'll kill yer, yer old witch, if yer hit my sister again!" I shouted.

Seeing I was in earnest, Black Arrow retreated and screamed that she would tell my father as soon as he came home.

"Tell him what yer like, I don't care what he does to

35

me. But I know what I'll do to you if yer hit any of my sisters."

Scenes like this were not unusual. My father used to punish me – if he caught me. His mind was often so dulled by drink that it was not difficult to dodge him. He was baffled by my behaviour. Like other parents before and since, he tended to regard children as bits of furniture that could be moved around rather than as individuals with emotions.

The long war ended not long after my mother left home. An air of excitement prevailed throughout Uxbridge and on our dingy estate. Everyone was singing and laughing. Flags and bunting hung from the houses.

I hoped that the arrival of peace would improve family life. My mother had always insisted it was the war that made my dad drink so heavily.

"Perhaps dad will stop drinking now, and mum will return," I thought.

Far from drinking less, dad got more drunk than ever before. By this time drinking had become his way of life.

There was one bright spot in this period. We had a road party to celebrate the end of the war. I'd never in my life seen so much food and made quite certain that I and my sisters had a fair share of all the good things.

It was a memorable year for other reasons also. I was growing up fast and was told it was time for me to transfer to the large senior school. This change – a source of pride for most youngsters – meant only further worry for me.

My tattered appearance had brought derision at the junior school. What would it be like at the posh senior school? My father and Black Arrow were not the slightest interested in my problems. Once again I had to face a situation all alone with no word of encouragement.

"Yah old ragamuffin! Look at the dirty gipsy!"

My first week at the new school was filled with abuse. I tried to ignore the remarks of the other children and decided to try to please the teachers – even pinching some flowers from a nearby garden for the classroom.

Although by no means unintelligent, I was thought stupid because I rarely put up my hand when the teacher asked a question. I felt it was no use – I could never win. If I showed that I knew the answer to a question, the children would say, "You're just a dirty cheat."

It was best to remain unnoticed as far as I could. I hated school from the day I entered its gates to the day I left. No one noticed that beneath the rags and tatters there could be someone of talent and sensitivity.

During the next two years, in which I battled my way through senior school, Black Arrow had two babies, one for each year. The house now seemed full to overflowing. More responsibility was thrust on my young shoulders. By the time I reached my thirteenth birthday I was certainly old beyond my years.

About this time in my life I attempted to improve my personal appearance and that of my four sisters. The school clinic provided toothbrushes and toothpaste, as well as a fine-tooth comb to help the removal of fleas from our heads.

I became somewhat preoccupied with cleanliness. Using the substantial bar of "sunlight soap" at the sink, I would take time to wash my four sisters, and when satisfied with their appearance, I would turn my attention to the other children in the house. There was little time left for myself, but I was determined to improve on the spit-and-hanky cat-lick that had been so much a part of my life.

I had two prized possessions: one a string of glass beads given me by a friend, the other an old jewelry box that my father discovered on the dust-cart where he worked when sober.

I remember stealing a tin of silver cleaner from Woolworth's and polishing the rusty old box until it shone. Then I placed the glass beads in it, deciding to wear the beads only on Sundays. Sometimes I would take the beads from the box and hold them up to the sunlight to watch the beads sparkle. These were my only treasured possessions. Not much, but *mine*.

The combination of my campaign of self-improvement plus deteriorating family conditions prompted an exciting thought: why not leave home altogether? I began to make frequent visits to the underground station in Uxbridge High Street. There I sat on a wooden bench with my faithful friend Bessie at my side and watched the trains come and go.

The sights and sounds of the station excited the imagination of this restless thirteen year-old. What happiness could be found at the end of the silvery line? I dreamed of going to London one day and securing a job that would permit me to return to Uxbridge in grand style to rescue my sisters. Then we could all live together in a lovely house somewhere – live happily ever after.

But the thought of leaving my sisters obscured my dreams. What would happen to them in the meantime? The walks to the tube station, the fantasies, might have continued longer but for one small – but to me, terrible – tragedy: my faithful dog Bessie died.

Bessie, who had been a faithful companion for years, was old, but to lose her – it was a cruel blow. First mum gone, now my dog. It was too much. No one shared my grief. My sisters were too small to understand the great void left in my heart.

I decided to leave home for good – the next time I walked to the station would be the last time.

My father and Black Arrow went out every evening, so I was fairly confident I could leave the house without being observed. The hard part would be getting on the platform without a ticket.

Carefully I wrapped the beads and jewelry box, my sole possessions, in newspaper. Promising the children not to be long, I set out. As an experienced fast worker I found it easy to slip onto the platform when the ticket collector's attention was elsewhere.

Since this was my first train ride, I had no idea of the length of the journey to London. I had no idea how to slip past the ticket collector when I alighted. My heart was thumping in excitement as the train pulled out.

At Hammersmith I decided I had travelled far enough. The station was quite busy, and the clock showed ten minutes past ten – an hour when many people in Hammersmith were having a good time. I must have looked a homeless waif, in my thin cotton dress and matted jumper with its lumpy shoulders. No one paid any attention to me as I once again slipped past the collector's barrier.

Outside, the busy streets of Hammersmith were ablaze with light. They fascinated me as I wandered about gazing into colourful store windows, hardly conscious that the evening was becoming colder.

"What are you doing out so late, young lady?"

I spun round to face a middle-aged man whose expression was a mixture of curiosity, humour, and kindliness.

"I've run away from home, and I'm gonna get a job in the morning."

The man nodded thoughtfully.

"Do you have anywhere to stay tonight?"

"No."

I yawned and suddenly realized how hungry and tired I was.

"Well, my mother will be pleased to see you," smiled the stranger. "It's been a long time since we had a visitor like you."

We walked along in silence until we reached the house. It was dark, and I was too weary to notice the exterior of the house, but inside was lovely.

The kind stranger explained the situation to his mother.

"Supper's ready now," she said. "We'll have something to eat and sort it all out in the morning."

It wasn't long before I was tucked in a lovely, warm bed, experiencing for the first time in my life the joy of lying between newly washed sheets. I was soon fast alseep.

When I awoke the following morning, I was at first puzzled. Then I remembered the adventure of the previous evening.

"I've done it! I've run away!"

After a hearty breakfast of bacon and eggs I offered to do some housework for the kind lady.

"Well, we'll see about that later on. I'd like you to tell me how you came to be in Hammersmith so late at night."

I told her the story, but I didn't speak in self-pity. However I was looking for encouragement in the task I now faced. The kind lady wiped her eyes when I finished.

"So you see I gotta find a job to get some money so my sisters can come and live with me."

I was eager to get going.

"I want you to promise me you will come back and have some lunch," said the lady. "Make sure you don't get lost now."

I made a careful note of the address and set out. On the main road to Hammersmith I noticed a cafe – not large, but clean and respectable looking. I made an inward nod of approval and entered.

The woman at the counter was busy polishing glasses with a clean tea-cloth.

"Excuse me. Can yer give me a job?"

The woman looked down at me in amazement.

"How old are you?"

I thought quickly.

"I'm fourteen. I know I'm small for my age, but I'll work hard."

"Well, I do need some help."

"Go on, give us a chance," I pleaded.

"All right. You come along tomorrow, and we'll see how we get along."

I was so overjoyed that my emotion quite overwhelmed the lady behind the counter. My expressions of gratitude lasted all the way to the door.

I raced back to the house, full of the good news. But – my face fell when I saw a policeman, a policewoman, and my father.

"What rotten luck!" I thought.

I might have known it wasn't going to be that easy for me. The lady of the house came to me.

"I'm sorry, Doreen. But you're only thirteen. You must go home with your father."

"I don't want to go home with him. I want to stay here." I began to cry.

"Don't cry, Doreen. I want you to tell the policewoman what you told me this morning."

I told the policewoman why I had come to Hammersmith – that I wanted to find a job so I could give my sisters a better life.

"And I got a job, too. I can start tomorrow if yer let me."

The policewoman took me to another room and questioned me carefully about my home background. She listened intently as I told her all, leaving nothing out.

The interview ended with me being escorted back to Uxbridge in a big police car. At home the neighbours and the kids came out to stare at the returning adventuress. I was the heroine of the day and was considered very brave. But my father gave me the biggest beating I'd ever received in my life.

"Don't you dare say another word to anyone," he threatened, "or you'll get another good beating."

Obviously the authorities had not entirely believed my father's denial of my statements, for the very next day an inspector from the local welfare department appeared at our house. Black Arrow, dressed in her best, blamed the shortage of money and other problems for the lack of care for the children.

Blankets and clothes were delivered by the children's department, and for a short time things improved. But the condition was short-lived. I was ready to run away again but wisely decided to wait until I'd reached my fourteenth birthday. I vowed then I would run so far that no one would find me.

It is uncertain whether my kind friend, the captain of the C.A.W.G. Messengers, heard of my attempt to run away, but she knew about my problems at home and encouraged me in my attendance at Sunday school. To everyone's amazement, including mine, I won a special prize for good attendance. (Note: not good behaviour.)

The captain often spoke to me about Jesus Christ.

"He has a purpose for your life, Doreen," she would say.

I didn't want to hurt the captain's feelings by rejecting Jesus Christ. On the other hand, I never accepted Him.

"I will always pray for you," the captain said. "We will never give up trying."

It was the captain who finally opened the door of the cage in which I felt imprisoned. She secured me a post as a domestic servant in the village of Cowley, not far from Uxbridge. I was to start as soon as I left school, living in as a maid. Although the wage was small, the position offered many advantages if I did well, the captain assured me.

The beginning of a new life awaited me. I looked forward to getting away from home at long last.

CHAPTER FIVE

Transformation

I T was late summer on a Sunday afternoon.
"This will be the last time I'll go to the mission," I thought,
for the day had arrived for me to leave my slum council
home and start my life as a domestic servant in Cowley.

I hoped to see my good friend, the captain, at Sunday
school, but she was away that afternoon. No one else
seemed to know about my imminent departure. As we have
seen, the captain worked on the biblical principle of doing
good secretly; so I said nothing about leaving.

After Sunday school I walked home. My father and Black
Arrow were out. Watched by my young sisters, I packed my
belongings in a battered carrier bag. The task was quickly
performed. I possessed no clothes other than those I was
wearing. But I had my jewelry box and glass beads, as well as
my prize from Sunday school: a copy of the *Golden Bells
Hymn Book*.

My band of faithfuls were in the recreation grounds to see
me off. My sisters looked rather downcast.

"Now don't worry, kids," I said as brightly as I could.
"I'll come back to see yer. Cowley's only a couple of miles
away, ain't it? It's not like going to Australia, is it?"

They waved good-bye to their little leader and watched
until I disappeared over the bridge. I was sad. But that's life.

Fortunately it was a fine afternoon. I had to walk all the
way to Cowley. The instructions were plain, and there was
no chance of getting lost. I felt nervous, however. What
would the place be like? Would my experience be anything

like that in Hammersmith? I had no idea what to expect.

Once again I was taking an important step all alone with no word of encouragement and assurance from anyone. On my solitary journey I had to pass my old school.

"Well, I don't have to go there anymore," I thought – and that was enough to cheer anyone up.

My heart beat faster as I quickened my pace. Soon Cowley came into view. It was a nice place; a bit posh, I thought, but nice. Peering carefully at the entrances to several houses, I finally discovered the number on my slip of paper.

The entrance gates were huge – something like the gates of heaven, only made of iron instead of gold. I walked slowly down the spacious drive and swallowed hard when I saw the large house.

I hesitated for a moment before ringing the front doorbell, half expecting the door to be opened by a butler in a black suit. After a few moments a rather elegant lady appeared. She looked at me in surprised interest.

"Yes, may I help you?"

"Um, I've come to be the new maid."

The elegant lady stared at me, then said quickly and politely, "Oh, yes. I've been expecting you. Please come in."

She took me into a huge hall, from which a wide staircase led to the upstairs rooms. I walked in wide-eyed, unable to utter a word. When I recovered, I said the first words that flew into my head.

"Cor, ain't it posh!"

The lady turned in shocked surprise.

"I suppose you would like to see your room, wouldn't you? Follow me, please."

I followed her up the wide staircase in silence.

"Your room is up here on the left, and I'm sure you will like it."

Like it? I loved it. Why, never before had I seen such a room.

I kept thinking, "Perhaps it's like heaven" – of which I had been singing (with little conviction) that very afternoon in Sunday school.

The room had a lovely fitted carpet and was sensibly and nicely furnished: a bed with a pink coverlet, a dressing table with a real mirror, a chest of drawers, a wardrobe, and a bedside table. In the corner stood a wash-basin.

My eyes were darting from one wondrous object to another. I had no idea such luxury existed.

The lady spoke again: "Now, Doreen – that's your name, isn't it? – I am your employer. This is your room. When you want a bath, your bathroom is next door."

My bathroom! I could hardly believe what I heard or saw.

"Your uniforms are in this chest of drawers. You may place your personal belongings in the dressing table drawers and wardrobe."

As if her words had reminded her that I had arrived somewhat empty-handed, she inquired when my luggage would arrive.

"I ain't got no luggage."

"You mean you own nothing else?"

"Yes. Only this what I got."

The lady was completely overcome by the realization that her new maid was all but destitute.

"Oh, dear! Well, something must be done. Wash your hands and come downstairs."

She disappeared through the pink painted door. I heard her footsteps die away.

I sat cautiously on the bed. I wondered if I was going to be sent home again. Then, recovering myself, I unpacked my few possessions and placed them on the dressing table. Pride of place was given to my *Golden Bells Hymn Book* on the bedside table. Always inquisitive, I tried the bedside lamp and was rather surprised to find that it worked first time.

I carefully examined the uniforms I would wear. I took

45

them out one by one and held them up against myself, looking at my reflection in the mirror.

Suddenly I remembered the instructions to wash my hands and go downstairs. I washed quickly, enjoying the fragrance of the scented toilet soap, then made my way downstairs – a voyage of discovery, for with every step I became aware of beautiful fittings and furnishings.

When I found the kitchen (another amazing sight) I thought I was dreaming and would wake up with a start any moment. Various gadgets, so clean and sparkling, were everywhere I looked. I was dumbfounded.

"Here is your supper, Doreen, and this is where you will eat your meals."

The good lady soon saw I had brought my appetite, if little else. She disappeared again. I enjoyed the fine meal, but it was rather eerie eating all alone in such a large kitchen. Fortunately my new employer returned before I finished my meal. Despite the strange beginning I somehow felt that everything would be all right.

When the lady had been told (probably by my good friend, the captain) that the new maid was from a poor neighbourhood, she had not anticipated a little girl in such obvious need. She herself had come from a prosperous family and married well. Her husband was a very successful businessman, and she had never known what it is like to go without. Now she was faced with a poor, neglected child of fourteen. It is not surprising therefore, that she hardly knew how to instruct me as to my duties.

But she put me at ease. I was beginning to like her already. She drew up a chair and sat beside me.

"I expect you would like to know something about your work. You must always call me Madam and my husband Sir."

She must have seen the look of resentment on my face and quickly went on to say that my wages would be twelve shillings and sixpence a week, payable on my first half-day,

46

a Thursday. I must have looked very pleased and interested in that detail, because that is how I felt. Madam gave me a general idea of my duties and added some timely encouragement.

"You will soon learn, Doreen. Don't be too impatient. Now, Doreen, do you have a night dress?"

"No Madam."

Oh, well, I think I can find you one for tonight. Tomorrow we'll fix you up with new clothes and shoes."

"Oh thanks, Madam! Thank's very much!"

I spent my first night in that marvellous house in my own room, sleeping in my own real bed. It was like a fairy story come true.

Next morning I was awakened by someone knocking on the pink painted door of my room. I turned over to go back to sleep. Then I remembered that I was a maid, and I sprang out of bed.

I wondered if I was meant to wear one of the uniforms. My own clothes looked shabbier than ever. Eventually I dressed in my old clothes and made my way downstairs, where a lovely breakfast awaited me. I was thoroughly enjoying it when Madam appeared.

"We are going to London as soon as you are ready, Doreen."

This prospect prompted me to conclude my breakfast quickly. I overheard a brief conversation between Madam and the daily cleaning woman, who had just arrived.

"She has come from the most appalling home and possesses nothing at all to wear. I'm taking her to London to buy her some clothes."

The daily cleaning woman – a person of a rugged and cheerful disposition – came into the kitchen to meet me. She stared for a minute before speaking.

"Hello, Doreen. I'm Mrs. Hill, the daily help. I hope we're going to be good friends."

There was a suspicion of a wink. I hardly knew what to say and just looked polite.

Mrs. Hill had been helping for a long time, I was to learn later. She was mainly responsible for cleaning the bedrooms. My work was to clean downstairs and to serve at table.

The household also boasted a cook, who was having a long week-end off duty when I arrived. I wondered how I would fit in with everybody.

Soon I was whisked away to London in Madam's big black car. She was driving and asked me lots of questions about myself. She seemed satisfied with my answers, if a little stunned. Although Madam had lived a somewhat sheltered life, she knew that honesty, rather than education, is of most value in a maid. I was completely honest with my answers.

We were soon in London. The car arrived at Harrod's just as it was opening. I was taken quickly in to the fashion department by a very embarrassed Madam. She was well-known at the shop and every effort was made to please her.

Madam quickly explained the difficult situation to the department head, who concealed her surprise professionally and sprang into action. Quickly she organized her staff so that I could be fitted out in one department, thus saving Madam and me further embarrassment in going from one department to another.

I was completely bewildered by the sudden burst of activity on my behalf – people running back and forth with boxes and packages of every shape and size. Vests, petti-coats, dresses, and other garments were brought to the private fitting room. I wasn't at all bothered what colour and style they were. After all, I had *never* before had new clothes.

Madam herself entered into the spirit of the unusual event. Indeed, it was as if the whole store had something of the spirit of Christmas. The experienced staff gave me smiles of encouragement as they ran back and forth with garments and suggestions for my transformation.

My old and shabby clothes were discreetly spirited away. I wore some of the new clothes and my new, shiny shoes, and the rest of the purchases were carried to the car. But the great adventure had not ended yet.

Madam took me to the hairdressing salon, where my hair was expertly washed and styled. When it was finished, I was invited to look at myself in the mirror. I was speechless, hardly able to believe that the bright, attractive person in the mirror was myself.

"What a transformation!" said Madam.

She was very pleased with the morning's work. As for me I thought I was dreaming and would wake up any moment to find myself on the heap of dirty coats in Uxbridge.

For a short time all who had played a part stood around me, pleased with their work. Then with waves of good-bye from the staff Madam and the new maid left the famous store.

The ride home was punctuated with my profuse thanks to Madam, who seemed to be taken aback by such earnest gratitude. To make sure I did really own all those lovely things, I continually turned round to gaze at the packages on the back seat of the car. I stroked my new coat and admired my new shoes. Yes, they were real enough. It was no dream. Life was not going to be so bad at all.

Back at Cowley, I met the cook. I liked her as soon as I set eyes on her. Cook and Madam helped me put on my maid's uniform – another thrilling experience.

My life as a domestic servant was to have its ups and downs. There were moments of despair for all concerned, but Madam and cook were determined to take the new maid in hand and make something of her.

In case all this sounds rather solemn, let me add that cook later told me she had never laughed so much in her life as she did after my coming to Cowley.

CHAPTER SIX

The Stranger

ONE of my first tasks was to cut bread for the evening meal. Here at least was one thing I could do with comparative ease. Why, I must have cut hundreds of slices for my hungry sisters!

I set to work and placed the ample slices on the plate. Madam, with eyebrows raised in obvious amazement and some distaste, surveyed the mountain of door-step slices.

"What on earth do you think you call this?"

"Bread, of course – what yer asked for."

I couldn't understand why Madam didn't like my healthy-looking slices of bread.

"Now, Doreen, I'll show you how to cut bread properly. Just get rid of those other slices."

"You ain't gonna chuck 'em out, are yer? My sisters will eat those."

Madam looked surprised but said nothing. Cook, hovering in the background, tried unsuccessfully to conceal a grin, while I somewhat sulkily watched Madam instruct me in the art of bread-cutting.

After making a flop of my first job I was rather nervous about future tasks. I was willing and eager to learn but difficult to teach, and disasters followed.

Take the case of the hall floor. I was instructed to polish it. Working on the principle that the job was best performed by using as much polish and elbow grease as possible, I quickly turned the hall floor into something approaching a skating rink, and just as dangerous, as poor Madam soon discovered, almost slithering across the hall on a small rug.

"It's far too dangerous, Doreen. You must scrub it all off and start again."

"Scrub it all off? After all my hard work? No fear! Yer wanted it polished, yer got it polished. If yer fink I'm gonna scrub it all off now, yer got another fink coming!"

A long dialogue followed between Madam and the new maid, with me using a few choice words from the back streets to express my feelings. Cook came from the kitchen to see what all the fuss was about, took one look, and hurried back to the kitchen, hardly able to restrain her laughter.

"You *must* do as you're told, Doreen. Now see that the floor is scrubbed!"

With that Madam departed to safer places, while I had to do as Madam said, but not without protests in loud Cockney lingo.

Soap powder was a commodity unknown to me. I used it unsparingly in the tasks I was given. I wanted to make sure that the tea towels were really clean and white and once used half a packet of soap powder and half a bottle of bleach to wash just two tea towels. It's not difficult to imagine the result: soap suds everywhere and two tea towels that were a very sorry sight.

Madam and cook were patient, really, although it must have been very difficult at times. Very often I would run into the garden or upstairs to my room, in tears or in hot indignation.

Not every job was a failure, though. Madam asked me if I could light a fire. I smiled, thinking, "I'll show 'er."

"Yer give me the sticks and the coal, mate, and I'll soon show yer."

"You must call me Madam, not Mate," said Madam very quickly.

"All right! All right! I heard yer!" I shouted.

It was not long before I had a fire blazing halfway up the chimney. Madam and cook congratulated me, even if the huge fire did look a bit dangerous.

Life at Cowley, then, was a mixture of disasters, tears, arguments, and a few successes during my early days. But what had been a well-ordered household was turned into a kind of chaos. The advent of this Cockney waif certainly added colour to the otherwise placid scene. Neither Madam nor her husband, neither the cook nor the daily cleaner had ever met anyone like the new maid, who caused so much concern, shock, frustration, and amusement all in a few days.

When I was sent into the other rooms to work, I was half afraid to touch anything for fear of breaking the lovely ornaments. Why they needed all those rooms puzzled me. At home in Uxbridge there were only two rooms downstairs, and both of them would have been lost in one of the large rooms at Cowley. Life was certainly different here.

The cook was a good friend to me and helped me no end but there were times when I felt lonely and lost in this large well-run house. I missed my sisters very much.

The cook had been with the family for some eight years. She looked as every good cook should – plump, with a round pink face that was always cheerful and bright. Cook and I shared our meals in the kitchen. I had never been so well fed, for cook always saw that I had plenty to eat. We talked freely together, and I always made her laugh.

She at all times looked neat and clean, never seeming to get her large pinafores dirty, whereas mine were very dirty and creased after a half-hour's wear – much to Madam's despair.

Cook's advice was simple enough: "Always look on the bright side. We have much to be thankful for."

I tried to take the good advice, but so many things kept going wrong, no matter how hard I tried.

Madam made an attempt at teaching me to wait on the

table at mealtimes, but decided to postpone this aspect of my work until I was better trained.

Answering the door, however, was another matter, a task that even this unpredictable young lady could manage without anything going wrong (Madam thought). But Madam was wrong. I managed to make a mess of even that simple task.

One evening I was told that guests were coming. I was to welcome them politely when they arrived at the front door and show them to the drawing room.

When the doorbell rang, announcing the arrival of visitors, I went to answer. Cook stood at the half-open door of the kitchen, hidden from view, to listen how I got on.

I opened the door very quickly and said in a very loud voice: "Come in – and wipe yer feet."

The two guests stared at me and stepped somewhat gingerly inside.

"Give us yer coats then," I said, "and I'll 'ang 'em up."

They did so in stunned silence.

I announced the guests by flinging open the drawing-room door and saying in loud Cockney tones, "'Ere they are, then."

I thought Madam looked rather strange. I marched back to the kitchen where to my amazement I found cook doubled up in fits of laughter, tears rolling down her pink cheeks.

"What's up with yer?" I asked.

Cook could not answer for laughing.

"I ain't done nothing wrong, have I?"

Cook only laughed all the more.

Madam was soon on the scene. If cook thought my performance funny, Madam certainly didn't. I, who had only been my natural self, couldn't understand what all the fuss was about. Cook, still in fits of laughter, fled upstairs to her room to recover. Apparently Madam objected (among other things) to having her guests told to wipe their feet.

At long last Thursday came round, and I was to have my first half day – and first wage packet.

"You are now free until tomorrow morning," said Madam, "but you must be back here no later than ten o'clock tonight."

"Oh, thanks, Madam!" I gasped.

Eyes shining with pleasure, I rushed upstairs to count my money: a whole clean ten-shilling note and a gleaming half-crown. Never had I owned so much. No wonder I felt like a duchess.

"Cor!" I thought, "won't I show 'em back at Uxbridge what a success I'm now!"

In my nice new clothes, money in my pocket, I set off proudly down the road to the railway station. The journey by train to Uxbridge lasted a matter of minutes. When I alighted, everything felt and looked different to me – cleaner, fresher. Could it have been Sunday, only four days ago, that I'd left the town for my new position? It seemed like years.

I bought sweets for my sisters and sat down in a cafe to relax with a cup of tea. I was experiencing a new sense of self-awareness. Something strange and indefinable had entered my life.

Quite suddenly I thought of cigarettes. I was no stranger to smoking. From the age of eight I had picked up fag-ends from the gutter and smoked them when no one was around. Sometimes I stole tobacco from my father's tobacco tin and rolled my own, merely copying others. Everyone, including children on the grimy estate, liked a fag. While I was in service at Cowley I had never even thought of smoking. Now that I was back in Uxbridge, the link with the past perhaps prompted my next action.

I bought my first packet of cigarettes at the counter and returned to my table, where I lit one. It was a very pleasurable sensation. No one seemed to care or have the slightest interest that this young girl was smoking.

"I'm really grown up," I thought. "I really can do what I like and go where I please."

When I left the cafe, I made my way to the council estate where I had spent so many unhappy and lonely years. At least I would see my sisters again. But my sisters, playing in the recreation ground, did not at first recognize me. Indeed I had to call their names several times before they gasped, "Hey! It's Dor! It's Dor!"

They bounded over with shrieks of delight. I took them up in my arms, overjoyed to see them – dirty faces and uncombed hair notwithstanding. It was wonderful to hear them talking all at once. My heart was filled with a deep and tender love for them all. I had missed those lovable rascals more than I realized.

Spellbound by my appearance, they finally took my hands and together we marched proudly down the road to my old home. As the procession proceeded, so it grew. All the gangs of children followed me.

The neighbours came to their doors to stare at the transformed Doreen. I stopped to tell them of my new life and, understandably, showed off more than a little. I was the centre of attraction that afternoon.

When I reached our down-at-heels house, my father was out. Black Arrow was speechless when I walked in with my lovely clothes and new shoes. Finding it impossible to stay inside the house, which now seemed dark and cramped, I walked around the estate, followed by my friends, the gang, and my sisters – just like the old days.

"Will yer take us back with yer, Dor?"

"Can we come and live with yer, Dor?"

They seemed to think their old leader had found a fairyland castle or a limitless chest of treasure.

At last my father arrived home. I realized I still loved him, but he showed no interest in me, just surprise that I bothered to return home at all. I wanted to ask if anyone had news of my real mother, but the question remained unasked.

I began to feel strangely out of place. As the hours passed, the stares seemed to turn into glares of resentment.

"I think I'll go to the pictures now," I told the gang of children.

The return home had turned into an anti-climax. As I sat alone in the cinema my thoughts were racing. Smoking cigarette after cigarette, I was hardly aware of the events projected on the screen before me. Over and over I felt I was a stranger to the people on the estate.

"I don't belong to the family anymore. I'm a stranger."

The word stranger sent a chill through me – a sense of emptiness. I had wanted to leave home, I had wanted to be free. Now I was – yet not free, for I was bound up in a new inner emptiness and loneliness.

"If it wasn't for my sisters, I'd never go home again," I thought.

But where would I go, if not there? I knew no one else.

As I walked to the station, my steps seemed to say, "I'm a stranger. I'm a stranger. I don't belong anywhere. I'm a stranger."

Awful depression gripped me as I walked alone back to the large house where I was employed.

"Did you have a nice half-day, dear?" cook asked.

I could only nod my head at what had been a shattering experience.

CHAPTER SEVEN

Departure

"YOU'RE very silly to waste your money on cigarettes," said cook, unusually serious. "If Madam catches you smoking in the kitchen, there'll be serious trouble."

"That'll be no change," I sniffed. "I'm always in trouble anyway."

Although I later confined my smoking to my bedroom whilst in the house, the habit was soon discovered by Madam. Neither she nor cook knew of the depression I was suffering. If they had known, perhaps they would have understood why I smoked so much.

Madam's attempts to create an efficient maid from the small bundle of humanity that had arrived at her doorstep continued. I was learning fast, although I continued to make the most awful mistakes.

Also, I was getting to know the two children. From the beginning Madam had been careful to keep the two children well out of my way, perhaps because of my occasional verbal explosions. She didn't wish the children to pick up bad language. The parents were not always successful, however, according to the occasional giggles outside the kitchen door. The sounds of scurrying feet would follow as the children were shooed away by a perturbed father or mother.

I got to know the children better one memorable evening. Madam decided to leave them in my care whilst she went out for the evening with her husband. Cook was having the evening off.

The children, as full of mischief as any of the back-street kids, decided to take full advantage of the situation. They complained they were hungry and begged me to give them something to eat. I led them to the larder to let them choose what they liked, and there was plenty to choose from. Helped by me, they got through a whole chocolate cake just baked by cook, some currant buns, some fruit, plus three bottles of pop.

We had a wonderful time together, chatting and laughing and getting to know each other better. The children knew that helping themselves to food was strictly forbidden, but I was completely innocent about the whole affair, thinking it was perfectly all right.

The next day Madam and cook missed the food from the larder and found the empty pop bottles. The children were closely questioned, and the whole adventure was blamed onto me. Madam was very angry, and I was really in trouble.

My anger blazed as I shouted, "If the little perishers wanted something to eat, why can't they? Yer can afford it, can't yer?"

"I suppose you had your share too, Doreen," said Madam quickly.

"Well, so what if I did! I'm fed up with yer and this place. And yer can take a week's notice."

I had got slightly tongue-twisted and was acting as if I were firing an inefficient employer. Cook, who was never far from mirth when I was around, roared with laughter. But I didn't think it funny. I was off upstairs to pack. Cook followed me, then Madam, then the children.

"You mustn't be too harsh on Doreen, Madam," said the cook. "She's had a hard life."

Then the children pleaded with Madam not to let me leave. I was quite a hit with them, it seemed. They later confessed it was their fault, and so the whole affair blew over and was soon forgotten.

My employer was a very patient lady. Any lack of understanding on her part stemmed from the relatively sheltered life she'd lived. The truth was I often felt like a caged bird. Since I had never been accustomed to any kind of discipline, my outbursts would occur – like the day Madam came into the kitchen to give me some small instruction.

I was depressed and turned on poor madam, shouting, "Oh, for God's sake shut up and get out of *my* kitchen!"

Poor Madam was so dazed that she retreated, but I soon learned that Madam was still the boss. She continued to correct me when necessary.

One morning about six weeks after my appointment as the new maid I came downstairs to find Madam, somewhat ashen in appearance, preparing breakfast. It was past seven o'clock, but there was no sign of cook.

"Where's cook?" I asked.

There was no reply, and I repeated my question.

"Doreen," she said very gently, "cook died in her sleep."

"Dead!" I stared at Madam in unbelief. "She can't be dead! You must be mistaken, Madam."

Poor Madam, who was obviously shaken herself, had a difficult time trying to convince me it was true.

Madam had gone to cook's bedroom when she failed to come downstairs.

"She died in her sleep, Doreen. It was very peaceful."

"Now, Doreen," went on Madam, "I want you to be a good girl and help me by being very quiet. I'm expecting the doctor any minute."

"Why call the doctor if she's dead?"

I was puzzled. I cannot recall Madam's reply. She had difficulty calming me down.

Everyone, including me, crept around the house in silence. It wasn't until hours later, when I was alone in the large kitchen, that the tears began to flow. The awful realization struck me that my good friend cook would be there no more. Everything in the room reminded me of her: her favourite chair, her knitting, her extra apron still hanging near the stove.

Cook, dear cook, my good friend, was gone. Whatever would it be like without her? The gap left by cook, loved member of the household, could never be filled.

Life went on, as life must. Cook was never replaced, and I was relieved. A new cook would have seemed like a usurper. Who knows? – Madam's decision not to get a new cook may have been because she saw the sadness in my face.

Now Madam did the cooking, helped by Mrs. Hill and sometimes by me. I liked cooking and learned a lot from the very patient Madam. She taught me to bake cakes, bottle fruit, and other useful things.

My half-days were spent in Uxbridge, where my appearance continued to cause ripples of excitement among the younger children. But I had no friends of my own age.

In my wanderings around the town I noticed that people were unwilling to speak or even smile – they were so preoccupied with their own lives. Often I would spend a half-day off in Uxbridge without speaking to one adult person.

Once or twice I visited the mission hall in Waterloo Road, but here too there was no communication, perhaps because on my solitary half-day a week there was seldom anyone around.

Often when children reach the school-leaving age and drop into a very busy world, they are lost in the great swirl. This happened to me, and it was a pity. Had a perceptive Christian befriended me or even written an occasional letter, I might have been won for the Saviour at this time.

Like most girls of my age, I began to dream about having a boy friend and getting married. It would be so wonderful to have someone who really loved me! I was growing up both mentally and physically.

In an attempt to meet young people of my own age and perhaps to acquire that Prince Charming of my dreams, I went to dances instead of the cinema. I was a little shy at first but I was so full of life it wasn't difficult to find boy friends. I became known as a girl who was fun.

Servicemen from the nearby RAF station went to the dances to acquire a girl friend. They were usually not slow in boasting about their casual romantic conquests. I had no illusions about the motives of some of the RAF servicemen. All I wanted was company.

As a small child I had seen and heard many things pertaining to sex. Acts of life were facts of life to me. In the neighbourhood in which I had grown up sex had no religious overtones, and marriage was sometimes a matter of convenience. I learned the facts of life by observing them.

Casual relationships with the opposite sex were nothing unusual, so I had no inhibitions. Furthermore, there was always the possibility that one of these men might really love me and I would live happily ever after in true story-book fashion.

I thought my search had ended at last when I met a young and handsome man who was also kind and considerate. For the first time in my life I fell head-over-heels in love.

My entire outlook was transformed overnight. Everything was wonderful – even the housework. There suddenly emerged a bright and shining Doreen. All my loneliness disappeared.

My head-in-the-clouds romance ended suddenly after three weeks, and I came back to earth with a painful jolt. My handsome boy friend informed me he was already engaged to be married. My whole world collapsed, and I thought I would die of a broken heart.

Time was the healer . . .

Why should some people have so much money and others so little? – this was the big question that now occupied my thoughts.

"It's all unfair," I thought.

Bitterness was filling an empty heart. A great chip was growing on my young shoulders. And I began to think that

61

the acquisition of a lot of hard cash would bring me the happiness I was searching for.

I decided to ask Madam for a rise. I thought that then I could save enough to run away to London, where I could earn a *lot* of money and get nice clothes and new friends.

The wage claim was still in my mental pipeline when another incident occured to astonish Madam and diminish me. It all centred around the telephone, an instrument that I regarded with a mixture of fear, awe, and suspicion.

One day Madam decided it was time her new maid overcame that fear. Patiently, carefully she explained how the telephone should be answered. Then she declared the next time the telephone rang I was to answer it.

A little later the telephone rang. Madam called to me:

"Go on, Doreen, pick it up and answer as I've told you."

Then she added: "If it is only Mrs. Winters, tell her I'm not at home."

I gingerly picked up the telephone, as if it were a stick of dynamite with a very short time-fuse. I repeated the number on the dial, just as Madam had instructed.

"This is Mrs. Winters here," began a voice at the other end of the line.

"Oh! Is it?" I interrupted quickly. "Well, Madam told me to tell you she ain't in today!"

With a mixture of relief and amazing confidence I slammed down the receiver on a very indignant lady. Madam nearly exploded. Needless to say, she never again asked me to answer the telephone.

Later I felt very silly. After all, if I had been more careful with the telephone, I could have asked for that pay-rise. It was no use asking Madam now. I would have to save harder.

London was my destination – the city that must be full of opportunities for young girls like me with ambition. Somehow I thought that my mere arrival in London would change my life for the better. I could hardly wait for my savings to grow.

When I believed I had saved enough to make my journey, I packed my case and left without telling Madam or anyone else that I was going. I boarded the train at Uxbridge with various emotions flooding my being. No one paid any attention to this tragic form with the grim look of determination on her young face.

Sad to say, the story is repeated today – so many teenagers, lonely and bewildered, running away from home, turning their sights toward London. Sadder still to think that often there is no one to care what happens to them once they arrive in that huge city all alone.

Little did I realize what awaited me at the other end of the line.

CHAPTER EIGHT

Streets of Paddington

THE possessions I carried with me to Paddington, London, were many more than those I had nine months earlier, when I trudged from my home in Uxbridge to the job in Cowley. But this time there was no job waiting for me. Furthermore, there was no bed in which to sleep.

I had been reared on uncertainty in the school of hard knocks; therefore I wasn't too discouraged. Best thing, I thought, was to think the whole matter through over a meal in a cafe. But I was no nearer solving the problem when I'd finished my meal.

Gullible as ever, I expected London to be a beautiful place. I was rather like Dick Whittington, who believed the London streets were paved with gold. After gaping in shop windows in the main shopping centre I wandered down the side streets. I was disappointed in what I saw: dark alleyways, blackened buildings, and semi-derelict houses in dirty narrow streets stretched as far as the eye could see.

"Why, it's worse than the estate at Uxbridge," I thought.

There was no turning back now. I stopped several people hurrying along the shadowy road and asked where lodgings could be found. Only one person stopped to give any helpful information – a woman who directed me to a large house in a nearby side street. A room in the house was offered after I paid a week's rent in advance.

It was a gloomy room, barely furnished, and the brown

wall-paper was peeling from the damp walls. Compared with the warm and pretty room I had left a few hours ago in Cowley, this was a real come-down.

I sat on the rickety bed and looked around. The place could always be cleaned up.

"I've had plenty of training for that," I said to myself.

Actually the large house was a hive of bedsitters. Hearing loud laughter from the next room, I decided to investigate. My knock on the door was greeted by a cheerful "Come in, love," and further laughter.

"Er, I'm looking for a bucket and some soap and a scrubbing brush, to clean my room with."

The girls stared at me, then at one another, and giggled.

"I wouldn't bother about it, deerie," said one of the three girls. "It's not worth it."

"Leave the kid alone!" interjected the apparently senior member of the trio.

Judging from the appearance of the room I had entered, I might just as well have asked for a chandelier. Much to my surprise the articles I had asked for were found – rather battered but usable.

"Thanks a lot," I said and retreated.

I heard them laughing again as I returned to my room. The sound of my scrubbing must have touched a chord of conscience, for one of the girls entered carrying a cup of tea. My room looked much cleaner, but I didn't. I was filthy.

"Here you are, love. You deserve it," said my good neighbour.

"Cor, thanks! I could do with that."

"You're new here, aren't you? I saw you arrive."

"I've run away from my last job. I was a domestic servant. My name's Doreen."

"Well, I'm Brenda, and there's six of us living here. Well, you're the seventh. Lucky seven. Maybe you're lucky for someone, Doreen."

Brenda and I exchanged further personal details. As I told

Brenda my life's story with gusto, the other girls crept in. Brenda, who was ten years older than I, did most of the talking when my story was finished.

"I'm on the game, see?"

"On the game?" I was puzzled.

"You know – we go with fellers at night for money. There's plenty of money on the game. The men pay up all right."

The other girls nodded in agreement.

"Who wants to slave at work all day," said one of the other girls. "We're independent. We get all we want."

They certainly possessed good clothes and jewelry. My eyes opened wide in amazement. I had never before met a self-confessed prostitute. I carefully noted they regarded the game in strictly commercial terms. Morality didn't come into it.

"Well," I sighed, "I've only been a domestic servant and I don't want to do that again."

"You don't have to, love. You're young and quite nice-looking. You could make a lot of money with us on the game."

"I'll think about it, Brenda, and I'll let you know in the morning."

When they at last left my room, I did think about it. After all, I reasoned, that's why I came to London – to make plenty of money. If the men wanted to part with their money for a bit of fun, what harm was there in that? And the girls seemed happy enough living that way. They at least took an interest in me – something no one had done before.

Not all the prostitutes had come from a poor and unhappy home as I had. Not all of them had been denied the love and care of their parents. But all seemed to have one thing in common: loneliness. All were looking for happiness and considered money the key to that happiness.

This is the way many prostitutes reason, never realizing the many hidden dangers and risks of such a life, none so attractive as the money. Disappointments and let-downs (especially let-downs by men) push other women along the same path: bitterness and loneliness, too, and an urge to hit back at society. All these things put together had certainly been mine.

Thus it was that I too, as a lonely fourteen-year-old, joined the ranks of the women of the twilight. I entered the world's oldest and most shameful profession.

The very next evening I accompanied Brenda on the streets of Paddington. I saw how easily she attracted men. She simply walked along swinging her hips, jangling a bunch of keys. It wasn't long before a man approached. Terms were quickly settled.

"Two pounds," I heard Brenda say.

The man nodded, and they both disappeared.

It looked easy, but I was far less experienced and much younger. Brenda had given me some hints and guidance on charges, contraception, and dangers to avoid. How would I fare?

The first time I ventured out alone I was very nervous indeed. Walking along the edge of the pavement, I jangled my keys. My heart thumped with every step I took, and I tried hard to act as if I were an old hand on the game.

I need not have worried about getting a start. Young as I was, I didn't have to wait long before a man drew up in his car. Taking a deep breath, I launched out on my new career.

My confidence grew as the weeks went by. I soon had plenty of money. I too had plenty of pretty clothes. Most important to me, I had plenty of friends, all of whom followed the same way of life.

I was an entertainer par excellence, full of fun and ready to exercise my quick wit. Little wonder that I was popular with other girls and older women on the streets of Paddington. Even the streetwalker has need of a laugh and some good clean fun.

Many of the girls, including myself, had a spirit of freedom, joy, and love. They had hearts of gold and would never see anyone treated badly. They would give away their last penny if they knew anyone in real need.

In spite of everything, real happiness still eluded me. But I never spoke of my frequent depression to the other girls.

Then came my first encounter with the Salvation Army. As I walked along the familiar street I noticed an open-air meeting being conducted by the local Salvation Army corps. A young girl in army uniform was singing unaccompanied, and her voice sounded as sweet as a bird's. I was arrested by her words as she sang:

> My Father is rich with houses and lands.
> He holdeth the wealth of the world in His hands.
> Of rubies and diamonds, of silver and gold,
> His coffers are full; He has riches untold.
> I'm a child of a King, I'm a child of a King.
> With Jesus my Saviour I'm a child of a King.

The singer's face, serene and joyful, gripped my attention. I suddenly knew that with all my easy money I was poor in comparison. She seemed so contented to stand there and sing. She was a child of a King.

"Well, what's the use? It's too late to change now. It's all right for them. They're nice people, but I'm a common prostitute."

Somewhat sadly I continued on my way. Like so many people today, I thought Christianity was a matter of being good rather than being made good. Although I became preoccupied with "the game", I never forgot that Salvationist singer. That short encounter was a memorable occasion in the hard pilgrimage of my life.

I later changed my name (it was easier to change one's name than one's life). I called myself Michelle in my professional activities, and my bank balance was growing.

Brenda and I were now firm friends. We often moved from the Paddington streets to other parts of London. My leanings towards mischief had hardly diminished – anything for a laugh. I threw soap powder and red dye into the fountains at Trafalgar Square, nearly getting caught in the process.

Because prostitution is illegal, I always had a wary eye open for the law. In fact, I became quite an expert at dodging the vice squad, but I never underestimated them. I knew how far to go in my daring.

Not so easily avoided, however, were my feelings of guilt as far as my little sisters were concerned. Long ago I had lost touch with the family at Uxbridge, but I often wondered how my sisters were getting on. Had my real mother ever returned?

Staring at the wall and preoccupied by such thoughts, I felt guilt and emptiness descend on me like a heavy, stifling blanket. Often I would shake my head and in a determined way push the guilty thoughts away, as far as I could.

One day Brenda and I went to Soho in the West End of London. Soho was to me the ultimate in pleasure and glamour. The sights and sounds intoxicated me. We walked aimlessly around the busy streets, but I was ready for some fun.

Suddenly I stopped to read a notice displayed in a shop window; MODEL WANTED, APPLY UPSTAIRS.

"Hey look, Brenda," I said. "Shall we go up just for a laugh?"

"I daren't. I'm past being a model. But I'll come with you if you want to have a go."

"Okay! I should have brought my ostrich feathers."

I joked and giggled almost every step of the way upstairs. A similar notice was tacked to the door. I knocked loudly, and Brenda and I stifled a further giggle.

We were received by two men in loud flashy clothes. They looked at me with keen, appraising eyes. An odd interview followed, the men taking my measurements accompanied by a few cheeky remarks from me.

I was told then to walk around the room. Not taking the

interview too seriously – after all I only went up for a bit of fun – I laid it on a bit thick. Next I was asked to dance to a record.

"Just move any way you please," said one of the men as he placed the record on the player.

My performance was, to say the least, slightly hilarious, but the two men laughed in approval, not derision.

"Have you ever stripped before?"

I stopped dancing, slightly out of breath.

"Plenty of times – but it depends on what yer mean."

"In a proper club, to music."

"No, but now I see what kind of model yer mean."

"We like you. You move well, you've plenty of life, and you're cheeky – just what the customers like."

"You're on the game, aren't you?" asked the second man.

"What if I am?"

"Oh, nothing. You'll find this an easier way of making money. The job's yours if you want it."

I stared in astonishment.

"Well, to tell yer truth, we only came up for a laugh, didn't we, Brenda?"

"You take the job, you lucky thing," Brenda advised. "I wish I had the chance, but I'm a bit old for it now."

"Right. When do I start?"

"Tonight. But you'll need a stage name, something that suits you. What is your name, anyway?"

"Doreen."

"No, that's not glamorous enough."

"Well," piped up Brenda, "she's daring, if that's any help."

I used my imagination.

"How about Daring Diana?"

"That's it! That's fine. It suits you. Daring Diana," the man chuckled.

He then explained that I was to report to the strip club that very evening to watch the routine of the strippers. I walked down the stairs with Brenda in a state of amazement.

Within a mere half-hour after seeing the advert in the shop window I was a striptease artiste (or very nearly).

It had been so easy – like prostitution. Not difficult at all. Straightforward and simple. Yes, straight forward into a life far more degrading than the one I had known, which was bad enough. How true it is that Satan can make the way so very easy. Once someone has started on the downward path, the way farther down is smoother still.

That night, instead of walking abroad in search of men, I sat watching a young girl doing her act in a Soho club. A keen observer, I carefully noted the way she moved. It seemed easy enough.

It wasn't long before I learned how to strip off my clothes to slow music. I was instructed to be as provocative as possible. Thus Daring Diana became part of a non-stop strip show, one of the dozens of such performances in the clubs of the area.

Eight girls worked on a shift system in the club which featured Daring Diana. A nude photograph of the new star was displayed outside the club to lure the men in from the streets. Once inside the club, the men were persuaded by the girls to buy expensive drinks.

For this nimble-minded Cockney kid the new life was a push-over. I was earning far more money than ever before. Prostitution was far more profitable too. I left Paddington back streets and rented a large flat in Mayfair. This meant I could charge more for my favours.

Soho was for me the best place on earth – plenty of clothes, money and jewelry. I even employed a cleaner to look after the flat. Now *I* was the Madam, in more ways than one.

"I'm really going up in the world," I thought.

In actual fact I was sliding downhill as fast as I could go.

CHAPTER NINE

Road to Prison

"WHAT am I doing in a dump like this? Is this what I was born for?"

These questions arose, sometimes right in the middle of my strip-tease act. Amidst the roars of appreciation from my audience I often felt completely alone. While my fame as Daring Diana spread through Soho, the softness that had been part of my nature was slowly disappearing. Soho and all the glamour had failed to bring the real happiness I yearned for. Despite the big money I received, I hated the life. But no one guessed it, as I lived up to my reputation of being good for a laugh – even if that laughter was hollow and empty.

"Coming to the party tonight, Diana?"

The invitation came from one of the girls of the strip club. Her wild parties were always good fun.

"'Course I'm coming, and make sure there's some nice fellers there!"

I was the first to arrive at my friend's flat and began to sort out some good records from the stack in the corner of the room (loud music was essential background for any party). I came across a very old and unusual record at the bottom of the pile and put it on the turntable. A man's clear voice began to sing:

I have lived a life of sin in this world I'm living in.
I have done forbidden things I shouldn't do.
I asked a beggar along the way if he could show
        me where to stay,
Where I could find real happiness and love that's
        true.

Across the bridge there's no more sorrow,
Across the bridge there's no more pain.
The sun will shine across the river,
And you'll never be unhappy again.

As I listened some of the old softness returned, some of
the old wistfulness came back. A sense of remorse filled my
heart.

"I wonder where the bridge is," I was thinking. "I wonder
where the river is. I would like to know where true happiness
can be found."

Somehow, somewhere, I felt, I had missed the turning
that led to real happiness and contentment. But then the
party began, and I put on my usual act of the good-time
party girl who kept things alive.

As the weeks passed I became harder and very often
suffered bouts of severe depression. Also I was rapidly
becoming a heavy drinker and got through over forty
cigarettes a day.

At the bar one day, where I'd just emptied my glass, a man
drew up a stool and sat beside me. He looked vaguely
familiar.

"You look fed up today," he said.

"Yes, I am."

"Try one of these then." He offered me a hand-rolled
cigarette.

"No thanks. I prefer my own brand."

"You feel fed up, don't you? this will make you feel better.
Of course, they're a bit more expensive than the ordinary

kind, but they're worth every penny. Why don't you try one?

I idly took the cigarette, and he watched carefully as I lit it and inhaled. A wave of contentment flooded through me within minutes.

"Whatever is it?" I asked.

"It's a reefer. Makes you feel good, doesn't it?"

"Yes. Can I have some?"

"Sure, as many as you like, and there's plenty more where these came from."

I wasn't interested in where they came from. They made me feel good, and that's all that mattered to me.

I took six reefers and paid the man fifteen bob for my first batch of drugs.

The man smiled and left. He was a pusher, and this encounter was undoubtedly well planned – as was his follow-up strategy some weeks later.

"I can offer you something better than reefers, Diana."

I was very interested, even though there was an element of mystery about his invitation to "follow me." I followed him down a small alleyway and into one of the many seedy bookshops of Soho. Nodding to the man in the shop, the pusher took me into a small room at the back.

"What's all the mystery?" I asked.

"Well, we don't want anyone to see, do we? Don't tell anyone, whatever you do, Diana."

I promised.

"It will mean a prick in the arm – nothing to worry about."

"Well, do it quick then," I said, rolling up my sleeve.

I turned my face away as he tied a tourniquet and quickly injected a shot of heroin in the main vein near my elbow. Within seconds I was high as the sky. I felt on top of the world. Indeed, I felt I owned it, floating on a cloud of happiness.

"It's heroin," the man explained. "Makes you feel even better, doesn't it?"

"Yes," I smiled stupidly.

74

For some hours I lived in a state of euphoria.

"At last," I thought, "I've found the happiness I searched for."

I was completely ignorant and totally unprepared for what was to follow. After several hours the happiness and contentment slowly ebbed away and were replaced by an intense, stark depression, far worse than anything I had ever known. I felt I was being pulled slowly and surely into a deep, dark, bottomless pit.

I couldn't understand it at all. Why, only a short while ago I felt so happy. What was happening to me? I began to sob and sob uncontrollably, believing I was going mad and would die.

Hardly able to walk, I dragged myself to the club, where I was supposed to work that evening. The girls stared at me as I stumbled into the dressing room. They had seen this thing happen before only too often to other foolish girls like me. No one had thought to warn me of the danger of drugs.

Then *they* did a foolish thing: they ran to find the pusher. Had they sent for an ambulance or got me to bed and sent for a doctor – anything but run for the pusher – I would have been all right in time, given proper care. But then the police would have been informed, and the management preferred such authority outside the door.

By the time the pusher was found I was wailing hysterically, a crumpled, shivering heap on the floor. The pusher gazed coldly at the crumpled form.

"You'll be all right. You just need some more dope. Got the money?"

Only after he was sure I could pay, did he give me another shot of deadly heroin.

I was hooked.

In such a simple way – hardly knowing what I was doing – I became addicted to hard drugs. Just another junkie joined the ever increasing numbers who exist from one fix to another, who depend on the needle to get them through each awful day.

It happens today in towns and cities everywhere. Many young people rush headlong to an early grave, all because of that first fateful shot in the arm, or the first reefer. Some, like me, do it in ignorance of the dreadful aftermath. Others, not so ignorant, go straight ahead, regardless of many warnings, into a life of sheer hell. Only when it is seemingly too late do they realize the warnings were only too true.

I realized early that it was too late for me. As the days passed I became utterly dependent on drugs – and more deceptive.

At first I had plenty of money to pay for drugs, but my bank balance dwindled as the pusher, who knew that I was in his control, asked a higher price every time we met. He sold me a syringe and some needles and showed me how to give myself my own fix – often a bloody and dangerous business.

I was losing weight rapidly and could not help noticing my deteriorating appearance. My waist-long hair lost its shine and began to fall out, whilst my skin became shallow and pitted. My good looks, my sole asset, disappeared. Often I had to stay in bed with liver infections and other effects of heroin.

One day the boss of the strip club gave me an ultimatum:
"Get yourself right or get out."

I was quite helpless. I knew only too well that I looked more like Deathly Diana than Daring Diana. I struggled through a few more appearances at the club before I was told to leave.

Jobless and faced with the daily problem of raising money for my drugs, I returned to prostitution. It wasn't an easy option. I must have looked like death warmed up – a very poor candidate for a good night out.

It was an awful ordeal, but what choice had I? It was drugs or die. I *had* to go onto the streets now, whether I wanted to or not. Believe me, I didn't – I was so ill.

What a picture of utter degradation I was, so steeped in

shame and misery, with no one to care what became of me. All my friends had left me and would not lend me money. They knew only too well I could never repay them now that I was a junkie.

I wasn't the only one. I saw and met many others just like me – mere shadows of people drifting round the streets like scraps of wrecked ships tossed in by a tidal wave of destruction. They are the flotsam and jetsam of humanity, blown along by the winds of misfortune and depravity, seeking shelter and rest from the cruel and bitter blows that life has dealt them – and finding none.

As I move down a silent, dusty street into the twilight zone, will you follow me? Let me take you behind the scenes and give you a glimpse into this twilight world.

It's a cold winter's evening. The few lamps down the gloomy back street throw out a dim, mellow light. There are not many people around. The bitter cold has driven everyone inside one of the many squalid public houses or dingy cafes.

I stop for a moment to pull my thin coat around my pitifully thin form. The coat's not nearly thick enough to keep the chill wind from piercing through me, but it has to suffice. Only a few days ago the last of my clothes and shoes had to be sold for drugs, a little food, and rent. My eyes are dull but ever watchful for the would-be customer that may pass by.

After what seems like an eternity a man appears down a side street. Eagerly I approach him, hoping he will be kind and generous and give me a little money. He takes pity on me and slips me a few extra shillings.

Watch now as I make my way into one of the squalid public houses. I know there will be a fire there to warm my weary, cold body. Sitting huddled by the small fire, I wish I had no need to go out and repeat the whole procedure. I present a perfect picture of sadness, loneliness, and despair. What a pity that I must go through the whole bit again, but drugs are expensive, and a must.

A pathetic picture, isn't it? But oh, so very true. This person could be your daughter, your sister – or you.

Although great efforts are made today to reach those who are trapped as I was, many are not reached. We cannot brush aside scenes like these and pretend they don't happen. They don't go away if we close our eyes.

I became too ill for prostitution every night and turned to shoplifting. When I was a child in Uxbridge, it was "steal or starve." Now it was "drugs or die." I had no choice.

Shoplifting was not easily carried out. I lacked the old confidence I once possessed and drugs had slowed down my quick reactions. Every excursion into a store caused me to shiver and break out in perspiration.

I hated selling the stolen merchandise. It made me feel even more guilty than the original act of theft. The prices I received were far below the retail value of the goods, perhaps 25% on average. When I did my purchasing, the price of heroin continued to spiral upward.

Because I was not apprehended I began to think I was quite an expert at shoplifting. Perhaps my over-confidence was the reason why I was caught red-handed one day. It was a wonder I wasn't caught earlier, for I must have looked suspicious many times as I gave furtive glances over my shoulder.

Leaving a store one morning with stolen jewelry in my handbag, I was quite unaware I was being followed by a store detective. Suddenly a firm hand gripped my shoulder.

"Will you come with me, miss? I believe you have taken something without paying."

He was not bullying or rude. Indeed, he seemed a little sorry for the poor bundle of humanity he had apprehended. I walked silently back to the store and was taken to the manager's office, where in the presence of a policeman my handbag was searched.

In addition to the stolen jewelry my handbag contained a reefer. Now I faced further trouble. Although I was evasive, the police seemed satisfied with the notes he made. He told me to appear in court the following morning and warned me to arrive on time and not to try to run away.

I had never before been in court on a criminal charge. I hardly slept that night and smoked many cigarettes, trying to think of possible alternatives. It was no use running away. In any case, where could I run? The police would only find me in the end.

The courtroom was a cold, bare place. I was advised to plead guilty by a stranger who disappeared after delivering this piece of advice. Apart from the court officials the room was quite empty. This was a surprise to me. I imagined that the seats would be filled to capacity with staring on-lookers, but it seemed no one was interested in me or cared what happened to me.

In the dock I was faced by a row of unsmiling faces, which looked carved from stone. An elegant man in a pin-stripe suit stood up and read the list of offences. I was surprised that the police knew so much about me, more than I could remember disclosing in the store manager's office.

"Do you plead guilty to these offences?" the man asked.

"Yes," I replied quietly.

There was a long pause, interrupted only by the rustle of papers and a muffled discussion amongst the magistrates. The silence seemed to last an eternity. Tick-tock, tick-tock — even the clock on the wall seemed sombre, as if it were counting up my crimes as well as the seconds.

"You have admitted that you are guilty, and you are therefore committed to serve a three month's prison sentence."

I was stunned. PRISON! The word sounded like a death sentence.

The court officials slowly filed out of the courtroom.

"This way, dear!" said a voice at my ear with some kindness. The policewoman at my side looked sad and sorry too.

A black van stood in the courtyard. I was escorted into it,

and the back door was firmly secured. Inside the van sat another policewoman. No words were spoken.

"Condemned to three months in prison, and no one cares," I thought.

When I look back at that time, I believe that God stepped in and allowed me to go to prison. I hesitate to think what might have happened had I continued unchecked on my old path. If drugs had not killed me, I could have ended up in the Thames. I now fully believe that God preserved me from a dreadful death.

At that time I could only think how uncaring everyone was. No one was concerned. No one.

No words were spoken during the journey that day as the van sped down the road to prison. My destination? Holloway.

CHAPTER TEN

Prison and Cold Turkey

HOLLOWAY Prison loomed into view, stark and menacing, like a great grey monster eager to devour its latest victim. I shivered in apprehension, wondering what it would be like trapped inside its jaws.

Nameless fears engulfed me as I passed through the black studded doors and caught the sounds that are a prison's own: loud banging of doors, jangling of heavy keys, clashing of milk trolleys.

Silently, fearfully I followed the prison officer down a dark corridor and into the reception area. Everything was very impersonal and formal. Orders were given in crisp tones to "have a bath". Then, dressed in my shapeless prison dress and black leather shoes, I was taken to the prison doctor.

"Hmmm."

The doctor examined me carefully, taking note of my eyes and the telltale marks on my arms.

"You are an addict. Is that correct?"

"Yes, I am."

I wondered why he asked the question, since he had the records before him.

"You will be looked after in the hospital wing for a while."

He gave a few instructions to the prison officer, and I was led away through a maze of corridors. My eyes were downcast, and I felt that invisible eyes were watching me with every step.

Clack! clack! clack! The sound of my heels on the floor sent weird echoes down the cold corridors. I shivered again. Keys jangled as doors were locked and unlocked. At last we reached the hospital wing.

Someone was screaming. The sound sent a cold shiver down my spine, and my fears mounted.

"This way."

The prison officer unlocked a cell door and ordered me inside.

I stood in the doorway for a moment, terrified. The officer gave me a definite push to get me inside and then slammed and locked the door. I was quite alone.

The floor, where I half fell, was thickly padded. It was not easy to walk or even stand on it. Padded to the ceiling, the walls had one small window, well out of reach and barred.

"Do they think I'm crazy or something? Why have they put me in here?" I thought.

The truth was I was to withdraw from drugs with no compensating medication. It was a terrible ordeal. I clearly remember the awful withdrawal symptoms which I suffered all alone, although I was watched through the spy hole in the door.

Delusions are very real indeed to the drug addict in the process of withdrawal. In my delusions the prison cell itself turned into an ugly monster that clawed at my body with hairy hands. When I screamed and kicked and fought the monster, prison officers rushed in to restrain me. I saw the officers as dragons, each with six heads. In my efforts to free myself from the monster's grip I pulled at the padded walls.

Sleep was short, and I suffered horrible nightmares, waking in a cold sweat to begin my fight all over again. When in short moments of sanity I saw a face at the spy-hole in the door, I thought:

"They've come to see if I'm still alive."

I cried to God to let me die.

"Let me die! Let me die!"

82

God never replied. I wondered if the Almighty could hear me through the padded walls.

During the three days of withdrawal, they brought me food on a plastic plate. In my wild behaviour I threw food, plate, tray, and all at the walls. As I began to recover I became aware that the cell looked worse than a pigsty. It literally stank.

I spoke aloud: "Oh, my God! What a fool I've been! What good are drugs, money, clothes, and jewels now?"

It was a most awful experience. I didn't think I would live.

The prison authorities had not encountered drug addiction on its present scale, and they used only one way to effect a cure. Even in the 1970s many say that "cold turkey," as the prison's method is called is the only realistic way of taking people off drugs like heroin or cocaine. But the suffering of the addict given this treatment is very terrible. Great care is certainly needed, or the patient will die.

After coming through the physical stage of withdrawal, I was taken out of my pigsty. I was very shaky and felt empty and dazed. As my footsteps echoed along the endless maze of corridors I vowed I would never again touch drugs. Never would anyone see me stripping in a low-down club. I'd live a good life when I got out, I was thinking. I had learned my lesson.

"I must be good! I must be good! I must be good!" my footsteps seemed to say.

"I wish I were you, with all your youth," said one of the older prisoners, who seemed destined to spend most of her life in prison. "You can make a fresh start, but it's too late for me."

"A new start. Yes, that's what I'd like when I get out of here. Start again and make something of my life," I said to myself.

The older woman's words cheered me. While in prison I lost some of my bitterness. I saw many sad people with even sadder backgrounds than my own – if that can be imagined.

Many of my fellow prisoners were alcoholics, shoplifters, prostitutes, and compulsive gamblers. A mixed and motley crew indeed -- some as hard as nails and others somehow wistful. Deserving punishment, they were also in need of compassion and guidance.

All suffered from the same disease as I: *loneliness*. I tried to help them in my way by cheering them up – even though I too was in need of that tonic. I was well liked and called Cheerful Dor. It reminded me of the old days at Uxbridge, where I had been the leader of many neglected children. Strange how history repeats itself!

I had been allowed to take a few personal belongings to prison, and they were now given to me – not that I had many possessions left. Most had been sold for drugs.

My Sunday school prize, the *Golden Bells Hymn Book*, was one of my possessions. In my cell at night before the lights went out I would read the familiar hymns of childhood.

> *Jesus, tender Shepherd, hear me.*
> *Bless Thy little lamb tonight.*
> *Through the darkness be thou near me.*
> *Keep me safe till morning light.*

I wondered, "What if the Sunday school teachers knew where I am now."

The screws (prison warders) were usually regarded as the enemy, not to be trusted, but I saw that many of them had a genuine interest in the prisoners. Quite a few took a great deal of interest in me.

At long last my three months' prison sentence ended. Some prisoners were sorry to see me go, but they called out:

"Don't come back if you can help it!"

Don't come back! As I made my way down the corridors, again my footsteps tapped out a message.

"Don't come back! Don't come back!"

Outside I looked at the grey stone monster of a prison and vowed I never would. I never did.

I walked away to search for the new life I'd resolved upon. Alas! I never found it. Once outside the prison walls I had no idea where to go or what to do.

My good intentions were blown to the four winds. The author now knows that one cannot "go it alone," without Christ's loving hand for guidance. One simply fails. As yet I had no Saviour to help me.

In the end I decided to look up my friends in Soho, and that was that. Within a short time Daring Diana was on stage again. Worse still, I returned to drugs. I told myself I would be in control of the situation this time, but I was back where I started from. "Little lady of the road" was stamped all over my young face.

It was like playing with fire. So many misguided youngsters think as I did they are bigger than drugs, only to find to their sorrow they were mistaken. I was just a junkie again. The slippery path downhill was beneath my feet.

During this period of my life the Salvation Army stepped up their work in Soho. They sent young officers to do practical work among people in great need. I was aware of their presence everywhere I went. As they spoke sincerely and honestly of the love of God for all mankind, I stopped to listen. But not for long.

Had I not heard this before, long ago at Sunday school? It was as if the past came back to haunt me. On one hand I resented the message of the Salvationists, and on the other I envied them. They had qualities I secretly yearned for and they all seemed so happy.

"But it's not for me," I thought. "It's too late now."

Sometimes after my performances at the strip club I would sit up in bed and read the hymns in my *Golden Bells Hymn Book*.

> *Tell me the stories of Jesus.*
> *Write on my heart every word.*

How simple the words were! I would close the book with a sigh.

"It's all right for them," I thought as I recalled the fresh, earnest faces of the young Salvationist officers, "but they have never lived my kind of life."

It may seem incredible that someone like me – a night club stripper and a prostitute – was reading hymns in the early hours of the morning. But God moves in a mysterious way.

To conceal my true feelings and to make an impression on my friends, I would often ridicule the Army girls.

"Salvation Army all gone barmy!" or "There goes Sister Anna carrying the banner."

This sport made not the slightest difference to the Salvationists. If anything it made them more determined than ever. Maybe they knew that this girl was somehow touched by their message.

Always ready for a laugh, my friend (also a stripper and drug addict) and I went to the Salvation Army Hall one evening. We sat at the back, giggling and making remarks throughout the evening. One of the officers invited us to go forward and kneel at the penitent form while the congregation sang:

> *Standing somewhere in the shadows*
> *You'll find Jesus.*
> *He's the only one who cares and understands.*
> *Standing somewhere in the shadows*
> *You will find Him,*
> *And you'll know Him by the nail prints in*
> *His hands.*

We used to sing that in Sunday school. It was all getting too much for me, and I fled, laughing and trying to push the whole thing out of my mind. My friend and I, who were searching for a different kind of fun, may have been laughing, but I at least felt I had almost come face to face with God.

Early one morning, about two a.m., I felt a gentle tap on

my shoulder as I emerged from the strip club, tired and rather depressed, for drugs were beginning to take their toll. I swung round to see the calm face of a Salvation Army girl. Oh, no, not again! I was in no mood for religion.

"Drop dead!" I said rudely.

The girl ignored my nasty remark.

"Jesus loves you, and He died for you."

"Look!" I shouted at her. "Just leave me alone, will yer! Just get lost."

"You are the one that's lost."

Her simple statement struck at my heart as surely as if it had been a well-aimed arrow.

LOST! LOST! LOST! I fled down the street like lightning, leaving the Salvation Army girl standing outside the club.

I knew somehow she was right. I was lost. Lost in my own darkness. Lost in my loneliness.

It would be some years before the Saviour would find me and claim me for His own. Looking back at that night, I realize that a wonderful opportunity was opened to me. I missed it.

CHAPTER ELEVEN

The Empire of Satan

Two girls were standing together in the semi-darkness of the strip club, whispering in hushed voices. What was it that made these two girls so different from the others?

I had noticed them before. They were always together, never making friends with anyone else. A strange bond held them together. In fact, I never saw them apart. No one seemed to know very much about them.

Yes, there was something different about them – something eerie and strange. Curiosity was my constant companion and I decided to investigate.

Since the club was always in semi-darkness it wasn't difficult to creep up behind them and listen. Standing in the shadowy doorway of the dressing room, I listened carefully to the two whispering girls.

Although I was unable to hear much that was said, I heard something about the Satanists' temple. I held my breath. It was impossible to hear more. If I wanted to learn what they were saying, I would have to disclose my presence.

I stepped out from the shadows and said brightly, "What's all this about the Satanists' temples?"

The two girls were startled.

"We can't tell you anything about it. It's a secret."

"I gathered that," I sniffed, "but I would like to know."

The two girls probably thought I had overheard the entire conversation. They looked at one another, and then one of them said, "If you promise never to say anything to anyone about it. . . ."

I agreed not to say a word.

"We are Satanists and worship at the temple of Satan."

"Can I come too?"

They again exchanged glances and then agreed.

"Be outside this club at six o'clock tomorrow, and we'll take you."

On the next evening I stood with bated breath at the appointed place. At six o'clock sharp a large black car drew up. The two girls were seated in the back. The driver instructed me to get inside.

"You will have to wear a blindfold, as this is the first time for you. No one must know where the temple is situated."

I had no objection. Indeed, the blindfold only added to the excitement. My heart was beating very fast.

The journey was soon over. I was led up a short flight of steps, and the blindfold was removed.

What I saw was astonishing and very mysterious.

I was standing at the back of a very large hall, filled with about five hundred people. A platform at the front was draped in black. On a throne-like seat sat a robed and hooded figure. His garments were embroidered with snakes, dragons, and flames of fire. Around him in a semi-circle stood some thirteen figures, also robed in black.

My first impulse as I took in the scene was to giggle, but because of the serious expression of the people I restrained myself. It was just as well that I did, for I had placed myself in a hazardous situation. The figures around the platform were the priests and priestesses of the order of Satanism.

My next impulse was to run away as far as I could, but I seemed to be glued to the spot.

The ceremony began. Priests and priestesses chanted in a strange rhythmic chant that grew louder and louder as the robed figure in the centre stepped down from the platform. Two of the priests removed his hood, and everyone bowed down and worshipped him, falling prostrate on the ground. I was just an observer, of course, and remained standing.

"That's the chief Satanist," one of the girls with me explained. "He must be obeyed at all times."

Unable to speak, I merely nodded and continued to watch in fascination.

"He represents Satan on the earth," said the girl, her voice trembling in awe.

Little did I realize that I had walked into the most ancient order of Satanism in the world.

"Watch, and listen carefully," said the girl again. "I will explain as the ceremony proceeds."

The whole congregation was now chanting prayers to the chief Satanist in that same strange rhythmic way. Everyone's eyes were on him. Priests and priestesses waited upon him as he kissed the vessels, the knives, and the emblem of Satanists that had been taken from the high altar.

"He is dedicating the temple and the vessels to Lucifer."

Suddenly the dim lights went out, and flaming torches were lit. For the first time I saw the effigies of Satan around the walls. They seemed to come alive as the ceremony continued.

A white cockerel was brought in, and its neck was wrung right on the steps that led up to the throne and altar. Blood was everywhere. Then the cockerel was offered to Satan in sacrifice with more chants and prayers. Everything was done in the name of Satan, "Diablos," and everyone was excited and in deadly earnest.

I was surprised to find the chief Satanist looking straight at me. It seemed as if his eyes were piercing right through me. I shivered.

The whole ceremony lasted some two hours. It had been an awesome, yet evil, experience.

The chief Satanist appeared at the back of the hall in street attire, and he came over to me.

"Do you want to join us?" he asked.

"I don't know. I was a bit frightened by it all."

"There's no need for fear," he smiled.

I could not help noticing the admiring glances he was giving me.

"I hope to see you again at the next meeting," he said and disappeared.

"He's interested in you, Doreen," said one of the girls.

"Yes. I wonder why."

I was puzzled. He sought me out from among five hundred people. Why?

I learned the reason later. Search for talent and potential members was energetically pursued – perhaps more so than in Christian churches. Besides, once a person has actually been present at a ceremony as a mere observer, there is danger that the proceedings will be told abroad. Very often the site of the temple was moved elsewhere if there was any danger of its being discovered by outsiders. Secrecy is a must in the order.

I wasn't sure that I would ever go again, yet some unexplained power drew me back to the next meeting. I had to be taken again as I didn't know the exact location of the temple.

I witnessed all manner of evil scenes, far worse than the last. I was more than a little surprised at the seriousness of those present. Apparently they believed earnestly in all they were doing. Strangely enough, by the time the hideous meeting was over I was no longer afraid.

I was rather flattered too when the chief Satanist asked me to join him for a meal. I felt a little nervous, and he tried to put me at ease. It wasn't long before I found myself telling him my life story. He didn't seem in the least surprised when I told him I was a drug addict, prostitute, and strip-tease artiste. Indeed, he seemed to know all about me. Probably one of the girls I'd seen in the club put him in the picture.

"All kinds of people are Satanists," he said. "From the high to the low – bankers, shopkeepers, teachers, nurses, prostitutes, drug addicts. There's no difference between us.

We are here to promote Satan on the earth whenever and however we can."

He had a strong personality and had no difficulty in persuading me to become a Satanist. I was taught that evil – as most people think of evil – is not wrong, but right and good. It sounded stupid to me, as indeed it is, but I started to believe it.

The Satanists twisted and distorted everything. A lie, I was told, was in fact the truth. All very confusing, but many believed it – even intelligent people. It was a kind of brainwashing. If you are told the same thing over and over again, you finally come to believe it, no matter how stupid it sounds.

My friendship with the chief Satanist grew. I attended all the meetings at the temple minus blindfolds or secrecy. I was eager to become a full-fledged Satanist.

Taking that awful step was not simple. One has to learn the rules of Satanism and believe every one of them utterly. These are samples of the rules I had to accept and learn:

1. Secrecy is the keynote for all Satanists. They must never reveal the whereabouts of the temples to an outsider or the things that go on inside the temple.

2. All must love, honour, and obey without question the chief Satanist, who is Lucifer's representative on the earth. Satanists must follow Satan all the days of their life and serve no other but him.

3. Satanists must never enter a Christian church unless sent in to spy by the chief Satanist. All new ideas and fresh happenings are to be reported back in full to the chief Satanist at the temple of Satan.

4. Satanists must never read the Holy Bible for their own edification.

5. The Holy Scriptures are to be mocked and burned in the Satanists' temple, also prayer books and hymn books – in fact, all Christian literature must be destroyed. (This order dates back centuries. In contrast, various old writings by ancient chiefs are carefully preserved. Relevations from

Hades, demons, and gods are often read in ritual worship in the temples of Satan.)

6. No one must arrive late at the temple. Punishment by whipping will be carried out on all latecomers by the chief Satanist in front of the whole congregation.

7. Lucifer must be highly esteemed in all situations, even while at work or in private. Lucifer sees, as he is with Satanists always, and he must be obeyed. Lying, cheating, swearing, free lust – even murder – are condoned.

8. Prayer to Lucifer must be made daily.

There are many more rules, and all who fail to obey them are punished by whipping in front of all Satanists at the temple. The whippings are carried out by the chief Satanist himself.

I soon learned the rules. Furthermore, I fully believed them.

The chief Satanist was by this time a regular visitor to the strip club, where I still worked. I was now his mistress. He would bring with him my supply of heroin and would accept no payment.

"It's a gift," he would say.

Some gift.

My addiction to hard drugs was just an extra one-way ticket to hell, yet drug addiction, stripping, etc. seemed to pale compared with Satan worship.

I asked no questions about the source of drugs. Although I was now his mistress, the chief Satanist didn't care about my prostitution. He believed the more evil he condoned or achieved on earth, the greater would be his reward. If and when he died, he believed he would be in charge of legions of devils, so the greater the evil, the greater the reward.

One day he informed me, "You are now ready to become a sworn-in child of Lucifer."

The ceremony would be complicated and lengthy. Many Satanists would be present, Satanists from other temples in England. When the time came around, about eight hundred or more Satanists were present, all punctual, since no one was ever late for any meeting.

I was dressed in a loose black robe, whilst hymns and prayers were chanted to the great god of darkness, death, and mystery. Flaming torches sent weird shadows racing across the walls and ceiling. The vessels on the high altar were dedicated one by one, and the silver knives kissed.

The chief Satanist rose from his throne and raised his hands, whereupon all, including also me, fell down and worshipped him. Two priests disappeared behind the black drapes at the rear of the raised platform and returned with the sacred white cokerel. Its neck was broken and split open, and its blood caught in a silver cup. More chants and prayers to Satan followed. The air was heavy with evil.

The chief Satanist approached me and made an incision in my left arm, and my blood was caught in the cup that contained the blood from the slain bird. The knife was again kissed, and the blood mixed. I then drank some of this blood and made my vows to Satan.

Next I dipped my finger in the mixed blood and signed a real parchment, thereby selling my soul to Satan for ever and ever, to be his slave for all eternity. I was now a true Satanist, and everyone rejoiced that another child of Satan was born.

The people went crazy, and all kinds of evil scenes followed. Much wickedness was done that evening.

To my surprise I was sworn in as high priestess, a high honour indeed in Satanist circles. When I protested that I wasn't ready for such a place of honour, the chief Satanist said it was a request of the great Lucifer himself, and he must be obeyed.

In this position I could serve my master better. I was qualified to handle the sacred vessels and wait at the high altar. I was known as the great priestess Diana. I felt very important.

From a bit of conversation overheard at the strip club I had become a leader in Satanism, and Satan was indeed my master. I even heard his audible voice and saw him materialize in front of me.

On more than one occasion Lucifer materialized in a black form before all Satanists in the temple. No one disbelieved; it was indeed Satan. We heard his voice speaking to us as a whole congregation.

We knew it was he saying: "I am Lucifer, your master. I speak unto you from my lips. Obey my voice, my children. Do all the evil you wish. Never fear – I will protect you at all times. Revel in your freedom of lust this night. It is pleasing in my sight."

We all obeyed without question.

In olden times one or two chiefs had power from Lucifer to perform operations on themselves and others. No drugs were used in these operations. Furthermore, no scar remained where incisions were made.

The power to go into deep trances is still practised today. I too could go into a trance and see powerful activity in the demon sphere. ESP (extra sensory perception) was one of my powers. I could read people's minds easily and know what they would say or do.

Readers may ask if it was really possible that someone steeped in evil as I was in my position as high priestess could be wonderfully converted to the Lord Jesus Christ. But the Bible says Jesus died for the who-so-ever. He died for Satanists.

The time was to come when I would change masters and serve the greatest Master of all. But not yet.

CHAPTER TWELVE

Queen of Black Witches

As the months went by my knowledge of evil grew. The practice of devil worship and my role as high priestess were the most important things in my life. Indeed, I thought of little else.

Even away from the temple the presence of Satan was very real. It was as if an unseen hand was pushing me further into the realms of darkness. For example, I needed very little sleep, and I was given a supernatural strength and endurance. I was truly a slave of satan and keeping my vows well.

Strangely, though, I kept my *Golden Bells Hymn Book*. By all Satanist rules I should have destroyed the book, but I couldn't do it. It was the only gift I'd ever received as a child.

Not that I read the hymns any more. I had given that up long ago. I had almost forgotten I possessed the book, carefully hidden from view. Many people came into my bedroom; the chief Satanist was of course always there.

One day I was having a drink with my lover and master, the chief Satanist. He seemed eager to impress me.

"I'm a black witch, Diana, and I practise black magic."

I nearly choked on my drink and then burst out laughing.

"It's not funny," snapped the chief Satanist.

"I'm sorry. It sounded funny," I said, still laughing.

My idea of a witch was a hook-nosed old hag riding on a

broomstick across the face of the moon. As I soon discovered, nothing could be further from the truth.

Witchcraft of the black kind is not far removed from Satanism. The main difference between the two is that Satanists worship the devil in the Satanist temple, whereas witches attend a coven of thirteen witches, one of whom is the head. They require no temple.

Witchcraft can be practised anywhere but preferably in a quiet, remote setting, such as a deserted house, a lonely beach, or a wood. The witching hour of midnight is also preferred, and activities are conducted by moonlight. "Warlock" is the correct name for a person usually called a witch.

Black witches have great power and are not to be taken lightly. They are able to call up, or call down, powers of darkness to aid them.

Very often they exhume fresh graves and offer the bodies in sacrifice to Satan. They break into churches, burn Bibles and prayer books. Whenever holy ground is desecrated, an emblem of witchcraft is left behind: goat's blood is splashed on headstones of graves, on walls, etc.

They hold nothing sacred and will stop at nothing to pursue their goals. NOTHING!

Black witches have power to put curses on people, and the curses work. People have been known to die because of the curse or spell of a black witch. Nude rites are another evil aspect of witchcraft.

All this may seem rather unlikely to readers who have had no encounter with witchcraft, so it's worth explaining. Black witches and Satanists believe that in the ultimate battle between good and evil, evil will triumph. They believe that Lucifer will one day conquer Christ and will retrieve what they call his rightful place. Satan, they affirm, will rule the earth, sea, and heavens.

Hell, for a witch of the black kind, is not a place of torment but of unlimited pleasure, with every lust fulfilled.

The more evil, the better is the motto of a black witch and Satanist.

Be warned: those who walk down the dark road of witchcraft lose their reason, often going completely insane. Good is called evil, which does not make sense. Minds are twisted and warped.

The chief Satanist's long discussion on witchcraft ended.

"You will make a fine witch, Diana. You have a great natural power."

I had known and felt that power often enough, but I believed it was not a natural, but rather a supernatural, power working through me. I was not born with it. The power was not my own but Satan's.

I was surprised at the chief Satanist's words. His dark eyes flashed as he spoke, almost hypnotizing me. His face shone with a strange, eerie light I'd never seen before. For one brief moment I wanted to escape, but the feeling subsided, and I agreed to accompany him to the witches' coven.

"It can be no worse than Satanism," I reasoned.

I had witnessed evil and ugly orgies in the Satanists' temple, but I was to see far worse in the witches' coven.

I always obeyed my master, the chief Satanist, and naturally I became a witch. At my initiation goat's blood was smeared all over my naked body. Things followed that were too evil to be brought to mind.

All meetings included awful scenes of perverted sexual acts, as sex plays an important part in witchcraft. Many black witches were Lesbians or homosexuals.

Sadism was practised frequently. Some even cut themselves with knives and felt no pain. Some swallowed poison, and no ill effects were experienced at all.

Imagine over one hundred black witches all taking part in such perversions at the same time. And this still goes on today.

My powers as a black witch were great, and I added to

my knowledge of evil every day. My ability to levitate four or five feet was very real. It was not a hoax. Demons aided me.

Killing birds in flight after they had been let loose from a cage was another act I performed as a witch. I could make objects appear and disappear. I also mastered apport, which is often used when witches demonstrate their powers before others.

I took part in everything a black witch would do, leaving nothing out. I practised more wickedness in a single week than many would in an entire lifetime.

I was not surprised when the chief Satanist suggested that I advance in witchcraft.

"You might even be queen of black witches one day, Diana."

"What, I?"

"Yes! I'll submit your name. But keep practising your powers so that you will be ready for the test."

The test of power to which the chief Satanist referred was to be held on Dartmoor in Devon, the centre of two large and active covens. Unaccompanied by my master (an unusual event), I exhibited my powers in a remarkable way one moonlight night. This action virtually confirmed me as queen of the witches – and points out the conflict between good and evil.

It was midnight, a bright, cloudless night, excellent for witching. The naked members of the coven were pursuing their rituals. I was among them. Suddenly we saw three men approaching over the brow of the hill. Although the intruders had not yet seen us witches, in a few minutes they would come upon the whole lot of us. There were no rocks or trees to hide behind.

"What shall we do?" asked the witches anxiously. "There's no place to hide!"

"Don't worry," I said. "I can make myself invisible."

"What about us?"

"If you put yourself in my hands, I'll make you invisible too."

There was no time to lose. Hastily the others did as I told them. Standing perfectly still in a circle, we raised our hands so that they touched.

I called up powers of darkness from demons and Satan himself. Within seconds a green swirling mist enveloped us. We could scarcely see each other as the three men passed us. I could easily have reached out my hand and touched them, one of whom had walked under our raised hands into the centre of our circle. My magic had worked.

What I have related is perfectly true. The other witches and I were invisible to the three men, who were not even aware of the thick swirling mist. They had not seen a single thing.

"Let's go home," we heard one of the men say. "There are no witches here. We're wasting our time."

When the three intruders were gone, the mist slowly disappeared.

The reason for the three men's appearance was explained when I read the local newspaper the day after. An article in the centre pages was headlined: NO WITCHES ON DARTMOOR. It related that a local preacher had taken two reporters onto Dartmoor the previous evening to investigate a rumour that witches would be present there.

The search had been fruitless, by all accounts. However, the local preacher was not convinced that witches had not been on the moor. He was right, of course. He had unawares been within inches of them.

We were all highly amused. The story was told in other covens, and my fame spread abroad. Some may think it strange that the Lord did not permit the local preacher to see the witches. Without questioning the Lord's will, we can be absolutely sure that He had His own purpose in not permitting His servant to see. The Lord certainly did not permit His servant to be harmed – for I tried to put curses on the preacher, but they did not work. There was a barrier between my power and the preacher, who was a man of great faith and courage.

I was puzzled. My powers had never before failed. I had no idea that far greater power than that of Satan was protecting this man – the mighty power of the Lord Jesus Christ, who conquered death, hell, and Satan at the place called Calvary.

Although the event on Dartmoor at first glance showed plainly the power of witchcraft and Satan, in truth it showed the far greater power of the Lord Jesus Christ.

The scene was set for the great ceremony at which the next queen of black witches was to be chosen. Black witches from all parts of England assembled, as well as witches from Holland, Germany and France. They arrived before Hallowe'en, when Dartmoor was a hive of activity. The influx of visitors at Plymouth certainly included many witches.

The arrived in smart cars, not on broomsticks, and booked in at hotels looking for all the world like successful businessmen and women – which some were. This was the new face of witchcraft – prosperous, almost respectable – a veneer that concealed tremendous forces of evil.

Taking drugs before the ceremony helped to quell my feeling of nervousness, and I confidently faced the ordeal.

The ceremony commenced with chants to the ancient gods and demons. The moon goddess Diana was my favourite, for obvious reasons.

After the rituals the great test of power began. Seven witches, including me, were competing for the title. Success would not be easy, for all witches have great powers.

A bird was released from a cage. I killed it in flight. It was something I'd done before, but I was the only one who did it in this test. Various other supernatural feats were performed that eerie night on Dartmoor, but the last was the greatest: fire-walking.

The test was to walk through a great bonfire (not a ring of fire, please note, but a great blaze). The successful candidate would meet Lucifer in the centre of the blaze, and Lucifer would be *seen* by the assembly to take the hand of the witch and guide her through the flames so that she would emerge completely unscathed.

I walked confidently into the flames of seven feet or more, all the time calling on my great master, Diablos. Suddenly I saw him materialize before me – a great black figure. I took his hand and walked with him to the centre of the great blaze. There I paused, the great flames leaping around me.

Only when I emerged at the other side of the blaze did my master Diablos disappear. Not even the smell of burning was upon my loose witch's robe or my long flowing hair.

Everyone was prostrated on the ground.

"Hail, Diana, queen of black witches!" rose the loud cry of over a thousand witches.

A crown of pure gold was placed on my head, a cloak beautifully embroidered with gold was thrown around my shoulders, and an orb of gold placed in my left hand. I took my seat on the throne, which had been prepared before the ceremony. These and all other objects used were of great value and were carefully preserved for the reigning queen.

Wild and frenzied celebrations followed: dancing in the nude and other sensual pleasures, drink and drugs. Diana, queen of black witches, was of course the centre of attraction, regarded with pride by her master and lover, the chief Satanist. After all, I was his protege. He had trained me.

Had reporters or anyone else ventured on the moor that night, they could hardly have been unaware that something strange was going on. The flames of the huge fire must have been visible for miles, yet none of the witches were interrupted. Perhaps there were individuals who knew something evil was in progress and kept well away. I don't blame them.

One can laugh at legends of witchcraft when evidences of evil are not at hand or ever witnessed, yet had anyone been on the moor that night, he would not have laughed.

I know that witchcraft is real. Was I not right at the top as queen of black witches?

CHAPTER THIRTEEN

No Way Out

"QUEEN of Black Witches." It was a title of high esteem, a standing of great importance. I was not a little envied by other witches who had great power. With the title went study, work, and travel.

And travel I did, in luxury, with the chief Satanist, who was also a black witch. Holland, Germany, France were some of the countries I visited. Foreign witches entertained the two honoured guests in grand style. We stayed only at the best hotels or sometimes in large, expensive houses situated in beautiful grounds, which were, of course, homes of witches.

The travels could aptly be described as a tour of sin.

There was no language barrier, for when I called upon Lucifer to help me, he did, and it was not long before I could understand the various tongues, not long before I could converse with ease. That old saying, "the devil looks after his own," is true only when it suits his evil purposes.

Many discussions were held, the most important subject being how to make black witchcraft more appealing. Many people, especially the young, were taking a fresh interest in the occult. It was important to give witchcraft a new look, and these guidelines were laid down:

Never frighten anyone. Offer new realms of mystery and excitement. Make witchcraft less sinister. Make it look like natural, innocent adventure. (Everyone is attracted by adventure and mystery.) Cover up evil with appealing wrappings.

New recruits were needed if evil was to conquer. Time was short. *Now* was the time to trap people. Once people were involved in witchcraft, it would be too late to get out. Fear would hold many back from retreating. There would be no way out.

We witches were very devout in our cause, and discussions went on for hours on end. We were not sparing with our time. Sharing experiences, demonstrating occult powers, and visiting covens were some of my activities on my full programme abroad.

When I returned to England, my time was spent visiting covens. Many new ones were springing up, and it was important to encourage new members. White witches were swelling their ranks; therefore we also had to attract new members. We didn't mention blood sacrifice – that would have caused fright.

White witches joined the ranks of the black witches, and we learned from them. I will mention here that although white witches claim never to harm anyone, I can say that I've known white witches who did so. Practices called voodoo by black witches were followed by white witches, who use "fith fath," a doll made of clay in the image of the person they wish to harm. They use a pin on this image to seal the lips of the person represented. They tie a cord to the legs of the image to inflict pain in the person's legs. When someone is rendered speechless or when he is made to suffer pains in his legs and is unable to walk, he is certainly being harmed.

I was queen of black witches for a full year. Then I willingly stepped down to allow someone younger to take the title, although I could have kept it had I wished. As soon as I gave up the title the chief Satanist found himself a new mistress. At first I was hurt and angry, but, after all he was the chief Satanist and no one questioned him. Best to accept it and go quietly.

I left London and drifted from town to village for a few years, visiting London now and then to obtain my drugs or to worship at the temple of Satan. Life was a little less hectic but still as dark as the grave. Prostitution was always something to fall back on if cash got short. As queen of witches I had lived a life of luxury and had been more of a call girl.

Perhaps my greatest power was my ability to deceive the many people I met. No one besides the Satanists knew of my darker activities late at night in a witches' coven, not even the man I lived with.

I managed to get away with the biggest lies. No one doubted them in the least. In fact, I often felt that if I were to tell the truth, no one would believe it. Lies were more readily accepted.

Those were unsettling years for me. I had one mounting fear – the fear of growing old and dying. As the fear grew, so questions arose in my mind. Was hell the wonderful place I had been led to believe? Suppose it was just the reverse. What then?

When the doubts persisted, I decided to try to break away from witchcraft and Satanism. Of course I would have to be careful, I reasoned – break away slowly so no one would notice, because no one leaves black witchcraft. It was worth a try at least.

While I was in the covens in the midst of rituals, I half believed that what I was doing was right for me. Then fear and uncertainty gripped me. In the awful confusion I felt I was trapped in a long dark tunnel. No glimmer of light could I see.

At this time of doubt and confusion I decided to visit a few Christian churches, just to see if they had the answer. Not that these visits were frequent. Far from it. But the fact remains, I at least went – something a black witch would never do. Always the fear of being found out haunted me. I constantly looked over my shoulder to make sure I wasn't being followed.

"What's the use?" I would think. "I've sold my soul to Satan with my own blood."

Why did I have doubts about my craft? Was it because I was not in the constant company of witches, seeing them only once or twice a week? Or was it that the Lord Jesus caused serious doubts about my craft to arise? I believe the latter.

Surely the loving Saviour was looking down on this captive child of darkness in great, tender compassion. One small link of the chain that bound me so tightly was beginning to weaken.

Eventually, after many roamings, I moved to Bristol. Because of the docks in Bristol it wasn't difficult to obtain my drugs, after a little help from London to make the right contacts. Again, in Bristol, Daring Diana was back in business as a prostitute, ready as ever with a laugh and a song.

I was quite popular with the street girls of Bristol, especially in the twilight area of St. Paul's, where I lived. Little did anyone realize my true feelings of loneliness and uncertainty.

Black witchcraft is widely practised in the west country, and before long I found the witches' covens. Some of the witches remembered me and had been on Dartmoor when I was crowned queen. I was put in charge of two covens in Bristol.

Still the doubts persisted. But life went on in the same sordid way. I had given up any thoughts of getting out. I knew it was useless trying. *There was no way out.*

Bristol is a city of churches, as I soon discovered. There seemed to be one on every corner. I visited a few, but my visits were extremely short. Indeed, I never stayed the whole length of the service. I cannot remember what was said or done there.

In my wavering, tossed-about way I forgot about my search for the truth. Instead I turned strongly against the churches as true Satanists should, regarding them all as a lot of hypocrites. At this point even the sight of a Christian church annoyed me immensely.

I stared at the name on the display board outside one of Bristol's churches. Wasn't he the preacher from Plymouth who tried to expose the witches on Dartmoor? I'd tried to cast spells on him, but they had never worked. Now he was coming to Bristol.

I hurried on. It was uncanny. Try as I might, I couldn't get his name out of my mind. God moves in a mysterious way.

One summer evening I was out as usual on the familiar streets. Two of my friends, also prostitutes, were with me. I suddenly stopped at the sight of another poster, outside yet another church. The poster proclaimed in large bold letters:

> *Blessed are the pure in heart,*
> *For they shall see God.*

The quotation affected me strangely. It was that word pure. It seemed to reach out. Anger and resentment swept over me.

"I'm not pure, so I'll never see God – if there is a God."

If there is a God – I was not sure.

Moving swiftly to the board, I tore the poster down, rather surprised when the entire poster came away intact. I dropped it quickly.

"Bloomin' load of hypocrites!" I said hotly.

"Good old Diana. She's at it again," laughed the two girls.

They were highly amused, but I was not laughing. I was furious. The truth was my conscience was pricked; God was pursuing me.

108

This incident was in the way of preparation for what was to follow, only I didn't know it.

Some months later I was out walking again, this time in the centre of Bristol. It was a Monday morning, an unusual time indeed for me to be out. Once again I was in the company of those of my own kind, wandering aimlessly around the streets.

I noticed many posters displayed in prominent places, unusual posters.

"Come and hear Eric Hutchings at the Colston Hall," read one. "Thousands hear. Hear you too," proclaimed another.

Yet the posters didn't say who Eric Hutchings was or why he was coming to Bristol. There was only a picture of his face.

At first glance I surmised he was an all-in wrestler. I was puzzled and determined to find out just who he was. I marched into the information bureau, followed by my giggling friends.

"Who is Eric Hutchings?" I asked the woman behind the counter.

"I haven't the faintest idea," she replied.

"Someone must know," I insisted, explaining about the many posters I'd seen.

"I do believe he is an evangelist or a preacher of some sort," spoke up another woman.

I nearly fainted. Oh, no! Not again. I couldn't get away from them.

"As if we haven't got enough preachers in Bristol without him poking his nose in."

I was angry and raised my voice in protest. By this time I had a small audience who were amused, if a little puzzled, by my outburst.

"Come on, girls. Let's get out of here."

They duly followed me, in fits of laughter.

As my giggling friends watched, I proceeded to pull

down every Eric Hutchings poster I could find. I was conducting my own crusade as champion poster-puller.

"Has everyone gone crazy in this city of churches?" I was saying. "Has everyone got religious mania?"

Much to my astonishment just a few days later even more posters had been put up. It seemed that six replaced each one I had removed. My anger flared again, but I changed my tactics.

Instead of pulling down the posters I drew a big bushy beard on the face of Eric Hutchings, or a huge handlebar moustache, much to the delight of my friends.

Billy Graham was in the news at the same time. In contempt I called the two preachers a pair of do-gooding hypocrites. By this time my friends were more than puzzled by my behaviour.

"What are you getting all steamed up about, Diana? They haven't done you any harm.."

"They haven't done me any bloomin' good either," I snapped.

Why indeed? My heart was filled with hate for anything Christian.

Lucifer, my master, was not at all pleased that the grand old Gospel story was to be preached in Bristol. A crusade was planned, to be held, not in a church, but in a large central hall.

I have related that I was trapped in my evil life and there was no way out. I was to hear of *the only way out*: through the love and salvation of the Lord Jesus Christ.

Unaware of what lay ahead, I continued in my shameful way of life, the only way I knew.

CHAPTER FOURTEEN

First Step to Freedom

IT was a lovely summer evening in June 1964. Three weeks had passed since I'd ripped down the posters announcing the arrival of Eric Hutchings. I had forgotten all about him. It was a Saturday, and I had other things on my mind in my business as a prostitute.

Daring Diana, dressed in keeping with her profession, was waiting for a client. Growing more restless as the minutes ticked away, I realized he wasn't going to turn up. I was high on drugs, and drink.

Just about to move on, I was suddenly aware of crowds of people, all heading in one direction. Curious as ever, I wondered why many people were in the centre of Bristol early in the evening. Then I saw the Bibles that some were carrying.

"It's all the religious hypocrites going to Eric Hutchings' meeting," I thought.

I fell in step behind a small group. At Colston Hall I paused, but not for long.

"I'll show him what I think of him and his meeting."

I was not in a very good mood. Wishing I had a few of my friends with me to back me up, I pushed my way through the vast crowds in the entrance hall. I had one purpose in mind; to punch Eric Hutchings on the nose.

I cannot recall how an observant usher managed to calm me down as I set out to do what I'd come for, but he did.

He showed me to an empty seat at the end of a packed row. My entrance caused no small stir, since the entire row had to stand up to let me pass.

I was dressed in a low-cut black satin dress, my face was heavily made up, and I flaunted an assortment of jangling jewelry. I could feel the curious stares in the audience.

I directed my gaze to the platform. Here sat a row of ministers and behind them a huge mixed choir, dressed in white. I was beginning to feel uncomfortable. People seated in front of me turned to stare at the decorative Doreen.

"Let 'em all look!" I thought. "Do 'em good."

They received a long, hard glare in return.

The meeting began with a rousing hymn, but I was not singing. I was thinking how I might make an exit without attracting too much interest – it had been bad enough when I walked in.

When at last the hymn ended, everyone sat down – everyone except me, for I saw my chance to beat a hasty retreat. At this precise moment a hush fell on the large congregation as a woman with a sweet voice broke into song, filling the air with lovely music. It caused me to pause and listen.

I would love to tell you what I think of Jesus,
Since I found in Him a Friend so strong and true.
I would tell you how He changed my life completely.
He's done something that no other friend could do.

All my life was full of sin, when Jesus found me.
All my life was full of misery and woe.
Jesus placed His strong and loving arms around me,
And He led me in the way I ought to go.

No one ever cared for me like Jesus.
There's no other friend so kind as He.
No one else could take the sin and darkness from me.
Oh! how much He cares for me.

112

Something wonderful yet inexplicable was happening deep down inside me – something I'd never experienced before. My whole life unfolded before me as if projected on a screen. My mind was very clear, and I was instantly sobered up.

I saw myself as a child in the Sunday school class and heard the teacher say, "Why not let Jesus come into your heart?"

I saw the Salvation Army lassie singing on the Paddington streets. I also saw the beds of shame and myself in the witches' covens.

As accompaniment to the scenes before my mind's eye I heard the words of that lovely song. The realization dawned on my black and sinful heart that no one really loved me – not the men on the streets or the men in the public houses, not the Satanists or witches. Yet the singer said that Jesus cared and that Jesus could take the sin and awful *darkness* away.

Oh, could it be true? Could it really be true that this Jesus really lived and really cared? Could He care for me, a common prostitute, drug addict, and witch? Oh, if it were true, I would surely love Him in return. How could I have missed such blessings all these long years?

After years of deepest shame someone was reaching out to me – Jesus, the tender Saviour who died in my place. For the first time in my life I felt dirty and really ashamed of the life I'd lived.

I had completely forgotten I was still standing up in the large hall. I was sorry when the solo ended. I wished there had been fifty verses. Betty-Lou Mills, the singer's, face shone with an inner radiance, a beauty not obtainable in any chemist's shop.

Whether the unusual sight of a worldly woman standing and listening so intently to the soloist made any impact on that gathering is not known to me. I was unaware of anything or anyone except the singer and her wonderful message of hope.

113

I sat down subdued and shaken. Eric Hutchings began his sermon thus: "If you do not know the Lord Jesus Christ as your personal Saviour, you are lost. You are dead in trespasses and sins. The Bible says you are BOUND."

He laid such emphasis on the word bound I nearly fell off my seat in fright. He was right though, and I knew it.

I jumped to my feet and shouted, "He's right. I AM bound!"

A shocked silence fell on the vast congregation, not to mention the evangelist himself, who was unable to speak for a few moments.

When he continued, he spoke with added fervour.

"If you go to church Sunday by Sunday and do not know the Lord Jesus Christ as your personal Saviour, you too are lost."

My ears pricked up at this statement, and I wanted to resound a hearty "Hear, hear!" but I was aware that people were watching me and I refrained.

"He's having a go at the church members," I thought, "so he's not such a bad sort."

Eric Hutchings went on to say that Jesus died for the who-so-ever, and if they turn to Him, He will set them free from the bondage of Satan. My heart was beating very quickly indeed. Could He set me free?

I remember no more of that powerful sermon. At the close the evangelist made an appeal: "Come to Jesus tonight. Come out to the front."

People began coming forward as the choir sang:

> *Just as I am, without one plea*
> *But that Thy blood was shed for me,*
> *And that Thou bidst me come to Thee.*
> *Oh, Lamb of God, I come, I come!*

Chains seemed to bind me to my seat as I heard the audible voice of Diablos: "You are MINE. You cannot go. It's too late for you. You are MINE."

I was shaking from head to foot. A great battle was going on, a battle with the powers of darkness and Satan. My evil master was fighting to hold on to me.

The choir sang another verse.

> *Just as I am, though tossed about*
> *With many a conflict, many a doubt,*
> *Fighting and fears within, without.*
> *Oh, Lamb of God, I come, I come!*

By some tremendous miracle I was on my feet, making my way to the front, all the while fighting the powers of darkness within and realizing too that someone greater than Satan had come to my aid.

Satan was losing the battle. Satan was losing his slave. Jesus, who cared for me, even me in all my sin and shame, was tenderly wooing and winning my black and sinful heart.

I was now standing at the front. Tears were falling down my painted face.

"I'm coming, Jesus," I said softly. "Please take the darkness away."

I had no understanding of how to pray. But do we need to know how? The Saviour heard the cry of my heart and accepted me just as I was. What rejoicing there must have been in heaven that night!

In the counselling room later all was different. I was not easy to counsel. My doubts and fears came flooding back in that changed atmosphere.

I even heard the voice of Satan say, "You cannot change. You are MINE."

A great struggle was going on within. What about my way of life? How could I live without drugs? How could I give it all up?

Several individuals spoke to me and showed me verses in the Bible, but I couldn't take it in. They presented the ABC's of the Gospel, but something was missing that I couldn't name. Those Bible verses applied to anyone who was seeking Christ, and of course they applied to me, but more was needed.

I was afraid to reveal the whole truth about myself, afraid they would turn me out if they knew I was a witch and a prostitute and a strip-tease artiste.

All I said was, "I'm a drug addict."

How was I to know they would not dream of turning me out?

They were at a loss in their counselling, only saying, "If you let Christ take over your life, everything else will just fall away."

I didn't think it would be as easy as that. I agreed to pray, though, trying hard to believe what they said was true.

"Perhaps they are right. When I wake up in the morning, maybe everything will be different," I thought.

But something was missing somewhere.

A woman adviser then spoke to me for a little while. She was Mrs. Mary Hutchings, although I didn't know it at the time.

"I will pray for you, my dear," she said.

She was gentle and kind. I liked her.

Eventually I left, clutching my copy of St. John's Gospel and a little book called *First Steps with Christ*. It was very late, well after midnight. Everyone else had left long ago.

A group of prostitutes were standing on the corner near Colston Hall.

"Hello, Diana," they chorused. "Where have you been? We've been looking for you."

"I have just got saved at Colston Hall," I answered simply.

They thought I was having them on. They roared with laughter.

"I'm not joking. I have given my heart to Jesus at Colston Hall."

They stared in unbelief.

116

"Come off it, Diana. It's us – your friends."

"I'm perfectly well aware of that. But it's true. I'm going home now to read my Bible."

I showed them my St. John's Gospel.

"Goodnight, girls," I said and went home.

Although I did not realize it, I had done a tremendous thing. I had just confessed with my mouth the Lord Jesus. No one had told me to witness in this way. Although I didn't know it then, I was on my way to becoming an evangelist. I knew nothing as well of the bitter struggle that would follow.

I was set on the right pathway. Jesus would do the rest, watching over me, protecting me, until at last I would obtain a great deliverance. My feet were on the narrow way.

I had taken the first step to freedom.

CHAPTER FIFTEEN

Search for Deliverance

WHEN I awoke the following morning, the events of the previous evening came slowly back to mind I hadn't slept well. Perhaps I've just dreamed it all, I thought. But it wasn't a dream, for there on my bedside table was the Gospel of St. John and the booklet *First Steps with Christ*.

I had kept my promise to the counsellor and to the girls on the street corner to read the booklets, for before going to sleep I'd sat up in bed and read the Gospel of St. John right through from beginning to end – not that I understood or remembered a thing, but I'd kept my word.

"Will life be different now? Will things change for me?" I wondered.

As the days passed, doubts filled my mind. How could *I* ever hope to live a Christian life? How could I give up drugs, drink, cigarettes, and my way of life on the streets? It would be far too difficult. And what about witchcraft? How could I get out of that?

A voice, the audible voice of Lucifer, said: "You can't get out of it. You are mine! It's too late for you."

"He's right," I thought. "Best to forget about it all straight away."

I pushed the Gospel of St. John into a drawer and went out to have a drink in a nearby pub.

As I sat drinking, I heard again the sweet voice of the singer.

No one else can take the sin and darkness from me.
Oh, how much He cares for me!

"This is stupid," I thought. "Why does that song come back and haunt me – here, of all places?"

"Forget about it," said Lucifer again in an audible voice. "Have another drink. It will soon go away."

But it didn't go away, even after several more drinks. How could I forget? Wherever I went I could hear:

Jesus cares for me, Jesus loves me.

While I was walking the streets in search of men, or drinking in pubs, or even while giving myself a fix of heroin, snatches of that lovely solo kept ringing in my ears, telling me over and over that Jesus cares.

"Take no notice," persisted Lucifer. "It's not for you."

"Am I going completely mad?" I thought.

Two voices saying two entirely opposite things. What was happening to me?

I was the battleground of a great struggle between good and evil, between the very powers of darkness and Jesus Christ, the mighty Son of God.

I was most surprised to receive a letter from the woman counsellor. No one ever wrote to me. It was a sweet letter, saying, "I am praying for you. Can you come again to the crusade?"

Although I was very touched to receive such a kind letter, I wasn't sure about returning to the crusade meetings.

"Don't go!" said Lucifer again. "You are mine!"

His voice was even more frightening this time. My mind was in a complete turmoil. But I did return. Some sweet power seemed to draw me back two nights later.

I hoped the soloist would sing again the song that kept ringing in my ears. Instead she sang something quite different. Still, her face was a picture of sheer joy, and I knew that I wanted what she had. Oh, to serve the Lord Jesus Christ fully, to be free from drugs, prostitution, and witchcraft!

That very night Lucifer stood by my bed. There was no mistaking him. I'd seen him often enough in the past and heard his audible voice many times. It was not imagination but very real indeed.

"You are MINE," he said. "You must obey me. Keep away from Christians, or you will die."

His form and face were black and twisted, his voice ugly with hate and threats. I felt great hairy hands reach out and grab my throat. I tried to shout out, I tried to pray. It was no use. The power of evil was too strong for me. It was all very awful, all very real.

"What's the use?" I thought. "I'm in his power and have been for years. I can never be a pure Christian."

No matter how much I wanted to be released, I was in Lucifer's dreadful grip. In another pendulum swing I decided to give up any idea of loving and serving the Lord Jesus.

Then again, and yet again, the words of the solo rang in my ears,

Only Jesus can take the sin and darkness from me.
Oh, how much He cares for me!

That did it.

"I'll fight until I'm free. I'll search until I find the freedom I need and want."

How wonderfully true it is that once Jesus Christ has begun a work in someone's heart, He never leaves him alone. Jesus was not going to let me go. I was His child now. Although the battle had only just begun Jesus was making me aware of His presence and nurturing my desire to be set free from all bondage.

The woman counsellor came to visit me.

"If you really want to love and follow Jesus," she said, "you must have fellowship with His children. Join an evangelical church."

"All right," I agreed. "Where is the Evangelical Church? Which one do I go to?"

"We're not allowed to advise which evangelical church you should attend. Go to any evangelical church. There are many around."

I at no time told her that I was a witch, prostitute, and strip-tease artiste. I was held back by fear of what would happen to me it everyone knew the kind of life I'd lived. That I was in real spiritual needs was all she and a few others knew.

As for finding a church to attend regularly, whatever would anyone like me know about churches and denominations?

Out on the streets as usual, I passed many churches, but I saw no sign of an Evangelical Church, although I looked closely at the names as I passed. I saw the Methodist Church, and the Baptist Church, and the Church of England, and many more, but not a sign of the Evangelical Church anywhere.

The counsellor had said there were plenty around, yet I couldn't find one – simply because I was looking for a label. What does the term evangelical mean to a complete outsider as I was? NOTHING!

But I wanted to know more about Jesus. I was earnest in my seeking, despite the fact I had not changed my way of life. But I could not change – and I knew it – unless I somewhere found something or someone who could help me, even if it meant going to church to find deliverence. Now, ask any prostitute to attend church, and she will laugh in your face.

"What, me?" she would say. "What would the likes of me be doing in church? They wouldn't want me in a place like that!"

You can imagine how I felt. How would it ever come about that I would go to church? I wondered. It seemed impossible, but I was determined to find what I was looking for.

I shall never forget my first experience of attending church. Giving up my efforts to find the Evangelical Church, in desperation I walked into the first church I saw one Sunday evening.

It was large and packed with people. I looked a little nervously at the congregation, who appeared so respectable and good. My reaction was an urge to run out again.

There were no empty seats at the back. The only empty pews were right down at the front of the church, and there were two whole rows of empty pews.

No one helped me. I had to make my way to the front to get a seat. It was embarrassing, and once again I felt that every eye was on me. I was dressed much the same as when I first went to the Colston Hall.

"Why does everyone stare so?" I thought.

The service began with a dreary hymn, not at all like the rousing hymn sung on the first night of the crusade. The minister then prayed a very long, complicated prayer. Another hymn followed, even more dreary and difficult to sing than the first.

Next came the Bible reading. I had my St. John's Gospel with me. The minister read from another part of the Bible, and I couldn't understand why I couldn't find his reading in my little Bible.

Eventually the minister began his sermon, but I couldn't understand one word of what he was trying to say. He used long theological phrases that didn't make sense to me. Nothing was simple or plain. I wanted to hear something about Jesus that I could understand, like: Jesus can set you free, Jesus loves you. But I didn't hear a thing I could understand.

I was becoming restless and very bored, and gasping

for a cigarette. I couldn't stand it a minute longer and jumped up and walked out. Everything became very quiet as I walked past the good, respectable-looking people and out of the door.

I lit my cigarette outside, but all the time I was thinking, "Perhaps I didn't give it a fair chance. Perhaps it's me. Better try again."

So in I walked, much to the astonishment of the congregation, who obviously thought I'd gone for good. I sat down again in the front and stayed until the end, jolly glad when we came to the closing prayer. I prayed too, hoping Jesus would understand me.

The people were standing around in small groups. The minister was shaking hands and saying polite farewells at the door. I tried to get past him without his seeing me, but I failed. He was very sedate and polite.

"Good evening," he said with a smile.

Somehow I liked him.

"We haven't seen you before, have we?" he asked.

"No, 'cos I ain't been here before have I?"

There was a stillness in the air. He was very startled by my reply. After a few seconds he continued.

"What made you come tonight?"

"Well, I went to the Eric Hutchings crusade at Colston Hall and gave my heart to Jesus."

He beamed.

"That's wonderful!"

And I knew he loved Jesus.

"Can I help you at all on the Christian pathway?"

I thought quickly: "Is this my chance? No harm in trying."

"Well," I said to the minister, "I don't know if you can. You see, I'm a prostitute and drug addict."

He looked very strange and went a bit white. In fact I thought he was going to fall over backwards. The people standing nearby became very quiet and gave me curious looks.

After recovering himself, the minister said. "Do come again. Good night."

"Come again?" I thought. "What for? What's the matter with these people? Can't anyone help me? Where is this Jesus they talk about so much?"

Looking back, I can smile, and feel a little sad also. Those people went to church Sunday after Sunday with nothing unusual happening to disturb their well-run meetings. It was rather a shock to have someone like me walking in – a rank outsider, someone so different from them.

One of the old-time preachers once said, "Be prepared for anything." They were certainly not prepared for someone like me. As a result, I was in no different state when I left the church than when I walked in – more confused, if anything.

"Where, then, do I go next? What do I do now? Where is reality found in this city of churches?"

Some weeks went by. I was still seeking. The battle was getting fiercer. Lucifer was stepping up his efforts to keep me chained and bound. As the battle grew fiercer, so other things happened.

I wandered into many different churches and sometimes heard the blood of Jesus mentioned. At that, a dark force within took control of me, and strange things occurred. I acted in inexplicable, Satanic ways. I snatched Bibles and tore them. I threw hymn books around the church. I knocked communion trays out of the hands of those who were taking around the bread and wine.

I would fall to the floor screaming, hissing, and slithering like a snake. Then, quite suddenly I would come to myself and remember nothing. Very often I would run out of church sobbing and crying.

People didn't understand what was wrong with me or

why I caused such disturbances. Some thought I was mentally ill. But I knew that it was not I myself that willed these actions. A dark evil within me took control.

Outside the churches I could feel an unseen hand pushing me into doing the very things I wanted to give up. Before I gave my heart to Jesus I took part in witchcraft, drugs, and prostitution without hesitation, but now that I was seeking to live a Christian life, the things I wanted to part with I sought out as if *against my will*. I was made to do them, controlled by some evil power deep within.

When in my wanderings in and out of the churches I heard the real Gospel preached, the evil forces within became activated. I went out undelivered.

I visited many churches. Many evil manifestations continued. I saw the bewildered and concerned looks on the faces of people when I came around, and I too was confused, more confused than the ministers themselves. I wondered why they didn't do something for me.

As the struggle didn't abate, I decided it was best to stay out of the churches. Perhaps I *was* mad, and there was no help for me in churches, or indeed anywhere. I was at the point of giving up my search for freedom from evil.

"Seek, and ye shall find," the Bible says. "Knock, and it SHALL be opened unto you."

"Jesus cares! Jesus cares!" In my dejection the words rang in my ears more clearly than ever. "I must get free. I want to live for Jesus if He loves me so much."

The Lord Jesus was speaking to me. Through the darkness. Through the confusion. The Holy Spirit was breaking through, encouraging me to seek, seek, seek, until I found.

One Sunday morning I decided to try again. I resolved to go to God's house and pray. The moment I entered the evil powers took control. When I came to myself, to my horror I saw smashed communion glasses and spilt wine, bewildered looks on men's faces.

125

I ran out sobbing and weeping, running down the road as if every devil in hell were at my heels. I was really desperate now. I was really in despair.

"Best to end it all, best to die, DIE, DIE, DIE," said Lucifer.

His voice was mocking me as I ran like a tormented, hunted animal down the road. I reached a small bridge. I jumped up onto the parapet and was just about to throw myself into the water below when a man suddenly pulled me down.

"What do you think you're doing, you silly woman?"

I tore myself away from him and ran again, not knowing what to do or where to run. Blindly I ran into a telephone box, shaking and sobbing for some time.

As I grew quieter, I saw on the wall of the telephone box the name and telephone number of a minister, Rev. Stanley Jebb. I read it again. Before I even thought, I was on the phone talking to him. I don't know what I said, but I was in a terrible state.

"Please come to the church," said the minister.

He gave me the name and address. His voice was warm and kind. So it was a short while later that I was at the Baptist church in Queen's Road, Bristol. Two men were waiting for me, one the minister, the other a Mr. Dennis Clark, an evangelist.

They were kind and very understanding as I sobbed out part of my sad story. They listened intently. They really understood me. I could hardly believe it.

They calmed me down a little and prayed for me. At that the evil forces within became active again and fought the ministers as they tried to pray and lay hands on me. The men didn't seem a bit worried at the reaction, but they stopped praying.

They spoke to me kindly and gently: "We know a man who can help you if you let him. He is minister of a Baptist church at Burnham-on-Sea. His name is Arthur Neil. We

126

know he can help you. We'll contact him for you and let you know when he can see you."

It was arranged for me to see Rev. Arthur Neil. At last, at last, I was on the right road to freedom.

This is a true account of my long search for deliverance.

CHAPTER SIXTEEN

The Finger of God

Rᴇᴠ. Arthur Neil arrived the following afternoon with the Baptist minister, Rev. Stanley Jebb. I watched them enter the front gate and proceed to the door.

Suddenly a voice said to me, "Don't open the door. Have nothing to do with them."

Frightened though I was, I was aware that the dark powers within me were more afraid than I. Somehow I knew that Mr. Neil was the man who could help me, so, although I was afraid, I opened the door to let the men in.

Mr. Neil was a complete stranger to me, yet I knew instinctively he was a pure and holy man of God. I felt as black as the night and as vile as the devil himself in his presence.

Straight away he tried to put me at ease. He was very kind and gentle, and love seemed to shine from his eyes. I had to drop my eyes before his gaze. Something dark within me rebelled against him, but it was not I myself that did so.

"Do these voices you hear have names?"

"No."

"Are there any unclean spirits?"

I became aware, suddenly, of the evil spirits within me. They actually possessed my body. The evil spirit spoke again, but only to me.

"Tell him nothing, nothing."

128

Now, I was no stranger to demons. Had I not often called on them to assist me in rites as witch and Satanist? For the first time I knew these demons were *within* me, not outside. It was a startling revelation.

But I said nothing, nothing about witchcraft or Satanism, or anything at all.

There was no need, for Mr. Neil knew I was demon-possessed, if he knew nothing else about me. He pointed his finger at me – yet not at me myself but at the demons within. He spoke in a strange tongue that the demons understood, commanding them to leave me in the name of Jesus.

I sat terrified in the chair.

But the demons within were even more afraid. Mr. Neil laid his hands on my head as Dennis Clark had done the previous afternoon. I made no attempt to attack Mr. Neil. I was fully aware of what was happening. I knew without the shadow of a doubt that the great kingdom of darkness within me was well and truly shaken.

Later Mr. Neil explained that he had used the authoritative tongue the Lord had given him in dealing with demons.

I felt very much easier in myself. Somehow I knew all would be well.

The two ministers left after an hour or so, but Mr. Neil knew that a long and deep ministry with me had only just begun. He was so right.

If I felt easier after my first encounter with this man of God, it was not to last very long. I had the most dreadful night.

In the early hours of the morning I awoke filled with the most awful fear, I was surrounded by evil powers. I heard the awful voices, but this time they gave their names. I was torn inside as if someone had taken a knife and was tearing me to pieces.

Tossing back and forth as the demons within tormented and tore me, I heard this:

"Have nothing to do with Neil. I am Doubt and Unbelief."

"I am not coming out."

Then many more voices cried out all at once: "Not me – not me – not me!"

It sounded like a mighty chorus growing louder and louder. I was perspiring, the bed clothes were soaking wet, my body was torn by the demons.

I heard again another voice say: "I am Lust. I am an unclean spirit. I am not leaving. I have been here for years."

"I am Lies," said another. "I'm not leaving either."

"And I am Witchcraft," said another very powerful demon.

"I am Pride," said another. "I am not leaving."

"No, nor I."

"Nor I."

"Nor I."

The demons spoke one after another. I thought I was going mad. I was not mad, yet I knew that if these demons were not cast out, I would go completely mad.

I wondered where Jesus was, where the light was. My eyes couldn't see the light at all. The darkness of hell seemed to descend upon me.

When I finally got up, I heard a voice say: "Phone the pastor of the Baptist church. Tell him not to come to the house."

I was expecting Rev. Jebb to call that morning to see how I was feeling. I telephoned, as the voice had bidden, but his wife answered and said he was already on his way.

I waited, smoking cigarette after cigarette. The disturbing unrest within would not let me sit down. At eleven a.m. I heard a knock at the front door, and I knew it was the pastor. He was as kind as ever.

I told him of the names I'd heard.

"Do not despair," he said. "I will contact Mr. Neil again, straight away."

I felt afraid. It was not just I who was afraid – once again I knew that the demons within me were afraid.

Rev. Jebb explained that because Mr. Neil did not live in Bristol but at Burnham-on-Sea, I couldn't see him immediately.

"I will let you know when Mr. Neil can see you again. Meanwhile do not worry. I shall pray for you."

It was some days before Mr. Neil was able to see me again. He was very busy, with a full ministry as a Baptist pastor. Those few days of waiting were like long years. I visited the old haunts – pubs, cinemas, the witches' covens – but I felt I was pushed to these places by the dark demons within. They actually controlled me.

At the same time I wandered into various places of worship. I visited the Spiritist church, then ran out halfway through.

I drank and smoked more than ever. Sometimes I remembered nothing of what I'd done or where I'd gone in my wanderings. I felt compelled to wander down dark streets – the darker the better – wearing only black clothes.

In the short moments of normality, when I was myself, I yearned with all my heart to be pure, to be free, to love and serve Jesus Christ and Him alone.

I was like a split person, like two people: one, the witch, prostitute, addict; the other, someone who wanted to be changed completely, to be happy and joyful.

I knew I was not ill, not mad. I was possessed by evil spirits and was almost constantly obeying their commands.

One Friday morning I had word that Mr. Neil would see me that very evening. I was told that my counsellor from the crusade and her husband would take me by car to the Baptist church in Queen's Road, Rev. Jebb's church.

At that news everything within me that was evil trembled. I literally shook from head to foot.

"Keep away from Neil," the demons demanded. "He is holy, too holy for us. Keep away. Don't go to the church."

131

A thousand voices, like hammers inside me, thundered out the same message.

The day of restlessness turned to evening. As soon as I saw Mr. Neil I again had the feeling, only more so, that he was a pure and holy man of God.

I was unnerved. I wanted to run away but couldn't. Mr. Neil smiled at me, and I was put at ease instantly, but it didn't last very long. I found I couldn't meet his eyes. They seemed to pierce right through to my very soul. I could sense his calmness and his power. It was most disturbing.

"This man could tell me more than I can tell him," I thought.

He was fully aware of what was wrong. He asked me to tell him the names I'd heard. I did my best to tell him all. As I spoke, my thoughts were being taken away. I was being held back by the demons. Mr. Neil understood perfectly.

Now he spoke in another tongue, pointing his finger in a very commanding way. I can remember no more, as the demons within took complete control.

It was not until later, when I was completely free from all demons, that Mr. Neil did tell me exactly what happened that night. And this is what he told me.

Six demons revealed themselves under close interrogation by Mr. Neil. They each expressed themselves through my lips, according to their individual nature.

The commander-in-chief was Doubt and Unbelief (one demon). It was most obstinate and violent. Apparently I had to be held by two Christian men while Mr. Neil cast out the demon.

He pointed his finger (see Luke 11:20) and quoted, "If I by the finger of God cast out demons, no doubt the kingdom of God is come upon Doreen."

He commanded in the name of Jesus, both in English and in the tongue the Lord had given him for the purpose

132

of exorcism, that the demon should leave and depart to Gehenna (hell).

The tremendous struggle that followed could best be described by Ephesians 6:12. Wrestling is the perfect description. The demon didn't want to leave my body and certainly didn't want to go to Gehenna before the time, but in the end it left with a loud scream. As it came out, it tore me.

The exorcism lasted three or four hours. In this time the demon Deceit and the unclean spirits of Lust, Lies, Pride, and Witchcraft were despatched to Gehenna.

The demon of Witchcraft, said Mr. Neil, was very noisy. Its nature was weird and gave expression by certain enchanted wailings.

"Do you know the witch of Endor?" it almost sang in weird, bewitching tones.

"It tried to bewitch me," Mr. Neil told me, "but I resisted it in the authority of the name of Jesus Christ, consigning it to Gehenna."

"Not there, not there!" wailed the Witchcraft spirit. "I must have her body. I will not leave her body. I need a body. Not there, not there! Not Gehenna!"

"You will not possess her body or any other body," said Mr. Neil. "I command you to leave her body and go now to Gehenna, in the name of Jesus Christ."

But the Witchcraft demon was very obstinate. The exchanges went on for some time before Mr. Neil with a final word of command opened the nearby door and commanded the spirit to leave and go straight to Gehenna.

It did – with terrific screams and wailings, saying: "All right, all right. I'm going."

I fell to the floor as if dead, said Mr. Neil. When I came round, I knew nothing of what had gone on. I knew only that I was free of these demons. They had been cast out and were gone forever.

I prayed and thanked the Lord Jesus for setting me free.

I was very tired indeed. My throat was bruised, and so were my ribs and my arms. But the six demons were gone. Mr. Neil prayed for me and went home.

I felt happy and free. It was wonderful. That night I slept like a baby – the best night's sleep I'd had for years.

But within a short time other demons revealed themselves to me. Some gave names, some didn't.

I was in deep despair. I thought every demon had gone. Instead, some remained. I was very confused, but Mr. Neil wasn't at all surprised. He knew that he had cast out just a few of all that had been within. A start had been made. The rest would go the same way as the first batch and to the same place. It couldn't all be done at once, at least not in my case.

This is a powerful ministry, a very deep and exhausting ministry. Sad to say, it is also a neglected one.

My life had been an open door to demon-possession. It would be some time before I was completely free, before every demon would depart. Not that Jesus Christ could not have done it all at once and altogether. He could have. But as I have said before, His ways are past finding out.

Undoubtedly He had a special purpose. Ministers and other Christians had to be shown the reality of demon-possession. I believe Mr. Neil had to teach others how to cast out demons. And I too had to learn many things.

A real work was being done in my own heart.

CHAPTER SEVENTEEN

Jesus Is Victor

TIME! It was something I had too much of, whereas Mr. Neil had precious little.

I wasn't so busy. The old saying that the devil finds work for idle hands is true. He certainly found plenty for my idle hands.

Besides, six demons were now gone, and it wouldn't be long before even more were cast out; the remaining demons, in danger of losing the dwelling place they'd occupied for many years, were almost constantly active, knowing that their time was almost up.

Casting out the rest of the demons was a long, exhausting ministry and had to be done at intervals, in special sessions. Mr. Neil fasted and prayed before each session. He knew he was coming into contact with powers of darkness in an actual, genuine way. Therefore prayer and fasting were most essential.

The demon Tormentor was the next to leave. It revealed itself much the same way as the others had done. It was a tormentor indeed, for I was tormented day and night, with very little let-up.

I experienced the most horrific dreams – dreams so vivid, so real, and so horrible. Ugly, hairy animals chased me to the edge of a dark, bottomless pit, hands clawed at my body, my throat. Marks were evident on my body when I awoke.

I was tormented in the daytime also, feeling compelled to wander for hours on end, seeking rest and peace and finding none. After wandering for hours, where I know not, I would at last return home to bed absolutely exhausted, only to experience dreams more horrific than before.

Another appointment was made to see Mr. Neil. The demon was now the one who was tormented.

"Take a knife and kill Neil," it commanded me.

Obediently I placed a knife in my handbag.

"Kill, kill, kill!" it demanded.

As soon as I entered the church, the demon went mad within me.

I learned something about demons at this time: they could not see Mr. Neil until I did. They had only my eyes to see with. They knew what Mr. Neil was about to do and every movement he made only through *my* eyes. That they had to rely on me is proof that they are limited.

"Kill, kill, kill!" the Tormentor ordered again.

I remember no more of what happened until this demon had gone.

Mr. Neil told me later that I brandished a huge knife with the express purpose of blinding his eyes. However, he snatched it away in good time.

Apparently this demon was exceedingly strong. I was difficult to restrain, having the strength of ten men. Strong Christians had great difficulty in holding me while Mr. Neil cast out the demon.

Long exchanges again occurred between Mr. Neil and the demon. It didn't want to leave, resisting again and again. After a long battle, lasting about an hour, the Tormentor left with loud screams to Gehenna.

"Jesus is Victor!" exclaimed Mr. Neil. "Jesus is Victor!"

Seven evil spirits were gone forever. A little more rest for me before even more were cast out.

As they revealed themselves – their name, their work, their time of possession – so they were cast out, never without a long, hard struggle, all hating Mr. Neil, all hating Gehenna. They knew that if they were cast out to Gehenna, it would be the end of them.

"Not before the time," they would plead.

But Mr. Neil insisted they all go to Gehenna, where they would never again torment man or beast.

Many of the demons quoted Scripture, many argued over Bible truths, and some spoke in other tongues. In the conflict they disclosed that some had possessed my body fifteen years, a few even longer.

"I'm not leaving her body," said one unclean spirit. "I've been here for years. I'm not leaving now."

Solicit was still another unclean spirit. Mr. Neil explained that this demon had entered my body at the age of fifteen, when I became a prostitute on the Paddington Streets. It even tried to solicit the ministers present at the exorcism.

After many verbal exchanges it eventually left with loud screams to Gehenna, along with Dark Enticer. Very smart this one, with a smart-sounding name, and works to match. It put up a very powerful display – showing off, trying to attract and allure the ministers. But it also was cast out in the more powerful name of Jesus.

Other unclean spirits, like Seducer, Stripper, Corruption, and Lesbian, were cast out to Gehenna. The Lesbian demon was most revealing, Mr. Neil told me, and quite startling in its dialogue. It spoke in a refined society voice (so unlike my own).

In the course of exorcism Mr. Neil mentioned Mary Magdalene, out of whom went seven devils. The demon immediately took it up, saying, "Don't speak to me about Mary Magdalene. Traitor! Traitor! Don't speak to me about her!"

Mr. Neil also mentioned Calvary, where Satan and all demons were conquered by Christ.

"Don't speak to me about Calvary. I was there, I was there. I saw it all. I was there years and years ago, long before I entered this body. I was there. Don't speak to me about Calvary," said this demon.

In spite of all protests it had to go to Gehenna before the time.

"Jesus is VICTOR!" said Mr. Neil over and over again. "Jesus is VICTOR!"

After each session, when the demons were gone, I prayed and thanked the Lord Jesus for all He had done. I thanked Him with all my heart for setting me free.

Mr. Neil often quoted these words, which I have never forgotten, for they encouraged me greatly: "Jesus is stronger than Satan and sin. Satan to Jesus must bow."

It was at one such occasion that I actually saw the Lord Jesus Himself, standing just behind Mr. Neil. The Lord was lovely, arrayed in shining garments and bathed in a radiant light, which filled the whole room. His face was gentle and kind. His eyes were filled with deep love, and He was looking straight at me. I *knew* He loved me. I *knew* I was His child. He was setting me free.

I will never forget it as long as I live. To think that Jesus should appear to such a one as I! Ah, the wonder of it all!

I needed that vision of Jesus, for the battle had not yet ended – far from it. But I knew that as long as I was willing Jesus would complete the great work He had begun.

Of course, Satan had not given up and tried hard to put a stop to this ministry, tried to stop Mr. Neil from continuing.

"Go back to witchcraft," said Lucifer. "Give up this nonsense."

I had no intention of doing such a thing. The demon Witchcraft had been cast out, and with it went the power of witchcraft in me. I lost my evil powers, and I was glad.

"No." I said, "I will never go back to the witches' covens."

". . . Unless," I thought, "I'll go back and tell them I am through with witchcraft for good. I'll tell them they will have to find someone else to run their evil covens."

138

The more I thought about it, the more it seemed the right thing to do.

Off I went.

It was a foolish thing to do, for their answer to me was a severe beating. They dragged me half-conscious to a car and drove me to a lonely spot, where I was dumped. They believed, I'm quite sure, that I was dead or would die within a short while.

But someone found me and rushed me to a hospital, where I stayed for four days – such was the extent of the beating I'd received. It was only by a miracle that my life was spared and Satan's plans for me were smashed. Jesus had His hand upon me, even if I was very foolish, and Satan was again defeated.

I learned a lesson, though. I would never again go near the witches' covens. I had not heard the last of them – but that came later.

About five months passed. Many demons had been cast out, but I was still not completely free of them. I felt discouraged. At times the fear and torment were unbearable. When would I be completely free? Five months was a long time. When would the last demon go for good? When would it all end?

Yes, I was flooded with discouragement. A few other Christians also lost heart. They said they could see no lasting effect of the ministry, and they pulled out.

Mr. Neil had the same feelings, but he continued with the ministry, against all odds. I'm very glad he did, or I am sure I would not be alive today. I would never have written this book.

At this time of discouragement, and between sessions of exorcism, Satan saw his last chance to finish me off for good.

I was in a terrible state one particular evening. Demons within me were really strong and active, mocking me and taunting me in an awful way. I was looking for the drug pusher, but I failed to find him. You see, I was still on drugs.

This no one knew, not even Mr. Neil, although he was certainly aware I had been taking some kind of drug. What he didn't know was that I was on the hard stuff, heroin.

Weeping and wailing and in a state of confusion, partly from withdrawal symptoms, I was taken to a mental hospital, and there I was put to sleep for over a week – sleep therapy, it's called. I tried to explain when I entered what else was wrong, but they wouldn't listen. They thought I was just very ill. I was ill indeed; but who and what caused the illness? Certainly not just the drug heroin.

"Demons! Don't be silly," said the doctor. "There are no such things as demons. It's all in your mind. You just need some treatment, and then you'll be all right."

So I was put to sleep for about ten days, and that was that.

When I awoke fully, I wondered if I'd dreamed all that had happened. But the thought came to me that it was useless to talk about Jesus in the ward. Such talk would be labelled religious mania.

I was now off heroin – a great advance for me. Sleep therapy had effected the cure. But now the doctors prescribed pills, pills, pills, and more pills. I thought that very stupid, but it was no use telling them anything. No one took the slightest notice of what I said.

"See," said Satan, "you *are* mad. You will never get out of here. Even if you do leave, you'll be madder still."

I was beginning to believe he was right about that.

"Ha, ha, ha!" laughed Satan. "Now you are done for!"

Everyone who was mentally ill acted pretty much the same all the time, but I didn't. I knew I was not mentally ill and told the doctors so. I even felt superior to the other patients – not that it was a good thing to feel. But I was convinced I was different.

No one believed demon-possession was real. No one. There is no such person as the devil, let alone demons, I was told over and over again.

Now what? Was I to stay locked up in a mental hospital for the rest of my life? Things looked very black for me.

"Where is your Jesus now?" mocked Lucifer.

"Yes," I wondered, "where is my Jesus? What will become of me?"

Electrical convulsion therapy came next, commonly called E.C.T., or shock treatment. But I knew it would not help me. Demons can't be shaken out that way.

Chatting with a nurse one day, I said, "Nurse, do you know that before I came here I was a prostitute, drug addict, and witch, but one night I walked into a meeting and heard about someone called Jesus and how much He loved me. I gave my heart to Him that night. What do you think about that?"

"You're just very ill, my dear," she said. "There is no Jesus. It's all a lot of silly nonsense."

"Well," I replied, "if you are a prostitute, drug addict, and so on, that is considered wrong by others, but if you want to live a different life and become a Christian, they say it's all a lot of silly nonsense. What then is right?"

She walked away quite baffled. Later she returned and spoke to me again.

"You know, you are right. You are different from many here."

Others noticed a difference too after a while, and I was watched very closely indeed.

The pills I had to take were nothing but a worry to me. I was slowly becoming addicted to *them*.

I couldn't sleep at night. Therefore sleeping pills were prescribed. I took three pills every night, and if I was not asleep before midnight, I was given another. Although I swallowed enough dope to knock anyone out for four days, I didn't sleep. I enjoyed the nice feeling it gave me and nothing else. I averaged about three hours' sleep a night.

Before very long I was first in the queue for tablets, especially the night tablets. I was now addicted to pills. One day I inquired what they were for.

"Well, this one is to calm you down, and this one is to pep you up."

"Crickey," I said, "make up your mind. What do you want?"

It was utterly useless and futile. I knew what was wrong with me. The rest of the demons had to be cast out and then I would be perfectly whole. But it was useless to say anything. No one listened. Religious mania – that's what they termed my case. I began to believe it myself for a while, ready to abandon all my beliefs just to get out.

My head was X-rayed when I complained of pain. The doctors found I had brain damage, caused, they said, by too many drugs. Now, that was a blow. Would I die? Satan was really having a field day with me.

One thing after another, just because I wanted to be a Christian. Why? Was it worth it?

"Jesus is Victor, is He?" mocked Satan. "Where is your victorious Jesus now?"

Then again, just when I needed it, that beloved solo rang out in my ears.

Jesus cares, Jesus cares.
He can take the sin and darkness *away.*

One thing was very clear to me: Jesus was the only answer. Doctors could do nothing for me now. I recalled that lovely vision of Jesus. Had I imagined that? Of course not. Jesus was real. He did care.

"I must believe! I will believe!" I said over and over again.

I clung to the promise that Jesus would see me through and bring me out of the thick darkness into His wonderful light. I had to, or I would have gone completely mad.

142

Much to my surprise, I was allowed to have a weekend away from the hospital. I was overjoyed to get away from the depressing atmosphere.

On that very weekend Mr. Neil was to preach in Bristol. The Lord was moving on my behalf – I knew it. I went to the church to see Mr. Neil.

"Please help me, Mr. Neil," I pleaded. "You must cast out the rest of the demons TONIGHT."

He agreed to minister again. Some Christians stayed after the evening service to back up Mr. Neil and assist him in prayer. It was now or never. Darkness or light. Satan or Jesus. Madness or gladness.

I was at the church to well after midnight. Mr. Neil says it was at the stroke of midnight that the last demon left my body with loud, piercing screams. It had been a long, hard battle with the powers of darkness.

Sixteen unclean spirits had been cast out. The name of the last demon was Dementia. Its work? To destroy the brain.

"Jesus is Victor!" exclaimed Mr. Neil.

What a night of rejoicing that was. I was free. Jesus had done it. His mighty power was felt in a tremendous way, by one and all. Mr. Neil's face was aglow with the glory of God, and so was mine. Such praise went up in that church, such as was never heard before. It was truly a memorable night.

The evening I write of was seven months after my first meeting with Mr. Neil – a long time. But it was worth waiting for. Mr. Neil knew, and I knew, that it was all over. Jesus had delivered me. I left the church after prayer a free woman.

Later I had a further X-ray taken of my head. No brain damage was found. My X-ray was perfectly normal. "It's nothing but a miracle," the doctors said. They were right – a miracle of healing by Jesus Christ my Lord.

Is Jesus a lot of nonsense? Is the devil just a myth? Are demons just superstitious fairy tales handed down from the dark ages? No, a thousand times no. Demon-possession is real, very real, and is increasing at an alarming rate in this present day and age.

But Jesus, who is stronger than Satan and sin, who defeated all demons and Satan at Calvary, is alive today and is still doing wonders on the earth. Still casting out demons. Still healing the sick in body and mind.

Yes, Jesus is real. Jesus does care. Jesus is wonderful, and Jesus is VICTOR.

CHAPTER EIGHTEEN

Peace at Bethany

AFTER that blessed deliverance in February 1965 I didn't meet Mr. Neil again for some two years because he moved to Brixham, where he is today.

I returned to the hospital for an additional two weeks until I was finally discharged. At first the hospital staff were just rather surprised to see me looking so well after my long week-end away. I wondered what they would have thought and said if they'd known about my experience. But I said nothing about it.

As the days went by their surprise turned into utter astonishment at the change in me. That something had happened they couldn't gainsay. The evidence was plain enough for all to see, but they couldn't understand it at all.

"You even look different," they said. "Younger, fresher, and more alive than before."

After such a mighty deliverance I hoped that I would be discharged straight away. I sensed that the oft-times depressing atmosphere in the hospital would be no help to me. To a certain extent I was right. Not until later did I learn that I need never have returned at all as I was a voluntary patient and under no obligation to go back if I didn't want to.

The Lord moves in a mysterious way, His wonders to perform. Perhaps the Saviour had a purpose for my return. Who knows!

No more shock treatment was given me. There was no need. Indeed, I was the happiest person in the whole ward – far happier than the poor overworked nurses.

If I felt sadness or loneliness overtaking me, I took an interest or a part in all that was going on around me: cheering up the depressed and confused patients; talking to the elderly and lonely; brushing their hair and doing little things for them that they were unable to do for themselves; generally making myself useful and helpful in a very busy, very full, and very noisy ward.

In a strange way it reminded me of my days in prison. History seemed to be repeating itself.

The sisters and nurses were amazed, as were the psychiatrists, who stood by almost open-mouthed in astonishment at the complete transformation.

One big problem remained to be solved – the problem of the pills. Undeniably I was addicted to them. Had the psychiatrists had full knowledge of how great a part drugs played in my life, they would never have prescribed so many pills in the first place. Now it was a matter of some concern to them – a bit late in the day perhaps, but at least they partly admitted their mistake.

Before I was discharged I was advised to cut down on the many pills, slowly, and in my own way. This I promised to do, for I really wanted to be free from all drugs. Easier said than done, as I was soon to find out.

When I was discharged from the hospital, I still needed a lot of care mentally, physically, and spiritually. Before long I began to regress – not so severely as before but all the same I was moving in the wrong direction.

I was still at the beginning of my Christian pathway and experience. Every Christian experiences some kind of oppression at one time or another, and I was now suffering from oppression, and Satan saw to it that it was intensified in my case.

Darkness seemed to descend on me once again. Instead

of taking less pills I was taking far more than in the beginning. Something was lacking in my life. What I needed was real love and understanding. I was, it seemed, at the crossroads and didn't know which road to take.

I often felt that Christians avoided me and were afraid to speak to me for any length of time. Perhaps my past was too fresh in their minds for full acceptance of me. Had they known about my past activities as a witch, matters would have been far worse.

The attitude of the Christians, the oppression, and the fact that I was still only a babe in Christ made things difficult for me. After all, I was just beginning to walk, so to speak. Instead of being thoroughly happy, I was once again confused and afraid.

Some Christian friends saw the need of convalescence away from the familiar surroundings of the big city with its many temptations. It was suggested that I should go to the countryside to rest, to be strengthened spiritually, and above all to be built up physically.

I wasn't at all keen about the idea to go away and stay with complete strangers. With people who knew nothing about me! No, thanks!

But how could I hurt those who were trying to help me? So despite my doubts and fears I agreed to be driven to the countryside in my friends' car. After all, I reasoned, if I don't like it, I can always turn round and come straight back.

Eventually I arrived in the village of Gamlingay in Bedfordshire. I received a warm reception but remained very cool toward the whole project. Not that I was ungrateful; I was afraid of the unknown that lay ahead.

I shook hands politely with my hosts, Mr. and Mrs. Parker. Mr. Parker's first impression of me was of someone very lonely and wrapped up in bitterness. He observed that I was preoccupied with my own thoughts and that an air of resentment surrounded me.

My face was a picture of sadness. My eyes, he said, were full of the pain and hurt I'd suffered and was still suffering. The unhappiness in my life, the tremendous needs could not be disguised.

Over the years since Mr. Parker had committed his life to Christ he had come to realize the great needs of the many lonely and unhappy people in the world. He realized that someone so obviously downtrodden in spirit as I would respond only to love and understanding. Only real love would get through to me.

Although a naturally talkative man and pastor of a small village church, he didn't preach to me. He knew that he must be a good listener to all I had to say.

Had I known Mr. Parker's train of thought, things might have been slightly different on my first evening in their company. As it was, I felt very uneasy, expecting him and his wife to start preaching or quoting Bible texts. As soon as I could, I asked if I might take Paddy, the family dog, for a short walk and inspect the village.

Once outside the house I lit a cigarette. As I walked around the small deserted village, my heart sank lower and lower. It seemed to me a very dull place. I wondered why I'd been so foolish as to allow myself to be driven to such an out-of-the-way dump as this – not even a cafe where I could sit and have a cup of tea and a fag in peace, away from everyone's eyes. I decided I would stay only a few days and make some excuse to return to the city.

During the next few days I spent my time taking Paddy out for walks. We became firm friends. I used to tell Paddy all my fears, and he would often look at me rather sadly with his big brown eyes, as if he understood every word I said. He'd never had so many walks before and must have wondered what it was all about. Memories of my childhood floated back, of the time when I used to speak to Bessie, the old black Labrador.

As the first week slowly passed, I began to change my

148

mind about the Parker family. No one preached at me or launched some great plans for my future. I waited for it, but it didn't come. In fact, the pastor and his wife did no more than treat me as a normal, equal person. Still more surprisingly, they accepted me into the family without question, without hesitation, and without any pressure whatsoever. They had two teenage children, a boy and a girl, and even they treated me as one of the family.

Love kept this family together, not rules or religion, for they all loved Jesus. It was simple, sweet, and so natural, and to me, so refreshing. This was the first time I'd encountered family life that was in no way unhappy or sordid. Much to my amazement, I was actually beginning to enjoy my stay.

Depression returned, however, despite the happy surroundings. Familiar doubts and fears filled my mind. My nights were often sleepless, in spite of the sleeping pill. Horrible dreams recurred again and again. In the daytime I was semi-doped, and my actions were very sluggish.

Although Mr. Parker noticed all these symptoms and was well aware I was smoking, he said nothing to me. Instead, he spent much time in prayer. He was waiting God's time, waiting for the barriers to be broken down. Slowly and surely he saw the resentment and mistrust disappear as I responded to the love of this Christian family. I realized that they really did care.

It was a wonderful step forward, therefore, when I asked if I might call them Mum and Dad. At last they had won my trust and affection.

"Of course you may, my dear," they said as they took me in their arms and openly wept.

How wise, how patient they had been! Not in any great rush to minister to my deeper spiritual needs. How Christlike, to wait prayerfully and patiently for me to respond.

As I became closer to mum and dad, as I now called them, I began to open up and tell them more about myself. They didn't rush me, and I knew I could trust them to treat anything I did say as confidential. As time went on, the evil spirits that had been troubling me during my stay were dealt with. So were the fears. Little by little. Slowly, prayerfully, and gently. Mum and dad dealt with it all as it arose in love and great patient understanding.

Indeed, this was just the beginning of long months of ministry to me – a tear-stained ministry. They often had to stay by my side day and night, not daring to leave me. Such was the onslaught on my soul by Satan. But the battle was the Lord's, and Jesus slowly and wonderfully brought me through to complete liberty. I began to live the Christian life to the full. Jesus was Victor once again.

When it was finally over, I saw Jesus again. Yes, I actually saw Him! This time His hands were outstretched toward me, His eyes were full of love, and He took me in His arms and whispered, "You are mine."

I knew without a shadow of a doubt that I was His. He would never let me go. He would bring me through all trials, all gloom, until one day I would see Him face to face for all eternity.

The village and the countryside that seemed so dull and lifeless before were now very dear and lovely to me. I called the place Bethany. It reminded me of that little town just outside Jerusalem where Jesus often went to visit Martha and Mary and their brother Lazarus. It too was named Bethany: a place of retreat, a place of peace and rest. It seemed an appropriate name for this little home in the countryside.

As you can see, I had begun to read my Bible. Whereas it was once unintelligible, now it was clear and plain and full of meaning. I would sit for hours reading the stories of Jesus – how He healed the sick in body and mind and made everyone He touched perfectly whole, just as He does today. Had He not touched my life, and had He not made me completely whole? It was all so thrilling. The Bible came to life.

My *Golden Bells Hymn Book*, given to me long ago in

Sunday school and even taken to prison with me, was now very precious indeed. I would sit and read, and sometimes sing, those hymns I had learned so long ago, captivated by the lovely words. They were so simple and plain.

> *Tell me the stories of Jesus.*
> *Write on my heart every word.*

Oh, yes! The words meant something to me now. Oh, how I loved those hymns!

I could look back and realize that Jesus had followed me with his tender eye of compassion right through the long years of deepest shame. He saw me on the streets as a prostitute. He saw me in the evil temples of Satan and in the witches' covens. Even then He loved me, even in my sin of darkest degradation. Then one day He called me and took me in.

Ah, the wonder! It filled me with great contrition, great wonderment, to think that He loved even me. It still fills me with wonderment today, and it always will.

At Bethany Jesus was drawing me closer to Himself. Removing the bitterness from my heart. Washing away the hurt and pain of years through the love in this little home. Erasing the horrors from my mind. Making me a new creature in Christ.

Everything was new – everything. It was as if I were born anew in the flesh as well as the spirit.

The whole world appeared beautiful. I loved everyone and everything in this great big wonderful world that God had made – the mangy old cat on the rubbish heap, the dandelion pushing its way through the rubble. Yes, even those things looked beautiful to me.

As I walked through the green fields into the thick woods, my heart sang. I danced for sheer joy at all I saw, at all that Jesus Christ had done for me and all he was showing me and all He was going to do for me in future days.

For the first time in my life I noticed the tiny flowers growing in the earth, the blades of grass. I noticed the colours. The sky looked as if someone had taken soap and water and washed it blue. Previously the sky had looked so grey.

It looked as if someone had also painted the trees and grass green, the whole earth with glowing colours. All this beauty, displayed before my eyes, I'd passed by before. Now I was looking at the world through different eyes.

> Heaven above is softer blue,
> Earth around is sweeter green.
> Something lives in every hue,
> Christless eyes have never seen.

I didn't know that lovely hymn then, but I'd experienced it in a very real and wonderful way.

Mere words could not express the immense joy that welled up within me. Mere words can never tell how precious and how dear Jesus was to me, how wonderfully sweet his presence was.

One day while resting at Bethany I felt the very presence of Jesus in an even greater way than ever before. I felt His presence at first drawing nearer and nearer to my side. Then I heard the audible voice of my Saviour as He whispered sweetly in my ear.

"You are a chaste virgin in My sight. You are My *modern* Mary Magdalene."

Dad happened to be nearby and saw the expression on my face. He too knew that Jesus was very, very near. I wasn't aware of dad's presence, only of Jesus' presence and the words He spoke to me.

Dad said later that he'd never seen anything like it in his life. My countenance was radiant, he said. Little wonder when Jesus was so near.

"Who is Mary Magdelene?" I asked dad.

With tears in his eyes he read from his Bible how Jesus had

152

cast out seven evil spirits from Mary Magdalene, a woman of the city, a street girl, a harlot until Jesus came into her life and changed her completely.

I wept and wept. Oh, how Mary must have loved Him! He had forgiven her so much. He had set her free. Now Jesus had spoken to *me* and said I was His modern Mary Magdalene. It was just wonderful, so very wonderful.

I was like her, a street girl possessed with many unclean spirits, and Jesus had set me free. Jesus was becoming more precious to me every day, yes, every hour.

"A chaste virgin in My sight." That's what Jesus had said.

Still weeping, dad turned to the second book of Corinthians, chapter 11, verse 2, where Paul is speaking to the church at Corinth:

"I am jealous over you with a godly jealousy, for I would present you as a chaste virgin to Christ."

The church at Corinth was noted for its backslidings and wickedness. Paul was grieved, for he wanted God's children to be pure and spotless.

I was overjoyed to think that Jesus Christ should speak to me – a former prostitute, black witch, strip-club girl – and say that in His sight I was a chaste virgin. In other words I was now clean and pure, washed in His blood, and justified in His sight. I loved Jesus even more after that. How could anyone forget such words! How could *I* forget such words, straight from the lips of my Saviour Himself.

Jesus continued to pour out his blessings on me. They were new every morning. I was filled with the Holy Spirit, praising, loving, and serving my Lord. He was now Lord of my life and Lord of all.

Imagine my further joy and wonder when I read the story of the woman of Samaria, how Jesus met this sinful woman at the well and gave her the water of life. At first I found it incredible that such true, simple stories were to be found in the Holy Bible. I could hardly take it in. Jesus was certainly making Himself very real to me, drawing me nearer to His side as I grew in grace and in the knowledge of the Lord Jesus.

I stayed at Bethany for some months. Jesus was teaching me Himself, preparing me for the ministry He had planned for me, assuring me over and over again that I was now a child of a King. No longer a child and slave of Satan. Now a child of God.

No, I could never forget Bethany, for it was there that love won through. Peace came in. Joy abounded.

A huge bonfire was lit one evening, and all my black clothes were burned along with cigarettes, drugs, and many other idols. It was a time of rejoicing as we ran around the bonfire, praising and thanking Jesus for everything He had done for me. It may have been a peculiar sight to others, but to us it was very meaningful.

Satan certainly trembled, but the angels were rejoicing with us, I'm sure. This was an outward manifestation and testimony of all that Jesus Christ my Saviour had worked inwardly, for Jesus Christ had chased away the fear and the dark shadows and brought me into the full light of His love.

Yes, I found joy, love, and peace in Christ at Bethany.

CHAPTER NINETEEN

A Rough Diamond

"A TROPHY of grace," "a rough diamond" – this is what Christians called me. I had now left the shelter of Bethany, returned to the city of Bristol, and started a new life.

In Mark 16:15 we read: "Go ye into all the world and preach the gospel to every creature." That little word "ye" included me, I knew. The Lord Jesus had called me, yea, chosen me, to work for Him in this world, and I now entered the pathway of service.

It was not easy. I had no Bible college education, but I had a tremendous testimony to what God can do in a person's life, which is far greater. I wanted to tell everyone what the Lord had done for me. I also had a growing compassion for the lost, especially the prostitutes and the drug addicts. Oh, how I yearned that they too might come to a knowledge of His saving grace.

"Here I am, Lord, send *me*!" was my cry. "I will go for You."

The Christians, however, were a stumbling block. Very few remembered me at all. Those who did hardly recognized me, for I was so changed. I dressed differently, spoke differently, and acted differently. Indeed, I *was* different, a new creature in Christ. Despite this fact, few believed I was a true Christian.

I couldn't understand it. Many times I suffered because of their distrust, and I shed many silent tears. Not because of what they actually said but because of the look of doubt and suspicion on their faces. It was the way they reacted in my presence. I got the impression they were afraid of me.

The apostle Paul had the same experience at first. His past was too fresh in the minds of the early Christians for them to accept him. Paul also must have suffered because of the lack of belief on the part of Christians. I knew how Paul must have felt.

But there came a time when Paul's past grew dim in the minds of others, and they saw he was a true disciple, a changed man. And so there came a time when Christians saw I also was a true believer of Jesus, and they accepted me. They realized my life was changed and I was free of the past bondage.

Then they called me either a trophy of grace or a rough diamond. Such expressions were entirely new to me. I'd never heard such phrases before.

Now, I didn't mind being called a trophy of grace. But a rough diamond! I wasn't sure about that. It was the word "rough" that put me off somewhat.

Well, this rough diamond was off on a mission. Back to the streets, but for a different reason than before. Where better to start carrying out the Lord's command than among my old friends and acquaintances? But they thought I was quite mad.

"Poor old Diana has got religious mania," they said.

But I didn't mind. I just kept on telling them what Jesus had done for me and could do for them if they would only let Him.

"We will give you three months, Diana," they said. "Then you'll be back on the game with us."

"Old Diana is dead," I replied. "You will never see her again."

My proper name is Doreen, but they went on calling me Diana. It didn't matter.

Oh, how I loved those girls! Many times I would stand

on the street corner with my arms around their shoulders and weep for their souls. In the end they had to admit I had what they lacked – real happiness and peace of mind.

"You look well on it, anyway," they said. "Your eyes are clear, and you look very happy."

So I was, but my heart ached for them.

"We can never change now, Diana," they often said.

How I wept, for had I not thought and said the same thing?

"If you let Christ take over your life, He would do it for you," I told them over and over again.

"Perhaps when we're older, we will think about it, but not now," they would say as they walked away.

Now I could really say, "There, but for the grace of God, go I."

Indeed, I had gone that way for many years. If anyone knows how a prostitute feels, I do.

Regardless of rebuffs (and I had plenty), I just went on telling them of the love of Jesus. Not once a week, but every single day and night. Often I went out late at night to contact them, for I knew just where to find them.

"Look out! Here comes Diana with her Jesus leaflets," I heard one girl say.

Very often I would see them shoot off down a side street when they caught sight of me approaching.

"You will walk the streets in different shoes, My child."

These are the words that Jesus had once whispered in my ear, clearly and sweetly. At the time I wondered what Jesus meant, though I believed it would be revealed to me later.

Now I knew exactly what Jesus meant. I was walking the streets in Gospel shoes. My feet were shod with the preparation of the Gospel of peace. (See Ephesians 6:15.)

This trophy of grace certainly lacked a little grace herself with the Christians. I wanted them to join me in witnessing to the girls on the streets. I recall saying to a group of Christians one evening:

"How about coming with me into the twilight area and speaking to the girls on the street?"

They all went very quiet and just smiled, almost as if they were sorry for me, and they didn't answer me.

"Oh, well," I said. "I'll go on my own. You are hopeless."

As an afterthought I added: "I only hope that someone comes along and tells you all the great importance of witnessing to the lost."

They just stared at me blankly as I marched off. Oh dear, not very gracious of me, was it? I needed to pray for more grace.

Later I said how sorry I was for the way I'd spoken.

"That's all right," answered one girl. "Don't be too sorry. Someone did come along and tell us about witnessing only an hour after you made that remark. It made us all think."

One evening while I was out witnessing as usual, this time in the public houses – the very ones I often visited as a prostitute – I was speaking to a man I once knew very well, speaking about Jesus and His love. Most people in this pub knew me, and they recognized that I was a different person.

"Don't take it so seriously, Diana," he said. "Have a drink and forget about it for an hour or two."

"No," I answered. "I cannot forget about Jesus for one minute."

All went quiet as I spoke openly and freely of what Christ meant to me. Not a clink of drinking glasses could be heard as I suddenly broke forth into song:

Things are different now, something's happened to me
Since I gave my heart to Jesus.
Things are different now. I am changed; it must be
Since I gave my heart to Him.

Things I loved before have passed away,
Things I love far more have come to stay.
Things are different now. I am changed; it must be
Since I gave my heart to Him.

Everyone listened in rapt attention. It was so wonderful, so thrilling, to sing for Jesus in that public house.

When I got outside, I leaned against the wall. My heart was full, my eyes were moist, as my gaze went over that twilight area, and I longed with all my heart that lost humanity would catch a glimpse of Jesus, just a glimpse of him. How different their lives would be!

The twilight zone was my first parish, the public house my first pulpit. My first convert? An elderly woman I'd met in a public house.

She always sat in a corner all alone, looking lonely and sad. I offered her a Gospel tract and sat down to speak to her. The tears started to fall down her brown and wrinkled face.

"I've been coming to this pub for ten years," she said, "ever since my husband died. I'm all alone in the world. No one has spoken to me for years. No one ever speaks to me in here – no one at all."

My heart skipped a beat. Jesus loved her and died for her. Here was a wonderful opening for me to tell her that there was One who cared, and His name was Jesus.

"May I take you home?" I asked.

"Will you? And stay and have a cup of tea with me."

I took her to her little house nearby. Her name was Vera, and she was sixty-three years old.

Over a cup of tea I told her how Jesus Christ had met my need. Vera was very moved. Taking my Bible, I showed her the way of salvation, perfect peace and rest. The result was we both got down on our knees, and I had the great joy of leading this dear lady to the Saviour. What a wonderful conversion it was!

When I visited Vera a few days later, she was radiant.

"I will never go back to the pub again," she said. "Instead I will get my comfort from the Bible you gave me. I'm now ready to meet my Maker."

Vera never did return to the pub, and one week later she did meet her Maker. The neighbours told me she died peacefully in her sleep. Vera went to be with her new-found Saviour. One day I will meet her again, in glory.

One evening, walking along City Road (known as Sin Street), I was giving out Gospel tracts when a car drew up and the man indicated he wanted to speak to me. He was an old client of mine.

"Hello, Diana," he said. "Out on business?"

"Yes," I replied, "but not the sort you think. I'm out on the King's business now. Here, have a Gospel tract and read about my king, Jesus."

He was so astonished he very nearly ran into the car in front of him. Although I saw him several times that evening, circling around in his car looking for a prostitute to pick up, he didn't speak to me again, but he gave me curious stares from the car. I prayed that he would read the tract I'd given him and find Christ as his Saviour.

Another evening I ran into yet another of my old clients while giving out Gospel tracts in the public houses. He was standing at the bar. I started to tell him how Christ had changed my life. His face went bright red, and his hands trembled so much that he couldn't hold his glass. Suddenly he rushed out of the pub, leaving his beer on the counter.

I wondered if he was a backslider or had been under the sound of the Gospel before. He acted very guiltily.

When I'd finished giving out the tracts and speaking for Jesus in this pub, I moved on to the next one. There was the man again, and as soon as he saw me, he rushed out again, leaving his beer. Later on we met a third time.

"Are you bugging (following) me?" he asked. "Everywhere I go, you're there."

"No, it isn't me that's following you," I replied. "Jesus is, and He wants you to surrender to Him."

At these words he rushed out again, this time nearly knocking over the people and the tables as he went. He never did get to drink his beer that night.

How I prayed that he would turn to Christ for peace and rest.

This, then, was how I first began my ministry for Jesus: walking the same streets I'd walked as a prostitute, preaching the Gospel to every creature, telling men and women that Jesus is alive and that Jesus cares for them.

One of my favourite words is "whosoever," for it means everybody everywhere, no matter who or what you are.

Satan tried to discourage me, tried to make me give up.

"Go on, have a little drink," he whispered in my ear. "Just one. No one would know."

No, but Jesus would see, and my testimony could be ruined if I listened to Satan.

"Resist the enemy, and he will flee," the Bible says.

So in the name of Jesus I said: "Get ye behind me, Satan."

And Satan fled.

One night the temptation was very strong.

"No one believes you," Satan said, "not even the Christians. You're wasting your time. Give it all up, and have a drink and a smoke. Relax in the pub for a little while."

In the name of Jesus I rebuked Satan, but still he persisted. In desperation I got on the telephone to dad at Bethany. Hearing about the temptations and how troubled I was, he prayed for me over the phone. He told Satan to be gone in the name of Jesus.

"Go home now," dad said, "and as you pass the public houses, take the hand of Jesus in faith. He will guide you safely home."

Whether he meant me to take him literally or not, I don't know, but as I passed each pub, as Satan tried again to get me inside to drink instead of witness, I raised my hand to heaven in faith, saying quietly:

"Lord Jesus, take my hand in Thine. Keep me from all wrong."

It worked. I never did succumb to those temptations of Satan. It must have been a strange sight for passers-by to see someone walking along with a hand in the air. Strange or not, Satan was defeated once again. Jesus was Victor. His hand guided me, kept me from falling.

Satan tried in another way to stop me in my work for the Master. The black witches sent me letters, threatening my life if I didn't keep quiet about witchcraft. They were awful letters, saying:

"You will die if you don't stop running down witchcraft."

Some of the letters were written in blood. It really frightened me at first, for I knew that black witches carry out their threats. Satan was pulling out every trick he knew to discourage me. Now what? Would I keep quiet about witchcraft? Would I stop warning people of the evil and dangers of the occult because my life was in danger?

No, most certainly not. People should be warned. Such letters only went to prove how evil it all was.

I took courage from Paul's epistle to the Romans, chapter 8, verses 38 and 39, where we read:

"For I am persuaded that neither death nor life nor angels nor principalities nor powers nor things present nor things to come nor height nor depth nor any other creature shall be able to separate us from the love of God, which is in Christ Jesus, our Lord."

"Nor witch nor Satanist," I added.

No, nothing can separate me from Jesus or the truth.

My Jesus was stronger than any witch or Satanist. The Lord Jesus Himself dealt with the witches that threatened me, in His way. No harm came to me. His hand was protecting me every hour.

As you see, I had my discouragements right at the beginning of my ministry. But Jesus was teaching me to trust Him, whatever situation came my way, whatever trial crossed my path, no matter how great or how small. Jesus would see me through. After all, He saved me and delivered me to serve Him.

How could I keep quiet about the evil web of witchcraft? Someone must warn people about the awful evil of it all. Who better than I?

Right at the commencement of my work and ministry Jesus was preparing me for even greater things. I didn't know it then, but I do now. He was teaching me to trust Him at all times, making plain His word, preparing me for greater spheres of service in the kingdom of God.

Day by day I was getting stronger, and so was my testimony. Next I began to give witness at Christian meetings. Starting in a small way, I was learning to speak publicly.

My cockney accent often caused amusement. Very often I got my tongue twisted. But far from making a mess of it all, these things made my testimony more natural and real.

Little by little, step by step, line upon line, the way was opening up for me to speak at bigger meetings. More and more people invited me to chapels, churches, schools, women's meetings, coffee bars, to give my testimony.

How it thrilled me to witness for Jesus in front of so many people! More thrilling still to see men and women, young and old, surrendering their hearts and lives to Christ.

As I progressed further along the Christian pathway of service, as I grew in grace, I thought again about the expression "a rough diamond." Now I saw it in a different light altogether and understood the deeper meaning.

Not that I knew everything there is to know about diamonds. But I did know they are found in the hottest and darkest parts of the earth, and when diamonds are first quarried, they are rough and unpolished. Not until they are put into the skilful and expert hands of the lapidary do they become perfect and beautiful. Rough edges have to be cut away and facets have to be cut into the rough stone to allow the glowing colours to shine through. Finally, they are polished. The result is a most exquisite jewel of great value.

As I thought about the processing of the diamond, I didn't mind being called a rough diamond. Did not the tender Saviour draw me up from the quarry of darkness and deepest shame to fashion and mould me, just like a rough diamond, to His likeness and for His glory?

I am still in the Great Lapidary's loving, skilful hands. He is still doing His own wonderful work on this rough diamond.

CHAPTER TWENTY

A Fuller, Deeper Ministry

THE Bible says: "I have set before you an open door, and no man can shut it."

Many doors have opened up for me to preach the grand old Gospel story and to testify of Christ's mighty transforming power in my life. It has been a joy and privilege for me to give my testimony at many crusades in this country led by Dr. Eric Hutchings.

The first crusade I took part in was at Leeds, where I gave my testimony in the form of an interview with the singer John Grant. I was very nervous, but the Lord Jesus helped me, and it was a great blessing.

It was strange to recall the night in June 1964 when I was ready to punch Dr. Eric Hutchings on the nose. If anyone had told me then that one day I would stand side by side with Dr. Hutchings and speak of what Christ had done for me, I would have laughed in utter disbelief. Yet I was sitting on the same platform with him and telling how on that very night in Bristol I surrendered my black and sinful heart to Jesus Christ.

"Jesus has brought me a long way since then," I thought as I sat on the makeshift platform in the old tram depot.

This was the first of many crusades at which I spoke, but I will never forget it. The congregation was not very large and was rather taken aback as I related only some of the evil in my past sinful life. Many eyes were opened to the awful reality of darkest sin and wickedness in this so-called enlightened age.

Imagine what a great thrill it has been for me to stand with Betty Lou Mills while she has sung again and again that lovely solo I heard in the Colston Hall at Bristol. Meeting Betty and getting to know her as a person as well as a Gospel singer has proved a great blessing to me. She is a very sweet girl and so understanding about the many pressures and responsibilities of being in the public eye. Her singing has remained a source of inspiration to me as well as to many others.

Between my public engagements I often go out into the highways and byways, compelling sinners to turn to Christ, who alone is the answer to the many problems in the world today. I did this not only in Bristol but in many parts of the country, especially London. Back down the familiar streets of Soho my heart has ached for the many lost souls that frequent the strip clubs and other dens of iniquity, as I returned with a message on my lips of hope, joy, and the perfect peace which the world and its pleasures can never, never give.

One such visit was to the east end of London, near the place where I was born. I was not scheduled to speak at any meeting in London. The Lord Himself sent me. It was a very special appointment.

"Go to No. 50 ———— Street, Stepney, and ask for Evelyn," the voice of Jesus spoke to me one evening in Bristol.

I knew the voice of my master Jesus, and the message was clear and plain. I'd never heard of ———— Street, and I wasn't acquainted with Stepney, but when Jesus tells you to go, you know that you can leave the details to Him.

Off I went to London on the train, praying all the way that Jesus would guide me to the street, praying for the right words to say when I did find the street. At Aldgate

East underground station I looked around at the immediate area and was amazed to see how run down it still was.

Never ask Londoners the way, it is often said, for although they may have lived in the city for years, very few can direct you. That old saying seemed too true in this case, for no one I approached knew where —————— Street was.

In the end I contacted a local minister and told him of my mission. Somewhat surprised, he and another minister took me to —————— Street. It didn't appear very hopeful. Indeed, it looked pretty hopeless. The street was absolutely filthy, with all kinds of rubbish littered everywhere, from dirty old mattresses to heaps of rags and rusty bedsteads.

The houses were boarded up, ready for the demolition squad. It didn't seem possible that anyone lived there at all. But right at the end of the road one house was still occupied – No. 50. It seemed incredible.

The tenant, a very large woman, was leaning out of the dirty window. She was so large she almost filled the window frame.

In her hand was a glass of wine, and a cigarette hung from her lips. After a quick silent prayer for guidance, I spoke to her.

"Good afternoon. My name is Doreen, and I've come all the way from Bristol with a special message for you."

"Oh!" she said vaguely and gazed at the three of us standing on the pavement, almost as if she didn't see us at all.

"Yes," I went on. "The Lord Jesus has sent me especially to you."

"Oh," she said again, just as if she hadn't heard me and was preoccupied with her own thoughts.

"Oh, dear!" I thought. "I'm not getting on very well."

Then I suddenly remembered that Jesus had said, "Ask for Evelyn."

"Thank You, Lord," I said, almost aloud.

"Does anyone called Evelyn live here?" I asked.

The woman came alive.

"Yes. That's my daughter. So you want to speak to her?" Then in the same breath: "Do come in."

The inside was most appalling. The walls were very damp, and the woodwork was rotting away.

"This place isn't fit for pigs to live in," the woman said.

I had to agree with her.

"It's overrun with rats," she continued.

I saw one run along the passage, and I shuddered.

"We're moving soon," she explained.

She showed us into a small, barely-furnished room. No rugs or lino covered the dirty floorboards, yet in the corner was the most expensive cocktail cabinet I've ever seen. A young girl of about eighteen was lying, fully clothed, between dirty bed linens on a very rickety double bed.

"Is this Evelyn?" I asked gently.

"No," said the woman. "This is Jane. Evelyn is upstairs on the top floor."

Slowly and prayerfully I explained how I came to be there. Then I spoke a little about my past life, especially about my unhappy background as a child, and related how the Saviour had picked me up from a life of prostitution and shame to make me over anew.

Tears filled the woman's eyes, and she said:

"I've not done the right thing by my children. I'm an alcoholic, my two daughters are prostitutes, and Evelyn's on drugs."

By this time both the ministers and I were weeping also as we saw how low Satan had dragged this family.

After we'd told this dear lady that Jesus died and rose again that she might live and pointed her to Calvary where Jesus shed His blood for all her sin, she agreed to let us pray with her. Right there and then she fell to her knees, and we got down with her and led her to the Saviour.

She repented of her sins and gave herself to Christ. There was no doubt that her conversion was real. Jane, her daughter, was very impressed as she watched and listened intently, but she was not yet ready to receive Christ as her Saviour.

The mother then called Evelyn and told her all that had happened in the room.

"Evelyn, darling, will you let Jesus save you also?" she asked.

It was wonderful to hear the woman speak and witness in this way. However, Evelyn was not ready, and she fled back upstairs. My heart went out to her.

We committed this family to the Lord in prayer and gave them a Bible and some literature before leaving. Later we heard that Jane was in prison. A minister called on her, and there in the prison Jane also surrendered her life to Jesus Christ.

The mother wrote to say that her husband had returned, as he saw that she was a new creature. Shortly afterward the family was rehoused, and we lost contact, but we know that Christ had performed a wonderful work in this family, and He would keep His hand upon them.

Whether Evelyn was ever converted I don't know, but Jesus had sent me, and we can safely leave the rest to Him. It is always worth being obedient to the voice of my Lord.

With Christ all things are possible. How wonderful it is that Jesus can reach anyone, wherever he may be. The Lord Jesus can speak to any one of His servants and instruct him just where to go – even to the number of the house and the name of the street and the name of the person who is in need. Nothing is too hard for the Lord; there is nothing that He cannot do. He is the same yesterday, today, and forever.

My ministry and work for the Master is full and varied. Not long after the experience in ———— Street I spoke at Brighton Teachers Training College, giving my personal testimony to many of the students there. When I'd finished speaking, I threw the meeting open for questions.

Only with the Lord's help have I been able to answer some of the questions put to me. It is truly wonderful to me how the Lord has taught me and helped me in this regard, and I give Him all the praise and glory. He alone has taught me to adapt myself to whatever environment I find myself.

Young students today have a great thirst for knowledge. I'm well aware that many have an unhealthy interest in withcraft and other forms of the occult. When I discern this, I am very careful what I say, for a little knowledge can be most dangerous.

There are, however, many Christians who are ignorant as to how to counsel those caught up with witchcraft. I do my best to teach them, putting them in the picture, so that they may be able to warn others in a far more knowledgeable and intelligent way.

My first television appearance was also an unforgettable experience. I was asked to appear on Southern Television in the news programme *Day by Day*. To say I was nervous is an understatement. To be given an opportunity to speak to thousands of viewers of what Jesus Christ had done for me was a great honour and privilege. My earnest prayer was that the Lord would be glorified and I would be asked the right questions by the interviewer, questions simple and straightforward. The Lord undertook to help me in a marvellous way.

"How can a prostitute, drug addict, and witch be an evangelist?" the interviewer asked.

"Such people cannot," I replied, "unless their lives have been transformed by the Lord Jesus Christ. I'm no longer any of those things, for my life has been changed by Jesus. I am now a new creature in Christ."

The rest of the questions were as simple to answer as the first one, and Jesus was glorified on television. Thousands heard of what Christ can do, and everyone at the television studio also saw and heard that Jesus can change a person's life. It has been my great joy and privilege to speak on many radio programmes also, telling out the same message that Jesus Christ is alive today and is still doing miracles.

Yet again I was invited to appear on a television news programme, this time on Harlech television. At the same time I was appearing at Cardiff Cory Hall with Dr. Eric Hutchings and his team. It was a tremendous interview, and once again the Gospel was preached on a television news bulletin. After all, the message of salvation is the greatest news of all.

My visit to Cardiff was cut short, however, as the very next night I fell and damaged my ankle in Cory Hall. I'm quite sure that Satan was trying to put a stop to all the Lord was doing in Cardiff. He was very annoyed that Jesus was getting extended news coverage on both television and radio.

But the Lord permitted the accident to happen and turned it into good. At Cardiff General Hospital I was surprised to find that everyone remembered seeing me on television the night before. I was in so much pain I'd completely forgotten my television appearance. The nurses and student doctors had not forgotten, and I was able to speak to them about my Saviour.

Everyone, including the patients in the casualty department, heard again the good news of salvation. The student doctors who examined my foot were absolutely amazed as I related to them all the Lord had done in my life.

"There's no known cure for heroin addiction," said one young doctor. "You're a living miracle."

"Well, preacher lady," said another student doctor as he looked at my X-Ray, "you will not be preaching again for a little while, for you've cracked a bone in your ankle."

I had to smile at his words, for I was preaching right there and had been for some hours, from a wheelchair.

A fine Christian doctor took me back to Bristol by car.

We had a wonderful time of fellowship on the drive.

Prior to leaving Cardiff I made a tape-recorded message for the next meeting in Cory Hall. I was told later that it made a bigger impact than if I'd been there in person. So I did preach the Gospel after all, and Jesus was once again glorified.

Later, when my ankle was healed, I returned to Cardiff. All things work together for good to them that love God, to them who are called according to His purpose. I didn't know that I was to see good resulting from the television appearance of my previous visit.

I was giving my testimony on a Saturday evening in a large church in Cardiff. Near the end of my address a voice rang out across the congregation:

"Can Jesus do anything for me?"

"Yes," I replied. "Jesus can do anything. Nothing is impossible with the Lord. Come out to the front now, and I will pray with you."

Out to the front ran a young coloured man, tears streaming down his cheeks. He dropped to his knees, and I led this young man to the Saviour. He was gloriously saved – there was no doubt about it whatsoever. It was a wonderful sight to behold.

A little later he told me this true story. His name was Samuel, and he had not long been released from Cardiff prison.

"While I was in prison," said Sam, "I saw you on the television, and I listened to all you said. When I got back to my cell, I said, 'Oh, God, if You're real, let me meet that woman.'

"I knew you had something I didn't have, and I wanted what you had.

"Then tonight I saw your name on the poster outside, and I came in. You spoke just the right word for me. My life was ruined, and I was a rejected man. My life's been

172

a real mess, but now I know I'm saved, and my past has been wiped clean by Jesus."

What a time of rejoicing it was when Sam's life was transformed by the power of God!

Sam is now a very fine Christian and always witnessing for his Lord. He came to visit me a few months ago. His face was radiant with the joy of the Lord, and his praises to Jesus rang out loud and clear. His prayer was a great joy to listen to.

Sam is a real trophy of grace. Giving his testimony at churches and preaching the Gospel himself, Sam is a great blessing.

Still growing in grace and in knowledge of Christ, I find my ministry is deeper and fuller than ever. So many people are lost and lonely without a single friend in the world, without a glimmer of hope, light, or love. I know just how it feels to be very lonely, so I have a special message for them.

The message is simply this: there *is* one who cares and understands. His name is Jesus, who said: "Come unto Me all ye that are weary and heavy laden, and I will give you rest. Take My yoke upon you and learn of Me, for I am meek and lowly in heart, and ye shall find rest unto your souls."

How I have proved His word time and time again! Jesus really does give rest, light, and love. He really is the truest Friend there is. He died alone on Calvary that men and women everywhere need never be lonely again. . . .

Holland – land of canals, tulips, and windmills. My destination was Middelburg, a small island just off Holland's mainland. There I joined Dr. and Mrs. Hutchings to take part in a Christian crusade, to tell the people of Holland what Jesus had done for me.

Middelburg has a beauty all its own: narrow, cobbled streets, old and picturesque churches with sweetly chiming bells, and Dutch traditional dress, which is worn all the time. Everything is touched with a quaint, old-world charm – a refreshing change from our modern noisy towns and cities.

Yet amidst all this beauty dozens of drug addicts existed. It hardly seemed possible. They crowded into the old music hall of Middelburg to hear what we had to say about Jesus Christ. Our words had to be translated into Dutch for the benefit of the non-English-speaking people.

How the Lord moved the hearts of these Dutch people is beyond description. When the invitation was given to accept Christ into their hearts, young people, mostly drug addicts, literally ran to the front and on to the stage. These dear ones opened my eyes afresh to the deep needs of young people today.

On an afternoon walk I met many more young addicts. I shared my chocolate and peanuts with them on Middelburg square. They shared with me their many problems. It was sad to think that all they wanted was someone to talk to, someone who understood them and cared. I understood, and I wished I knew the Dutch language so that I could speak to them in a much plainer way. They really made me feel wanted by them. Some of them knew I was once a drug addict myself, and that alone was a help to them.

Language is not an impossible barrier. People feel, and they sense if you care or not. Some of these dear young addicts gave their lives to Jesus Christ at the Middelburg crusade. My prayer was that they would receive the correct care afterward, both spiritual and physical.

In Holland I made quite a few friendships that proved lasting. It was a joy to return to that land in 1972 to make a documentary film for Dutch television, which also proved a great blessing to many.

I have given just a glimpse at the full and deep ministry that the Lord has graciously bestowed on me for the glory of His name and the extension of His kingdom. It still goes on today and will continue to go on if I am willing to give my all for the service of Jesus my Lord.

I have had the joy also of witnessing to my dad of the change in my life. He said he is very proud of me indeed. As yet he has not yielded his life to Christ. I am still praying for him.

I have never seen my mum since she left home when I was eleven. I haven't been able to find her, but I believe that one day I will meet her again. Jesus knows where she is, and – who knows – maybe I'll meet her sooner than I think.

As for my four sisters, I've seen two of them. They are well. One is happily married with three children, the other works in Portsmouth. They too know of the great transformation that Jesus Christ has wrought in my heart and life.

I know this: prayer changes things. My life proves it. I always pray for all my sisters, for mum and dad. God is still working out His purposes. I leave it all to Him, who knows the end from the beginning.

So far I have not mentioned my husband, David, because this has been the story of my own life, conversion, and ministry. But I am married to a fine Christian, who stands by me, helping and guiding me in every possible way in the work of the Lord.

David is a man of prayer, and when I have to travel without him, I can be sure he is spending much time in prayer on my behalf. We both know that if our lives are fully and wholly surrendered to Jesus Christ, there is no limit to what He can do in us and through us.

Many people in need visit our little home. Some need encouragement and guidance on the Christian pathway. Some are in need of a mighty deliverance from demons and powers of darkness. Some need practical help. We thank God that we have seen quite a number of people helped and blessed in our little house. We know that prayer changes things and that Jesus can meet all needs and problems, no matter how great or how small.

My husband is a great personal worker for the Lord behind the scenes. I thank God for him and for the help and encouragement he gives me at all times.

My earnest and sincere desire is that the Saviour will lead me higher yet, and deeper yet, into even fuller service for Him and others.

CHAPTER TWENTY-ONE

A Spiritual Warfare

For we wrestle not against flesh and blood but against principalities, against powers, against the rulers of the darkness of this world, against spiritual wickedness in high places.

– Ephesians 6:12

"Is it a harmless, dotty craze, or is there something in it?" asked one of our national newspapers in a recent series of articles on witchcraft and the occult.

Far from being harmless, witchcraft and other forms of the occult are harming, yea, wrecking and ruining lives today to an alarming degree – driving men and women to suicide, mental hospitals, utter fear, and a living hell. If people saw only half of what I've seen in the country and overseas, they would think again before writing it all off as a harmless craze. It is not a craze that will finally fizzle out.

We must face up to facts. In the past eight years witchcraft, Satanism, spiritism, and other evil cults have trebled in their number. The occult has spread over the world like a malignant cancer.

I cannot conclude this book without giving a sober warning against such grossly evil practices, for I have met young people whose lives have been ruined by getting mixed up with dark and evil things. We must ask ourselves why do people, especially young people, get involved with witchcraft and the occult?

First of all, consider the fast-moving events in the world today: bloodshed, riots, strikes, and terrible unrest. Undoubtedly a huge question mark emerges in people's minds. Why? they ask.

Man caters for the mind, for knowledge is increasing daily, but can man cater for an empty, broken heart? Can man ever fill the huge void? *Never*.

Young people are looking for an answer. They are looking for something to fill the gaping void. I know, for I looked for years for something to fill my empty heart. Young people will go anywhere and try anything to find that *something*. In their desperate search for the answer, in their search for the truth, they are turning to drugs and occult practices, especially witchcraft.

The element of mystery and excitement is one great factor that adds to the pull away from the truth, away from the one true God. Everyone is looking for a bit of excitement and mystery. Many are looking for a supernatural sign.

Where better to find these elements than in some witches' coven or Satanist temple? So Satan sees to it that the searchers do get signs – evil signs and lying wonders – in such places. I ought to know, for I have seen these evil manifestations.

The Bible warns us against witchcraft, divination, and other such diabolical practises. In Deuteronomy 18 God forbids all such practices, not because He is a cruel, forbidding God but because He is a good God, a kind and loving God. He knows these things are grossly evil. Therefore He warns us in love. He wants only the best for the men and women He made.

It is not the manifold manifestations in themselves that are the greatest evil, evil though they are. It is the *diversion* away from God that constitutes the greatest evil of all.

178

Many Christians shrink back in fear and trembling whenever witchcraft, demons, or evil manifestations are mentioned. Occult practices frighten them.

"We don't want to hear about such things," they say. "It gives us the creeps."

Why all the fear? This should not be so. We must always remember that Jesus is far stronger than Satan and sin, remember that Jesus conquered Satan and all demons at that wonderful place called Calvary.

The Bible tells us we should not be ignorant of the devil's devices. How ever can we expect to reach the lost and help those in the very grip of evil if we do not know what is going on in the world today?

This is a spiritual warfare. We cannot hope to fight the good fight of faith in this spiritual warfare if we do not know our adversary. We must know just what we are up against on this spiritual battlefield. The Word of God plainly states that unseen forces of evil are at work, and wickedness will wax worse and worse as the coming of the Lord draweth nigh. We do not have to look very far to see that wickedness is far worse today than ever it was, with more and more people in the trap of the occult, with more and more people in the evil web of witchcraft.

Some Christians have no idea how wicked some evil is. We are bound to encounter evil such as was never known before. So it's wise to be alert to it all now. We are going to come across it one way or another, whether we like it or not.

Even little children are playing devil games like ouija boards. I have been requested to visit especially junior schools to warn children of the dangers of dabbling. Christian school teachers and parents have been alarmed to learn that children dabble in awful, evil practices.

Children's minds have been tortured and twisted in fear when dire things have actually happened while they were playing with ouija boards. Parents have been distraught

179

with worry when their little ones were terrified to attend school, had nightmares, and refused to eat their food, all because of ouija games.

Dabbling like this is extremely dangerous, not only to souls but to minds and bodies also. One of Satan's tricks is to come as an angel of light and deceive people into thinking it is all perfectly harmless. I myself have been shocked and appalled at some of the things that go on in schools.

One Christian school teacher told me that fifteen out of twenty in his classroom were playing devil games. It was an awe-full privilege to warn the boys and girls at this school of the dangers. It is only one of the schools where ouija boards are played with.

Christians should never be afraid of the devil's devices Never fear witchcraft dolls, voodoo practices, or demonic threats. Greater is He that is in you than he that is in the world.

Christians everywhere should be up and doing, strong in faith and scornful of fear. We can go forth into a world of woe clad in the whole armour of God, not in fear, not in any way ignorant of the many diversions that Satan has put in the way to allure, trap, and pull away men and women, boys and girls, from the narrow pathway of life and light.

Part of my ministry in this spiritual warfare is to warn people against deceitful diversions, no matter what form the diversion takes, and to point them to the right pathway, which is Christ of Calvary, the great and mighty Deliverer.

Having said all this, I am well aware, however, that there are some poor misguided people who have what I call demon or devil mania. They can think and speak of little else. Demons seem to make up their main spiritual diet, for it's demons at breakfast time, dinner, and tea. They see demons in everything and everybody – demons in the cat, demons behind every hedge, demons everywhere.

These poor people seem to think it their sole life's work

to cast out or deal with so-called demons. Sad to say, they do untold damage and cause confusion and chaos.

To be obsessed with the subject of demons is very dangerous indeed. I have come to the conclusion that people who can talk of nothing but demons and what the devil is doing are in need of deliverance themselves. Many, however, lack the right kind of Bible teaching, and sad to say, do not want any Christian discipline at all.

Although part of my ministry is to expose witchcraft and warn of the dangers of the occult, I can assure you I am not always talking about demons and witchcraft. Only when I am requested to give my full testimony do I speak of demonic powers, and then it is to expose the devil and all his works, not to glorify him in any way. I am at my happiest when I am preaching the grand old Gospel story, talking about Jesus and His love.

In Revelation 12:11 we read: "And they overcame him (the devil) by the blood of the Lamb and by the word of their testimony."

I often quote this verse before I give my testimony. It is a wonderful fact that wherever we give testimony to the glory of God we once again overcome Satan. Satan hates to see God's children give glory to God through a personal testimony.

Although there is danger of the extreme as far as demons are concerned, it is also a fact that some Christians do not believe that demons exist at all. When Jesus was here on earth, He healed the sick and cast out evil spirits – two entirely different works altogether.

Jesus Himself said in Mark 16: "Go ye into all the world and preach the Gospel to every creature. In My name you will cast out devils (demons), ye shall lay hands on the sick, and they shall recover."

Many more people are demon-possessed today than when Jesus was here on earth. Jesus Himself said that wickedness shall increase. There are more open doors for demon-

181

possession in men's and women's lives than ever before.

So then, we have the two extremes: some who talk and think of nothing but demons and the devil, some who deny the very existence of demons or even a devil.

Very often poor people in genuine need of deliverance from demons within go undelivered and neglected because of this unbelief. We must have balance in all things and not be lobsided in any way. We must embrace the whole World of God, not just part of it. Put on the whole armour, says Paul, in the spiritual warfare, for it is not a carnal warfare but mighty through God to the pulling down of strongholds. Strongholds of Satan.

Yes, demon-possession is real. Very real. But thanks be to God, Jesus also is real. His word tells us so, and I have proved it so. Demons can be cast out in the name of Jesus. At the name of Jesus devils fear and fly. Sick bodies can be healed today.

Jesus said: "Go and preach, saying, 'The kingdom of heaven is at hand,' heal the sick, cleanse the leper, raise the dead, cast out devils. Freely ye have received, freely give."

We are His disciples, I am His disciple. He has freely forgiven me *all* and has set me completely free from the power of the devil and demons. He has filled me with the Holy Spirit. Therefore I will freely give my all to Him. He has forgiven me much, therefore I love Him much.

All my past He has put behind His back forever more, never to be remembered against me anymore. He has washed me whiter than the snow and says, "It is just as if you never sinned at all." JUSITIFIED.

Isn't it wonderful? Instead of witches' robes, instead of filthy rags of sin and shame, He has clothed me with the garments of salvation. He has covered me with the robe of righteousness – new garments for a new creature. He has given me a new song and placed my feet upon a rock, even Christ Jesus my Lord.

No wonder I get excited. I have new life, new love, new clothes, and a new song. I have something to be excited about. Indeed, when I am preaching, I get so filled with joy I often burst forth into song and have been known to dance with the sheer joy of the Lord.

Jesus said: "Go and preach the good news of salvation to every creature, and in My name do exploits."

Furthermore, Jesus said: "Greater things ye shall do than I, because I go to the Father."

Tremendous, isn't it?

Let me relate one example where the Lord used me to cast out devils in His name – just one example, for the Lord has used me in this field many times.

I was conducting a tent crusade in Liverpool. It was a huge tent, and it was packed every night. Every night souls were gloriously saved, and sick bodies were instantly healed. Christians dedicated their hearts and lives to Christ. It was a week I shall never forget. God's Holy Spirit was in operation in great power.

One evening the television cameras were set up, and I appeared again on television. Once again Jesus was glorified on television news. Jesus was hot news in Liverpool, not only on television but on radio Merseyside also.

Near the end of this week of blessing another wonderful thing happened. A dear old Christian lady came up to speak to me.

"I want you to pray for David, my grandson," she said. "Once he was a fine Christian boy, but now he is involved in black magic."

Tears filled her eyes as she went on.

"He has lived with me for years, and I love him dearly, but he has put years on me. I cannot rest until he is completely restored."

"One night," she continued, "I was waiting for him to return, for I can never go to bed until I see him safely home. I was sitting in my rocking chair praying when I felt an evil presence in the room. Suddenly I saw an evil, ghost-like figure appear. I called upon the name of Jesus and it left.

"When David returned, he saw I was upset, and I told him what had happened and begged him to turn again to Christ. David was so frightened he decided to finish with his evil practices.

"But he can't get free. Every night I hear him pacing up and down in his room. He's in a terrible state. I always pray for him. I've asked him to come to the tent, but he refuses. He thinks it's too late."

She was in a very disturbed state of mind. After I prayed with her and assured her of my continued prayers on David's behalf, she left in a more contented frame of mind.

The next night David was present at the meeting. When I'd finished preaching, I appealed to those who needed prayer to come forward. Many responded to the appeal. Some needed healing for their bodies, and some came to give their hearts and lives over to Jesus Christ. The Holy Spirit was moving again in a tremendous way. Souls were saved and bodies healed.

Among the many seekers was David. I had no idea that the boy I'd prayed for the night before had come forward. As I moved along the prayer line, I reached David and spoke to him.

"What is your name, son?"

"David," he replied.

The Lord showed me that this was the grandson of the little old Christian lady.

"You have broken your poor granny's heart, David," I said.

He nearly fell over backwards in surprise.

"You have played with fire," I went on, "practising witchcraft and voodoo. But if you repent tonight, Jesus will set you free."

"How did you know?" he asked.

"Your grandmother told me all about you last night. And tonight the Lord showed me you were the boy."

Yes, among the five hundred people present the Lord had directed me to David.

The boy stayed behind, and I had to talk to him for hours, pointing out the seriousness of what he had done. David truly repented in floods of tears. But it was long hours before he was completely free of demons.

With the prayerful support of other Christians I cast out seven demons into Gehenna in the name of Jesus. It was a tremendous battle, yea, a spiritual warfare with the very devil himself.

The demons were very strong and contested and fought for their ground, but Jesus was stronger, and David was finally delivered, set free by the power of Jesus Christ, the mighty Victor.

At three o'clock in the morning David was baptized in water in the baptismal tank under the big top. He was also baptised with the Holy Spirit. How he praised and prayed in a heavenly language! It was a joy to listen.

His dear old grandmother was beside herself with joy and thanksgiving to God when I met her in the evening meeting. This time tears of joy ran down her cheeks.

"I can rest easy now," she said. "He has been praising God all day at the top of his voice. He has burned all his books of magic and charms. Praise be to God."

But in the spiritual warfare on God's battlefield it has not always been victory, victory, victory, all the way. There have been failures and mistakes also. There have been times when I have fallen headlong to the ground in defeat with a great crash. There have been moments when I have lacked grace, foresight, and wisdom.

Then Satan has laughed and said, "You are nothing but a failure. Throw down your sword now, and give in."

Instead of staying down in defeat and failure, I have allowed the Lord to pick me up – and then I have fallen down at the foot of the old rugged cross and admitted my failure.

I have wept and cried: "Jesus, I'm a failure. I've made a mess of things, but I still love you. Have mercy on me, and help me to go on."

I have learned from my mistakes and failures. By God's grace I have learned to look my failures and defeats squarely in the eye and face up to them.

Does God ever get a big stick and chase us out of the fold because of our defeats and failures? A thousand times no. He gently picks us up if we confess our faults and puts us back on our feet and tells us to go on.

Failure and defeat have brought me to a place of utter dependency on Jesus, the mighty Captain of my soul.

It's no use staying down in the dust when we fail and make mistakes, for Satan would only tread us further down than ever. We must not give up when we have failed the Lord. Satan is always ready to pounce on us like a vulture when he sees us fall. One of his favourite tricks is to convince us we are not perfect enough, or he tells us we will never rise above our failures.

In the Bible we read that some of God's greatest men have failed Him at some time. King David was a mighty warrior and a singer of psalms. Yet David sinned and failed God. He saw another man's wife and coveted her for himself. He deliberately sent Uriah, her husband, to certain death in the forefront of the battle in order to have this woman for his wife.

But David repented, he faced up to his failure, he confessed his sin. We read in the Bible that David ran into God's house and caught hold of the horns of the altar and found forgiveness and peace with God. Then he went on to face and win many more battles.

Jacob too was a man of prayer, who once wrestled with an angel. Yet he too failed, he too had his faults and failings. He deceived his aged father, stealing his brother's blessing

186

and inheritance. He despised his wife Leah because he was in love with her sister Rachel. Jacob was caught up in a web of trickery, deceit, and unfaithfulness of heart, yet Jacob was also a great man of God.

Peter too failed Christ at the time when He needed him most. Peter repented and went on. He rose above the ashes of denial to lead a church to Pentecost.

These men and others rose above defeat to serve God with renewed peace, power, and greatness.

Everyone makes mistakes and has failed God at some time or other. No one is absolutely perfect.

Even the apostle Paul says in Romans 7: "For the good that I would I do not, but the evil which I would not, that I do."

He goes on to say: "Oh wretched man that I am! Who shall deliver me from the body of this death?"

The answer? I thank God through Jesus Christ our Lord. Only by Christ can we overcome.

Christians, look upward, not inward, when you fail and make mistakes. Face up to your failures. Cry aloud to Jesus. Lean hard on Him. Get things right. Get up, and go on with God, as I have, to higher heights and deeper depths with Christ.

I am still on the battlefield for my Lord, still in this spiritual warfare. Not alone, for Jesus my mighty Captain of salvation goes before me and fights for me. Without Him I could do nothing but fail. As long as I have strength I will serve Him here below. As long as He lends me breath I will praise Him and speak of all His love, grace, compassion, and power.

I want the whole wide world to know I love Him. I want the whole world to know Him too. I want to tell everybody, everywhere, that my Jesus lives, my Jesus cares, my Jesus is wonderful and can do anything. Nothing is impossible for Him. *Nothing!*

Another battle has been won as I finish this book. It

has been a battle – a big one. At first I didn't want to write it at all. Besides, I didn't think I could.

Many people asked me: "Why don't you write a book?"

Easier said than done, I thought. When would I find time to write a book? It was only after much prayer that I began it at all and then only by God's help and guidance. I've written it between preaching engagements. I trust and pray that it will be a blessing to all who read it.

With the completion of this book another spiritual battle is over. Other battles will follow, but with Jesus beside me I am confident that I will conquer every foe. With His mighty hand in mine and by His strength divine, I will fight the good fight of faith, clad in the whole armour of God: my helmet of salvation, my breastplate of righteousness, my loins girt about with truth and my feet shod with the preparation of the Gospel of peace, and in my hand and heart the sword of the Spirit, which is the Word of God, my Bible. How can I fail?

When I was a child – so lonely, so unhappy – I often wondered why I was born. When I was in the padded cell in Holloway Prison, I wondered why I was born.

Now I know why I was born. I was born in the flesh to be born again by the Spirit of God. I was born to preach the Gospel to every creature. To love and serve Jesus. To comfort the lonely. To love the unlovely. To fight for Him and serve Him here below with the great and mighty army of the Lord until one day I see Him face to face and tell the story: *saved by grace*.

And the end is not yet, praise the Lord . . . Even so, come quickly, Lord Jesus. Amen.

Afterword

Like many others I read *From Witchcraft to Christ* some years ago. I never dreamed that someday I would have the author of this powerful testimony in my congregation, but that is the case today. Doreen commands the respect and love of those who know her and we are delighted to have her worship with us.

Because of ill health Doreen is no longer able to follow the intense itinerant preaching engagements of former years. She has seen much physical suffering and the enemy has not left her unchallenged in other ways. This is not surprising: one who has left his camp and done such damage to his kingdom could not expect to be left alone. Rumours have circulated that Doreen had gone back into the occult, but these rumours are quite false and spring from the father of lies. Doreen has never gone back to the dark life she knew —she walks with God and exercises a ministry of prayer. She and her husband Dave live here in Bromsgrove, and their four children—Julie, Stephen, Mark and Ruth—are all Christians.

Although limited in her activities Doreen continues to serve the Lord as he enables her. I thank God for her spiritual wisdom, for her encouragement to me and the rest of the pastoral team in New Road Baptist Church, and for her ministry of discernment.

In the latter years of her public ministry Doreen raised quite large sums of money, sometimes at great cost to herself. Something over £60,000 was raised for the Bristol City Mission to build a home for street girls. Unfortunately staff could not be found for such a home and the money was redirected into a Christian coffee bar for street girls, down-and-outs and other needy people in the area.

Even under the restrictive pressure of painful illness Doreen and Dave have done what they could for God, and Doreen's books, *Spiritual Warfare* and *Set Free to Serve Christ* remain effective in communicating vital information and guidance to present-day believers. Few people I know are more able to help us all to be alert and wise and strong to see the way of victory over all of Satan's devices.

We in our church fellowship pray for further blessing on the reissue of this book. May many be set free from bondage and brought into the glorious liberty of the children of God through Jesus Christ—the one and only Way to eternal life and peace.

The Revd Keith Blades
New Road Baptist Church
November 1994

Set Free
to Serve Christ

DOREEN IRVINE

KINGSWAY PUBLICATIONS
EASTBOURNE

Contents

Foreword

WHEN the Gadarene demoniac was emancipated by the supernatural action of the Lord Jesus Christ, there was recognized a state of harmonious equilibrium and normality of personality, wherein the man knew the profound sanity and sanctity of peace with God and peace within himself. *"Then they went out to see what was done; and came to Jesus, and found the man, out of whom the demons were departed, sitting at the feet of Jesus, clothed and in his right mind . . . "* (Luke 8:35). Instead of asking the delivered and healed man to keep quiet about it all (as in many other instances), the Lord dispatched him with the instruction, *"Return to thine own house, and shew how great things GOD hath done unto thee. And he went his way, and published throughout the whole city, how great things JESUS had done unto him."* (Luke 8:39) His witness was authorized and advocated by the Lord for the glory of God.

It is my privilege and joy to introduce this present volume and up-to-date testimony by Doreen Irvine. In my Foreword to her previous book, *From Witchcraft to Christ*, I have referred to the background and the nature of the diabolical conflict with supernatural forces of evil, in which it was my terrible responsibility to be implicated. Throughout the years since Doreen's gracious deliverance from demonic possession, I have had periodic contact and fellowship with her. I have marvelled at the way she has been brought through many circumstances which have been contested, at times viciously and violently, by the strategy and power of Satan. In view of the fact of the Devil's dominion over her and use of her in the past, can you wonder that she has been subjected to abnormal and supernatural reaction from him and his agencies? However, it has been wonderful to recognize the victory of the Lord Jesus Christ as she has sought, through evil and good report, by His grace, to witness clearly and courageously for her Lord in exposing the works of the Devil. **This to me is as important a miracle as her deliverance itself.**

Doreen has had her struggles, heartaches, and failures. She would be the first to admit that she is no paragon nor is she an angel out of orbit. Some Christians have been quick to criticize her for her imperfections. But surely every believer in the Lord Jesus Christ knows that sanctification is a continuing process as well as a definite crisis, the Holy Spirit acting in and through us to conform us more and more to the image of the Son of God. And I know that Doreen's great desire is to know increasingly such purity of heart, clarity of mind, and holiness of life which honours the Lord and commends the Gospel. When I remember her in her tragic state of demonization, and compare what she is now by Grace with what she was then by debauchery, I marvel that she is as she is. And her passion is to continue to grow in Grace and in the knowledge of her Lord Jesus Christ.

I am delighted that now there has been set in motion by men and women of God the process to establish a Rescue Home in the Bristol area, and my prayer is that is will be a veritable means of Grace for the deliverance of despairing captives whose plight is as Doreen's was—humanly hopeless.

As I recommend this book, I pray that the Holy Spirit will use it to the glory of the Lord Jesus Christ and the blessing of many.

Rev. Arthur Neil, Principal
Faith Mission Bible College of Edinburgh

Summer 1978

Introduction

"But grow in grace, and in the knowledge of our Lord and Saviour Jesus Christ" (2 Peter 3:18).

"AND the end is not yet. Praise the Lord." With those words I ended my first book *From Witchcraft to Christ*. How better way to introduce my second book than with those same words. The end is not yet, still; indeed it is only just beginning. In my first book I talked mainly about my past life as drug addict, prostitute, and witch, and how I was miraculously saved by Christ Jesus from a life of sin and hopelessness. In my second book I want to take the story further and to share with you my experiences as a Christian and a servant of God. This is the story of one no longer a slave of Satan, but a servant of God.

Not only do I want to share the blessings of my Christian journey thus far, but also the lessons I have learned and the battles I have fought and won with Jesus by my side. As I begin writing I am praying for guidance over each chapter, for without prayer and without the guidance and inspiration of the Holy Spirit, I would be unable to write one sentence, let alone an entire book!

Inside my Bible I have written the initials K.I.S.S. They stand for "Keep it simple, stupid", and remind me to keep my words plain and simple. I am sure that many Christians use a language which is largely incomprehensible to those outside the faith and so I will try to keep my language as simple as possible in order that all who read may understand. It is my hope that all who read my book will find it helpful, inspirational, and a source of blessing for themselves and their families.

As the Holy Spirit brings events and people to my remembrance I pray that my writings will be for His glory alone. The blessings of the Lord are great and numerous. No book could contain all that the Lord has done for me.

The Bible says "Grow in grace" (2 Peter 3:18). Every day

of my life I am growing in grace and learning more about Jesus and His love for us all. If we plant seeds in a box and wait for them to grow we see that as soon as the shoots emerge from the soil they automatically turn towards the light. No matter where you put the box, the shoots will always turn towards the light. This is how we all should be, ever leaning towards the light of Christ Jesus. He is the "light of the world" (Matt. 5:14; John 8:12; 9:5) and He lights the Christian pathway. We should not look elsewhere lest we do not grow at all.

To grow, we should be in touch with the Lord every day of our lives. Start every day with God, look upwards to Jesus, have fellowship with Him and put your trust completely in Him. Imagine if a child went off to school every day without speaking to his father! Would the father not feel unloved and unwanted? Yet how many Christians treat their heavenly Father in this way every day? I have met many Christians who have admitted that they do not pray in the morning and indeed have frequently gone all day without speaking to Jesus. Prayer is the simplest thing and yet is perhaps the most important. It should never be neglected and indeed should be a priority in the life of every Christian. It is no wonder that so many Christians have stopped growing in faith and have faced setbacks.

If you love Jesus you will want to speak to Him as often as possible. You will count it a pleasure and a privilege to speak to our Lord rather than a daily chore! I am sure that if all Christians knew the joy and blessing they were missing by not talking to Jesus, they would be sorry. I do know that it would change their lives. They would have the power to overcome all obstacles and solve all problems and be armed to fight the Devil in all of his various forms.

What an honour to be able to speak to the Creator of all things. Look around you at the majesty of His works, the sun, the mountains, the rivers and seas, and remember that we, humble as we are, can talk to the Creator of all these wonders. So often Satan distracts us and wastes our valuable time. We then realize, too late, that we have thrown away valuable time which might have been spent in prayer.

Many Christians have admitted to me that they do not actually appreciate their salvation as they should. The things of God and the Church have become familiar and they have lost the joy and wonder of worship, or reading the Word of God. This is very sad.

Prayer and the reading of the Scriptures are the two most important factors in our Christian lives. If these are neglected, the light in our hearts grows dim and may even be extinguished completely. We have free access to the Bible in our society. Many Christians are not so fortunate. Christians in Communist countries run the risk of persecution for possessing the Word of God. How foolish that we who have open access to the Bible so frequently neglect our readings. How much more should we study the Scriptures and speak to God in prayer, growing in His grace and pointing others to Him.

There are so many precious jewels of truth to be found in the Book of Life and we have a duty to seek them out and apply them in our lives. Satan certainly does not want us to understand or derive power from the Bible and will put all manner of distractions and hurdles in our way. He knows that the Christian who feeds daily on the Word of God is strong and out of his evil reach.

Satan hates the Bible. He once ordered me to burn Bibles on the high altar of a satanist temple. I held them in the flames until they were ashes. Satan protected my flesh while the pages flared in the white-hot heat. Satan knows the power of the Bible. So all Christians should appreciate the privileges they have. They should devour the Word of God constantly.

I love the Bible and I treasure every sacred word therein. The Bible is the Word of God and the Word of God is the sword that all true Christians can use to cut down the strongest enemy. No wonder Satan hates and fears the Bible so much. We need the Bible to help us grow.

We must also glow. Having been saved we ought to show the wonder and thankfulness in our faces. A bright smile can warm the coldest heart and we, as children of God, have so much to smile about. Christ has set a blaze within me and this fire will burn until Jesus comes again. Sometimes my heart has been so full of burning love I have wanted to climb to the rooftops and shout into the crowded streets, "Jesus loves all you people and so do I. Will you let Jesus into your hearts and lives?"

How often have I wished that I could get the whole world under one roof and tell them of the love of Jesus and how much he means to me. This is, of course, impossible but with His grace I will reach as many as I can and tell out His praise by word of mouth and by my writing. I am one of His mouthpieces and I have a living message that burns in my heart. I am aglow for the Lord.

"Grow, glow, and go." But go where? Go to a lost and needy world. Take with you the living burning message of Salvation for all men. Millions are looking for the answer. Millions stand in the valley of decision. Go to them with your message of love, truth, forgiveness, and Salvation. You can meet them on any street and in any town. For my part I must go for Jesus has commanded me to go.

He said, "Come ye after me, and I will make you to become fishers of men" (Mark 1:17). I have been set free to serve him, to follow Him, and to serve others in His name.

Let us be strong in the Lord and let us go where He would send us and go with a joyful heart.

This book is for saint and sinner alike, so let me take you on a spiritual journey and show you how God has blessed and used me. Some of my experiences may help and encourage you. I pray that they will. I am still pressing on, ever upward towards the light. I am still growing in grace and still glowing and going with God. I would never wish to do otherwise.

Let us all go forward for the glory of God. Let every Christian grow, glow, and go for Jesus.

December 1978   DOREEN IRVINE

CHAPTER ONE

Jesus in the Twilight Zone

Then Jesus answering said unto them, . . . to the poor the gospel is preached (Luke 7:22).

ALL was strangely quiet and still as I made my way down the grimy back streets of the twilight zone. It was early evening and the streets were deserted. This was unusual as this area was normally filled with people coming and going about their business or just standing around on street corners. "Where are all the people tonight?" I wondered. It felt as if the area had been evacuated—all the people gone. And they could hardly have been blamed for wanting to leave such a bleak and inhospitable place. A few cars were passing through, but even they seemed to accelerate in order to get out of the area as fast as possible.

"To get away from it all," I thought with a sigh. "Away from all the heartaches and problems that come from merely living in an area like this." As I walked on I wondered, "Where are all the young women that walk these streets at night?" I knew their problems. I had come to this area to share them and to tell them about Jesus. For the moment, however, I was alone.

It had not taken me long to get to this area as it lay quite close to my home. It houses a multi-racial community whose main problem is unemployment, especially among the younger people. For them life is frustrating. They have nowhere to go and nothing to do.

As I walked on, my mind went back to the time when I frequented these same streets as a prostitute. It all seemed so long ago, almost as though it had never happened. I had even forgotten that even the most notorious areas, like the one I was walking through, had their quiet times, and that early evening was one of them. The people were here, somewhere, and so were the problems. I would simply have to wait a short while before they emerged from behind closed doors and entered the grim streets.

The fact that you cannot see the army of young prostitutes that operate in this area does not mean that they are not there. Many work in brothels or even in their own homes! They often go off to another part of the city for a while before returning to their home territory. Most prostitutes own their own cars and as such can travel easily from city to city. Often they go away for days on end, returning just when you think that they have gone for good. This mobility is a great help in avoiding the Vice Squads of major cities.

I had often contacted these girls and told them about Jesus and I hoped that tonight I would again be successful. Lost in thought I wandered off the main road and into a small side street. I almost fell over a group of men that were half lying and half sitting on the pavement. There were newspapers spread out to offer meagre comfort and even in the half-light I could see that they were all hopeless alcoholics, the outcasts of society.

What a pitiful sight they were. Their eyes were glazed and blank and their faces bore the marks of sleeping rough and constant inebriation. These men slept where they could, in old derelict houses or warehouses, or even by the side of the road. They were constantly moved on by the police and they had nothing but the rags on their backs which were filthy and foul smelling. These men were on the bottom rung of society. They were in the gutter. What had started them on the downward spiral to degradation and hopelessness? What personal tragedies? Bereavements, broken homes, rejection, failure. Whatever the first cause, Satan had seen to it that their

14

decline led them to the very bottom.

Downtrodden miserable forms of humanity—Jesus Christ had died for these men! These men were the bottom of the pile. They were hopelessly addicted. They would drink any liquid that contained alcohol even in its crudest form. Methylated spirits, paraffin, metal polish, and other similar horrid concoctions were their daily sustenance. The stench was unbearable. Despite my natural wish to leave them, I knew I had to stay and talk to them. They were human beings and Jesus loved them. He had died for such as these.

I offered to find them shelter but they were not interested. They seemed to prefer their own wretched wandering way of life and were suspicious of any sort of help. Instead they asked me for money. "I have no money," I answered truthfully. After a pause I began to talk to them about Jesus and His love, telling them as simply and as plainly as I could that Jesus could change their lives completely. "He can give you peace and joy, such as you have never known," I said. They all listened but whether or not my words were making any impact I knew not. "He can chase away the dark shadows and give you everlasting life," I went on.

I began to pray in my heart that Jesus would open up their hearts and break the chains that bound them, so that they might begin to see His love and glory. I knew that nothing short of a miracle could change these men. I asked them their names, but only two of them could remember. I then asked if I could pray for them right there and then individually. They were obviously surprised, but they agreed. I laid my hand on each man's head and prayed for the Lord to come to them. I rebuked the powers of darkness in the name of Jesus. "Loose them, Jesus, from all bondage. May they see Thee in all thy love and power. Make them willing to be free that they might find peace in trusting Thee as their own Saviour."

Many organizations do a wonderful job in helping these unfortunates. They provide food and shelter and try to solve the basic human problems of the men and women who come to them. But mostly their help is temporary and limited and in a short time their subjects have returned to their wandering and wretched way of life. Man can solve some of the problems, but only Jesus Christ, the great and mighty deliverer, can set them completely and wonderfully free.

After I had finished praying the men thanked me most earnestly. I was deeply moved. Suddenly it began to rain and the small group of men got up and went off to find shelter for the night. Once again I was alone in the now dark streets.

I looked at my watch and was surprised that I had been with the men for over an hour. As the darkness came down it was as if a signal had been given. People began to come out from behind the closed doors and soon the streets presented their usual busy sight.

Some people were purposefully hurrying, while others were simply drifting aimlessly. They all had the same anxious look as though they were looking for something or someone but were uable to find the place or person that they were seeking. One lady walked towards me and I spoke to her. "I wonder if I could talk to you for a minute?" I asked her. She looked puzzled and said, "What about?" I smiled. "About God's love and His plan for your life." She replied, "I'm sorry, but I just haven't time tonight." I asked her if she would read a Gospel tract when she did have time and she said she would. She pushed the tract into her pocket without looking and hurried away. As I approached others in the same way, some took the tracts while others politely refused. I continued to walk the streets searching for men and women for Christ.

As I walked, a poem began to take shape in my mind which aptly described my experiences that night.

> I walked the lonely streets tonight
> There was not a single soul in sight
> Yet I knew that every single day
> Lost and lonely people passed along that way
> And all I could do was to pray.

Oh Lord please walk along this street
Lord Jesus please rest those weary feet
May they know that somebody cares
May they know that it is You.

Suddenly I knew that I was right
For suddenly there burst upon my sight
A group of human beings on the ground
With faces sad and lonely, huddled all around
And all I could do was to pray
Oh Lord please walk along this street
Lord Jesus please rest their weary feet
May they know that somebody cares
May they know that it is You.

The rain came tumbling down
And the wind went whistling around the town
I thought about the people living all around
Knowing some were lost, knowing some were bound
And all I could do was to pray
Oh Lord please walk along this street
Lord Jesus please rest their weary feet
May they know that somebody cares
And help me to tell them it is You.

Help me to tell them Lord. Help me to tell them it is You. Little did those poor helpless men know how much encouragement I had received from talking to them that night. My heart was filled with an even deeper love and compassion for a lost and sinful mankind. I shall never forget that encounter in the twilight zone. "Help me to tell them it is You," was my prayer that night and indeed still is. Jesus said, "to the poor the Gospel is preached". I still pray for those men that heard the Gospel of Salvation.

Some time later I walked into one of the many public houses in the area. "What's a nice girl like you doing in a place like this?" asked one dark haired woman to whom I had begun to speak. "Surely you should not be here!" Gently I told her, "Jesus sat with sinners. Jesus was a friend of sinners. He cares about everyone and He cares about you. He is alive today and He still loves the lost and the lonely." The woman, whose breath smelt strongly of drink, but who was still quite sober said, "You remind me of my daughter." I smiled and continued to talk to her. As I did a group of people gathered around to listen and eventually everyone in the public house was hearing about the great love and power of the risen Christ. What a thrill it was to witness in such a place. Many were surprised that I took the trouble to come to them and they thanked me for my concern. The dark haired lady kept saying how much I reminded her of her daughter. It seemed that for a moment a curtain had been drawn aside to reveal a wistful mother's heart. This woman and I became firm friends after that first meeting and she always listened to what I had to say about the Lord Jesus. Under all the hardness and the laughter and the glitter was sadness and pain that was never spoken of.

We should all be good listeners. Very often we can see a little of what is hidden from view, praying all the time that one small word may be the means of bringing someone to the knowledge of the Saviour. I remember the words of an old song that my mother used to sing many years ago:

> City of laughter, city of tears,
> What are the secrets you hold.
> What are the sorrows beneath the joys,
> The pain 'neath the glitter of gold.

How often does a seemingly happy face hide an empty and broken heart.

My constant prayer is, "Lord, keep me watchful and discerning. Help me to see that which is hidden from view. Keep me tender and broken so that by Thy spirit I may catch a glimpse beneath the surface and see and feel the pain and sorrow that is never knowingly shown." When listening to people in counselling rooms, in churches, in public houses, or on street corners, with the help of Christ we can see and feel a little of what people are trying to say and cannot. What is needed more and more today is a tear-stained ministry. Sometimes a tear shed on someone's behalf can help them more than mere words. Often when confronted with tragic problems and enormous heartaches all I have been able to do is to weep for the people concerned. Not that anyone can simply turn on tears like a tap. Compassion must stem from deep inside the soul. Then and only then can we weep a soul into the Kingdom of Heaven.

After speaking for Christ in this particular public house I moved on to another that I had frequented in the past. I knew that there I would meet prostitutes as it was a favourite meeting-place. They gather there while the evening is still young and relax and talk among themselves before commencing work. As I walked in I saw the barman who I remembered was called Charlie, polishing the glasses behind the bar. He did this every night in readiness for the evening trade. He knew me well from the old days and he remembered me. Charlie never missed a thing that went on in that area.

The bar was fairly busy and I turned to see a group of prostitutes sitting in the corner. I caught my breath as I recognized one of them. We had once been friends and had often sat together in that very corner. I did not go over straight away, but mingled with the people on the other side of the public house, praying quietly for the right moment to go and speak to the women in the corner.

I began handing out Gospel tracts and they were very well received indeed. My presence was not questioned at all. After a short while I walked over to the girls in the corner and said, "Good evening girls, I am giving out these little Gospel tracts telling about the love of Jesus. Will you each take one and read it?" One of the girls looked up and said, "Leaflets about what?" I repeated, "About the love of Jesus." They all burst out laughing. From the corner of my eye I could see Charlie, still polishing his glasses, rooted to the spot, watching and listening. His face was a picture.

My former friend, Valerie, had not yet recognized me. She laughed loudly, "That's very funny. That's really very funny." Suddenly she stopped laughing and said, "Here, don't I know you from somewhere?" I answered, "Keep on looking and perhaps it will come to you." She stared at me closely and then said, "It's never Dianna, is it?" I smiled, "That's me Valerie, but my name is Doreen, not Dianna." She nearly choked on her drink. "Don't tell me you have gone all religious." "Yes Valerie, I have, if you choose to call it that. Personally, I prefer to call myself a Christian." Valerie laughed again, "Give her a drink Charlie, I think she needs one." Poor Charlie was unable to utter a word. He kept looking at me, then at the girls, then back at me again. "Don't bother Charlie," I said, "I don't need a drink." Charlie had been polishing the same glass for quite some time and he continued to do so. He was quite unable to comprehend the situation.

Valerie chirped up, "Is it more profitable than what you were doing before? Do you make more money doing this? If you are we all might join you." Peals of laughter came from the corner at Valerie's sarcasm. Her taunts had no effect on me. "No, Valerie, I do not get paid for doing this, but it is far more profitable in other ways. I don't need drink or drugs to get me by any more, because Jesus has given me real love, peace, and happiness. And you ought to know that money can't buy those things." Valerie was unrepentant. "I don't believe in all that religious rubbish. It is all just a money-making racket if you ask me." I replied that her words were ridiculous. "The Christian Church really cares about people and does a tremendous amount to help." To my surprise one lady piped up, "Hear, hear." This took me quite by surprise and gave me the courage to stand my ground. "Jesus really loves you. He died that you might have real life and have it more abundantly." Valerie snapped back, "She's gone a bit crazy in the head, or else it's one of her big jokes." Looking straight at her I said "It's no joke Valerie. I am more sane than you are. When you wake up tomorrow, you will have one of your giant-sized hangovers and will spend the rest of the day ill in bed. Then you will get up and come out and do the whole sad thing again." One of the men who had been listening said, "She's got a point there."

Valerie had run out of arguments. She told the girls that it was time that they went out into the streets for the night's work. Suddenly one of the girls said, "Can I have one of those leaflets to read?" I smiled at her. "Certainly my dear, and I will pray for you . . . is there anyone else who would like one?" At once they all crowded round and I could not give them out fast enough. Most of them sat down right there and then and began to read them. Charlie behind the bar had one as well and settled down to read it. Suddenly someone said, "They want some in the other bar." I moved into the next bar and to everyone I gave a tract. When I walked out of the pub I did not have one single tract left. Someone called after me, "Come back again, and bring some more of those leaflets with you." I smiled and replied, "Don't worry, I will be back." I went on my way rejoicing at how the Lord had used me in that pub. I have since returned to the same pub several times to witness for the Lord.

One day I had a wonderful vision. I saw the King of Kings walking down a grimy back street and graciously move among the overflowing rubbish-bins. He had a look of tender compassion on His face and He stretched forth his nail-pierced hands to the poor people in the slums. The scene changed and I saw Him walking down a broad street among the milling crowds and the bright lights. Then I saw Him walking on the sea beside huge passenger liners and smaller merchant ships. The scene changed again and Jesus was standing on a high platform stretching forth His hands to a congregation of many thousands. My vision ended and I heard a sweet voice saying, "I will walk with you on the side streets. I will walk with you down the lighted highways. I will be with you on the platforms. I will be with you for evermore. Go then and preach the Gospel to every creature."

It was so real, so very real. This was a true vision and I will never forget it. Jesus walks down all streets. He walks down *your* street. Isn't that just like Jesus! Never will I forget those words, "Go then and preach the Gospel to every creature." Jesus means everyone, rich or poor, high or low, of every race and colour. He means everyone . . . everywhere. In the Bible we read: "And they went forth, and preached everywhere, the Lord working with them, and confirming the word with signs following" (Mark 16:20). It is wonderful to know that the Lord is with us. He works through us and in us. As mere men we can do nothing of our own accord. With Him we can do anything. Nothing is too hard for the Lord. Nothing.

Like Paul I must preach this wonderful Gospel of Salvation. I must tell of all His wondrous love and power. Furthermore, Paul says, "Woe unto me if I preach not the Gospel." This is how I feel. I cannot live unless I preach the Good News of Salvation to everyone. Every evangelist and every Christian worker should go into the highways and byways as the Lord has commanded. There is little point in sitting in our secure comfortable pews or in confining our preaching and witness to the pulpits of churches alone.

What is the point of praying in prayer meetings for people to come into the church if we are not prepared to got out to where the people are. To many people, the presence of people praying for them inside the church is of little importance. We must go out to the people with the message of Salvation. We must reach the lonely and the lost. We must go out to those that are steeped in sin and shame and preach to them the Gospel of Salvation with power, simplicity, and great compassion. We must follow in the footsteps of the Master remembering that He stooped down to touch the lowly. We must love people and genuinely care about them. We must talk with them and try to understand them. We must lift up the fallen and help to bear their burdens. We must be a friend to sinners in the same way that Jesus was. Only then can we hope to reach the millions that will otherwise never know eternal life.

I am sure that if Christians only knew how people respond when you bother to meet them on their home ground they would make more effort to take the Gospel to the people. People can tell if you care. Your words may be few and stumbling, but they will listen to what you have to say about Jesus Christ. I have seen even the toughest of men melt like snow in a furnace when the love of Jesus has shone through and the barriers have been broken down by the Holy Spirit.

Take Margaret, for example. Margaret was really tough, or so it seemed at first glance. Nothing seemed to get through to her as I witnessed week after week. Very often her loud laughter would drown out every word I said and she usually tried to put off other girls from listening to me. But I knew her laughter was false and that inside she was tremendously lonely, unhappy, and confused. I never seemed to be able to talk to her on her own, as she was always sitting with the other prostitutes. One evening, however, I managed to see her on her own and I spoke to her about my unhappy past life as a drug addict and prostitute. As I was speaking I could feel the harshness slowly fall away revealing the real Margaret. I saw the fear, the confusion, the bitterness, and the sadness very clearly in her young face. Gently and prayerfully I told her how Jesus had saved me. I told how He had changed me and told her that He would change her also.

She began to listen intently to my words. Suddenly she burst out crying and said, "That's done it. I will never go on the streets again." I explained that that was not enough and that she needed the help and guidance of Jesus. She could never succeed on her own. She took the Gospel tract I handed her and said, "I know." With that she ran off and I was not able to catch her. I called out after her, "Jesus loves you Margaret." I got some very strange looks from passers-by, but I did not care. I was doing the Lord's work and that was all that mattered.

How I prayed that Margaret would find peace in Jesus. I knew that He and He alone could put her on the right way. Margaret disappeared from the streets. When I asked about her, one of the other prostitutes told me, "She is not on the game any more. She's given it all up and got herself a job." You can imagine how I felt. "Are you sure?" I asked. "Positive," the girl replied. I prayed even harder for Margaret after that.

One day I was getting off a bus when who should I see coming down the stairs, but Margaret. She had a happy smile on her face. "Hello, Margaret," I said, "how are you?" Margaret turned and said, "Oh, hello, Doreen. I am very well indeed. Actually I am a Christian now." I almost fell off the step with surprise. Margaret helped me off the bus laughing at my obvious astonishment. "And that is not all. I am engaged to be married to a wonderful Christian boy and we are very happy." I was overjoyed and we stood in the street hugging each other with excitement. Passers-by must have been looking at us but we were quite oblivious to them.

As we walked up the road Margaret continued, "I never did go back on the streets after you spoke to me that night, and the next day I went into a local church and heard the Gospel preached. The words I heard were almost identical to your words." She paused for a moment then continued, "That night I gave my heart to the Saviour and became a regular attender at the meetings. I met my fiancé there and we fell in love. Isn't it wonderful?"

And wonderful it was. It was absolutely tremendous. Tears filled my eyes and I was overjoyed to see Margaret so radiantly happy and serving the Lord Jesus who had transformed her life so wonderfully. Margaret is now very happily married and has a beautiful baby daughter. She also teaches in the Sunday School.

It was worth it all. All the rebuffs, all the tears, all the trials, just to see one life changed by the mighty power of God. One so seemingly hard and unreachable had been touched by Jesus. He had been able to reach her and to save her.

The Lord Jesus also reached me, and I was harder and farther from God than she was. I suddenly remembered the vision I had had of Jesus walking along the dirty side street. Yes! Jesus walks with us everywhere, even down the sad dark and dirty streets of the twilight zone.

CHAPTER TWO

A child of a King

"My praise shall be of thee in the great congregation"
(Psalm 22:25)

BRISTOL Temple Mead Station was very busy when I arrived to catch my train to Weymouth. When the train came to a halt at the crowded platform, I wondered whether or not I would be able to find a seat. "It's a good thing I don't have to change trains," I thought, when I eventually I found a seat and settled down to enjoy the journey. Every compartment was full with buckets and spades and holiday suitcases piled high on the luggage-racks. Every available space was taken. Happy smiling children ran up and down the corridor, chattering excitedly while anxious parents tried hard to exercise some sort of control. As the train pulled out of the station the warm August sunshine streamed through the carriage windows adding the finishing touch to the gay holiday scene. Everyone was in happy holiday spirit and indeed my own spirits rose and I felt as excited as those children, although I myself was not on a pleasure trip. I was visiting Weymouth for a very different reason. In fact, I was going to speak at a special week-end meeting organized by the Salvation Army. This was to be my first speaking engagement with the Army and I was really looking forward to it.

As the train sped on, my mind went back to the time

when, as a young prostitute, I had made fun of the Salvation Army as they stood on the streets of Paddington proclaiming the Gospel. I smiled to myself as I remembered the drummer in the band who used to beat the drum with such fervour that I felt that at any minute he would bang a big hole right in the middle of it. I also remembered that secretly I had admired the men and women in their smart uniforms, especially the girl who sang alone in the middle of the open-air circle, "I'm a child of a King, I'm a child of a King. With Jesus my Saviour, I'm a child of a King." I wondered if the Salvation Army still sang that lovely hymn.

I cast my mind back to the time when as "Daring Diana", a striptease artiste, I had encountered the Salvation Army in Soho. How fiercely I had rejected their message and how wonderful it was that now, many years later, I was on my way to speak at the Salvation Army Hall in Weymouth. I, too, could now sing "I'm a child of a King". No wonder I was excited. Wouldn't you have been too?

I was still deep in thought when a voice beside me brought me back to the present. The lady sitting next to me was offering me a cup of tea from her flask. She observed that deep in thought my face had presented such "a picture" she could not but help remark upon it. I accepted the tea and we began to talk. So it was that I was able to witness to my travelling companions. The lady and her husband and teenage daughter listened intently as I unfolded the story of my life. When I came to the experiences I had had as a black witch and indeed as Queen of the witches they were truly astonished. I went on to tell them of the wonderful saving power of Christ and how He and He alone had taken away the darkness from my life and shown me His wonderful light. I told them that what He had done for me, He could do for all men. It was thrilling to see how this family responded to my story.

Her husband said, "If a stranger had approached me and spoken about religion or God I would have been offended, but somehow it is different with you. With you

26

I am impressed. Your life must be very interesting and rewarding now." I replied that it was and I said a silent prayer that the Holy Spirit would touch this family that they, too, might know Jesus is alive and real and able to change their lives. I mentioned that I would be taking part in a beach ministry on the following day and they promised to come and hear me speak. This was a wonderful start to my week-end ministry and I thanked the Lord for making it possible.

I have been asked many times by sincere, concerned Christians "How can I witness?" There is a very simple answer. Let God lead your conversation. If it is His will that you witness, then He will provide the opening for you. If you take that opportunity, He will give you the words to say and will lead you according to His will. However many times do we allow the opportunities that God has created slip away through lack of faith. Those opportunities might never come again, so we must always be alert and ready to use the opportunities that God creates for us.

Eventually the train pulled into Weymouth Station, where I was met by Brigadier Richardson, the officer in charge of the Weymouth corps. We went to the officers' quarters where he introduced me to his wife. They are a lovely couple, full of the joy of the Lord and we were all in complete harmony from the moment we met. After lunch we walked down to the crowded beach to conduct my first open-air meeting. It was wonderful to witness with the Salvation Army in the summer sunshine, telling out the Good News of salvation to the crowd. I told how the Saviour had lifted me out of the mud and mire and had made me a new creature, setting me free to serve Him and in turn others.

That evening in the packed Salvation Army Hall I gave my personal testimony. The experience of ministering with the Army was as uplifting and exciting as I had hoped it would be. What a thrill to stand on the platform and look down on the congregation, the band, and the songsters. I had great liberty in my ministry that night and the Holy Spirit was working in a real and wonderful way.

It rained the following day which meant that our Sunday open-air meeting had to be cancelled. However the meetings that were held in the hall more than made up for this disappointment and were a great blessing to us all. Needless to say the songsters sang "I'm a child of a King" and my eyes filled with tears as it brought back memories of my former life and of the Paddington streets where I had first heard it sung. I also heard another hymn written by William Booth, the founder of the Salvation Army, which I had not heard before:

Oh boundless Salvation, deep ocean of love
Oh fullness of mercy Christ brought from above.
The whole world redeeming so full and so free
Now flowing for all men, come roll over me.

The words of this hymn moved me greatly. They could not have been written without a deep and personal knowledge of Jesus Christ. William Booth certainly knew what he was writing about. It is obvious that he loved the Lord with all his heart and soul. When listening to the hymn I could almost see the great ocean of love rolling over me. What a blessing. What a joy!

When I had finished my testimony, I invited those who needed Christ in their lives and who had not yet made a commitment, to come forward and kneel at the penitent form. Many came as well as many others acting in faith to re-dedicate their lives to God and to reaffirm their faith in Jesus. It was a real joy to kneel and pray with them. There was a group of young people at the meeting who were on a camping holiday. They had arrived late and had not heard all my testimony. I was asked if I would speak to them in the minor hall and, of course, I readily agreed. Once again it was wonderful to lead two of the young girls to Christ especially as one of them had had contact with spiritualism and was very confused. What a joy to see this girl finally set free by the power of Christ. She too had become a child of the King.

That week-end God changed many lives and it was a wonder indeed to behold.

My next preaching engagement with the Salvation Army was much nearer home, in Bath. I had a busy schedule, appearing on the B.B.C. local television news magazine *Points West* before meeting a reporter who wanted to interview me for her paper. She listened intently to my story, taking notes in shorthand and obviously impressed at what the Lord at done for me. She stayed to hear me preach and when the article was published it was very comprehensive indeed, not forgetting to give all the glory to the Lord Jesus Christ for my changed life.

As the meeting began I was pleased to see thirty or so boys from a local boarding-school in the congregation. When I had finished preaching I asked those who needed Christ to come forward and fourteen of these boys came to kneel at the mercy seat. I was aware that the seed had already been sown by faithful witness on the part of Christian boys at the school as well as the Christian master who had brought them to the meeting. I was proud to see them come forward in faith.

Many people criticize this practice of public confession but I whole-heartedly believe that it is a necessary confession of faith. The Devil will try to stop a person from coming forward. "What will my friends think of me?" But if this temptation is overcome, the person concerned will be even more ready to accept the love of God. I remember when I made my public confession of need in the Colston Hall in Bristol in 1964. The Devil tried to stop me, but still I went and the Lord blessed me greatly for my faith. These boys overcame the temptation and it was wonderful to see. The seed that had been planted was now starting to grow and would, with the Grace of God, eventually flower into a deep personal relationship with the Saviour. We read in the Gospel of John, "And herein is the saying true one soweth and another reapeth" (4:37). And Paul says, "I have planted, Apollo has watered, but God gave the increase" (1 Cor. 3:6). The Lord had worked His miracle in these boys and it was wondrous to behold.

It is a great joy to preach before large congregations. I always give the praise and the glory to God, for He alone is worthy of honour and praise. One of my favourite scriptures is found in the Book of Isaiah: "Hearken unto me, ye that follow after righteousness, ye that seek the Lord: look unto the rock whence ye are hewn, and to the hole of the pit whence ye are digged" (51:1). When I look back to the dark pit from whence Christ pulled me, I know that alone I am powerless and that only with God working through me can I hope to bring the lost to the knowledge of Christ's saving love and forgiveness. It is good to look back to what we were and who we were before Christ saved us and made us new. This helps us realize that we are nothing and that He alone is worthy of praise and honour. That He, the Lord Jesus Christ must increase and that we must decrease.

Stoke on Trent was my next port of call. I was no stranger to the pastor and his wife who had invited me to speak at a special three-day mission. I had first met them in Blackpool where I had ministered at their previous church, so it was a time of renewed fellowship for us all. The meetings were packed to capacity and as I gave my testimony many wept openly they were so touched and blessed. I preached the plain and simple Gospel bringing in personal experiences to highlight my discourse.

While in Stoke on Trent I was able to speak on the local radio station and thus reach a much larger congregation. In my broadcast I warned of the dangers of dabbling in occult practices—spiritualism and witchcraft. The area known as The Potteries is a stronghold of practitioners of the occult and I prayed that my message would be widely heard and would prove effective.

On the third evening of the mission there were so many people at the meeting that many were standing outside the church. So vast was the crowd that I could hardly get to the platform. When eventually I got to the platform I found that here, too, were people sitting at my feet! Before I spoke the Salvation Army band and songsters gave praise to the Lord in music and song and we were all greatly inspired. During my testimony I could see that many in the congregation were deeply moved by my words. Many Christians were encouraged to serve the Lord with more vigour and it was thrilling to hear such comments as, "Hearing your testimony has encouraged me to go on for the Lord and to witness for Him in a better way." Little did they know that I myself received tremendous encouragement from their words which increased my resolve to serve the Lord with all my heart. It is indeed sweet to serve the Lord and to be the means of blessing but it is also very good and necessary to receive encouragement. Joy in service gives the strength to forge ever upward. This glorious week-end was one I would never forget.

From Stoke on Trent I travelled to Manchester, where I met the Reverend James Song, a Chinese minister, on this, the last leg of my journey to Morecambe. We were to speak at a special conference entitled "The Strategy of Evangelism". This week of teaching had been called to examine new ideas and new areas of evangelism. The Reverend Song and I were leading a special course on the occult. We got on very well together and had a wonderful feeling of fellowship. Isn't it amazing how two complete strangers from entirely different backgrounds can be in perfect harmony and work together for the Lord in complete unity.

At the conference the Reverend Song spoke very powerfully on the recognition of demonic possession. I followed and spoke about my personal involvement with witchcraft, Satanism, and the occult. I told of Satanic ceremonies and methods, and most important of all how the Lord Jesus Christ, working through an evangelist, had cast out the many demons that were within me, to Gehenna (hell). I stressed the fact that demons hate His name and that if banished in His name they are powerless and must obey His will.

The audience of Christian workers and ministers learned about the nature of demonic possession, oppression, and obsession in the twentieth century. They were all anxious for a deeper understanding of the problem to enable them to counsel more effectively. Many ministers are deeply concerned about the increase in occult practices and feel it their duty to learn how to recognize and combat them when they come across them.

Indeed, I feel that all Christians should be forearmed with this knowledge as the chances of them encountering the problem at first hand are increasing year by year. Many Christians have, however, been put off this ministry by a handful of insincere practitioners, ever eager to jump on the bandwagon, and seeking publicity through sensationalism. Fortunately these are the minority and there are many devoted Christian ministers doing invaluable work in this field. They never seek publicity and their work goes largely unnoticed.

Unfortunately, there are also many over-zealous people who seem to see demons in everything: the cat, the dog, and under every bush. These people, however sincere, can do immense harm. Often they convince a person that he is demon possessed, when in fact he is not. The psychological damage that can be done in these cases is self-evident. I have met people in a terrible state, convinced that they were demon possessed after spending time with these misguided "demon-chasers". In fact they were not possessed at all. Often I have been the last in a long line of counsellors and advisers and have had to undo a great deal of harm. This frequently proves to be an arduous task.

I myself have been demon possessed, but God has given me balance. I do not see demons everywhere and in everything as some do. Many Christians have been apprehensive about meeting me, thinking that I would be a fanatic taking a very real problem to extremes. Some clergy have hesitated to have me witness to their congregations for the same reasons. Understandably they were afraid. God however leads my life and His perspective guides me. I speak about demons and Devil worship only to show the saving power of the Lord Jesus. I am far happier preaching the Gospel but I know that God wants me to tell of my past and to show what depths our Saviour will plumb to save one of His children.

The Strategy of Evangelism Conference was an edifying experience. Christians from all denominations shared their knowledge and experience and went back to their home areas renewed and rearmed. On the last evening I was asked to give my testimony at the closing ceremony of the conference. Although this was unexpected I readily agreed. The Reverend Song introduced me to the audience and supported me in prayer. The hour was very late but the audience were eager to hear my words. I had great freedom that night and Christ was glorified. Even some of the catering staff at the conference stayed to hear me speak and many of the non-Christians among them posed interesting questions which I answered as carefully and as prayerfully as I could.

Through my ministry at Morecambe several other doors were opened to me and I spoke at many new churches. But perhaps the most thrilling engagement I had at that time was in Somerset. Two meetings were organized by the Yeovil and District Council of Churches. The meetings were held in the local technical college, and at last I was able to realize a long-held ambition. Sharing the platform with me was the Reverend Arthur Neil. Readers of my first book *From Witchcraft to Christ* will remember that it was the Reverend Neil who cast out forty-eight demons from my body. He also wrote the Preface to that work. Ever since my deliverance he has been the kindest of friends, always ready to help and encourage me in my work and in my Christian development. He is now the Principal of the Faith Mission Bible College in Edinburgh.

You can imagine how thrilling it was for me to stand on the platform beside him and share with him the work of the Lord. On the first night the Reverend Neil told what the scriptures say about demon possession, the spirit world, and the forces of darkness. He was able to speak from personal experience as God has used him many times as His instrument to cast out demons from frightened people. The following evening I gave my personal testimony to a packed hall. I was more nervous than usual with the Reverend Neil beside me, but in faith I spoke freely about my past life of utter degradation and of how the Saviour had set me free from my unspeakable bondage. What an experience to have the man who delivered me—who had refused to give up when others saw my case as hopeless, who had brought me through torture, and who had set me on the path that led to this platform and to this very evening—standing beside me as a friend and colleague.

I was also blessed at this meeting by the presence of two other friends, Mr and Mrs Deakin, once pastors of a church in Bristol. They, too, had spent many long hours with me as I struggled towards the light and because of their kindness I loved them both very much and thought of them almost as my own mother and father. They moved away from Bristol and we had lost touch, but I never forgot them or stopped loving them. It was wonderful to see their dear faces that night in Yeovil. After the meeting, I stayed with them and we spent a long time talking over old times, shedding more than a few tears in the process. They have helped many like me and still are helping other unfortunates today. They both have a wonderful sense of humour which is very necessary in the work they do.

Isn't it marvellous to belong to this great family of God. Oh that we as a family could live in unity and really love one another as the Saviour prayed we would in His time of testing in Gethsemane. For there is nothing greater, nothing sweeter than to live in unity and love. If we belong to Jesus we are all children of the King, members of one family. For me the Christian life is truly a great and exciting adventure. That is how I see the Christian life. It is an adventure. It is to be lived without reservation. I am sure that non-believers would quickly seek the Lord if all Christians lived the Christian adventure in a courageous and vital way. So many non-believers see Christianity as dull and humdrum, acting only to dampen the innocent pleasures of life. The Christian pathway is full of pleasant surprises. I have experienced more joy and more adventure through my faith than I ever did in my sinful past. Although the path is frequently hard and demanding, the blessings and joys far outweigh the hardships.

Once I thought I was rich. As a prostitute I was prosperous but the price I had to pay in terms of peace of mind and indeed health was much too high. As a striptease artiste my earnings were substantial. I had furs and jewellery in excess. And what good did it do me? No good at all. The baubles were eventually sold or pawned to pay for my drug habit. Did money bring me love and happiness? No! It brought me only pain and sorrow. Money can't buy health, peace of mind, happiness, or fulfilment. But with Jesus as Saviour I am rich beyond the dreams of man.

My heavenly Father owns the cattle on a thousand hills. I'm a child of a King and His royal blood flows through my veins. I am heir to a mansion, heir to a kingdom with riches too great to comprehend. I am certainly not rich by earthly standards but because He is mine and I am His I have wealth beyond comparison. I would rather belong to Him than be a slave of Satan. I have tasted the pleasures of the world and I understand their attraction. But compared to the wealth I have since found in the service of God I was indeed a pauper. I served Satan for many years. He was my master and he gave earthly riches. The price I was paid was simply "hell on earth". I know that life in the service of the King of Kings brings joy unbounded and that the world with its gilded toys and all its pleasures can hold no attraction for those who have experienced the love of God.

Now I am in the service of the King of Glory. I am no longer bound to Satan. Oh yes, I can now sing "Praise God, praise God, I'm a child of a King."

CHAPTER THREE

He tears the bars away

"The Spirit of the Lord God is upon me, because the Lord hath anointed me to preach good tidings unto the meek; He hath sent me to bind up the brokenhearted, to proclaim liberty to the captives, and the opening of the prison to them that are bound" (Isaiah 61:1).

THESE are the wonderful words that Jesus Himself read in the synagogue. All eyes were fastened on Him as He went on to say, "This day is the scripture fulfilled in your ears" (Luke 4:21). And it is still being fulfilled today. This is exactly why Jesus came and He is still the same. He has not changed. Following in His footsteps as His disciples we can do what Jesus did. We can try to be like Jesus. There are so many lonely and broken-hearted people living in the world. There are so many that are captive. Everywhere you look, everywhere you go you can see sadness and pain and people burdened with enormous problems. By meeting and talking to some of these people I realized again that Jesus Christ is the *only* answer to their problems and needs. He alone can bring them real love, joy, and peace.

I have often wished that I could solve all their problems myself, but I know that I cannot. The Lord has taught me to take all problems to Him. I used to try to bear the burdens myself and spent many sleepless nights trying to solve the insoluble. I still try and help but now with the Lord as my main support. At the very least I can show that I care and I can point people to Christ who cares so much and to whom no problem is insoluble.

The Lord has told me time and time again, "Do what you can and leave the rest to me." It is impossible for us to do everything and go everywhere. We can only go where the Lord leads us and do what He wants us to do. When Jesus sees that you are willing to follow Him, He will lead you to people that need you. You then do what you can and leave the rest in the Lord's hands. The question is, are we ready and willing? I have made myself available to the Lord Jesus Christ, to go where He wants me to go and to do what He wants me to do.

Some time ago, the Lord led me to a Borstal for boys and being taken through the numerous locked doors and gates was an experience that is etched on my mind. My whole being was flooded with a deep and tender compassion that words cannot express when I saw the sad looks of resignation on some of the young faces. I wondered where I should begin.

Winning the trust and confidence of the boys was the first big obstacle. Once this had been overcome the rest would be simpler. Only total reliance on the Saviour's divine wisdom and guidance for every word spoken could break down the barriers. The very fact that I had once served a prison sentence myself made it easier for me to be accepted.

Queuing up with the boys for a meal was an unusual experience and in fact made a very good start for me. I was treated in exactly the same way as the boys and given the same food. I was very glad about this as I knew it could be the start of my being accepted by the boys. I took my tray and walked into the main hall. "Come and sit with us," came a chorus from the tables. I hardly knew which table to choose and eventually I chose the noisiest. The conversation was unique.

"What's it like in a women's nick [prison]," asked one of the boys.

"Much the same as a men's nick I suppose. It depends which nick you are in. Some nicks are worse than others."

This all sounded so funny that we all started laughing. As far as I was concerned the barriers were gone and I had been accepted by the boys.

"What's it like in this nick?" I asked.

"Oh it's not too bad," said one boy.

Another piped up, "Speak for yourself. I shan't be sorry to get out of here."

The first boy replied, "It all depends what you make of it."

I had to agree that the Borstal was like a palace compared with some of the places I had seen. The subject changed and one of the boys asked me, "What did you get done for?"—that is why was I imprisoned.

I replied, "For shop-lifting."

They were all surprised, "Is that all, fancy putting you inside for that."

"That was not all," I replied, "I was also in possession of hard drugs."

One of the boys looked at me, "It's not worth it is it, taking drugs I mean?"

I had to agree with him on that point and told him, "It is very foolish and dangerous to meddle with drugs of any kind!"

A voice at my side said, "You're not kidding, look where it's got me, and this is not the first place I've been in. But I am going to go straight when I get out of here!"

I quietly prayed that this would be true for him. "Have you ever thought about God and prayer?" I asked him.

"No," he replied, "does it work?"

"Yes," I said, "it certainly does. I tried to go straight and failed. I didn't succeed until Jesus Christ had changed me from the inside."

One of the boys quietly and thoughtfully said, "I think I know what you mean, but it's not so easy in a place like this."

I turned to him and said gently, "I understand just how you feel. I've been inside and I know how lonely you can be. Perhaps we can talk about it later, but I have to move on now."

He replied, "OK, I would like that."

After this conversation I felt I had won a great deal of their confidence and had been accepted by them as an equal and as a friend. Later I gave my testimony in the prison chapel and quite a few lads came along. Some of them came out of curiosity, some for a laugh, and a few were serious. What a mixed crowd they were. Most of them had come from sad and tragic backgrounds. Many of them were from broken homes and were largely victims of the circumstance that had finally landed them on the wrong side of the law.

I had been told that despite their youth, most of them were hardened criminals who had been in and out of Borstals from their early teens. It was hard to believe, but facts are facts. Hard or not, they were not too hard for the Lord. Other Christians were there with me, singing and witnessing for the Lord and these people didn't think the boys were too hard for the Lord either. They regularly came to the Borstal to witness to the boys.

It was a tremendous privilege to witness in such a needy place, to tell how Jesus had set me free from vice, drugs, and witchcraft and all the terrible misery that went with these evils. You could have heard a pin drop when I spoke of the loneliness and unhappiness I had suffered as a child. Bowed heads and sad eyes spoke volumes to me. These boys knew what I was talking about.

When I had finished speaking they crowded round me and asked lots of questions and many wanted to talk with me privately. I spent the next hour or so visiting the various wings of the Borstal and the boys' rooms so that they could show me their latest hobbies. I wanted to take an interest in everything that they were doing. The Lord was once again showing me the great importance of being a good listener. We never stop learning. If a time ever comes when you think that you know it all, then that is the time to think again for something is wrong, somewhere. I certainly learned a lot from listening and talking to these young men.

I returned the next day and by then the word had gone round and the chapel was almost full as I once again gave my testimony. Again silence reigned as I told of all the things the Lord had done for me. When I had finished there were many questions.

"I can't believe that what you say is true," said one of boy. "No one can change like that."

I told him, "I agree with you, but if you remember I also said that I did not change myself, Jesus did it."

Another asked, "Do you really have the will power to keep off drugs?"

I told him, "Yes, but it is not my own power and strength. With Him I overcome every day. Without Him I would fail."

Another boy asked, "Have you ever seen the Lord?"

I replied, "Yes, I have."

The boy was interested, "What does He look like?"

I smiled and said, "My words cannot fully tell. He is so kind and tender. His eyes are full of love and He is altogether lovely."

The boy asked, "Do you see Him very often?"

"No," I replied, "I do not see Him every day—not with my natural eyes, but I know that He is with me, for He has promised never to leave or forsake me. It doesn't matter how I am feeling, whether I am happy or sad, uplifted or downcast, I know that He changes not. He never fails. My Christian life and experience is not based on emotions or feelings, but simply in faith in Him. He cannot break His word for His word is true."

It would be an understatement to say that these young men were stirred by my message. They could not get over the fact that I now devote my entire life to testifying to the power of a risen Christ, even in prisons.

In the afternoon, after I had rested and prayed, I returned yet again to the Borstal and had the tremendous joy of leading two of the young men to Christ.

"Excuse me," a voice said politely, "may I speak to you?"

"Certainly," I replied.

The boy continued, "Well, I want you to pray with me because I want to become a Christian."

I was overjoyed and after some simple counselling, illustrating from Scripture the way of salvation and making quite sure that the boy knew and understood just what it meant to commit his life to Christ, we knelt down together and prayed. He gave his heart to Jesus Christ.

"Will you pray with me as well?" another voice asked. "I too want to become a Christian." I turned to see the thoughtful young man to whom I had spoken the day before. At that time he had expressed a wish to talk to me again and here he was. "I've been awake all night thinking about all you said and now I believe the Lord is the answer. Will you pray for me?" So it was, with tears of joy, that I was able to lead this dear boy to the Lord. It was truly wonderful to see this life fully committed to the Saviour.

There is no joy on earth that can surpass the joy of leading a soul to the Lord Jesus Christ. What rejoicing there must have been in the presence of the angels as these two dear souls were born into the wisdom of God. The Prison Chaplain and many others do fine work in that very needy place. It was an honour to work with them and to know that they would follow up and continue to help and encourage these two young men.

Two men sat behind prison bars,
One saw mud, and the other saw stars.

This old saying kept ringing in my ears as I left the Borstal. There is great depth, truth, and meaning in these words. It all depends in which direction you are looking, for no matter where you are, or what situation you are in, if you look upward to Christ, you will find hope and light. If you continually look downwards at the conditions and the circumstances you will see nothing but darkness and hopelessness. As I travelled back to Bristol, I prayed that those young men would look upward into the face of Jesus, the bright and morning star.

There are many types of prison and many kinds of prisoners. Many of these prisoners have never been inside a prison cell, yet they, too, are prisoners. I meet them everywhere. Prisoners of loneliness, isolated inside their own private prisons without a glimmer of light. You don't have to be strictly alone to be lonely. Many of the loneliest people live in our great cities and millions of nameless people pass them by every day. Many of them could cry out, "I'm lonely too", but they do not and go unrecognized amidst the teeming masses.

There are prisoners of fear. Fearful of the future, afraid of death, afraid of losing their jobs or their loved ones, they are in fact afraid of everything. There are prisoners of drugs, hooked by the daily "fix". There are prisoners of alcohol who just cannot get along without a drink. There are prisoners everywhere and I must tell them that Jesus can set them free and can burst their bonds asunder. He can tear the bars away, dry the tears, drive away the gloom, and bind up the broken-hearted. I want to tell the world about the Lord Jesus Christ, the great and mighty deliverer.

As the train wheels rattled over the track on my way back to Bristol, they suddenly seemed to take on the rhythm of a well-known hymn that I love dearly.

> He breaks the power of cancelled sin
> He sets the prisoner free,
> His blood can make the foulest clean
> His blood availed for me.

Had the compartment not been so crowded I would have sung the hymn in time to the rhythm and movement of the train. I looked at the occupants of my compartment and wondered what kind of prisoners they all were. I must say, none of them looked very happy, in fact just the opposite. Most of them looked thoroughly fed up and miserable. Others looked extremely worried. The plain truth is that so many people are living under terrific pressure and it shows. People everywhere, on trains, buses, in shops and offices, and in the busy streets look worried stiff. As I looked around that compartment I wondered what impression people got when they looked at me! We cannot go around with a perpetual smile on our face, but I hoped that I didn't look as if I had the cares and troubles of the world on my shoulders. Somehow, looking back, I wished I had sung that hymn. I wonder what the reaction would have been? It's food for thought!

Very often when I travel by train or car, I find great peace and rest for mind and soul by looking out at God's wonderful creation. The peaceful countryside, the winding, rippling streams running through leafy glades, the tiny flowers growing in the rolling fields and on grassy banks, the tall green trees, swaying gently in the breeze and the song-birds on the wing, so gay and carefree. As my eyes feast upon such beauty, words like those used by Jesus come into my mind, "Consider the lilies, how they grow; they toil not, neither do they spin: And yet I say unto you, That even Solomon in all his glory was not arrayed like one of these" (Matt. 7:28-29). Yes, in a very busy and restless world amid the toil and woe, we can find peace and rest, by trusting in Jesus. As Christians we can cast all our cares upon Him, for He careth for us.

I often wonder why people don't find more time to stop and view God's handiwork and all the lovely things He has made for our enjoyment and pleasure. People crave for beauty, but are largely blind to the beauty that exists all around them. Perhaps it would be different if they knew the Creator. Years ago in Sunday School, I remember singing a little chorus that meant nothing to me then, but it does now. It goes like this:

> Said the robin to the sparrow,
> "I would really like to know
> Why these anxious human beings
> All rush around and worry so."
> Said the sparrow to the robin,
> "Friend I think that it must be,
> That they have no heavenly Father
> Such as cares for you and me."

A bondage of anxiety and care can be so heavy as to blot out completely the beauty of creation. We are truly sanctified if we help to reveal the surpassing beauty of Christ to this lost and troubled world. We can radiate Christ in all we say and do, reflecting His grace in our lives to those around us in bondage.

On another occasion, I visited a probationary home for young women. All of them had been in some kind of serious trouble. Needing a good deal of protection as well as discipline they had to reside at this home for a year. Most of them had jobs outside the home and returned in the evening. There were no locked or barred doors here. It was so different from the Borstal I had visited. However, their needs were just as great, their bars being of another kind.

The large drawing-room was filled with girls and a few Christian workers, some of whom were also members of staff. Right from the start I was aware of an atmosphere of indifference and scepticism. No one had been forced to come to my meeting, it was all quite voluntary. In a way I found it more difficult to speak to these girls than I had to the boys at the Borstal. As I began, I noticed the withdrawn and guarded expressions on their faces. I could almost hear them thinking, "Who is this do-gooder, what can she say that can possibly mean anything to us?" I threw myself entirely on the Lord Jesus for Divine guidance, wisdom, love, and understanding. I knew that every word I would say would be of the utmost importance.

Even as I was speaking I was praying, "Lord help me. Don't let me say the wrong thing. Please take over my thoughts and let every word spoken be Your word to these girls." And, as always, the Lord did help me. As I continued to speak the atmosphere of hardness and indifference slowly ebbed away to be replaced by an element of surprise. The hard look softened. Some looked sad for they like the boys in the Borstal knew something of what I was speaking about. You could see it written all over their young faces.

What bitterness of tragedy was theirs I will never know. No one came to speak to me after the meeting or even asked a single question. At first I was sad but then I realized that probably more work was wrought in their hearts than I will ever know. They were so astonished at what they heard for never before had they heard such a story of complete liberation from a life of sheer hell. It impressed them and they went away stunned to think about it all.

Oh how I prayed that the seed that had been sown would take root and grow so that these girls would find the liberty and freedom of a new life in Christ. I prayed that Jesus would tear the bars away. I had done what I could and now I had to leave the rest to Him. He alone could tear away the bars of doubt, bitterness, and darkness and bring them into the light. The Christian staff were encouraged to carry on in the great and very needful work among the girls.

There are still thousands of prisoners to reach for Jesus. The world is full of them. Jesus knows just where they are and is sending forth His labourers into the field which is the world. The fields are ripe unto harvest and the labourers are few. We must rise up and work while it is yet day, for "the night cometh when no man can work" (John 9:4). The time is *now*, not tomorrow. We must go forward into the world with the living message that Jesus Christ the Son of God can set the prisoners free, tear down the bars, and give glorious liberty, light, hope, and everlasting life to captives everywhere.

I am just one of His labourers in the field of service and the Lord needs many more. The time is short. Will you make yourself available to Christ, ready and willing to go where He sends you? He has work for you to do among the prisoners of Satan, to speak the words of deliverance and to help tear down the bars.

In Northern Ireland

"And God shall wipe away all tears from their eyes; and there shall be no more death, neither sorrow, nor crying, neither shall there be any more pain . . . " (Revelation 21:4).

NORTHERN IRELAND is always in the news. Hardly a day passes without reports of bombings, shootings, and intimidation impinging on our lives. Our consciences have been touched by the fate of the innocent, the old and the very young, caught up in a world of seemingly unceasing violence and horror. My heart had often gone out to the people of that troubled land and I had long hoped for an opportunity to go there and see the problems at first hand. This was not idle curiosity on my part, nor a chance to gain favour in the eyes of others. I simply wanted to let some of the people know that I cared. I wanted to preach Jesus Christ in all His fullness and to testify to all he has done for me. I wanted to tell them that many in the rest of the United Kingdom cared, and were praying for an end to the troubles.

When at last the opportunity came I was overjoyed for I felt sure that the Lord had opened this door and that it was His will that I go. Many friends were apprehensive about my journey and said, "Aren't you afraid to go, when there is so much violence?" I could only reply that not only was I not afraid, but that the dangers had not even entered my mind. I knew that the Lord would protect me from the dangers in Northern Ireland as indeed He protects me from the threats and curses of witches in England. But the more people expressed their fears, the more I began to waver in my resolve. Satan is the father of lies and he was doing his best to stop me going. However my faith was too strong for him and eventually I arrived at the airport to start my journey.

For security reasons, everyone was searched before being allowed to board the aircraft, and coupled with a few minor delays the flight was late in taking off. On the plane I talked to a young woman who was returning to Belfast after a short stay in England. She was very friendly. "I wonder what time we will arrive in Belfast," she said anxiously. "I can hardly wait to see my two young children again." I replied that I expected the captain would make an announcement soon. As we talked she told me that her husband was in the Services and was currently stationed in England. She had been visiting him but had been unable to bring her children with her. "Did you enjoy your stay?" I asked. She replied that she had and she wished she could have stayed longer. Her words were very revealing. "It is so different in England. It took a few days before I settled down. Once when a lorry backfired my instinctive reaction was that it must be a bomb or a shot and I forgot I was in England for an instant. Unfortunately my children have known nothing else but the sound of explosions and rifle-fire as well as the constant fear that pervades every aspect of life in the Province." Her words brought the problems of Belfast home to me in a powerful way and gave me valuable insight into the daily lives of those to whom I would be speaking. And I had not even reached Northern Ireland!

As we talked, the Lord opened up another opportunity for me to witness in His name and I told her about my past life and more importantly, about my new life in Christ. There was great empathy and harmony between us and in a very short space of time we had become friends. "Perfect love casteth out all fear." I spoke on: "Jesus can fill your heart and life with peace and joy, even in the darkest day. If we commit our hearts and lives

47

entirely into His care this is His sure promise."

We said goodbye at the airport and she thanked me for our conversation. She said, "I really needed someone to talk to and I will remember all that you said." This was indeed a marvellous start to my tour of the Province.

Mr Michael Perrot, who is the General Secretary of the Y.M.C.A. in Belfast, met me at the airport and took me to his home, where I met the rest of his charming family. Michael had arranged my itinerary. When I arrived at the Y.M.C.A. I was given the warmest welcome I have ever experienced. These grand Irish people obviously appreciated my coming and thev showed it.

Later I was interviewed by a reporter from the *Belfast Telegraph*, who coincidentally was also a Londoner. To my surprise, her report made the front page of the paper. It was great to see Christ glorified in such a dramatic and effective way. "Christ transformed my life" read the headline, and there among all the sad news of bombings and suffering was the name of Christ praised. Praise the Lord! He is still the best news of all and that is wonderful.

I began my tour in Newtownabbey, which is a suburb of Belfast. There, at the church of which the Reverend Samuel Workman was pastor, I spoke to an enormous congregation. It seemed as though all Belfast had turned up to hear me speak. Not only was the main church packed full, but also all the adjoining rooms. A loudspeaker relay system had been installed and many people stood outside, or sat in their cars and heard my message. I have often been asked if I feel nervous speaking to a large crowd, and the answer is "Yes, always." I am often so nervous that I feel that my words will stick in my throat or that my mind will go blank. Here was no exception and my tummy was behaving in a most peculiar way. But what an experience to see so many people eager to hear my story. I thought of their problems and their fears and I was so deeply moved. These people had ventured out and driven through the dangerous streets of Belfast at night, just to hear me give my testimony. I was so overwhelmed that I shed tears. I gave heartfelt thanks to the Saviour for this wonderful experience and opportunity to glorify Him. He had done so much for me, and now, this! I felt it almost too great a joy to bear. When the Holy Spirit moves in a mighty way, stirring our souls to the very depths, it is a feeling beyond human expression.

You can always tell when the Holy Spirit is moving and you always know that it is for a great and Divine purpose. We may not understand what that purpose is, or see any obvious demonstration, but we know that He is moving. We can sense that something magnificent is happening, although we may not actually see the evidence at the time. Our hearts tell us that God is working out His purpose and that we are involved. So often Christians expect instant results from missions and crusades. They expect miraculous mass conversion and are disappointed when this does not happen. However in the Book of Isaiah we read the word of God: "For my thoughts are not your thoughts, neither are your ways my ways . . . For as the heavens are higher than the earth, so are my ways higher than your ways and my thoughts than your thoughts" (55:8-9). We may never know what work has been done in people's lives. God works in His own way and accomplishes in His own time. As Christians we must believe and trust that God knows His own purpose and is accomplishing it in His own way. After all it is His word and His work that is important. We are merely His instruments.

After this highly successful meeting I was invited home by a member of the church. There I met his wife and we had a delightful supper. I could sense a spirit of expectancy in the air and it soon became apparent that his wife, although a regular church-attender had not yet been saved. Nevertheless, she had been very moved by my sermon. It is a sad fact that a person can hear the Gospel preached Sunday after Sunday and yet not experience a personal relationship with Christ. We must remember that in these cases, the seed is still being faithfully sown. I knew that in the case of this lady, the seed had fallen on good ground and was now ready to be reaped. As we talked she said, "I have put off becoming a

Christian for many years, but just lately an old song has been coming into my mind again and again. I hope you won't think me silly." I reassured her and asked to hear the song. "Well," she said, "it goes like this:

> Oh, I wonder, yes, I wonder,
> When the poppies bloom up yonder
> Will the angels play their harps for me?

"Tell me," she said, "do you think God is speaking to me through that song?" I replied that I was sure that He was speaking to her. She was puzzled by the fact that God seemed to be using an old song to communicate with her, rather than a verse of scripture or a hymn. I told her, "Well of course you know the Lord works in mysterious ways His wonders to perform!" We talked on and she told me about her mother, who had been saved. "I wonder if I will ever see her again?" she sighed. I replied, "You will if you, too, know her Saviour, if you, too, know the joy of sins forgiven and have the peace of knowing that you are on your way to heaven to be with the Lord and the multitude of the faithful." She was really surprised at the way I spoke of Jesus. "You speak as if you really know Him. Can He ever be that real to me?" I told her that He could and that He had obviously been speaking to her for some time, yearning for her response to His call. We spoke for a long time and I was privileged to show her the way of Salvation through the blood of Jesus Christ shed for the remission of sins. It was wonderful to kneel with her and pray for her as she finally yielded up her life to God and was truly born again by the Spirit. There are many whose loved ones are not yet saved. Do not lose faith, but keep praying. This woman's husband had been praying for many years and he now saw his prayers answered. Prayer changes things. Very often I have heard of people being converted weeks after I have left the district. There are no time restrictions on the Holy Spirit.

I receive many letters and here is one which gave me a great joy.

Dear Doreen,

This is to thank you personally for coming to give your testimony. On Saturday night in my own home, I received the Lord Jesus Christ as my Saviour. It is just wonderful to be a Christian and I know that the Lord will never leave me. I am reading my Bible every day and I want to tell you that I am also telling my friends about the Saviour and His love. Please pray for me.

It is wonderful to receive letters like these and they give me real encouragement.

The next meeting was held in the Y.M.C.A. It was good to see so many people there, as it is right in the heart of Belfast where there has been a great deal of trouble and danger. There were people from all denominations and all walks of life and it was a great joy to counsel some of them after the meeting.

It was at this time in 1973 that my first book *From Witchcraft to Christ* was published. I was quite overwhelmed by the sheer volume of sales. I had known the book would be a success as I had written it for the glory of Jesus, but even my expectations were surpassed. Praise, honour, and glory to the Saviour! I pray that God will continue to bless, encourage, and save through my book.

Some time later I returned to Northern Ireland for a second tour. Again the Lord moved in a mighty way. I was really happy to return to Northern Ireland as I had come to love the land and the people. Most of all I loved their seemingly irrepressible sense of humour which shone through despite all the troubles and hardships that they had to bear. They can make you laugh so much that the tears run down your face. Isn't it strange that some people cannot appreciate a good sense of humour, and even frown on it! Where does our good clean sense of humour come from if not from God? Surely He knows how valuable it can be, especially to see us through the dark days when everything goes wrong. I fully believe that a sense of humour is one of God's gifts to mankind. My own has helped me through many a dark and difficult day. I thank God for a good sense of humour and I pity those who neither have it, nor can appreciate it in others. Perhaps they are the victims of frozen theology!

One incident sticks in my mind. I arrived at a very crowded church—so crowded in fact that I had difficulty getting in myself! A major traffic jam had built up and, while my escort tried to park the car, I was asked to enter by the side door. I walked round the church, but to my surprise the door was locked. I could hear the hum of conversation inside the church, so I knocked on the door. No answer! I knocked again and again and finally a man came to the door and asked me to go away as the church was completely full.

I laughed and said, "But I am the speaker." The man looked at me suspiciously and replied, "Oh yes, anyone could say that just to get in." By this time I was laughing at my inability to convince him who I was. Suddenly he realized his mistake and apologized most profusely. The poor man was acutely embarrassed, but he soon relaxed when he realized that I had seen the funny side of the incident. People in the small ante-rooms were also laughing. Someone said, "It could only happen in Ireland." That was definitely the first time I have ever been turned away from my own meeting!

On the same tour, in a country church, I invited those who wanted to speak to me to stay behind after the meeting. A farmer walked in and out of the blue said, "Do you think God would heal my horse?" I though I had misheard him. "Sorry, did you say house or horse?" "My horse," he said and went on to explain. "You see I have had my old horse for years, but he is getting very old and tired and the vet has advised me to have him put to sleep. Trouble is I've had him for so long that I can't bear to part with him." I subsequently found that the sole reason for his visit to the church was to ask me to heal his horse! He was not a Christian, never went to church, and yet here he was with his strange request. Although ostensibly a comical situation, there was also an element of sadness. The man had sat for over an hour hearing how the Lord had saved me and healed my body and wondering if any of this applied to his poor old horse.

I told him that I would pray for his horse and he thanked me and started to leave. "I will pray with you now," I said. This took him completely by surprise as prayer was obviously something of a mystery to him. He really did look funny sitting there, fumbling with his hat and bemused by the whole process, and my heart went out to him. I realized how serious all this was to him. I began to pray: "Dear Lord Jesus, please reveal yourself to this dear soul for whom you died. Let him see you on the cross of Calvary. May he see his own need for your Salvation and Lord please heal his horse, that he may know that you are alive and real. For Thy name's sake and for Thy glory, Amen."

When I had finished praying, he thanked me and said that he felt a lot better. "I believe that the Lord has healed my poor old horse." His face was a picture of joy. I don't know if the horse was healed or not, but I do believe that the Lord started to work in the heart of that farmer that night and I prayed that He would keep His hand on him and that the Holy Spirit would work His wonders upon him.

On the second week of my tour I visited many churches and met many people. One of the places I visited was Carrickfergus. The church was very large and, as had become usual on this tour, it was packed to capacity. I had great liberty in my ministry and my reception was very warm and gracious. Once again I was aware that the Holy Spirit was working during the meeting. Many came forward for counselling including a believer who had brought along her neighbour. The neighbour was as yet unsaved and although they had never been to this particular church before, 'they had thoroughly enjoyed the service. The neighbour gave her heart fully to Jesus that night as did her mother who had also come to the meeting. What a wonder to see mother and daughter brought to the Lord in this mighty way! Later the mother told me that she had wanted to give her heart to Jesus once before but that her husband had stopped her from coming forward. He had told her not to make a fool of herself and she had been guided by his feelings. She was so overjoyed that at last she had given herself over to Christ for the rest of her life.

The lady who had brought these good people along also had a very heart-rending story to tell. At one time she had been a Catholic and her son had been a member of the I.R.A. "But he left the movement when all the bombing and killing started," she said. "Then one night he was abducted and had the sign of the cross branded on his back. He was then shot through the head and left dying in the street." The tears ran down her face as she spoke. "I feel no bitterness for anyone, not even for the men that murdered my son." What an incredible lesson in loving forgiveness. She obviously really loved the Lord and, of course, God is love. Only the power of God could keep a poor mother's heart from hatred and revenge.

This dear lady had been the means whereby a mother and daughter had come to the Lord. This could only be a miracle, for the greatest miracle of all is that a person can be born again in the Holy Spirit! I spent a good deal of time with these dear souls helping them to grow further in the Lord and in the knowledge of their Saviour, Jesus Christ.

Others were waiting to see me, but I never rush or hurry when counselling. I feel it is God's will that the people who I counsel are at peace and are assured of their salvation. This assurance, of course, is later confirmed as the person reads his Bible or shares in the fellowship of other saved Christians. It was good to spend time with these three ladies and to leave them fully assured of their salvation and of their future in Christ.

I am sometimes asked, "Do these converts stand?" We can, of course, never completely know, but we are assured that if a real act of grace was done in their hearts, then the Lord will guide them in His own way. We do not really need to know what happens afterwards. We simply trust in the Lord. He drew them to us in some way and if we do our work properly, trusting in the Lord, then we can leave the matter in His hands. We may never hear of them again, but the Lord knows where they are and He knows their need. The Lord Jesus is very patient and sometimes woos a soul for many years before that soul finally surrenders to His glory. Who can tell what work is done in a person's life. We ourselves may be instrumental in the very first work within the life of someone.

During my tour I also visited Larne. Again the meeting which was held in a local hall, was packed. It was wonderful to see so many people of different denominations, backgrounds, and persuasions all worshipping together in complete unity. No one came forward at this meeting, but I could tell that the Lord had indeed spoken to many of the congregation. This feeling was confirmed later as I stood by the door shaking hands with people as they left. One lady shook hands with me and said, quietly, "I should have come forward tonight when you asked, but I was afraid to." I looked at her and said, "It is not too late. You can be saved tonight before you go home. Please stay and talk to me for a while." She said that she could not and quickly made her way out of the hall. Silently I called out to her in prayer, "Dear Lord Jesus, please send her back, please save her soul tonight." While I was praying she returned. I continued, "Thank you Lord for answering my prayer, now please help me lead her to you."

I smiled at her. "Have you come back to be saved?" I asked. "Yes," she said. "I could not go home. I felt compelled to return and I want to be converted tonight." And saved she was that night. When she left her face was radiant and she was a new creature in Christ. This lady had been under the sound of the Gospel for many weeks and a lot of people were praying for her. Their prayers had also been answered as another soul was born into the Kingdom of God.

Before I left that night two young people had also been led to Jesus. They, too, had been afraid to come forward and had waited to see me privately. When they left they, too, were radiant in the Lord. They, too, had found Salvation. Praise the Lord!

Before I conclude this chapter, I would like to say this. It may have been said many times before, but it can never be repeated too often. There is only one lasting solution to the troubles in Northern Ireland, and that is a mighty revival of the Spirit. When people can be seen wending their way to the foot of the rugged cross of Calvary, in full repentance, only then will we see a lasting peace. When the sectarianism and bitterness is left behind and when lives are transformed by the power of God, then and only then will the world see a lasting and constructive peace.

Transformed lives are possible. My own life is a prime example. Take for instance also the life of John Houston who I met at the Y.M.C.A. John was once a compulsive gambler and an alcoholic. Then the Lord laid His hand on John. He is now a trophy of grace and a wonderful person, full of the joy of the Lord and always ready to lend a helping hand to anyone. He now works full time for the Y.M.C.A. in Belfast. It was truly a great joy to meet John and his wife and have fellowship with them in their home.

When my tour was ended I returned home. More wonders were to follow. As a result of my article in the *Belfast Telegraph* a lady was converted. I literally danced with joy. Isn't Jesus wonderful! To Him be all praise and glory.

Yes, it was wonderful to work for the Lord in Northern Ireland.

CHAPTER FIVE

In Europe for Christ

"One Lord, one faith, one baptism, One God and Father of all, who is above all, and through all, and in you all" (Ephesians 4:5-6).

SWITZERLAND is a small country, yet it has four different languages and four distinct cultures. It was certainly a challenge for me to go there and give my testimony. It never ceases to surprise me how with modern transport, the world has shrunk. Switzerland is just one hour from London by air, and yet in that short time you are in a different world. The languages are different, the currency is different, in fact the whole way of life is very different from our own. I have found the same to hold true of all the countries that I have visited and I expect this is why I find travel so stimulating. My ministry has taken me to many European countries including France, Belgium, Holland, Germany, and Switzerland.

I had visited all these countries before when I was Queen of black witches. At that time one of my powers was fluency in both French and German. I was even able to instruct in these languages. This Satanic power is no more and I am very glad. When Jesus set me wonderfully free from the evil demons that possessed me, all my powers vanished. Now, as a new creature in Christ, I was returning to these countries with a new message and a new purpose. I was bringing the message of Salvation and of deliverance through the shed blood of Jesus Christ.

I had been invited to Switzerland by Pastor Alan Morris, a Welshman who had been ministering the Gospel in Switzerland for about twelve years. At least I would have no language problem with Pastor Morris or his wife. A tour had been arranged which would take me to the German-speaking part of Switzerland. As I could no longer speak the language, everything I said would need to be translated. This was all new to me and I wondered how I would get on.

The welcome I received was really tremendous and everywhere I went these dear Swiss people made me feel at ease straight away and helped me in every way they could. Theirs is a most beautiful country and it was as though I was visiting it for the first time in my life. When I had come to Switzerland as an agent of Satan, I had not noticed the beauty of the countryside at all. My eyes were blind to it all. But now as a servant of Christ my eyes were open and, oh, the sheer joy of the beauty filled my heart with wonder. The snow-capped mountains and the tall fir trees standing out against the clear blue sky; the sweet meadows and the lush green fields and valleys with rippling brooks made my heart sing with sheer joy. Oh, yes it was all so different now.

My first meeting was to be in Zürich and it was here that I met Mr Henry Schoch, a fine Christian businessman, who was to be my interpreter. He is a fine man yet so humble and gracious. He is also a superb interpreter. He had acted as interpreter for David Wilkerson and Nicky Cruz when they toured Switzerland and although my accent was very different from theirs, Mr Schoch had no difficulty in understanding me at all. It certainly was strange to speak to an audience through an interpreter but I soon got used to it. God took over in a marvellous way and, of course, when He does, we have no need to worry. When we seek to serve Jesus and bring glory to His name, He will always take over. Then we can stand aside and see for ourselves that it is Him who is working with us, in us, and through us.

Mr Schoch was very quick in interpreting my words and everything flowed very smoothly and naturally and the Spirit of God was in operation in a very real and wonderful way. We worked side by side in perfect unity of spirit, often for long hours. After each meeting there were hungry, seeking, and troubled souls to counsel, to help and to pray for. Many of these people had deep-rooted problems that only Christ could solve and I believe He did meet their many needs. "Seek ye the Lord while He may be found, call upon Him while He is near." This is God's Word. Jesus was near and many called upon Him, some in tears, and God heard and answered their cries.

I next went to Berne where I met the Pastor and his wife Veronika, who interpreted for me at several meetings. It was a great blessing to stay at their home and share fellowship with them as well as others like Pastor E. Luthi from Olten, a real man of God with a marvellous sense of humour. We certainly had some laughs together especially as we strove to understand each other. He spoke no English and so we had many funny moments. Isn't it great to have good clean fun and laughter. You can when you belong to Jesus. The laughter of the non-Christian is often hollow, false, and empty, and often the things being laughed at are not very pure. But when you are a child of God you find a sense of humour that is pure and that can be shared. Since I became a Christian I have had more fun and laughter than I ever did before. And the laughter is God given.

I moved from Olten to Zuz, and then to Glarus, Ruti, Signau, and eventually Gunten where I was to meet many other servants of God at a ministers' convention. It was a joy to speak to this convention and to share with my brothers and sisters in the Lord all that God is doing today. God is moving, by His spirit, through all the earth. God is doing wonders, moving among the hearts of men and women, transforming lives that were marred by sin into shining lights for Jesus in this dark world of sin and sorrow, showing the world that Jesus is alive today and is the same today as He was yesterday.

From Gunten I moved on to Wadenswil, then back again to Zürich and Berne before moving on to Beil. I covered a lot of ground for Jesus in the German-speaking part of Switzerland and it was joy, joy, joy, all the way. Joy to see hearts stirred and blessed. Joy to see sinners repenting and receiving Christ as their personal Saviour. Yes, there is joy in serving Jesus no matter where He sends us. No matter how hard the way Jesus puts a song in our hearts. He giveth us songs in the night, songs of love Divine, and songs of souls set free.

As a result of my first visit to Switzerland, I received many letters from people with deep spiritual needs. Many of these people were physically ill, or had been involved in some way with the occult. Many others were oppressed and on the verge of a mental breakdown and some were even on the brink of suicide. When I answer such letters I never do so in haste. I sometimes get so many letters that the temptation to rush off replies merely out of courtesy is at times strong. I always seek the Lord before answering such letters and ask Him to give me the words to write—words of comfort and words of life. This side of my ministry is just as important as the public side and sometimes even more so. Often I am dealing with a life or death situation and the responsibility can at times be awesome.

I next journeyed through the French-speaking part of Switzerland, two tours having been arranged for me by Pastor W. Droz and others. It was with great thankfulness to Jesus I accepted the invitation and returned again to that lovely country, for it was clearly God's will that I should return.

Pastor Droz is a true pioneer in his own country with great zeal and vision for the Master. From morning to night he is as busy as a bee, and yet despite many setbacks and discouragements he is always smiling and laughing. I never saw him with a long sad face! His sense of humour was a constant source of encouragement to everyone, including me. I believe that even if his church were blown down in a sudden hurricane he would just say, "Praise the Lord, let's build another one."

Pastor Droz acted as my interpreter for most of the meetings, and what a superb interpreter he proved to be. He not only interpreted my words, but also my tone of voice, my seriousness, my humour, and even my actions. As I spoke I was aware that he was not only listening intently to my words, but was also watching me very closely to get the full effect of my words, my mood, and my actions. If I raised my hands, he raised his. If I was serious so was he. If I was joyful, he in like manner was joyful. He put real feeling into his translation of my words. This was so refreshing, so powerful, and so real. Sometimes I was so engrossed in his actions when he was speaking that I forgot to carry on. He was also so quick. I had hardly finished a sentence before he was translating it into French. He knew by the Spirit of God what I was going to say before I had said it. This took me by surprise at first and, indeed, caused some amusement in the congregation. I can remember on occasions bursting out laughing myself which set Pastor Droz and the rest of the congregation off, laughing good-naturedly at the situation. The message was not lost in the good humour or in the difference in the languages. Indeed the message was even more powerful, real, and mighty and people from all denominations were aware that Jesus was alive and that He was real.

My main ministry in Europe was to build up the faith of the Christians. Wherever I went I met so many Christians that were discouraged, downcast, or downtrodden. I felt it was my job to build them up, to revitalize them, and to encourage them to go on for God.

One young woman said, "I have no faith. I have no joy anymore. Once I really believed God's Word, but now I find it hard to believe anything. What is wrong with me?"

I looked at her, thought for a moment and then said, "Do you believe that the chair that you are sitting on will hold you up, or are you afraid that it will suddenly let you down with a big bang and you will fall on the floor?"

"No," she replied.

"Well neither will God let you go, even if you no longer believe."

"But you see I am always failing Him," she said sadly.

"That may be true," I said, "but He never fails us, even when we fail Him. He remains faithful, never changing. He still loves us no matter how much we fail." I continued, "Have you told Him about it and asked Him to increase your faith?"

The woman sighed, "Yes, many times, but I just feel the same."

I looked closely at her and said quietly, "How do you feel?"

She thought for a moment and then said, "I feel like a useless failure."

I asked her gently, "Do you think that Jesus has given you up then?"

"I don't know," she replied.

I looked straight at her and said, "Well I do know. I know that He never will. Failure is not final with Jesus. You can rise above feelings of defeat by turning to God's written Word. Satan always makes the most of our failures and tells us that we will never rise above them. But Satan is a liar, and remember he is the arch accuser of the children of God. His mission is to keep us wallowing in the dust of despair. Jesus is above all, yes, even our defeats and failures. He does not get out a big stick and chase us out of the fold when we fail Him. If He did, the fold would be empty, because we all fail Him. No one is perfect. There is something wonderful about Jesus. He knows everything about us and yet He loves us just the same."

Jesus has great lessons for us to learn and one of them is that we must keep our eyes on Him. He alone knows from beginning to end. The Apostle Paul says these lovely and simple words: "Looking unto Jesus the author and finisher of our faith" (Heb. 12:2). I am glad to say that this young woman regained her faith and trust in Him and in His Word, by simply looking to Him.

In Belgium and Holland it was a great privilege to work with "Teen Challenge". This organization does splendid work among drug addicts and meets them on their home ground in the streets or in coffee-bars. I was made to realize afresh the many needs of the youth of this day and age. It was so good to do work for the Master among these troubled youngsters remembering that I, too, was once like them. What the Lord had done for me, He could do for them. It gave me fresh love for sinners and my brothers and sisters in Christ who work for long weary hours seeking the lost in order that they might be brought to the Lord.

Drug addition has not disappeared. It may not be headline news like it used to be, but believe me the problem is even worse today. The problem has not gone away, indeed it has never been so serious in every country in the world including our own. I have an advantage. I was once an addict myself and I know how it feels and how hard it really is to give it all up and to become a Christian. The struggle is long and hard. Because I have experienced the problem at first hand I am in a privileged position to help drug addicts today. They will listen more readily to someone, like me, who has been in their shoes and who has come through the struggle. This is such a serious problem that I am sure that no matter how hard you work with drug addicts, only a miracle of grace can save them from an early grave.

It gave me great joy to teach the workers of Teen Challenge many things concerning the reaching of those caught up in drugs or in occult practices. There was a tremendous unity of spirit with these dear young workers, who really do know how to love people. They really want to know how to help others in a better way. Of course the only way is the way of love. Love never faileth. You can work for months, even years helping drug addicts, and those with deep personality problems and at times you will think you are getting nowhere. It is only when you are full of love and compassion that you persevere, no matter how discouraged you feel, that you will succeed in reaching them for Christ. I learned a lot from these young Christian workers, and they learned something from me.

Rose bushes have to be pruned every now and then to

allow even stronger and more beautiful growth to occur. So it is with our Christian life and behaviour. The things that stop us from being the way Jesus wants us to be have to be cut away. But when Jesus holds the pruning-knife we can be sure that He will make no mistakes, for His hands are gentle and kind and yet very strong. What better gardener could we have for our souls than Jesus! I remember a little chorus that I learned a long time ago in Sunday school, many years before I became a Christian. I enjoy gardening and I often sing this little song as I potter around my own garden at home.

My heart may be like a garden fair
Loving thoughts and words and deeds are blossoming
   there.
Or it may be a place of poison weeds
Growing into ugly thoughts and words and deeds.
Lord Jesus make my heart a garden fair
Come down Thyself and be the gardener there.

Are not these words very beautiful and full of meaning? We know that when Jesus is the gardener, there is nothing to fear for He will in His own sweet way, weed out the thorns and thistles and make our souls beautiful, if we let Him.

Jesus must always come first. When we really love Him with all our hearts, then we will learn to love others. Jesus told us to love one another as He had loved us "then people will know you are my disciples". I have spoken to so many who have said, "You Christians are always quarrelling. You can't even get on with each other let alone with outsiders like me." There should be no jealousy or back-biting gossip among the children of God as this will be instantly noticed by non-Christians who will then want nothing to do with us. Let us be shining examples to the outsider and learn to love one another.

The Bible teaches us that if we have total knowledge, and a faith such as could move mountains but have no love, then we are nothing (1 Cor. 2-3). Love is long-suffering and kind. Kindness to our brothers and sisters in Christ is most important and often it is just this kindness that is sadly lacking. Love envieth not.

I remember speaking to a young man in Brussels who told me he had left the Church because people were envious of his ministry. I was very sad and said, "Lord, please forgive my brothers and sisters." This took him completely by surprise. "I expected you to tell me I was in the wrong," he said. "Well," I replied, "I am sorry that you did leave your Church and I am sure that those that hurt you are now very sorry about it all too." This made him think about his life. It had not been better since leaving the Church and the Lord's work. I knew my words had struck a chord deep within him.

Love vaunteth not itself, is not puffed up; Doth not behave itself unseemly, seeketh not her own, is not easily provoked, thinketh no evil.

Faith, like holiness is progressive. The more faith you practice the more you will receive and while you build up the faith of others, your own faith is being strengthened. It is the same with love and grace which increase as you grow in His grace and love. This is the grace and love of Jesus Christ Himself bringing out the truth of the words of John the Baptist: "He must increase, but I must decrease" (John 3:30). The Lord knows what He is doing and He will perfect that which concerneth thee and do the needed work in our hearts and lives.

Men and women everywhere—of all nations, colours and creeds—are looking for direction in a world that seems to be drifting aimlessly. What a challenge this should be to those of us who know where we are heading. Christ is coming soon. This is the hope of all Christians, but we cannot use this hope as an excuse to ignore our present responsibilities and our present opportunities.

I want to work for Jesus *now*, while I have the time and the opportunity.

It was certainly a tremendous opportunity to go to Europe and tell about Jesus.

CHAPTER SIX

The power of praise

"Oh that men would praise the Lord for His goodness and for His wonderful works to the children of men" (Psalm 107:8).

THERE are all kinds of power. Men thirst after power in politics, in business, in sport, and in many other areas of life. There is nothing intrinsically wrong with ambition, but when it becomes an obsession and the sole driving force behind a person, and when that person has no scruples in how he achieves his ambition, then this is wrong. Unbridled ambition engenders many evils. For instance ambition leads to skilled craftsmen being asked to cut corners and produce sub-standard work, in the interests of speed and productivity. Someone pushes someone else who in his turn pushes another, and so on right down the line. Very often people give way under this pressure and certainly the constant strain imposes a heavy burden on mental health and family relationships. Pent-up emotions and frustrations often lead to unexpected emotional explosions with violence often the end result.

Have you ever studied a crowd at a football match? Many go not only to watch their team play, but for comradeship and because they can shout and gesticulate as much as they like. This is, of course, a safety-valve, but frequently it gets out of control and violence breaks out. There can be no doubt that the pace and pressure of twentieth-century life is the underlying cause of many of our current social problems. No wonder so many people are on tranquillizers, or are regular visitors to the psychiatrist!

Before I was delivered of my evil spirits, my mental state was such that I was advised to consult a psychiatrist. The irony of the situation was that he looked as if he should have gone to see a psychiatrist himself. As I unfolded my story he was clearly disturbed and even stopped to take some pills. By the end of the interview he was quite clearly shaken. I wondered at the time who needed the most help, him or me!

It is difficult not to get caught up in the frantic pace of life. Many try to escape from its worse effects, but few succeed. The only real and lasting solution is Jesus Christ. Those outside His loving protection and guidance are at the mercy of the winds of "progress" and have little control over their lives. The Christian, however, has the power and strength of God to help him and in praising God that bond is strengthened. Unfortunately this power of praise is something that a lot of Christians do not utilize to its full.

I learnt a lesson while in the United States. I was staying in an apartment in Buffalo and was horrified one morning to see a team of men arrive and begin to cut down a huge beautiful tree. I could see no reason at all why that tree should be cut down and I was so angry that I went down to the garden to the foreman. "What's the trouble, Ma'am?" he politely asked. I was still furious and rather testily replied, "I want to know why you are cutting down that tree. It gives a lot of shade in the hot weather and besides it is beautiful." He was startled both by my question and by my English accent. He answered, "Do you see those young saplings over there Ma'am?" I said, "Yes, but I can't see what they have to do with it." "Well," he continued, "this old tree may look harmless enough, but the roots have spread to such an extent that it is stopping those young saplings from growing as they should. Because of its low branches it keeps the sun from them and prevents them from growing upwards. Then take a look at that pavement, the roots are also breaking up through the concrete. This tree has grown out of all proportion Ma'am, and so it's just gotta come down." Having heard his reasons I walked away feeling not a little silly. However that incident taught me a lesson. How many things have we allowed to take root in our lives that are contrary to the will of God?

I was once counselling a young Christian girl, when she said, "I wish I had had a conversion like yours." I asked her why and pointed out that her testimony and conversion were as important and as meaningful as my own. "You don't understand," she said. "You see I come from a Christian family and I cannot really clearly remember a time when I was not a Christian. My experience has been very dull and uninteresting, I may as well not be a Christian at all." It was plain that she needed to unburden herself and remaining silent I allowed her to continue. "I'm a complete failure. I have no power at all in my Christian life. I used to witness for Christ, but not any more. I hardly ever read my Bible these days, and once I used to love reading the scriptures. It seems to me that prayer is nothing but a sheer farce as every time I try to pray, my mind goes completely blank and my heart is cold and unresponsive. I don't even bother to pray much now. I go to church regularly, but purely from habit. I only go because people would talk if I didn't. I just feel a complete hypocrite. I take the Sunday school class, and I used to really enjoy it and put in a lot of work and preparation, but now I don't seem to really care. It has all become such a bore. I am certainly not helping the children and I feel I might even be hindering them. I've been thinking of giving it up for some time now. Mind you, if I had a testimony like yours things might be different and I might have more power in my faith."

What a sad situation. This young Christian was joyless, powerless, and useless. The manner of her conversion should not have been important. Once she had had joy and power but now she had none. It was as if all the lights had gone out as the result of a power failure.

What she needed was to be reconnected. But what had caused the power failure in the first place? Through conversation it became apparent that in her case the power failure had been caused by disobedience and disloyalty. She had allowed worldly pleasures to take up that place in her life that truly belonged to the Saviour alone. I told her the story of the tree and the saplings and it spoke deeply to her.

The various aspects of her life that were wrong looked innocent enough, just like that tree, but they were choking out all the spiritual power that should have been available. Just like that tree, these things in her life had to go. The workmen hadn't just cut down a few branches here and there, they had cut down the whole tree. She needed to understand why this had to be done in her case in the same way that I had to finally understand the reasons for felling the tree. She had quite a lot of tree-felling to do in her own life and it was not going to be easy. Part of her problem was worldly companions. "Can't we have any friends apart from Christians?" you might ask. "Yes we can." But in her case she never spoke to her friends about the things of God although she had often had plenty of opportunity to do so. Therefore instead of her bringing them into the light, she was allowing herself to be drawn into their world. She was an avid reader of novels. Obviously there is nothing wrong in that, but in her case she read novels to the exclusion of everything else including her Bible. No wonder her heart was cold and she felt little else but hypocrisy as she sat in church on Sundays. Her line of sight to the Lord had been obscured by other diversions. I gave her another little example and perhaps it will help others who are feeling powerless and defeated.

Have you ever tried to keep warm, huddled right up to one of those old-fashioned stoves? I have. On this particular day something was wrong with the stove and the fire simply smouldered. It was a bitterly cold day. The trouble was that the stove was choked with cinders. These cinders were stopping the fire from burning properly. There was no strength in the flame. It needed to be raked out, reset, and rekindled. So it can be with our Christian lives, which can so easily become choked with the cinders of sin. St Paul says, ". . . Let us lay aside every weight, and the sin that doth so easily beset us, and let us run with patience the race that is set before us, Looking unto Jesus, the author and finisher of our faith" (Heb. 12:1-2). How proud the human heart is. If we can find a scapegoat for our own wrongdoings we will, even if it is God himself! We can give many plausible excuses. "I must have some relaxation"; "Is there no place for pleasure at all?"; "What harm is there in it?" What excuses we make to keep our trees. They give us shade so that we can slumber beneath them. How clever Satan is. He will use any means possible to keep us powerless.

In Chapter 6 of the Book of Judges we read how God commanded that Gideon should pull down the altar of Baal and also the grove of trees that surrounded it. Gideon, of course, obeyed the Lord. This girl hesitated when she was shown clearly that she had to review certain aspects of her own life, but eventually she did so. She threw out all the offending books that she had so avidly read, she saw less of her worldly friends and more of her Christian friends, and today she is a radiant joyful Christian and an inspiration to all she meets. Her Sunday school has increased in numbers and she now also sings for her Lord at church gatherings. The fire of love for Jesus that was in her has been rekindled to the glory of God.

Lack of praise can reduce the power of any Christian. Praise brings the victory. Praise strengthens our faith and renews the inner man. Praise works miracles!

In the Book of Psalms we read how David praised God in every circumstance. By the very act of praising, his faith was strengthened. He never doubted that God had the battle won, even before it commenced. Praise brings faith and faith brings hope. Therefore praise, faith, and hope will always be intertwined. Faith helps us accept the promises of God in their Divine reality. Hope goes on to embrace the treasures which have already been accepted.

Faith is the substance of things hoped for and the evidence of things unseen. If we praise God in faith, He will honour us. David shouted the victory against overwhelming odds. He knew that God was on his side. He says in Psalm 41, "I will praise the Lord at all times. His praise shall continually be in my mouth." No matter what may befall us on the Christian pathway, we should praise God for it. When everyone and everything is against you, praise the Lord for the challenge. You will be amazed at the difference it will make to you. Think of the disciples, so discouraged, so fearful, because Jesus their beloved Master had been crucified and buried. Imagine them as they gathered behind locked doors for fear of the Jews. At this time they were living on the dark side of the cross, the side of defeat and despair. Many Christians are doing just that today and Satan uses this to the full. Discouragement is one of the most effective weapons he has. It can knock us flat as Satan well knows.

Many a Christian has given up a Sunday school class, or some other work that the Lord wanted them to do. Discouragements can often come from fellow Christians through a word or a look. I myself was nearly flattened by the discouragement that I experienced when, shortly after becoming a Christian, I found that some of my fellow Christians were afraid of me, or avoided me as they believed that I could not be a real Christian. Satan told me, "You may as well give up, the Christians don't believe you and they don't want you."

Paul must have also felt discouraged. His past was fresh in the minds of the Christians of his day, and many must have taken a long time to accept him as a Christian and a new creature. But through it all Paul went on preaching that Christ had risen from the dead. Even when you are sorely discouraged, "Praise the Lord!" and another "Praise the Lord" will surely follow. Your faith will rise and the discouragements will melt away like snow in the sunshine. Giving praise to God drowns out all discouragement and the victory is won. Praise the Lord when people, even Christians, spread rumours and lies about you. Remember what Jesus said, "Happy are you when men insult you and mistreat you, and tell all kinds of evil lies against you; rejoice and be glad, because a great reward is kept for you in heaven; this is how men mistreated the prophets who lived before you" (Matthew 5:11-12—*Good News for Modern Man*).

But are we happy when these things happen? Very often we grumble and feel sorry for ourselves, but when we experience the power of praising God for everything, great and small, good and bad, then we can pass the blessing on to someone else. People, yes even Christians, have spread all kinds of hurtful rumours and lies about me. Some even said that I had gone back to my old ways, to witchcraft and black magic. At first this upset me more than I could admit. Then I started to praise God for it and said, "Praise you Jesus for the lies and the rumours. Thank you and praise you for it all." It was amazing how the peace and joy of Jesus flooded into my soul. Rumours didn't matter any more. It was senseless to worry and fret about things, but in praising Jesus the hurt and the pain vanished and gave me new strength to go on for God. Man can lift you up one minute and then drop you the next. Jesus is not like that and praising Him lifts you above earthly values and gives you the victory.

So, reader, if you are downcast and everything looks black and you can see no way out of your problem or circumstance, look up and praise the Lord. He will surely lift you up. Are you at the midnight hour? Start praising Jesus and he will see you through in victory. Remember Paul and Silas, beaten, bruised, and bleeding, their feet held fast in stocks for preaching the Gospel. There was one thing they could not confine and that was their tongues. They prayed and sang praises to God and the other prisoners heard them. What happened? Suddenly there was a great earthquake and the foundations of the prison were shaken. Immediately all the doors were opened and everyone's bonds were loosed.

As a result, the keepers of the gaol were converted and the entire household rejoiced and praised God. Praise is infectious. Even the sinner can be set free from his sin and darkness through praising God. He can be filled with wonder when he sees the joy of God's children praising their Lord. If you are called upon to suffer for the Lord, accept it gladly and with joy, for you are indeed privileged. By suffering with Him you will reign with Him and that is truly something to look forward to isn't it? No one suffers pain from choice, so surely it follows that if we do not plan it then it must come from God. He is above all and has the power to stop anything from happening, so he must plan it for a reason. Perhaps He wants to see if we are made of the stuff of martyrs. Are we willing to die for our faith if need be? If we cannot stand up to the few problems and sufferings that we face now, how will we fare if suffering really comes?

It is my opinion that Christians will in the future experience persecution and suffering such as has not been known for centuries. Jesus himself said that this would come to pass: "Then they will deliver you up to tribulation and put you to death and you will be hated by all nations for my name's sake. And then many will fall away and betray one another and hate one another . . . But he who endures to the end will be saved" (Matt. 24:10-13). We have seen evidence of some of the persecution and suffering that has taken place in Communist countries, but it surely must become much stronger before Jesus returns to catch away His bride. But we are assured that Jesus will meet our need. In the strongest persecution He will give us the power to overcome. A great and mighty outpouring of the Holy Spirit will be apparent and with praise ringing from the voices of the faithful, victory will be assured and the flame of faith will burn brighter than ever.

We often hear people say, "I can't go on any more, I can't stand it any more." We have even said it ourselves, yet often this is exactly where Jesus wants us to be. He wants us to be in the position where all we can do is to cling entirely to Him and say, "Lord, I give up." When we say "we can't" in our hearts we know that the Lord "can". He wants us to trust in Him. When we have vainly tried to work things out for ourselves and have failed miserably, then Jesus stands waiting to help us. Man's extremity is God's opportunity. Then we can start praising the Lord. He alone has the answer. Praise God for the answer that He gives when we are totally at a loss. He will always guide us.

Depression is another strong weapon in the hands of Satan. It has been proved beyond a doubt that when the body is sick, there is a grave danger that the mind will also be adversely affected. Satan is very quick to capitalize on our depression. It can render us powerless, joyless, and utterly useless. When a Christian is depressed the first thing that Satan does is to cast doubts into his mind about spiritual matters. As Satan is the accuser of the brethren, he jumps at every opportunity to make the Christian belittle his brothers, their work, and their faith.

While in New York I came into contact with a retired minister. This dear man of God was in failing health, but nevertheless he was a very cheerful person, always ready with a smile and a word of encouragement. Eventually he had to go into hospital for an operation and I went to visit him often. Despite the fact that he was in great pain and discomfort he was always cheerful and bright. After his period of recuperation he returned home where suddenly he became very depressed. He felt the Lord had forsaken him. Having once been a minister he knew only too well the promises of the Bible, but they did not seem real to him any more. He never spoke much about this depression, save to say that he no longer felt the presence of the Lord. His depression deepened even though many people, including myself, were praying for him. As I prayed for him daily, I asked the Lord to show me plainly the root cause, and He did just that. The Devil was tormenting this man with thoughts that he had outlived his usefulness and really had nothing left to live for. What was needed then? Above all else LOVE. God's children needed to encourage and reassure him that he was needed and that he was loved. It is all very well to talk about love, but you need to tell people you love them.

How often do you say to your children or your spouse,

"I love you". We all ought to express our feelings verbally much more often. Our family may know that we love them by our actions, but it is so important to express that love in words as well as actions. So it should be with brothers and sisters in the Lord. Kind deeds are necessary, but "I love you", though sometimes hard or embarrassing to say, is a great power and we ought to use it more often.

This dear man needed to be told that he was loved and needed. Then his faith would be strengthened. He also needed to praise, no matter how depressed he was. A word of warning, when trying to help people in this situation, commit every word and every action to prayer in advance. Let God speak through you. Acting on a purely "human" plain could make matters much worse, despite good intentions. Always ask for wisdom and compassion.

Eventually this dear man was taken to a meeting where God's people really knew how to praise. They left their seats and moved about the church talking to complete strangers, shaking each other by the hand and saying, "Brother I love you", and "I'm so glad to see you here." This was not mere emotionalism, this was real. The Holy Spirit was working in that church and in that congregation. Slowly, the man began to enter into the spirit of the meeting and eventually his face was a vision of joy and wonder. Praise and love had effected a cure. Once again prayer was made for him and the victory was claimed in the name of Christ Jesus. He began to feel the presence of God once again.

I still felt a burden for him and the Holy Spirit showed me that constant prayer was needed as well as consistent Christian love and encouragement. After prayer I spoke to him on the telephone and said, "Brother I love you", and I did. I told him to fight the lies of Satan and to keep on praising God. I could tell by his voice that he was in tears, but his tears were tears of joy, and so were mine. What touched and spoke to me more than anything else was his thankfulness that I should be burdened for him and that I had allowed the Lord to show me what was wrong and what should be done.

We can never love more, nor give more than the Lord Jesus Christ. Let us try to care more, give more, and love our fellows more. Let us have time for everyone that needs us. The power of praise brings faith strong enough to move mountains and to turn a hill into a smooth plain.

Praise not only brings faith, hope, and joy, but also thankfulness beyond words. Praise brings a greater love for Jesus and a greater love for our fellow men. The power of praise can calm the fiercest storm and blow the winds of doubt far away. It may sound silly to praise the Lord in the face of suffering, persecution, poverty, depression, or any other bitter struggle, but believe me praise works wonders. God honours praise, for whoever offers praise, glorifies the Lord and pleases Him.

I remember another Christian that I met some time ago. She had a particularly nasty growth in her neck, but as a Christian she believed that God could heal her. She asked for prayer and so strong was her faith that she told everyone that the Lord had already actually healed her. This was despite the fact that it was obvious that the swelling was still there and that she was in considerable discomfort. At first people were embarrassed when she insisted that she had been healed, and as she persisted in praising God for the healing he had done they began to take her for a religious fanatic. They avoided her, and even laughed at her. After months of praising God in this way, she woke up one morning to find herself totally healed. There was no trace of the growth and doubters who had not seen her in her suffering, refused to believe that she had ever been afflicted at all! She had honoured God in praise and through that praise she had witnessed a miracle of healing. Such is the very real power of praise.

I myself have proved time and time again the power of praise. There are things that I am praising God for at this very minute and I know that if it is His will, He will give me the desires of my heart. My life is in his hands and only He knows what the future holds. I praise and thank God every day, even for the things that I do not understand. I have praised Him for the way ahead, even though at that time I knew not what the way ahead actually was. I have praised Him for the answer, when I knew not what the answer was. Through praise I eventually knew the way ahead and the answer. Praise His name.

God has done so much for me and I have much to praise Him for. There will be many golden days ahead, as well as many dark days. There will be times when tears will come and I will fail. But I know that my God is good and kind and merciful. I praise Him for all His goodness. I will say with David, "But I will hope continually, and will yet praise Thee more and more" (Ps. 71:14). I will prove again and again, the great power of praising God. PRAISE THE LORD!

CHAPTER SEVEN

The dangers of dabbling

"Now . . . in the latter times some shall depart from the truth, giving heed to seducing spirits and doctrines of devils" (1 Timothy 4:1).

MANY books have been written about the occult. The bookstalls are full of them and they sell in large numbers. I am sure that there cannot be too many warnings given of the dangers inherent in any contact with the occult, even the mildest contact.

Speaking as a former Satanist and witch I can say with some authority: "DO NOT DABBLE—DO NOT PLAY WITH FIRE"; the danger to mind and body and soul is immense.

I am frequently asked questions about the occult, particularly by young people. There is an unhealthy interest in all aspects of the occult and the practice of it is clearly on the increase. There has been Devil worship for many centuries. It is driven underground, but every now and then it surfaces and becomes almost fashionable and acceptable. This unfortunately is true today. Young people, especially, seem to be drawn into the web of darkness that is the occult. The Bible tells us that wickedness will increase before the final victory. As Christians we are aware of "the other side" and we must be equipped to cope with its many manifestations.

What makes people turn to the occult? First of all let us take a look at our world. We find it fast moving, violent, insensitive, full of war and disaster. People try to find an answer to what seems insoluble problems. We know that turning to God is the answer, but many turn to Satan instead. In an increasingly dehumanized world the psychology of the clique is very important. People want to be part of a special group, one of a privileged few, and the occult seems to fill this need. We are bombarded with films, television and radio programmes, and novels based on the occult and it is not surprising that people who are disenchanted with the world are turning to the occult to find a solution. Medical science can cater for sick bodies and even sick minds, but a disenchanted or broken spirit is another thing entirely. Signs are wanted. Something different, something supernatural. Where better to find these signs than in the occult. Satan makes sure that these fledgling converts *do* see signs—*evil* signs and seeming wonders.

The element of mystery is another powerful magnet drawing people into the darkness. The great and evil diversions that take place in secret, the promises of earthly power all serve to draw the unsuspecting into the web of intrigue. It is far easier to join the ranks of the occult than it is to leave! The Bible tells us that Satan has the power to transform himself into "an angel of light". He can deceive us into thinking that he is harmless and it is only when dire and dark events happen that the truth is realized. Often by that time the person is so enmeshed that he is powerless to leave.

If people were only aware of some of the things which I myself have actually seen and heard, then they would certainly give serious thought to the consequences of occultism. As a former Queen of witches I speak from personal experience. I am not a scholar or researcher piecing together bits of second-hand information. I know, because I have seen with my own eyes. Deuteronomy 18 forbids witchcraft, divination, and necromancy, not because God is cruel, but because He is love. Like the loving Father He is He does not want to see His children harmed. Therefore in love He clearly says, "Thou shalt not". God wants only the best for His

creatures and like a father He says, "Thou shalt have no
other gods before me, [or] make unto thee any graven
image . . . for I the Lord thy God am a jealous God"
(Exodus 20:3-5).

There is much confusion. People ask me, "Why are
mediums and white witches evil. Surely they do good
works and help people?" One need only examine the
source of their power. They do not derive their power
from God, since they never make mention of Him or of
the shed blood of Jesus Christ. It is clear that their power,
if power it be, comes from Satan. Many so-called
"healings" are short-lived and the patient, in fact, in time
becomes far worse. He then has to seek further "help"
and so is drawn deeper into the web of the occult.
Mediums are often the one means of introducing people
to the occult. Mediums claim to put people in touch with
their dead relatives or friends, but as a former witch I
know that demons are wonderful imitators and are con-
vincing enough to make a person believe that he is
speaking to one of his dead relations or friends. The Bible
clearly warns us *not* to consult with those in contact with
"familiar spirits". These spirits are very knowledgeable
and know much about the departed dead. They are able
to imitate and thus deceive.

Witchcraft in whatever form it comes, frequently leads
to suicide. If you knew what went on in witches' covens
and at satanist temples, you would not be surprised at
this. Witches have been known to exhume bodies from
newly dug graves in order to mutilate them or offer them
to Satan in sacrifice. Imagine how dark and twisted a
mind must be to do this! Then imagine that same person
many years later as his mind begins to dwell on some of
the abominations that he has readily been party to! An
act of suicide must seem like the only possible relief to
him.

Black witches believe that demons must be obeyed and
appeased at any cost. They dare not disobey orders from
demons or from the leaders of their circle. They live in
perpetual fear. They, like Satanists, believe that one day
Lucifer will rule the earth and that the Christian Gospel

will be vanquished. The more evil that they do on earth, the quicker will this final victory be accomplished. Their doctrine is the complete antithesis of Christianity. Whatever is preached in the Christian Gospel, they believe the absolute opposite, always. Vile initiations and sexual ceremonies are part and parcel of their way of life. Even white witches, with their area of respectability, when closely examined are seen to be no different to their black counterparts. Their god is the horned god of fertility and they perform sexual initiations in a like manner to black witches. Witchcraft is pure paganism with a history going back many centuries.

Certain aspects of white witchcraft dogma can be traced back to some of the world's oldest religions. The Druids for example use runic incantations that have been handed down from generation to generation. There are no good spirits save the Holy Spirit of God. All other spirits proceed from Satan! The works and methods of witches, black and white, are the works of darkness. *All witchcraft is evil!* Witches do not believe in the Bible or accept the Lord as God. They worship their own demons and gods and are a law unto themselves. They offer more licence than the permissive society ever can, and they exploit that licence in the extremes of degradation. They are evil and corrupt to the core. Most people have a comic-book picture of witches. The old hags riding the skies on their broomsticks, for instance. This childish façade hides the reality, the dark and sinister reality. A normal person cannot really imagine the depths to which witches sink. The web of darkness leads them to the very pit of Hell itself.

Apart from the outward manifestations of witchcraft, equally distasteful are the deceptions that are employed to lure gullible recruits into the fold. Jesus said, "I am the way, the truth, and the life: no man cometh unto the Father, but by me" (John 14:6). People who go the way of the occult, often in complete sincerity, place themselves under the direct influence of demons and are in danger of becoming oppressed, obsessed or, worse still, possessed by evil spirits.

During the earthly ministry of Jesus, He healed the sick and cast out demons. Two entirely different acts. Demon possession is much more prevalent today than it ever was before. This fact obviously goes hand in hand with the increase in occult practices of all kinds. So the great deception continues. Imagine the despair if there were no solution to this problem! But fortunately there is a path of deliverance and I myself have trodden that path. I found deliverance through Jesus Christ who set me free from darkness, demons, and an early death. He alone was able to break the bondage of witchcraft and the evil power of the occult, and fill me with His glorious power. And I know that one day Satan, the great deceiver, and all his host, will be cast into the lake of fire for eternity.

In my ministry for the Lord Jesus Christ in schools and colleges I am asked many questions about the occult. I always consider my answers very carefully, I realize that a little knowledge can be dangerous especially to youngsters at the most impressionable time of their lives. I always answer questions so that no one will be ignorant of the Devil and his deviousness. Often the answers are not quite what the questioner hoped! I always bring in the Bible and, of course, Jesus Christ. For example I have been asked, "What does the Devil look like?" Even though I know what he looks like because I have seen him, I am sure it will not benefit the questioner so I answer, "What does it matter how he looks? A creature of such evil cannot look very nice no matter what disguise he uses. I am more interested in how Jesus looks, for He is good and altogether lovely." Many other questions keep cropping up. "Do you still retain your powers of witchcraft? Can you still kill birds in flight?" and so on. My answer, of course, is "No!" When the Lord Jesus Christ filled me with His holy spirit and set me free from Satan's evil power, all my witchcraft skills vanished. For that I am truly glad as the peace and power I have from Jesus is wonderful. It can bring life, love, joy, and peace, whereas Satan's power can only bring hatred, disgrace, and death.

Jesus said, "But ye shall receive power, after that the

Holy Ghost is come upon you; and ye shall be witnesses unto me both in Jerusalem, and in all Judaea, and in Samaria, and unto the uttermost part of the earth" (Acts 1:8). In the Gospel of Mark we read of the wonderful signs that shall be manifest to those that believe. These signs are for today. Those that witness and experience these signs know that the power that Jesus gives surpasses any power of the Devil or his agents, or any power on earth. Human beings are by nature sceptical and they have always demanded signs and proof in a visible form. It was the same in Jesus' day. Certain Scribes and Pharisees said, "Master, we would see a sign from thee." And Jesus replied, "An evil and adulterous generation seeketh after a sign; and there shall no sign be given to it, but the sign of the prophet Jonah: [who] was three days and three nights in the whale's belly" (Matt. 12:38-40). Jesus was alluding to his forthcoming Crucifixion and Resurrection.

We, therefore, have two areas of power. The good which emanates from God and the evil which comes from Satan. It is an odd paradox that while many people who have no personal knowledge of God will readily admit that God is good, they will not accept that Satan is evil. They usually are of the opinion that evil comes from man himself. Here is the greatest of the Devil's deceptions. As long as people do not think he exists, he is free to act as he wishes. I suppose that the idea of evil is so abhorrent to most people they tend to bury their heads in the sand when it is raised. They are able to accept that good comes from God and that there is a God of some kind, but the idea of the Devil and evil is beyond their comprehension. More importantly they cannot accept that as sinners outside the power of God, they are in fact under the power of the Devil to a greater or lesser degree! They think they are "reasonably good people" and do not wish to change their way of life. Jesus knew this: ". . . men love darkness rather than light because their deeds were evil. For every one that doeth evil, hateth the light, neither cometh to the light, lest their deeds should be reproved" (John 3:19-20). Witches, Satanists, mediums, and others of their ilk fully believe that they are in the right and in the light but the Bible says, "There is a way which seemeth right unto a man, but the end thereof are the ways of death" (Prov. 14:12). These people are twisted and living in darkness.

The Bible states: "They call evil good, and good evil; that put darkness for light, and light for darkness; that put bitter for sweet, and sweet for bitter! Woe unto them that are wise in their own eyes, and prudent in their own sight!" (Isa. 5:20-21). The situation is made very clear by the Scriptures. From personal experience I can endorse those words whole-heartedly. The occult is nothing but a deep and dark bondage of satanic nature, origin, and inspiration. Nothing short of Divine intervention can turn these people and make them see the evil that they do. I am fully convinced that every Christian church should hold Bible classes in which the true facts of demonic activity are discussed, and refuted by the Word of God. So many Christians are totally ignorant of the dangers, simply because they have no means of discovering the true facts. I have even met Christians who tried without proper knowledge to help someone with a demonic problem, not fully appreciating the seriousness of the situation or the personal risks that they were running. As a result of uninformed meddling one or two have themselves suffered obsession and possession!

Judy was just a babe in Christ when she visited a hypnotist. She was a bright and attractive student with a wonderful future before her. However, her fellow students persuaded her to go and see the hypnotist, somehow believing that he could see her through her final exams with flying colours. They had apparently been to him themselves. Three or four days after visiting the hypnotist, Judy became severely depressed and would burst into tears at the slightest provocation. Within a few short weeks she had changed from a normally happy girl into a sullen, withdrawn, bad-tempered, and irritable person. Her ability to concentrate had vanished completely and she became irrational and in every way unreliable. Suddenly she had become the exact opposite of her true self.

About this time she came along to one of my meetings and stayed behind to speak to me. It was very difficult to talk to her as she was scarcely able to concentrate enough to explain her problem. I knew that Satan was robbing her of her thoughts and did not want me to discover the root cause of her troubles. Judy was utterly confused and very frightened. I rebuked the Devil and the power of darkness in the name of Jesus and asked the Lord to show me what was wrong. I paused for a few moments, then I asked her if she had been in contact with a fortune-teller, medium, or hypnotist. As soon as I mentioned the word "hypnotist" she became hysterical and began to sob and shake from head to foot. The presence of evil was obvious and it was with great difficulty that I kept her from rushing out of the room and into the night. Laying my hands on her head I again rebuked the forces of darkness and she slowly calmed down and was then able to tell me of her visit to the hypnotist and how she had been affected by it.

It was plain to me that Judy was being oppressed heavily by the same evil influence that controlled the hypnotist. In the name of Jesus I commanded every demonic power to depart and never to return, and they did so immediately. Judy had been set free. The evil atmosphere that had filled the room was dissipated and the peace and presence of Jesus could be felt in a very real way. Judy's face changed from fear, to relief and joy. She later told me that if something had not been done that day she would probably have tried to commit suicide! Well, praise God something had been done—Jesus had set her free.

Isn't it sad to think that young Christians like Judy can be so easily lured and trapped through lack of correct teaching? In the end Judy passed her finals with flying colours through the help of her Saviour. Judy said, "I didn't see anything wrong in it at the time", but it is sheer folly to place yourself completely in the power of a stranger as she had done. Even more dangerous still is to go to someone who may be involved in all kinds of dark practices as well. Who can tell what happens during a trance? Young Judy had no idea. She could remember nothing. There are many like Judy all over the world and we must warn them and teach them that dabbling is dangerous. The dangers of oppression, obsession, and possession are very real. A door can be opened which will let in demonic activity and domination. Witchcraft and Satanism are the most sinister forms of the occult, but even the seemingly innocuous forms like hypnotism can be equally as dangerous.

Yes, these are the "latter times" that Timothy speaks about when he says that "some shall depart from the faith giving heed to seducing spirits, and doctrines of devils" (1 Tim. 4:1). Timothy indicates here that some of those already in the Christian faith will leave it and turn to occult practices and false doctrines. Many are doing just that today and the tragic thing is that they are not aware that many seemingly innocent things do in fact border on the occult. Little things like celebrating Hallowe'en, for example, and dressing up like witches. Making jokes about the curses of witches and acting out these so-called "harmless" pranks. All so seemingly innocent, but they may lead to much less harmless activities.

I have heard about people play-acting the reprisals of witches and even going so far as sticking razor-blades into apples and offering them to their friends. All seemingly innocent, but all extremely foolish and potentially dangerous. Real witches find these "games" amusing, especially when they are played by Christians. They laugh at the thought that Christians are celebrating Walpurgis Night at the same time as they themselves. Hallowe'en is one of the most important dates in the calendar of a witch. All kinds of evil manifestations are seen by witches on that night and evil spirits are very active. They can be seen to take over a person's body, completely controlling all that person's actions. If Christians saw even a little of these evils they would never again celebrate Hallowe'en.

In America, Hallowe'en is a big occasion. Shops display all kinds of witches' costumes and a kind of

Hallowe'en fever sweeps the country. Children go from door to door crying "Trick or treat." Simply put this means that householders either give them some form of treat, for instance an apple or some candy, or they will play a trick on them which could be anything from whitewashing the windows to slashing the tyres on the car in the drive. One group of youngsters literally terrorized an elderly couple who had no "treat" for them by shouting obscenities and smashing windows. When the police arrived the youngsters said they did not know what had come over them to act in such a way. They were not hooligans or rowdies and were from respectable homes. None of them had ever been in trouble before. So what had come over them? I fully believe that demonic forces took control of them for a short while transforming an innocent children's custom into something more sinister.

Witchcraft, spiritualism, Satanism, and all other forms of the occult are a direct affront and a rebellion against God, Jesus Christ, and the Christian Church. Those involved curse God and laugh at the Scriptures. No Christian should celebrate Hallowe'en!

The ouija board has for long been a popular party game and many people are unaware of the nature of the fire they are playing with or of the havoc their frivolous behaviour could cause. The ouija board is a device whereby a group of people try to communicate with the dead without the help of a medium. Questions are asked and an upturned glass or pointer spells out the answers letter by letter. This do-it-yourself spiritualism kit is terribly dangerous and should never be resorted to.

Mary and her friends played with a ouija board with terrible consequences. The spirit spelt out through the letters on the board that Mary's pet dog would die and that Mary herself would die shortly afterwards. Sure enough the dog died and the girls were filled with fear. Then Mary herself became ill. She had a temperature of a hundred and three degrees and yet the doctor could find nothing physically wrong with her! She was about to be moved to hospital when the ouija board incident came to light. Her parents contacted me and asked me to go to her and pray for her. When I saw Mary she was filled with fear and dread and was convinced that she was dying. She was writhing about in terror. I rebuked the demons of fear and destruction in the name of Jesus and the demons within her struggled and fought. There was much fighting for the ground that they had taken and they refused to come out of Mary quietly. Eventually they were beaten and with a loud scream, Mary was delivered. Within an hour her temperature was normal and all fear had vanished. Mary and her friends will never again play with a ouija board. Mary herself had to repent of this sin before she was set free from the power of evil.

I could go on and tell you much more about the evil onslaughts of the Devil and about the many times that I have come face to face with demons of darkness. Ouija boards cause a tremendous amount of harm, but this is just one aspect of evil to be met with on the spiritual battlefield. I think every Christian minister should be conversant with such matters in these "latter times"! We should neither be ignorant of the evil devices nor should we be fearful. "Perfect love casteth out fear" (1 John 4:18). We should be on the alert and ready at all times to minister and warn, in love, all those that are caught up in these devilish diversions. The occult is a multi-million-pound industry, turning out ouija boards, tarot cards, as well as thousands of books on voodoo and other vile practices. Satan is working overtime in his attempt to defeat Christianity. Men's hearts are failing through fear of the evil encompassing them.

Increased crime, violence, unemployment, inflation, pollution, and the ever-present threat of nuclear war are the fears menacing the stability of our society. It is all very frightening when everything seems to be falling apart. But the child of God need have no fear for God has everything under control. The power of the Devil is limited and even babes in Christ can put him to flight by the word and by the precious shed blood of Jesus. Resist the Devil and he will flee from you. All power is given us to cast out demons, tread on scorpions, and overthrow the enemy. Does this sound like defeat Christians? Why, the Devil is already defeated. Two thousand years ago at Calvary he suffered a massive and crushing defeat. He knows his time is short so he is using every trick and device to trap and lure away men, women, and children from the Saviour. But Christians, look up on high, the coming of the Lord Jesus Christ draweth nigh! God is in total control and only He knows when the time will be right to send Jesus to us again to cast Satan and his host into the lake of fire for eternity. Nothing can harm those who live in the shadow of God. He is stronger than any other power and His message is clear. "For God hath not given us the spirit of fear; but of power, and of love and of a sound mind" (2 Tim. 1-7). The children of God need fear no evil, nor fear any demon or power of the occult.

God is raising up a people who are launching out in faith to pull down the stronghold of Satan. Be assured, there is a growing army of consecrated and dedicated Christians marching forward fully armed to combat the legions of demons that swarm over the earth. If God is before us, then who can stand against us? No demon of Hell, no witch or Satanist, no man or woman, no power can overthrow the great army of the Lord. Jesus our mighty Captain and King goes before us and He is far stronger than Satan or sin. So Christians, let us shake off the cloak of apathy, ignorance, and fear and let us march forward clad in the armour of God to do battle with the Satanic host. Let us warn the faithful and rebuke and crush the Devil.

To be inspired is a process of the heart, but to be involved is a personal decision. Let us involve ourselves in the great battle to save the lost, deluded, and dying souls of mankind. Let us go for God.

The Lord is looking for new recruits. Will you dear reader say in faith: "Here I am Lord, send me!"

CHAPTER EIGHT

Happy reunion

"And they shall be mine, saith the Lord of hosts, in that day when I make up my jewels" (Malachi 3:17).

IN my book *From Witchcraft to Christ* I told how, as a child, I had attended the Waterloo Road Mission, which was just round the corner from the Uxbridge council house in which I lived. My parents were certainly no churchgoers, indeed the Lord's name was usually taken in vain in my house. My upbringing was rough and tough and there were a great many problems in my home. My sense of humour saw me through, and I really needed it. I had to be both father and mother to my younger sisters. Sunday school for me was just somewhere to escape the problems and pressures of life at home. Often my sisters and I would be turned out of Sunday school for bad behaviour, and yet the teachers were always very kind and understanding for they knew something of the problems we faced at home. Their kindness went largely unnoticed by my sisters and I. Sunday school was one of the few places where we could let off steam, and where we could have a laugh and some harmless fun. It did not matter how many times we were turned out, the door was always open to us the following week. Despite the problems, I have never forgotten those happy days at Sunday school. Nevertheless, when I left school at the age of fourteen I felt too grown up for

Sunday school and I never attended classes again.

After a short time in domestic service, a period full of ups and downs—although I remember more downs than ups—I left for London where I eventually became a prostitute on the streets of Paddington. Strangely, even at this time, when I saw a street meeting of the Salvation Army, scenes of Sunday school came flooding into my mind. So you see, the seed sown in my heart had not been sown in vain. When a happy-go-lucky and often confused little girl fooling around in Sunday school, I never imagined I would end up on the streets of London as a prostitute! My teachers could not have envisaged that outcome either. And who would have thought that the uneducated and difficult Doreen would one day be hailed as Queen of black witches! How important it is that we pray for those who teach and instruct. I am glad that I went to Sunday school for it was there that the seed of Christianity was sown in my heart. I know that my teachers prayed for me while I was in their care.

As a girl I also attended the C.A.W.G. Messengers' group whose meetings were also held at the Waterloo Road Mission. While I may have been unruly at Sunday school, I really loved the Messengers and I was as good as gold. We were taught many skills and crafts in the Messengers including first aid, nature study, cooking, and even the morse code. Our meetings always opened and closed with a prayer and the Captain was very kind and was loved by us all. She certainly knew how to manage girls, even the difficult ones like me. She was always patient and had a wonderful bright smile. All the girls, including me, used to run along the road to meet her. What wonderful work she and her helpers did among us girls. No. I never forgot Sunday school and the Messengers, no matter where I went or what I did. I remember that even during my striptease act, suddenly one of the choruses we sang would spring into my mind.

> Hide God's word in your heart,
> Hide God's word in your heart.
> The word of love sent from above,
> Hide god's word in your heart.

Fancy thinking of that in such a situation! Just imagine that the loving Saviour was speaking to me even in such a place and when I was so steeped in sin and shame.

Some time later when I had become a drug addict, I turned to shop-lifting in order to raise money to support my habit. I remember that while I was in Holloway Prison, I had with me a copy of the *Golden Bells Hymn Book*. I had been given this at Sunday school and I treasured it. I would sit in my cell before the lights went out and read the familiar hymns of childhood. How simple the words were, but they spoke volumes to me. I always thought: "It is too late for me now!" Of course it was not too late. It is never too late. As long as we are in God's day of grace it is never ever too late for anyone! But at the time I did not realize this and I went on with my shameful way of life. Here again we see the tender loving heart of the Saviour gently wooing a sinner. Yes, I am glad I went to Sunday school, and I am convinced that in this field is seen some of the most vital work being done in the Christian Church today.

Little did I know how far I would have to go before I found Christ as my Saviour. When I left prison I tried to change my way of life, but like so many others who have tried to "go it alone", I failed. Indeed I slid further and further into the realm of darkness. I became a Satanist and a witch and I worshipped in temples and covens. Eventually I became the head of thousands of witches in Britain and on the Continent. Satan was now my master and the Christian Church was my number one enemy. It was not until sixteen years later that I found the Lord Jesus Christ as my Saviour. I changed masters and began to serve the greatest master of all—Jesus, the Son of God. What a miracle of love and grace! And then all that I had been taught in Sunday school and the Messengers came back to me. Things long forgotten came back to me, including the hymns and choruses and even the Laws of the Messengers:

A Messenger reads a portion of Scripture every day.

A Messenger prays daily.

A Messenger is loyal to God and the King.

A Messenger is useful and helpful.

A Messenger obeys orders.

A Messenger is courteous and kind to all.

A Messenger is thrifty.

A Messenger smiles under all difficulties.

A Messenger is pure and truthful in word, thought, and deed.

The Messenger's motto is "By love serve."

These laws are very good and very scriptural. When Jesus saved me he set me free to serve Him and others. I am now a true messenger with a true sense of the living message. Imagine then my joy when many years later I met my former Messenger Captain.

I was on a speaking tour in the London area, and one night I was in Hounslow, which is not too far from Uxbridge. The church was full and as I was giving my testimony I had no idea that my former Captain was sitting in the congregation along with other members of the Waterloo Road Mission. After the meeting I was told that some old friends wished to see me and when I greeted them I could hardly believe my eyes. Miss Olive Maynard, my ex-Captain, looked no different though we had not met for all of thirty years. What a happy reunion it was. By now Miss Maynard had retired, but her work, and the work of many others, will never be forgotten. The Waterloo Road Mission is still in existence, telling out the Gospel and of Jesus and His love for all men.

If I thought the reunion with Miss Maynard was wonderful, can you imagine what it was like for me to return to the Waterloo Road Mission to actually give my testimony? And what a reunion that proved to be! Before the meeting, Miss Maynard had arranged a special tea and had contacted about thirty of the old Messengers. My dear old Captain and her helpers had worked very hard to organize this reunion and they were as excited as I was. I wondered if the old Messengers would actually remember me? Would I remember them, after all it was over thirty years since we had met. Truly this reunion was one of the happiest moments I have experienced in my ministry for Jesus. It was at this very mission hall that the seed was first sown in my young heart and it was wonderful to return home. Naturally I was excited and even nervous. If someone had told me as a child that I, the unruly and difficult Doreen, would one day stand up on the platform and preach of the wondrous love of Jesus, I would have doubled up in fits of laughter and thought them mad. Yet here I was after all those years of sin and shame, doing exactly that.

When I walked into the Mission, memories came flooding back to me. The main hall had hardly changed in all those years save for a new extension at the back. The seats were the same and so was the platform. It was quite an experience to see it all again and scenes from my childhood came flooding back. Some of my childhood antics brought a smile to my face. I remembered particularly that on the nights when prayer meetings were held, I would stand on the top of an old oil storage-tank which was outside the window and as the congregation were singing "Showers of blessings, showers of blessings we need . . . " I, much to the delight of my little band of followers, picked up handfuls of the small pebbles that lay outside the hall and threw them through the open window. The congregation certainly got their showers, only they were showers of pebbles, and at that time they were not much of a blessing!

The reunion tea was wonderful. The tables were beautifully laid and we all chatted and laughed about the old days. I was very moved when I was presented with the gift of a blue dressing-gown, which is so handy to pack when like me you do a lot of travelling. I was too moved for words and all I could manage was "Thank you everyone, thank you."

The meeting was tremendous and I will never forget that evening. The main hall was packed to capacity as was the new extension. All had come to hear the story of a local girl, a girl from Uxbridge. An amazing story, but not as amazing as the story of Jesus and His amazing Grace which though old, is ever new. Hasn't the Lord been good to me? Hasn't the dear Lord been good to us all?

On the night that I preached in Hounslow, word came to me that my father was seriously ill. I went straight away to his bedside at Hillingdon Hospital, but he was asleep. I returned the next day and his hand gripped mine very tightly as tears ran down his face. "Please forgive me, Doreen," he said. I was also in tears since, despite all that had happened in the past, I still loved him. "There is nothing to forgive," I told him, "so please don't worry Dad." He then asked me to pray for him. Words cannot describe how I felt as with tears running down my face, I asked the Lord to save my father. I also asked the Lord to heal him if it be His will and my dear old dad was very touched. My dad passed away some time later, but I know that the Lord took him as his own and that one day there will be another happy reunion when I see him again in glory. "Goodnight Dad," I said, "I will see you in the morning, over there."

Some months later I was again in the London area and it was a great pleasure to speak at my old school, the Greenway School in Uxbridge. I had not exactly been a willing scholar and I could never have dreamed that one day I would return there to speak. The boys and girls heard about my sinful life and how the Saviour had made me a new person. The school has been enlarged since I was a pupil and I took the opportunity to walk round the old part. It was strange to walk down those corridors thinking about the old days when I was there. I knew the corridors better than the classrooms as I had seemed to spend most of my time standing outside the classroom for some misdemeanour or other. It is wonderful how I, who left school with so little knowledge, now visit many schools and colleges every year to tell my story and warn of the dangers of drugs and the occult. It is even more wonderful that this is my second book dedicated to the Saviour! Walking round the old school made me wish I had been a more attentive pupil. Nevertheless the Lord has been good to me and has taught me many things. When I speak at schools it is just like being a teacher!

When the meeting at Greenway School ended, I went to the home of Miss Olive Maynard, and over tea we talked about old times. It was really marvellous. Not only has it been thrilling for me to meet my old Sunday school and Messenger teachers and helpers, but it has also provided further inspiration and encouragement to Sunday school teachers of the present day. Let me give you an example. The venue was Bournemouth and I was preaching with Dr Eric Hutchings and his team. Through lack of time I had not made acquaintance with many of the people with whom I was sharing the platform. To a crowded hall I firstly gave my testimony in the form of an interview.

"Doreen, having led the life of a prostitute, drug addict, and Satanist was there ever a time when you came under the sound of the Gospel?"
"Yes, when I was a child I attended the Waterloo Road Mission in Uxbridge, but I am afraid I played up a lot."
"In what way?"
"Well, I and my band of followers disrupted the meetings. We used to put our own words to the hymns and choruses and giggle and make loud remarks all through the open meetings which were held before the classes. Eventually we had to be turned out. I well remember the Superintendent coming out to chase us away and then we threw stones at the windows and kept opening and slamming the door. He never did catch me at it as I was always too quick for him."

The congregation roared with laughter. Little did I know that sitting right behind me on the platform was the very man of whom I had been speaking. What a surprise it must have been for him! I then went on to give my full testimony and it made a considerable impact on the congregation. Many people came forward at the end of the meeting to give their hearts to the Lord. When the meeting was over, an elderly man came up to me and said, "My name is Mr Lunn. I was the Superintendent at the Waterloo Road Mission." I very nearly collapsed, but I soon got over the shock and we were both excited to meet again after so many years, and in this way. "It seems you have caught me at last," I said, and we both started laughing. These proceeding were going on in full hearing of many people who had not yet left the hall. They must have wondered what was going on up there on the platform.

Some of the people on the platform were also wondering what was happening and, eventually, Dr Eric Hutchings came over to see what was going on. His face lit up when we told him of our reunion and he called both of us over to the microphone. Meanwhile those left in the hall and those remaining on the platform were looking at us with great curiosity. Dr Hutchings spoke, "Ladies and gentlemen, may I have your attention." He called upon Mr Lunn to step forward. "This ladies and gentlemen is Doreen's old Sunday School Superintendent. He has been sitting with us on the platform all evening and Doreen knew nothing about it." You can imagine the reaction that followed. He continued, "Hands up all those who are Sunday school teachers or youth workers." We were all surprised to see the number of hands raised. What a wonderful end to an already happy evening. Mr Lunn and I were photographed together and I treasure that photograph. I know that many of the Sunday school teachers present were encouraged to go on sowing the good seed in the hearts of those young who come under their guiding hands. So, teachers, take heart. You never know who you are teaching or what they will become. A typical class might contain future missionaries, pastors, and evangelists, or even someone like me! Sometimes the most difficult child will turn out to be the most loyal and fervent Christian with a real passion for God's work.

When I was first converted, someone referred to me as a rough diamond. I didn't fully understand the meaning of that phrase, but now I do. The diamond has to be dug from the darkest parts of the earth. When it is first quarried it is rough and unpolished. However after being placed in the hands of an expert it begins to assume a more attractive form. The skilled lapidary transforms the rough unfinished stone into an object of beauty. The rough edges are filed away and facets cut to allow the glowing natural colours to shine through with an undreamt-of brilliance. Only then is the true value of the diamond to be seen and appreciated. When Jesus digs people from the dark pit of sin, they, too, may be rough and unpolished. They are, however, very precious and when His loving work has been wrought and the true colours show through then the true value of His work can be seen. He has wrought a miracle in my soul and He continues to do so. Should you ever go into a jewellers to purchase an expensive stone, it is probable that the jeweller will place the stone on to a dark velvet cloth. The resulting contrast enhances the beauty of the stone. We are like His jewels set against the dark background of sin. The stars shine brightest in the darkest sky. Let us be as lights, burning ever brighter as sin darkens the background.

As a child one of my favourite hymns ran:

When He cometh, when He cometh,
to make up His jewels,
all His jewels, precious jewels.
His loved and His own,
like the stars of the morning,
His bright crown adorning,
They shall shine in their beauty
Bright gems for His crown.

Little children are just like jewels and are very precious in His sight. Jesus said, "Suffer little children to come unto me, and forbid them not: for of such is the kingdom of God" (Luke 18:16). Jesus took little children into His arms and blessed them. It is sad that all too often children are merely tolerated or are regarded as nuisances. This is very wrong. Sunday school is very important as it gives the Christian Church an opportunity to take an interest in children, it particularly helps children from difficult homes. Therefore the Sunday school should never be the Cinderella of the Church, indeed it should be constantly before the whole Church reminding Christians of the presence of the children and encouraging prayer.

My Sunday school teacher often referred to the City of God, that bright place where no sin could enter. I tried to imagine what it would be like to dwell in such a place where there would be no need for candles or even for the light of the sun, "for the Lord God giveth them light" (Rev. 22:5). No sin, no tears, no night. Oh, how wonderful I thought as I tried to visualize the golden street as we sang:

> There is a City fair,
> Closed are its gates to sin.
> Naught that defileth,
> Naught that defileth,
> Can ever enter in.

Closed to me I thought, knowing full well that there was sin in my heart. What's the use I thought, I will never get in because I am a thief and a liar, and the Sunday school teacher had said that if you were a thief or a liar you could never enter through those pearly gates. But very often there was no food in the house and as we had to eat, I stole, not only for myself but for my sisters and others. So how could I enter that City or walk down that golden street?

I thought that if I told the teacher of my sin I would end up in real trouble, so I simply gave up hope. But, nevertheless, I had got the message, proof that I had learnt something at Sunday school, despite all my misbehaviour. The gates of that City seemed a long way off, completely out of my reach, but I often thought about it all. I imagined myself approaching the gates in my old dress carrying my burden of sin. Two angels with flaming swords would block the entrance and shake their heads, indicating that I could not enter. Wouldn't it be wonderful to walk those golden streets. I knew how dirty the streets of this earth could be. I spent most of my time as a child roaming the streets, often until late at night. At that time it seemed that nothing would ever change my way of life. I longed for the light that outshone all others. No candle! I had often had to light a candle at night, as our electricity was usually cut off and my young sisters were afraid of the dark. When the candle went out they would cry and cling to me as we lay on a pile of dirty coats. Those old coats piled on to the bare floorboards provided the only bed we ever possessed. It was always a blessing to have a candle to dispel the darkness, but how I longed to live in a place where not even a candle was needed. Things got worse and eventually my mother could no longer cope and she left us. That broke my young heart. By the time I was fourteen I felt old beyond my years and the City of God seemed further away than ever.

It was not long after this that I became one of the youngest prostitutes on the streets of London. If I had thought the streets of Uxbridge were dirty I was soon to discover that the back streets of Paddington were far worse. Walking the streets alone at night is part and parcel of the life of a prostitute. A prostitute sees many things as she goes about her precarious business and so did I. The scrawled graffiti on walls indicating the confusion in peoples lives; rubbish blowing about in the wind; peeling walls, broken window-panes; and the drab dwellings where people lived in squalor and despair. By this time I had almost completely forgotten the City of God. I began to walk down many streets and found that they all led to degradation. The road to prostitution led to emptiness and guilt and utter loneliness, while the road to drug addiction led me eventually to prison. The darkest road of all, led me to demon possession and near suicide. This was the road of witchcraft.

Then in 1964 I heard of another road; the narrow road that leads to everlasting life. Could it be that one so wretched and vile as I would one day be transformed and walk the golden street arrayed in fine white linen, in that City of God. *Yes*, it was possible, wonderfully possible because Jesus Christ the Son of God died to redeem our souls from death and Hell. At last I found the way, the true and living way through the Lord Jesus Christ who died in my place at Calvary. Wonder filled my heart as I read for myself the Word of God in the Scriptures—those

Scriptures that I had once despised. The more I read about the City of God, the more real it became until I almost felt I could reach out and touch it.

Some time later I had a wonderful vision which confirmed to me that I, Doreen, was bound for the City of Zion. I was resting one afternoon when I was caught away in the Spirit and was carried in my mind to the City of God. I was dressed in a pure white robe. I was barefoot and in the distance I could see the City. As I was carried nearer I saw three gates inlaid with pearl, and the light from the City was brighter than the sun. The walls were made of precious jewels and the colours were more brilliant than any colours I had ever seen before. As I came nearer I saw two beautiful angels standing on either side of the gates, just as I had imagined as a child. They were dressed in fine white robes and their wings were a fine delicate gold. As I was carried nearer one of the angels looked at me and smiled a wonderful smile, the radiance of which was too wonderful to describe. He raised his hand towards his mouth and with a loud cry said, "No condemnation, let her in." As he did this the pearly gates swung open wide and I was carried through into the City while the angelic host took up the same cry, "No condemnation, no condemnation." The cry echoed through the City like the sound of mighty waters mingled with the road of thunder and the sound of sweet music.

Suddenly I was standing alone on the golden street in the City of Zion. A clear pure stream ran down the centre of the street and a big tree grew in the stream. The light was brighter than any earthly sun and a sweet peace filled the air. Before I had time to take in any more, I saw a woman coming towards me. I knew at once that it was Mary Magdalene. I ran to meet her and we threw our arms round each other and went skipping happily down the golden street. Then quite suddenly I saw another woman coming towards us. I recognized her as the Woman of Samaria and we ran to embrace her. "I have preached about you both," I said and we all went down the road skipping and singing. The Woman of Samaria said to me, "Look!", and she pointed to the stream. She stooped down and drank of the water and then we all splashed about in the stream in complete joy. It was all so real and so wonderful.

"Where is Jesus?" I asked. "He is coming soon," said Mary Magdalene, and even as she was speaking the two women disappeared and Jesus was standing beside me. His face was so beautiful and His eyes burned with deep love as He looked at me. I saw the scars that were made for me and then gently He took me by the hand and led me slowly back to the pearly gates. The gates swung open for me to leave and I was very sad. "Look yonder," said Jesus. I looked and saw a narrow pathway winding its way up towards the City. "Will you go and bring others into this City?" Jesus asked. I bowed my head. "Yes Lord," I replied and straight away I was standing on that narrow path outside the City.

The next time I saw the City, it was far away, but I could see the angels guarding the gates. The stones beneath my feet were very sharp and my feet were bleeding. The way was long and hard and I was very lonely. Yet, in my heart I knew I was not alone for the presence of Jesus became very real to me. In the distance I saw others coming along the narrow path. Many were weary and tired and I knew I had to help them along. Some were sick and I knew I had to comfort them. Others stumbled and fell and I knew I had to help them to their feet. Some were not on the pathway, but were walking alone along another pathway that ran parallel to it. It was a broad and easy road and I knew that it was the road to destruction. I knew that I must point the way and lead them to the City of God. The vision ended. But I carry that vision with me always deep in my heart.

How gracious the King of Glory is to show us such things. Often it is to prepare us for what He has in store for us in the future. Jesus loves us so much. Jesus is all love and He longs to visit us and commune with us. Often He comes in the dead of night when His children feel that they are walking alone. When dark shadows cross our pathway and when discouragements weigh us down, Jesus comes. He cannot do otherwise because

He loves us so much. He comes today. He will come tomorrow. One day He is coming back in power and glory to snatch away "His waiting bride".

When I ponder on God's great love, my heart is filled to overflowing. Oh what manner of love the Father has bestowed upon us that we should be called the sons and daughters of the living God. What love can be more merciful, more pure, and more kind, than the love of Jesus. "But where sin abounded, grace did much more abound" (Rom. 5:20), and reader, if you should be in the grip of the controller of Hell, Jesus can lift you up. His love is like a never-ending river that knows no bounds but flows on and on, giving joy and blessing. Human love, wonderful though it may be, pales into insignificance compared with His Divine love. Human love is restricted, its ability to express itself is limited, but the love of God which comes from above is immeasurable. Human love can be debased by lust or deteriorate, or be degraded by jealousy or envy. Many a heart and home have been broken in the pursuit of human love. But in His great love there is no darkness at all. There is no forgetfulness, no unfaithfulness, and no disappointment. His love is unfailing.

Some types of love have no vigour or height. They are weak and sickly. They have no power to uplift. The purer the love is, the higher it is and such love always uplifts and never degrades. Restricted love is like a stagnant pool—confined—it cannot flow out. The higher form of love is liberal and generous. Have you ever watched a waterfall and seen the sunlight play on the waters as they cascade down? A beautiful sight isn't it? The beauty is the result of the height of the fall. If we want our love to be an inspiration to others it must have height and be able to reach down.

God's love also has depth. Jesus stooped low to wash the feet of the disciples. He sat with publicans, tax-collectors, and sinners. We read, "But [He] made Himself of no reputation, and took upon Him the form of a servant, and was made in the likeness of men" (Phil. 2:7), Jesus humbled himself and was obedient even unto death.

God's love can reach down to the shame of prostitution and witchcraft and lift people up to sit in heavenly places beside Christ Jesus. That is what He did for me. What a Saviour.

God's love is as high as the heavens and is broad enough to encompass the entire human race. His love is as deep as the deepest ocean and is eternal.

Some people try to limit the love of God. They try to impose restrictions of social status, colour, sex, and denomination on His love. But God's love is not limited in any way and is forever free and boundless. What an amazing wealth of love. Yet despite this millions are starving in the midst of plenty. They long for love and do not seem to realize that they can taste the love of God and eat at His table. I was like that. I yearned for love as a child and also as an adult. All I found was a low, puny, and degraded form of love which was insignificant and impermanent. It did not lift me up at all. Then I tasted the pure, deep, real love of Jesus and His Divine love lifted me up from the very depths of Hell itself. What He has done for me, He can do for all men, no matter how low they have sunk or how far from the narrow way they have strayed.

I can never fully express how great His love is or how much I love Him in return.

My love for Jesus is a bridal love and my heart and eyes are firmly fixed on my Heavenly Bridegroom and the Eternal City. When I think that Jesus chose me to be part of His Holy Bride, my soul is flooded with the deepest praise and adoration.

The Christian's hope is—the return of Jesus. Yes a glorious day is coming when Christ the Heavenly King will come with a shout of triumph and those that are waiting and ready will be caught up in His arms. What a glorious day that will be when we see Jesus face to face and be recognized as His children. When the crooked paths are straightened and the dark things made plain. I want to be ready for that wonderful day. I want to keep myself pure and unsoiled by earthly things in preparation for that day. I want to walk through the gates and into the City of Zion that John saw. There will be no more tears, no more pain, no more sorrow, and no more darkness. There will be no parting and, as such, no need for reunion. Will I see you there? Will you be in that happy, holy band of saints? If you are not already on the narrow way bound for the City of God then place yourself there for I would love to meet you in the greatest reunion ever known.

CHAPTER NINE

A brand-new life

"Therefore if any man be in Christ, he is a new creature: old things are passed away; behold, all things are become new"
(2 Corinthians 5:17).

IT is a wonderful thing to wake up in the morning ready to face another new day in Christ. But it wasn't always like that. There was a time when I used to dread having to face another day. A day of constant fear and worry. Would I be able to get the drugs I needed? Would the pusher turn up and, if he did, would I have enough money to meet his price? And if I managed to get hold of a supply, would I be able to find a vein that I could "fix" into? What an awful, dark, satanic bondage. Yes, it is wonderful to wake up without those terrible fears. I do not need drugs anymore and I am free from that awful bondage. When I think back to those dark times I often wonder how I managed to survive all those years. I should have been dead long before I was set free. I firmly believe that the Lord Jesus Christ preserved me and kept me from certain death so that He could work the miracle that He did in my life. Even after I was saved, the doctors could do nothing to help me. But Jesus healed both my body and my mind.

So, every morning when I wake up I say, "Good morning, Jesus, thank you for another new day of loving and serving Thee." And when I hear the birds singing I often join them and dance and sing with complete joy, full of the sheer wonder of living. Every night before I go to sleep I say, "Good night Jesus, thank you for everything you have done for me today."

I am living a brand-new life in a brand-new way thanks to Jesus. It is like being born again in the flesh as well as in the spirit. I get excited about my brand-new life and, indeed, I have much to be excited about. There is nothing exciting about the life of a drug addict—a dreadful life full of misery and fear. There is nothing joyful about plunging a needle into your arm three or four times a day. Believe me, it is a hell on earth. For the drug addict there is no rest or peace for mind or body. Is it any wonder that I am excited about my salvation? But no words of mine can ever begin to express how wonderful it feels. Jesus gives a sweet peace and rest that all the world and its pleasures can never give and can never take away. When I served Satan, I served him through fear. But I serve the Lord Jesus Christ willingly because I want to—and that is love. As a Satanist I spoke to Satan because I was afraid what would happen to me if I refused. As a Christian I speak to Jesus because it is sweet to have fellowship with Him and He blesses me for it.

Satan wanted a token of blood, so I gave him of my own. In contrast, Jesus shed His precious blood on Calvary and gave Himself for me. What redeeming love!

Satan loves no one. I have actually heard him speak in the temples of his followers and never once did he say, "I love you." Satan is incapable of love and is afraid of the power of love. Jesus on the other hand loved me, even in my shameful and sinful state. Jesus loved me long before I knew and loved Him, and that is real love.

Satan died for no one. Christ died for the entire human race—past, present, and to come. If you offend Satan in any way you will surely be punished. If you offend Jesus and then truly repent, He will instantly forgive you. That is Grace. When Satan materializes in one of his vile temples he could be nowhere else since, unlike God, he is not omnipresent. My God is everywhere and Jesus Christ never leaves His children lonely. He is with us always; all of us.

Satan is a deceiver and is the father of lies. Jesus is the epitome of grace and truth. Satan destroys minds and bodies. Jesus restores bodies and souls.

One young Satanist I knew actually gave one of her hands to Satan. Her hand was literally chopped off as she stood at the high altar in the temple. The hand was then offered to Satan as a sacrifice. Many of the Satanists who witnessed this abomination, collapsed while others were violently sick. The girl herself, as well as many of the others present were in a trance. The girl felt no pain and this was seen as a miracle. I was neither sick nor in a trance. I was simply revolted by the entire spectacle. How stupid that girl was. I dared not voice my opinions at the time for fear of reprisal. Others in the temple gave fingers or toes in sacrifice. I am glad that I never fell into that trap. Jesus kept me safe even at that low point in my life. These people were maimed for life, and for what? *Nothing!* Satan gave them nothing! What kind of a miracle do you call that? What use has Satan for dismembered limbs? *No use at all!* There was no miracle, just futile and ugly sacrifice serving no purpose.

In the Gospel of John, Jesus says of the Devil that he is a thief and a robber who comes "to steal, and to kill, and to destroy"; and goes on to say, "I am come that they might have life, and that they might have it more abundantly" (John 10:10). Jesus heals and restores minds, bodies, and souls. He mends empty, broken, and shattered lives. He healed and restored my life. Which master would you rather serve? No one can tell me that a life in Christ does not work, for I have the proof that it does. I am living proof that it does! One ounce of personal experience is worth ten tons of theory.

Once I was witnessing to some prostitutes when one of them said, "We will give you three months before you are back on the streets again with us." That was thirteen years ago and I am still full of joy in the brand-new life that I have been given by Christ Jesus. What more proof is needed? Christ's keeping power is real and permanent. With this new life I have a new heart and a new spirit. The Lord has taken away the stony heart from my flesh and has given me a heart of love (see Ezekiel 36:26). Before I knew Christ I cared for no one. I led a totally selfish life dominated by drugs, and caring only for my own pleasures. My life was dominated by the word "Me", and nothing else mattered at all. But when Christ took control of my life He changed my stony heart into a caring heart. I care about people now. I care what happens to them and I try to help them in any way I can. Who could have been responsible for this transformation if not Christ?

Christ liveth in me, and it is Him that makes the difference. Only He can change a selfish and hard heart into a tender, loving, caring heart. We may try to change ourselves, but we will fail. Only if we have Jesus with us can we change. I have even spoken with Christians who have said to me, "I am not the Christian I used to be. I have tried to change but I have failed. Why? I have tried to pray more and have more patience and understanding. Why do I always fail?" They fail because their own strength is not enough. They should rely on the Lord Jesus Christ, and let Him change them from the inside. The more we depend on Jesus, the more problems we offer up to Him, the more He can help us. We must allow Him to help us. If we try to achieve radical change in ourselves, by ourselves, we will surely fail.

Only Christ can change a hard unloving heart into a compassionate and caring heart. He takes away all the old grievances and grudges. I had had many "chips" on my shoulder as a child and during adult life these had grown into "logs". My heart was full of hatred and bitterness, but Jesus took away all these. He swept away all the ugly cobwebs of hate and filled their places with His love which gave me a new heart and a new spirit. He has given me a new song to sing. "And He hath put a new song in my mouth, even praise unto our God" (Ps. 40:3). I no longer want to chant and wail to Satan or his demons, as I used to. This was the music of the Devil, if, indeed, you can call it music. It is inspired and written by Satanic forces. The wailing has the ring of death about it and it is uncanny. If you have heard it in horror films, then what you have heard is an accurate representation.

In sharp contrast to this but just as evil, are the modern rock and roll groups whose beat and rhythm rejects any kind of moral restraint. Aggression, rebellion, and sexual promiscuity are stimulated or heightened by this kind of music. It numbs the senses and induces a state of moral oblivion. With writhing, palpitating bodies, thousands are carried away, gripped by the ceaseless beat and with an uncanny light in their eyes and a seductive smile on their lips. This type of music has corrupted the youth of the world with its morally erosive force. The truth about such music and its origin is further confirmed when you hear that often such tunes are composed while under the influence of alcohol and drugs. Now we have what is called "Punk rock", the spitting, swearing, bottle-throwing, savage rock of rebellious youth that is sweeping teenage Britain. Performers swear and spit on stage and their songs often lead to acts of violence. Audiences get very tense and excited and "fans" are often seriously injured in riots. Punk operates on a very short time-fuse. Scuffles and fights break out in an atmosphere as unpredictable as a home-made bomb. During one concert a girl lost an eye after being hit by a flying bottle. At another, a girl bit off her boy-friend's earlobe and the audience, in a trance-like state, watched as the blood flowed. It is the voice of rebellious youth. It is the voice of a rebellious generation.

Jesus gives us different songs to sing. Music that comes from the realm of the spirit. Music that is directly inspired by the Holy Spirit. These songs bring us closer to God and make His holiness, love, and mercy very real to us. They inspire us to love and serve the Saviour, to follow in His footsteps, and to keep His laws. Spiritual songs strengthen our faith and encourage us as we do battle against Satan and sin. Some of these songs have a joyful beat and rhythm, ringing with the notes of victory and triumph, as befits soldiers of the Cross. These songs always have the mark of the pure Holy Spirit of God upon them. As new creatures in Christ and members of the holy body of the Church of Jesus Christ we should "be filled with the Spirit" and speaking to ourselves "in psalms and hymns and spiritual songs, singing and making melody in [our] hearts to the Lord" (Eph. 5:18-19).

As a creature who is new in Christ I have a song. I love to sing the songs of Zion. My song shall always be of Jesus and all His wondrous love.

He has given me new garments to wear. These are my spiritual clothes. No longer do I wear the black robes of witchcraft. I burned all those evil robes as well as other evil objects on a huge bonfire and I ran round the bonfire praising Jesus. "For He hath clothed me with the garments of salvation, He hath covered me with the robe of righteousness" (Isa. 61:10). I now dress in a way that becomes a Christian. I wear modest and decent clothing. My new garments are "the whole armour of God" (Eph. 6:11-17).

As Paul concludes his Letter to the Ephesians, he depicts the Christian way as a war. As Christians, we are called forth to fight. Our repentance and faith are not the end, but rather the beginning of a new way of life which is essentially a struggle and an active fight with Satan and his forces. In this fight, however, we strengthen ourselves by resorting to the vast might of our God. We are faced with the forces of evil and we need spiritual weapons to arm us in this spiritual struggle. We need not fear for ourselves for we have to protect us the whole armour of God. With this defence we can stand against anyone and anything, even Satan himself.

Jesus is the author of our salvation and the mighty captain of our souls. We are His soldiers, and we ought not to be ignorant of the tactics of our enemy. Every soldier must be properly equipped for battle. As soldiers of Christ, we are instructed to put on the whole armour, literally the panoply of God. Paul urges us to an awareness of the nature of the fight. He warns us against "the wiles of the devil" (v. 11) and urges us to know his strategy. Guile and insinuation are the Devil's trade marks. He is a subtle foe for he schemes and plots, not openly but by stealth and cunning. He is also a powerful enemy (v. 12).

The principalities and powers of which Paul speaks appear to be beings and forces that originated in creation. (Cor. 1:16) but that now stand against God. These are coupled with the world rulers of darkness who according to the Book of Daniel appear to be demonic forces who control the evil ambitions of nations and rulers in an attempt to undermine the will of God. Satan and sin are not the results of a badly adjusted society, or the failings of a few petty individuals. Satan and his hordes are a mighty force trying to govern a world system against the will of God.

If we minimize the power of the Devil or of evil, we do so at our own risk. The enemy is spiritual and the foe we face attacks mind, body, and spirit. His sphere of operations is described as being in "high places". Literally, "heavenly places", meaning the sphere in which believers know full blessing in Christ (Eph. 1:3). The place where the sinner is raised by the quickening effects of salvation (Eph. 2:6). There Satan attacks us in the very region of the soul. He seeks to poison our sanctification, to damage our faith, to block the process of holiness, to penetrate the realm of our thoughts, and to pervert the very high calling of God. This is spiritual wickedness in high places.

The enemy is very real, and the effects of his activities are very real and often devastating. He enters our day and insinuates his purpose into our very thoughts and actions. Never underestimate him for to do so would mean that you lack awareness both of the nature of the constant battle against Satan and the forces of darkness with which we contend. So the Christian is instructed to put on every piece of the armour in order that he can face the enemy who seeks to destroy our souls. Notice that Paul tells us to put on the *"whole* armour of God", not just part of it.

The first and perhaps most important part of that armour of God is the helmet of salvation. First of all you must be born again by the Spirit of God—"But put ye on the Lord Jesus Christ" (Rom. 13:14) and "that ye put on the new man" (Eph. 4:24). Here is the helmet of salvation which must be worn by the warrior for Christ. We have known salvation or deliverance from the penalty of sin in the past and we daily experience salvation from the power of sin. As we wear this helmet, "the hope of salvation", we shall have deliverance in the future from the presence of sin, when the Church Militant becomes the Church Triumphant. The helmet of salvation is my daily protection against evil. I have been transformed by the power of God and I am instructed in God's Word to be "transformed by the renewing of [my] mind" (Rom. 12:2).

Next we must don the breastplate of righteousness. When we experience salvation, we then walk a new path. Jesus, our Captain is also the Good Shepherd and as we daily follow Him, He will lead us to truth and righteousness. We are instructed to follow after righteousness, faith, charity, and peace with those that call on the Lord with a pure heart. John makes this very plain, "whosoever doeth not righteousness is not of God" (1 John 3:10). Christ is our righteousness. We do have righteousness of our own selves; but as we follow Him this will grow. We must put on the breastplate of righteousness as a deliberate act, in obedience to God's Word. The righteousness that Paul speaks about in verse 6 of his Letter to the Ephesians, seems to be not so much the righteousness of Christ imputed to the believer, as that of the believer's character and practice springing from Christ's imputed righteousness. Basically the believer doing that which is pleasing in God's sight and avoiding that which is not. Righteousness is another vital part of the protective armour of God.

The next part of the armour of a Christian is the belt of truth. At the time of Paul, the belt was a symbol of soldiery. The girding up of the loins; the gathering up of the long flowing garments under the belt, was a vital prelude to marching or, indeed, fighting. The soldier was made more comfortable and more mobile and also, naturally, more effective.

We, as Christians, must don the belt of truth. Jesus rejoices when He sees His children walking in the truth. We must always speak the truth and we should hate lies and deceit and cast away all that is false. We cannot afford to be hindered by dishonesty, disloyalty, or deceit. If we are so hindered, we may well falter on the field of battle. We must walk in the truth. "I greatly rejoiced when the brethren came and testified of the truth that is in thee, even as thou walketh in the truth. I have no greater joy but that my children walk in the truth" (John 3:34).

The Christian soldier must also be well shod as were the Romans in the time of Paul. We must be prepared to use every opportunity to bring the gospel of peace to men and women. We must be alert and ready to tell of our Saviour. Paul speaks of our "feet shod with the preparation of the gospel of peace" (Eph. 6:15). In his time, gall traps or sharp pointed sticks set into the ground were often used to impede the progress of marching armies. Soldiers needed to be well shod to surmount these obstacles. We, too, by constant renewal in the Gospel of Jesus Christ, must be well shod if we are to be enabled to march forward, sure-footed, to victory. The Christian soldier, clad in his armour, now needs his shield and sword. In Roman times, the shield was very large and was made to cover the entire body. In combat, missiles first dipped in tar and then ignited were hurled through the air at advancing armies. The shield protected the soldiers from these fiery darts and, indeed, being made of leather, not only stopped the missiles, but extinguished their flames.

The shield of faith performs the same function for the soldier of Christ. With faith as our protection we can render all opposition harmless. Finally, we need the sword of the Word of God. This is indeed a deadly weapon. The Word of God is quick and powerful and more effective than any permissiveness, paganism, indifference and opposition to the Gospel, and most important of all the private onslaughts of Satan against our life and the Church of God. To use our sword effectively we must know the Word of God.

Thus the soldier of Christ is fully armed and protected, but he needs one other vital element. Prayer is the force by which the armour is held together. It must be earnest, constant, and all-embracing. Salvation, righteousness, truth, the Gospels, Faith, the Word of God, and finally prayer. This is the armour of the Christian soldier. This is *my* armour.

All Christians must ask themselves, "Am I fully equipped today?" We must all examine ourselves and ask, "Am I completely armed in full assurance of salvation, or am I naked and defenceless in the face of the enemy whose aim is my downfall and my destruction?"

Are you wearing your armour? If not, buckle it on now and *never* take it off.

Christ has given me a new perspective, a new vision, and new aspirations. Before I knew Jesus I never noticed the beauty of nature or pondered the sheer miracle of creation. All I thought about was drugs, drink, and witchcraft. When I was set free to serve Christ, I saw for the first time the beauty of the earth that God had provided for us. The splendour of blossom in the springtime and the tall trees swaying in the summer breeze, the tiny birds rising high in a summer sky and the majesty of a sunset. I had previously been blind to all these things and now Christ had opened my eyes you can imagine my joy.

The first time I properly "saw" a carpet of bluebells in the lush, green wood I literally danced among them with joy. I now also "saw" my fellow human beings. People with heartaches, sorrows, and burdens. People with no hope and with no heavenly pilot to guide them across life's troubled sea. Many people are blinkered and have only limited vision. They see only those things that are directly in front of them; their own needs, their own problems, their own families. They are not able to look around and see the problems and needs of others. This "I'm all right Jack" attitude is very prevalent today and, indeed, it was at one time my own approach to life. But now my vision is wide and all-encompassing and I can see need all around me. My vision extends beyond the immediate horizon to distant lands and peoples with different creeds and cultures. I can say, with John Wesley, "The world is my parish." We read "Where there is no vision, the people perish" (Prov. 29:18). This is so true. Moses turned aside when he saw the burning bush and when the Lord saw this he spoke directly to him from the burning bush (Exod. 3:3-4). Let us do likewise. Let us turn our heads to see and hear what God wants us to see and hear. Let us ignore the earthly things that distract us so easily. Let us look away from the small and petty things and let us instead have a new and fresh vision. There are so many distractions that can divert our attention from God and His perfect will for our lives. We must guard against them.

If your vision is limited, ask God to remove the blinkers or the distraction or whatever else blocks your view. He will give you new sight and open your eyes to eternal and spiritual truths to which you were previously blind. He will show you new paths of service for Himself and others. Do not be content with limited vision. Do not be content to paddle in your own tiny pool. Instead, launch out into the vast ocean of God's fullness of blessing and service. Here are some of the new things that are to be found in Christ Jesus.

There is brand-new life—abundant and everlasting life.

There is a brand-new song.

There is a brand-new heart and a brand-new spirit.

There are brand-new clothes to wear and there is brand-new vision.

On top of all these things, for those that love and serve Him here below, there is a brand-new name written down in glory.

I cannot be content to keep all these joys to myself. I want to share them with others. I want to share them with you.

CHAPTER TEN

Yielded clay

"For I reckon that the sufferings of this present time are not worthy to be compared with the glory which shall be revealed in us" (Romans 8:18).

I RECEIVE many letters from Christians, and others, who are, or who have been, suffering, so I write this chapter especially for them. I write for those travelling through the shadowy valley in the hope that it will help to bring them through the darkness and into a deeper and sweeter relationship with God. I have experienced suffering in mind and body and I can, therefore, in some measure understand and help those that are in darkness. If we ourselves do not suffer, how can we really help those who are suffering.

Suffering often brings meekness. This is the key which opens the door to prayer. The meek and humble in spirit find it much easier to pray. Not many of us are willing to humble ourselves in our normal lives. If, however, external events turn against us and through failure, disgrace, or great physical pain and fear we are humbled, we will have no choice in the matter. When this happens we must take advantage of it.

Jesus was tempted and put to the test, just as we are. He was despised and rejected of men. He was a man of sorrow and He was well acquainted with grief. There is nothing that Jesus does not care about, His eyes search every dark corner of the earth. Jesus was tempted many times by the Devil. All through His life on earth He was put to the test. Let us look at the particular temptation that happened in the wilderness. Think of it! The Divine Son of God suffering in the desert wastelands with only the Devil for company. For forty long blistering hot days and for forty freezing nights He underwent test after test. He knew hunger, thirst, and pain but He never wavered. Look how humble Our Lord made himself. He knew that He had to experience as a man the things that men would experience, only in greater degree. Right from the beginning the King of Kings was lowly and humble. He left His Father's house, laid aside the glory that was His and took a lowly Jewish maiden for His earthly mother and a cattleshed for a birthplace. That is how humble Jesus was!

Paul wrote: "But He made Himself of no reputation, and took upon Him the form of a servant, and was made in the likeness of men" (Phil. 2:7). Only Jesus could forsake absolute heavenly majesty for absolute earthly meekness, so that mankind might be lifted up. This was a deliberate act. Jesus "took" the form of a servant. He might have come as a King dressed in silken garments, but He chose to come as a lowly born Jew in a country oppressed by foreign masters. In the Gospel of John we read that after Jesus had taken supper with His disciples, He laid aside His garments and took an ordinary towel and girded Himself with it (13:4). We see the Saviour surrounding himself with things of the earth, with things of man. He then stooped so low as to wash the feet of His disciples. He was willing to be humble to do so.

As Christians, we often fly high into the air on wings of inspiration, but we must also be prepared to come down and be humble in the way that Jesus was. Jesus came down from the mountain where He had been transfigured and went into the valley to face the mocking crowd. He then went to Calvary where in death He was glorified. The disciples wanted to stay on the mountain but Jesus bade them follow Him down into the valley where the first person they met was a demon-possessed boy. We too live in a demon-possessed world with sin and sorrow all around us. We must be prepared to follow Jesus down into the valley where we will come to grips with grief and pain and often even humiliation.

We will face problems that have no easy answers and some questions that perhaps cannot be answered on this earth, but face them we must. We have all been thrilled by large meetings where we see God move in a great and mighty way. At such times we are on the mountain and it is indeed wonderful. But very often we are brought back down to the valley with great suddenness and forced to face things that are not so beautiful and full of blessing. As true Christians we must also know Jesus in the dark valley. We must know what He means to us in suffering and humiliation.

God cannot make use of us if we simply stay on top of the mountain. The problems and the people that need our help are down in the valley and that is where we must go. It is easy to have faith on the mountain, but does our faith burn so brightly in the dark shadows of the valley? What use are we as disciples if we cannot walk with Him through the dark places as well as through the sunshine? A true disciple is one that can live in the midst of suffering and grief, trusting and calling on the Lord and daily surrendering to His will. Suffering moulds our character and makes us more beautiful on the inside. It gives us more compassion to help those in need. When we suffer ourselves, we are more able to help others who are also suffering. In suffering and humiliation we find our true worth and are given opportunities to put our faith to the test. Are we willing to descend and do the menial tasks with a smile? We should be willing if our faith is strong enough. We should be willing to work with no thought of self-sacrifice and with complete humility. However, we should never flaunt our "humility". This is the worse kind of pride. We must be totally sincere and servants of God and of those to whom He guides us.

For the Christian, suffering brings this lowly humble spirit. We may not even be aware of it but a most beautiful work will have been done in our souls by Jesus Himself. Many Christians will ask, "What have I done to deserve this?" It is not what you have done, but what the Lord wants to do in you. We do not have to know the reasons why, but we can be sure that there are reasons and that in His time God will reveal His purpose to us.

In Paul's Epistle to the Hebrews (12:11) we read: "Now no chastening for the moment seemeth to be joyous, but grievous: nevertheless afterward it yieldeth the peaceable fruit of righteousness unto them which are exercised thereby." Often it is afterwards, when the darkness has passed and the light is shining, that we understand the reason why the Lord permitted the period of suffering. The Lord allows many things to happen to bring us to a better relationship with Him. Very often the Lord has laid aside His servants in sickness, or caused difficult circumstances to arise and dark shadows to cross their ways, simply to bring them back into closer fellowship with Him. Many children of God have had their faith renewed and their souls restored in the dark shadows rather than in the bright green pastures.

But as Christians we can sometimes be so involved in "doing" the Lord's work that we neglect the Lord Himself. I can say from personal experience that suffering has in the end strengthened my faith and helped me to face future valleys of disappointment and discouragement with greater assurance and with increased faith that my Saviour will see me through.

"Why am I so tempted?" many Christians ask. The Bible tells us clearly, "count it all joy when ye fall into divers temptations; knowing this, that the trying of your faith worketh patient" (James 1:2-3). And who has not wished that he had more patience. I know I have and in fact it is one of my daily requests in prayer. I remember once I almost gave up praying for patience and then it dawned on me that I had to have more temptation and more testing of my faith in order to obtain the patience I sought. Being human I felt that I had been tested more than enough. I was frankly put off by the realization that only by further temptation would I achieve my aim. I realized that if I didn't ask for more patience, then I would have absolutely none at all, and that that would be far worse.

We need patience more and more today. Our world is going faster and faster and the sheer pace of life imposes terrific strains on the little patience that we have. It seems that everyone is always busy and has little or no time to spare and that patience is largely a forgotten virtue. Even when people are on holiday, supposedly having a rest, they rush madly from one place to the next in an attempt to cram as much into their time as they can. We have to live in this busy, restless world. Jesus said that we were to be as lights in this dark world of sin. It is very easy to get caught up in the hustle and bustle of the world and to neglect the first basic truths that we were taught as babes in Christ. We must spend time in God's presence. We must have a "quiet time" when we commune with the Saviour and bring our problems and fears and joys to Him in faith. The words of a favourite hymn of mine sums this up perfectly.

Take time to be Holy, the world rushes on.
Spend much time in secret with Jesus alone.
By looking to Jesus, like Him thou shalt be.
Thy friends in thy conduct, His likeness shall see.

Suffering brings a quietness upon our hearts and a mellowness which pleases the Saviour. He can then speak to us more easily and draw us nearer His presence.

Let me share one of the experiences I had in the dark valley. It may help you if at present you are walking the same road in the same valley. When I first started my ministry I faced opposition. I was told that I should have a meek and quiet spirit and not be standing up in public giving my testimony. "You should do little jobs in the church and not travel away from home. A woman's place in the church is to be quiet and in the background." Naturally I was disturbed by this criticism and I turned as always to the Scriptures. Perhaps I should keep silent and give up preaching. I even at times wished I had been born a man, as so many people seemed to object to a woman preaching. I felt that then I would not be frowned upon. All I wanted to do was to tell others of the good things that the Lord had done for me but if people were going to be against me for so doing, then I did not think that I could carry on.

I am by nature a sensitive person and I can very easily be hurt if people talk about me or unduly criticize me. I was further confused as many doors were being opened for me to give my testimony. Surely it would be wrong to stop now! I became totally confused and at one point I even began to doubt my own salvation and deliverance. This, of course, was exactly what Satan wanted. I eventually decided to stop preaching and to bow to the opinions of those whom I thought knew better. Very soon all my joy ebbed away. I lost all confidence in myself and was convinced that everyone was against me. I became hypersensitive and was constantly on my guard, afraid to open my mouth for fear of saying the wrong thing. Jesus seemed very far away and my prayers did not seem to get further than the ceiling. In a very short time I had changed from a happy, trusting person, to a sullen, withdrawn, and very depressed woman. I even became sorry for myself and that is very bad.

This state of affairs continued for weeks. I would occasionally be bright, but then the doubts and fears would descend on me again. Then slowly, very slowly, the light came stealing through the shadows and Jesus Himself showed me the way that I should go. Jesus spoke to me and told me where I had gone wrong. In the first place I had listened to the voices of men and not to the voice of God. I had also taken parts of the Bible and tried to live up to them, while neglecting other equally valuable truths. I was trying to become meek and mild, to change myself in order that I might be acceptable in the eyes of men. I was not embracing the whole Word of God. I tried to force myself to pray. Previously I had prayed naturally and with no effort at all. Because of the opinions of men, I had examined myself to such an extent that it was like pulling a plant out of the ground in order to see if the roots were growing properly. I had forgotten that to be at perfect peace and rest with Jesus I had to abide in Him and as my Father, trust Him to guide me.

In the Gospel of John Jesus says: "Abide in Me and I in you. As the branch cannot bear fruit of itself, except it abide in the vine; no more can ye, except ye abide in Me. I am the vine, ye are the branches. He that abideth in Me, and I in him, the same bringeth forth much fruit . . . " (15:4-5). The fruits of the spirit are Love, Joy, and Peace. All of these fruits were missing from my life because I was wrenching myself away from the vine—Jesus. I had hurt my Lord as well as myself and I repented of this sin.

Slowly the light became brighter and brighter in the dark valley and eventually burst upon my anxious soul with a wonderful radiance. Like a potter, the Saviour placed me on the wheel and began to mould me into a shape pleasing to His sight and purpose. "Behold, as the clay is in the potter's hand, so are ye in mine hand, O house of Israel" (Jer. 18:6). This verse in particular spoke loudly to me and I rejoiced. It was not for me to criticize God for the way He had fashioned me. I should not say, "Look here Lord, why did you make me this way. I am not satisfied." If Jesus was happy with me the way I was then it was foolish of me to want to change myself into something else.

The Lord taught me a great lesson at this time. He showed me that He simply wanted me to be myself. He made me as I am and if He wanted any changes, then He would make them, *not* me. The Lord said, "Be yourself and shine for me." He wants this for all His children. He wants us to speak to Him in a simple childlike way and to tell Him plainly how we feel. Jesus understands.

He showed me the great women of the Bible and how they had been used for the glory of God. He said to me, "Will you do my bidding my child and go where I send you, no matter what men think or say?" I replied, "Yes, Master", and immediately the peace and love and joy of the Lord flowed into my soul. I felt like preaching to millions right there and then. I was back to my natural self, only better and stronger. My fellowship with Jesus was now even sweeter than before. To abide in Him and to do His will means perfect peace for soul, mind, and body.

About this time I attended a prayer meeting. By pure coincidence one of the hymns that was chosen applied to me and the turmoil that I had been in.

> Free from the fear of what men think or say,
> cleansing for me, cleansing for me.
> From ever fearing to speak, sing or pray,
> cleansing for me, cleansing for me.
> Lord in Thy love and Thy power make me strong,
> that all may know that to Thee I belong.
> When I am tempted let this be my song,
> cleansing for me, cleansing for me.

I very nearly jumped out of my seat for joy.

I am still sensitive, but I have learnt that it is better to please God than to please man. You cannot please everyone, no matter how much you try. "It is better to trust in the Lord than to put confidence in man" (Ps. 118:8).

If I have to suffer scorn for preaching about Jesus, then that is how it must be because I will talk and preach and sing about Jesus wherever I go. We must pass through many different valleys, but Jesus will see us safely through them all. This He has promised so we know that it is true. If you want real help and comfort, get down on your knees and pray. Prayer changes things. If you solely rely on man, you will be let down. Jesus, however, never fails.

Take your Bible in your hand and read it in faith. The Bible caters for every need and His Word is true from beginning to end. Remember Jesus has promised that He will not let you suffer beyond the limits of your endurance. He will always give you the means to bear whatever comes your way. If you abide in Him, He will help you to overcome any crisis, conquer any pain, solve any problem.

Jesus shapes and moulds in mercy, the clay that He loves so much.

124

The valleys of bereavement and great pain are the darkest valleys of all. When we think of the compassion of Jesus our own ability to sympathize is seen as a paltry thing. Day after day Jesus gives Himself unceasingly in a way that we will never fully comprehend.

While on earth He was frequently moved to compassion. He saw the leper by the roadside. A man hideous and repulsive, an outcast shunned by his fellows. Yet Jesus reached forth His hand and touched him. The King of Kings and Lord of Lords actually touched those leprous sores and made them clean. That's Jesus! That's the Lord I love and serve. He felt the grief of the broken-hearted widow, mourning the loss of her only son. He said, "Weep not" and raised her son from the dead. He spoke the words of life to the lonely sinful woman in Samaria. Others avoided her and brushed their garments aside when they saw her. She, too, like the leper was an outcast. No one wanted to know her. When she wanted to draw water from the well she had to wait until no one was around before coming alone to fill her pitcher. What loneliness she must have suffered. Can you imagine her sad dejected form? I can. I was once like her. No one wanted to know me.

We read in the Bible that Jesus must need to go to Samaria. Yes, to speak to this lonely woman. When Jesus came to the well, He approached her and spoke to her. Jesus was weary, but he found time to speak to this sad woman. Then began the longest recorded conversation that Jesus had and with such a sinful woman as this! She had come to the well for water, but Jesus gave her the water of life and I am sure that thereafter she did not hide from her fellows or skulk in the shadows. She could hold her head high, not in pride but in gratitude because her sins had been washed away by Jesus. She like me had known many men, but this man was different. This was the Messiah. Her life was completely changed when she met Jesus. Jesus came to seek and to save that which was lost and He saved her. He sought her out and saved her in the same way that He sought me out and saved me! This woman of Samaria became the first woman evangelist.

125

She went about telling men of Jesus in the same way that I do. When I was saved I went back to my former sinful companions and told them about the saving power of Christ. How could I keep such good news to myself?

If you are lonely, lost, and in sin, remember that Jesus came to seek you also and that He wants to speak the words of life to you, too. Jesus knows that even the truest, bravest, and purest soul must come to the hour of grief and agony. He not only sees the pain and sorrow that man sees, he also sees deep into the soul. He knows how fiercely the stormy seas are raging within the troubled breast and gently whispers, "Peace, be still." He sees the tears in the long, dark, lonely night and whispers, "Fear not."

So dear suffering ones, call upon Jesus right now wherever you are. He *will* help you and He will never leave you without comfort. He will always come to you.

Jesus who knows and orders the bounds of your trials also knows and orders the hour of your deliverance. When that blessed hour comes and when Jesus reveals to you His shining face and His presence is so near that you actually feel his gentle touch on your fevered brow, then you will know the full meaning and truth of His words, "My grace is sufficient for thee" (2 Cor. 12-9). Yes! In the dark and through the gloom there will be light. You will no longer be alone and the light of His Divine presence will break forth in a glorious radiance that will outshine the midday sun. How precious it is to trust Him, for your times are in His hands.

It is very saddening to think of the thousands of lonely and unhappy people that are suffering in mind and body, many isolated from the world and without a single friend to care for them. It is tragic that these people do not know the love of the greatest friend of all, Jesus Christ. If you, dear reader, are lonely and suffering, I have a special message for you. "Jesus really loves YOU. He really cares for YOU. Will you in your loneliness and in your emptiness cry out to Jesus? If you do He will abide with you and never leave you. You need never be lonely again. Jesus will be with you for eternity."

CHAPTER ELEVEN

Telling the world

"Go ye into all the world, and preach the Gospel to every creature" (Mark 16:15)

IT WAS raining hard when I left London Airport. My destination was the United States of America.

Up, up, and away the Jumbo Jet roared into the grey cloudy sky like a great silver bird. The higher we went, the closer I felt to my God and His heaven. Above the rain clouds, the sky was blue and the sun was shining brightly. It made my heart sing and it felt so good to be alive. Somehow I knew that good things were in store for me in the great U.S.A.

Travelling to different countries where the customs, climate, currency, and language are so different from our own is always a great challenge. There would be no language problem in America but the great sense of challenge was very present as we winged across the Atlantic.

I had been to America before, but this time it was all different. I was going there for Jesus and I really prayed that He would make me a channel of blessing and that His name would be glorified in all things and His kingdom extended.

Many questions were whirling round in my head. Would the Americans like me? What would I think of them? Were they curious to meet me as I was to meet them? I expected they were. After all it is not every day that you get to meet an ex-queen of witches. At least they knew I was coming by aeroplane and not by broomstick! I chuckled to myself as I thought of the welcome I would get if I did arrive by broomstick. Why the entire population of Michigan would be there to see me arrive. And look at all the money I would save on the air fare!

I often wonder what people really expect when they see me for the first time. I suppose they expect to see someone very unusual indeed and they are probably surprised to find me quite ordinary, with no broomstick, no long black cloak, no long pointed hat.

There had been a strike at London Airport and the plane was late in leaving which would mean missing my connection in Detroit. I was going to Kalamazoo. Yes, there really is a Kalamazoo. I later saw tee-shirts with just that slogan on them in many of the shop-windows. Due to engine trouble we made an unscheduled landing at Boston and by the time I reached Detroit I had been travelling for nineteen hours! I began to wonder if Kalamazoo really did exist and if I would every get there.

After a wait at Boston I eventually caught the last flight of the day to Kalamazoo where I arrived after a journey lasting twenty-three hours in all. I began to wonder what other problems faced me. To my utter astonishment a small crowd of Christians were waiting for me at the airport. It was a joy and a relief to see their smiling faces. Now I knew that something good was in store for me in America.

Despite the long journey my spirits rose. They gave me a great welcome and I was so happy to have arrived at last. I was really glad to see a nice comfortable bed again and I thought I would sleep for hours. Perhaps because I was excited and overtired I did not sleep as long as I would have liked, but nevertheless I had a good rest and awoke refreshed in mind and body and ready to go.

First impressions are important and I wanted to make a good impression and be the means of blessing to these dear American people who had been looking forward to my coming for months. Pastor William Smith had invited

128

me to his church some months earlier and had arranged all my meetings in America. He had worked so hard to get me there and my first meetings were to be held in his church, The Full Gospel Community Church.

Imagine my surprise when at the first meeting they all sang:

> We're together again, just praising the Lord.
> We're together again with one accord
> Something good is going to happen
> Something good is in store
> We're together again just praising the Lord.

I could hardly believe it. I wasn't even aware that such a chorus existed so I knew that the Lord had spoken to me on the plane when I had had those self-same thoughts in virtually those self-same words. Something good had already happened and so much more was in store. I felt I had known those dear Christians for years and that we had been gathering together to worship the Lord like this every Sunday morning.

They certainly knew how to praise the Lord. The Saviour was present at that meeting and we worshipped Him in Spirit and in truth. No matter where you are you will always feel at home with God's children when you know the same Heavenly Father.

Everyone always says that everything in America is so much bigger, but it is not until you actually go there that you realize how true this is. It is so big and very beautiful that it is breathtaking. With so much open space and so much room to move you feel compelled to go on and on to discover what other marvels lie ahead. And there is so much to see. The cars are bigger, the roads are wider, the shops and homes are much larger than we are used to, and there is so much space between buildings. The churches are very large and superbly equipped and even the butterflies are much larger than in Europe. All the jokes you hear about the size of everything in the U.S.A. are in fact true. Everything is much much bigger.

What struck me most of all though was the beautiful

warm summer climate. As soon as you step off the plane the warm air hits you and it feels good to be alive. At night the sound of the crickets make you feel as though you are in another world. I was told that in winter it becomes very cold with a lot of snow but I would be back in England long before winter and so I had no worries. I meant to enjoy the warm sunshine while I was able.

Six weeks of ministry lay ahead of me so there would not be much time for relaxing in the sunshine but I did enjoy travelling in the warm climate and found it really pleasant. This was just as well as I had a great deal of travelling to do and, of course, many people to meet.

People, their problems, their hopes, their sorrows, their fears, and their joys are the same all over the world. The dear Lord helped me to help them, to talk to them, to listen to them, and to pray with them and for them. Most important of all He helped me to love them.

The first week I was there I was given a little trailer home, that is a caravan which was parked in the church grounds. It was very comfortable and well equipped with all modern conveniences. I was very happy there.

One night after the service ended I was just about to go to bed at about twelve o'clock when I heard the sound of many motor-cycles coming down the road. They came to a screeching halt outside the church and some fourteen teenagers all laughing and shouting loudly made their way to my trailer. I knew I was in for a spot of trouble. They then started to bang on the side of the trailer shouting, "Hi, there, old witch, come on out." They then shouted, "Are you there witch, come out and show us your magic powers." They must have seen the posters and the advertisements in the local paper and they had come to have a bit of fun at my expense.

At first I decided to ignore them, but the noise was so great and the banging on the trailer so loud that this was impossible. Their language got worse and the whole thing was becoming very ugly. What should I do? There was no telephone inside the trailer so I could not call for help. I knew it would be foolish to leave the trailer, but I had to get rid of them somehow.

With a flash of sudden inspiration I slowly wound the window down stuck my head outside, and making my Cockney accent as croaky as I could I shouted out, "Go away or I will turn you all into toads." I've never seen people move so fast in my life. They were almost falling over one another as they ran to their motor-bikes and they sped up the road at full speed. I laughed so much I couldn't sleep for hours. My plan had worked.

I was privileged to appear on several television programmes while I was in the U.S.A. They were not all religious programmes either, so once again I was able to reach many thousands who never set foot inside a church. I believe that we should use every means at our disposal to spread the Gospel. After all, there is so much violence on television as well as crime, sex, and horror that it is good for some of the time to be given over to the Lord.

Television is a very powerful medium. Young people especially are very much influenced by what they see on the small screen. Millions of people are slaves to the television set in their living-rooms. I've seen people run around like maniacs during the adverts getting themselves something to eat. I've seen children cease working on their vital homework until a programme has finished. For so many people it has become the focal point of their lives. Family communication has broken down because, of course, you cannot talk while the television is on!

I am not against television. If I were I would never appear on it myself. I enjoy watching television but, like everything else, in moderation.

In America you can tune into as many as fourteen channels and in many homes the choosing of programmes is a constant source of family friction. Some families have television sets in almost every room and it is not unusual to see the family scattered all over the house, each watching their own personal favourite programme alone. This is very sad.

Television is here to stay and it is a part of all our lives. So it is good to appear on television now and then and to be able to tell people that there is something more to life than television and other wordly pleasures. I have known Christians who have sold their television sets when their family life seemed to be being adversely affected. I am not sure if this is the right thing to do. Often the children simply go into other people's houses to watch their favourite programmes or else roam around the streets aimlessly with nothing to occupy them. Personally speaking I would rather have my teenage children inside their own home watching television than at a loose end out in the streets, where many other dangers, far worse than television, await them. I am sure that moderation is the only answer. Find a happy medium through common sense and television need not be a problem.

The major problem which I encountered in America, especially among Christians, was depression. I meet this universal disease everywhere I go, but in urban America I came across depression and oppression far worse than I had encountered anywhere else. Perhaps because the pace of life is so much faster.

Depression is a serious disease. It often leads to broken marriages, total separation from friends and family, utter despair, and sometimes suicide. People suffering from depression tend to be very irritable, especially when they see people happy and in good health while they are in the pit of gloom. Small petty things seem to irritate them. Things that would otherwise pass unnoticed. There is normally a deep spiritual cause for depression among Christians as is shown by the following example.

She was a fine Christian and a tireless worker for her church. She was also subject to dark bouts of depression. Indeed, when I spoke to her, she was in the deep throes of a depression and she wanted me to pray for her. I found as I counselled her that she was hostile towards the church in which she worked, bitter towards the other workers, and even at times rebellious against God. She was angry at God for not healing her in the way that she wanted Him to. At times she had almost demanded that He heal her! Because God had not answered her prayers exactly as she wanted she became bitter, apathetic, frustrated, and critical of others. At these times she was gripped by a deep depression. She was obviously unaware that she had a greater problem than that of her lifelong illness. Her main problems were rebellion and pride.

Instead of repenting, she had persisted in her rebellion and her condition has become steadily worse over the years.

"Do you come daily to Jesus for cleansing?" I asked her.

"But I have been a Christian for years," she replied.

"Yes, but we still need Jesus to forgive us our sins. And we all commit many sins even after we have become Christians. Being a Christian does not make us perfect."

She snapped back, "No, I know that. But I am no worse than the others in the church!"

"Never mind about the others, it is you we are concerned about and you need to come again to the foot of the Cross and repent of the sins you have committed. Then, the blood of Jesus Christ will cleanse you from all sin."

I showed her the passage from Scripture beginning "And he is the propitiation for our sins" (1 John 1:2-9). In order to obtain and maintain complete deliverance, we must repent of the sins we commit or we will build up a great wall between ourselves and God and Satan is like a roaring lion walking about, "seeking whom he may devour" (1 Peter 5:8).

"But I have worked in this church for years," she persisted.

That was true but she still needed deliverance from all the things that bound her and that were holding her back from living a victorious Christian life and being a real blessing in the church. She was full of resentment towards everyone in the church. Pride held her back from putting things right and she could not see it.

"Don't you see that Satan has robbed you of your true inheritance as a child of God with joy, peace, love, and life in the Spirit?" I continued, "Tell me honestly, was there a time in your life when you realized that you were a sinner and needed salvation. Have you ever repented and accepted the Lord Jesus Christ as your personal Saviour?"

"Oh yes," she replied, "but that was years ago."

"How often since then have you really spoken to Jesus and told Him all your doubts and fears and asked Him to help you to live for Him?"

"Not very often," she admitted.

For the first time I caught a trace of sorrow in her voice and I could see that her resentment and pride were beginning to slowly slip away. Her lips trembled and her eyes filled with tears. I put my arm round her and said, "Do you know that Jesus still loves and cares for you and longs to set you free from the depression, oppression, rebellion, fear, and pride that you have in you. He wants to bring you into His perfect liberty and to make you a real blessing to your church."

"I don't know," she said, "I am not an easy person to get on with and people just don't understand me."

"Jesus can change all that and then people will marvel at the change in you."

"Do you really believe that?" she said quietly.

"I know it for certain. If you humble yourself and confess your sins He will also heal your body."

So it was that for the first time in many years, this woman repented and entered into the right relationship with God, confessing her great need of deliverance. As I watched her make her peace with God, my eyes too were filled with tears. I then laid my hands on her head and rebuked the oppression, fear, rebellion, and pride that was in her. Jesus set her free that very night.

It was worth going all the way to America just to see this woman, who had been bound for so long and robbed of her inheritance, completely delivered from the grip of Satan whose job it is to rob, oppress, frustrate, afflict, and wear down the saints.

While in America I spoke to many Christians who got very upset when I told them that Satan can deceive them and seduce them and cause them to backslide, and said that the Devil could not get through the blood line. And I agree, the Devil cannot get through the blood line, if the blood line is in fact there! These Christians were taking an un-scriptural view, that once a child of God and once washed in the blood of Jesus, we are immune from the wiles of Satan. These Christians refused to believe that Satan can afflict, worry, oppress, suppress, frustrate, confuse, or lie to a child of God. I pointed out that continuous freedom from Satan is not automatic and neither is freedom from sin. I do not believe that once delivered is always delivered. It all depends on a close walk with God as well as deliberately turning your back on all that is wrong. The Bible says, "Resist the devil, and he will flee from you" (Jas. 4:7); "Neither give place to the devil" (Eph. 4:27), and did Jesus Himself not say "Go, and sin no more" (John 8:11), and again, "Behold, thou art made whole: sin no more, lest a worse thing come unto thee" (John 5:14)

I have often had to pray for Christians who were once gloriously delivered from demonic power, but who had chosen to backslide and to return to their old ways. The demons have returned and they ended up in a far worse state than prior to their conversion. It has been extremely difficult for them to be delivered a second time. In many cases it has taken long days and nights to complete their deliverance.

This ministry, that of casting out demons, is one of which has been sorely neglected by the Christian Church. This is probably due to fear and ignorance. I am pleased that this particular ministry is becoming more prominent in this latter-day revival.

Many Christians have little idea what a demon actually is or what it can do. As Christians we are familiar with the ministering work of angels. These are spirits sent by God to do His work on earth (Heb. 1:14). But we often forget that there are evil angels, those who fell with Lucifer from their first high estate. Those who betrayed the trust of Jehovah. In the Bible we read: "And the great dragon was cast out, that old serpent called the Devil, and Satan, which deceiveth the whole world: he was cast out into the earth, and his angels were cast out with him" (Rev. 12:9).

Satan was created by God. He was beautiful and he held the position in Heaven. But through his rebellion and pride he tried to usurp the very throne of God, his creator and was cast out of Heaven. The Devil is not omniscient or omnipresent. His powers are limited. He thus uses the innumerable company of wicked spirits or fallen angels to do his bidding. He cannot do it all himself. There is no doubt about that. He has a well-organized army which is very well disciplined and which operates on his order alone. The only way that we can be safe from these terrible powers is by being constantly covered in the blood of Jesus. His blood means absolute defeat to the demonic host. There is no other protection other than the blood of Jesus. It is wonderful to know that God's children have a far greater and far more powerful host of angels to help and protect them, than Satan has demonic agents.

This is our victory. We have authority over the Devil and his demons. This is part of our glorious inheritance through Jesus Christ the risen Lord. If we walk in the light and obey His word, the Devil and his demons cannot harm us in any way. Indeed we can do much more harm to them! We are able to command them to depart in the name of Jesus and when we do this, they must obey. This was part of my message to Christians in America who were afraid of the Devil. And this is my message to all Christians everywhere.

I have met many Christians who enjoy playing cards for pleasure. I was asked what my view on this was and I gave this answer. The first deck of playing-cards was invented in 1392 for King Charles of Frances, who incidentally was insane. The Puritans later called the pack of cards, "The Devil's picture-book." Here is the true meaning behind the innocent-looking pack of cards and perhaps you will think again about using them once you have read the next paragraph.

The "King" represents the enemy of God and all his unrighteousness. He is thus the Devil himself. The "ten spot" cards represent the spirit of lawlessness and are in direct opposition to the Ten Commandments of God.

Associated closely with this card is the symbol of the "Club". These cards represent murder. The "Jack" or "Knave" represents the lustful libertine, the sort of man that lives on the earnings of prostitutes. This card thus represents a moral leper. It also represents sin. The "ace" stands for death, blackness, and horror.

Not many people know that there is a game called the "Brothel game". In this game the players converse with each other in extremely obscene and secret language, merely by dropping a card on to the table. Now we come to the wickedest part of all. The "Queen" represents the Virgin Mary, the mother of Our Blessed Lord. In this game she is called "the mother of harlots". The "Joker" stands for the Lord Jesus Christ. Therefore Our Lord is portrayed as a fool. As if this is not enough the secret language of the cards goes even further and declares that the "Joker" is the offspring of the lustful "Jack" and the "Queen" (the "mother of harlots").

What utter blasphemy! I would not have a pack of cards in my house. I know the evil that they represent. Witches and those closely associated with the occult use cards to trick and delude men and women into vice, error, deceit, and finally Hell.

Can you in all honesty, my friend, go on playing with the sinful pack of cards?

When my work at Michigan was finished I flew to Virginia Beach, where I stayed overnight at a luxurious hotel prior to appearing on a television programme called *700 Club*. This programme is networked throughout the U.S.A. When I arrived in Virginia Beach I was overwhelmed by the beauty that I saw all around me. The houses were beautifully built with lush green lawns around them and with shrubs of all varieties. It all took my breath away. It was rather like discovering a picture-book land, one which you thought did not really exist. But it did exist and you were in it.

My hotel was fabulous. I could never have afforded to stay there myself, but all this had been paid for. When I was shown to my room I just stood and looked around in utter disbelief. What a pity I was only staying for one night! My room had everything that you could ever wish for, even in your own home. My little overnight suitcase seemed lost in this large luxurious room. I felt rather like Eliza Doolittle in Bernard Shaw's *Pygmalion*. No sooner had the porter left me than the telephone rang. I nearly jumped out of my skin. Who on earth could be wanting me? Nervously I answered it.

"You are expected in the Hotel restaurant in fifteen minutes, Madam. Please come to the desk in reception and you will be escorted to your table."

"Thank you very much," I replied, and put down the phone.

I decided not to change my clothes and went into the bathroom to freshen up before going downstairs. The hotel was so huge that it took me at least five minutes to find my way to the reception desk, where I made myself known to the clerk. I was then escorted into the most exotic restaurant I have ever been to in my life. Smiling faces greeted me as I neared my table. These belonged to people who were also guests of the *700 Club* programme and who were to appear on television with me.

My fellow guests had come mainly from New York City, where they worked among drug addicts and drop-outs, seeking to lead them to a new life in Christ. They were as thrilled to meet me as I was to meet them especially when they found out that I had once been an addict myself and now share their work. We all knew that the Lord was going to bless the television programme the next day and we were all looking forward to it immensely. After a period of group prayer we retired to our rooms for the night.

The next day at the studios we were given a very warm welcome and made to feel at ease straight away. Our hosts gave us great encouragement and strength. I was interviewed by a lovely Christian who gave me freedom to tell my story of the saving grace of the Lord Jesus Christ. I know that the Saviour blessed my testimony and witness and I gave Him all the praise and glory. The witness of the other Christians was also wonderful and all our testimonies tied in with one another. This proved to me yet again, that it is worth serving Jesus in this world today and to tell of all His wondrous mercy.

After the programme I flew back to Michigan and re-commenced my ministry. I spoke in many churches as well as talking every morning on a radio programme. I enjoyed every moment of this work and there is truly great joy in serving the Lord. Pastor Smith was a great help and encouragement to me and accompanied me to most of the churches I visited, where he introduced me to the congregations.

One visit that was truly memorable was to the Calvary Temple Worship Center in Fort Wayne, Indiana. The Reverend Paul Paino is pastor of the church there and has a congregation of almost two thousand. What a thrill to see so many people and to tell them what Jesus has done for me. My testimony was also relayed live on radio and I thus was able to reach hundreds of thousands more throughout the States. Yes, something good was happening in America. Telling out the Good News of Salvation and the goodness of Jesus must be good, mustn't it?

My next stop was in Illinois where I attended a tent crusade. Once again I was hitting the sawdust trail for Jesus! People who do not go to church will often come to a tent crusade because of the more informal atmosphere. I feel this ministry should be more widely used today to reach people for Jesus. I met many people under canvas that week. People with problems—it was a joy to help them. People with burdens—it was a joy to share their burdens and pray with them. People who were strangers to Jesus—it was a joy to introduce them to Him and they were strangers no more.

I will say again, "There is *joy, joy, joy* in serving the Lord." The Bible says, ". . . in thy presence there is fulness of joy; at thy right hand there are pleasures for evermore" (Ps. 16:11). At these meetings His presence was very real, His joys were full, and it was the greatest pleasure imaginable to serve Him, and others.

One night a group of boys from a local remand home were present at the meeting. They had been brought by

139

one of their counsellors. They were rather boisterous at first, but as the meeting progressed they became involved and listened intently as I gave my testimony. Before I had finished my appeal for those in need to come forward to the front where I would pray with them, some of these boys were already there, waiting. What a wonderful sight it was!

They were kneeling on the ground in front of me, with bowed heads and earnest seeking faces. My heart skipped a beat and filled me with an overwhelming desire and longing that they would really prove to be trophies of grace for the Master. One Negro boy stood out from the rest and I went over to speak to him.

He began to speak in a frustrated voice, "I hate everybody. I hate my father and mother, I hate those who try to help me, and I hate the whole world."

"Do you hate me?" I asked him.

"No," he replied.

"Well then, you don't hate everybody in the world do you!"

Needless to say there were reasons for all the hatred in his heart. No one had really ever shown him love. His father had done nothing but beat him and his mother had probably given up in despair. He had grown up with hatred, violence, and revenge and in fear and anger, he simply started to hit back. After running around wild in the back streets he eventually teamed up with others in the same situation and embarked on a life of crime, stealing first from local stores and then graduating to motor-car thefts.

All attempts to help him had failed and he was eventually taken away from his home area. But every time they took him away, he absconded. He was crying out for help and yet when help was offered it came too late for him to accept it and he regarded it with distrust, suspicion, and hatred. What a sad story, but it is not an unusual one. This sequence of events is being repeated time and time again all over the world.

"Do you want to stop hating?" I asked him.

"Yes, I do, but I don't know how. I just can't stop

feeling the way I do."

His big brown eyes never left me as I gently told him of the great love of God who sent His only Son Jesus, to die for him on the cross of Calvary, that he might live.

"If you let the Lord Jesus Christ come into your heart, He will drive out all the hatred and fear and help you to forgive those that have hurt and wronged you."

He was not very sure about that, so I went on to say, "Jesus was crucified in hate, but He responded with love and with words like these, 'Father forgive them for they know not what they do'."

I knew I was getting through to him so I continued, "Hatred is a breeding ground for more hate. Hatred causes wars, bloodshed, and untold misery. Hate for hate only ends up in a vicious circle of hatred. It cripples and paralyses, but love releases and heals. Hatred darkens our lives, but love illuminates it. Only love can conquer and drive away hate, just as light drives away and dispels darkness. By its very nature hate tears down and destroys, by its own nature love creates, restores, and builds up. We can never overcome evil with evil. But evil can be overcome with good. As we commit our lives to Christ and experience the forgiveness of our sins, and walk in His way of love, we are then able to forgive others. You need a deep and lasting relationship with God, who is love. When you know Him, His love will cast out all fear, all hatred, and all darkness."

All the time I was speaking I was aware that his dark solemn eyes had never once left my face and I knew that he was thinking very deeply about what I was saying. This was something he had never done before as he had always been too busy hating, to do any serious constructive thinking.

"Will you give Jesus a chance and let Him come into your heart tonight?"

At once he answered, "Yes, I will."

That night he indeed received the Lord Jesus into his heart and life and for the first time he knew that he had a personal Saviour that cared for him.

What a joy it was to lead this dear boy to the Lord. His

decision had a considerable impact on the other boys and strengthened their resolve to make the same decision.

Next day I went to the remand home and gave my testimony to others that had not been at the meeting. The Negro boy was there and he was radiant, his big brown eyes shining with joy.

"I don't hate anyone anymore," he said, "I know everything will be all right now that I have become a Christian."

I did not want to leave, but when it was time for me to go I prayed that Jesus would keep him and guide him into more truth, more light, more love, and more faith as the days went by. Before I left I asked him, "Will you promise me something?"

He said that he would.

"Will you promise me that you will give these good people a chance to help and guide you, just as you gave me that chance last night. And will you read the Bible that I gave you every day and always ask the Saviour to help you? And remember that I will be praying for you."

He said he would, and he meant every word of it. In my heart I wished that I could have taken every one of those boys home with me and shown them how the love of Jesus guides me in my everyday living, but, of course, this was impossible. But I knew that the Lord would keep them safe.

The time had come for me to say good-bye to beautiful America, at least for a while. I was going home! It sounded so good and I could hardly wait to get back to see my family again after such a long absence. I knew that they felt the same, even though my time at home would be short. I would have only three days before I had to go abroad again on another mission. But that is what working for Jesus is all about. It often means sacrifice and always means obedience. But when you think of all the dear Saviour has done for us, then our work and sacrifices pale into insignificance.

There is no point in working for the Lord unless you are prepared to go where He leads and if necessary to make sacrifices. He makes up for this by pouring out all

His blessings upon us in abundance and by strengthening us for all that He has prepared us to do.

I was so looking forward to meeting my husband at the airport, but an industrial dispute at Heathrow meant that our plane was diverted to Brussels. We had to remain on the plane without air-conditioning or even food for a full three hours before we eventually took off for London. So you see it is not always easy. I then had the further disappointment of not being met at the airport and have to travel on the train to Bristol alone. Of course there are disappointments and discouragements, but it is so worth while serving Jesus that these do not matter. He is never a disappointment.

Imagine the thrill when at last I arrived home. I was bombarded with questions about America from my entire family who had come to greet me. Everyone was talking at once and I knew I was finally home. It felt wonderful.

My five-year-old granddaughter piped up, "Granny, are you going on that big aeroplane *again*?"

"Yes poppet, *again*!" I laughed as I swung her up into my arms and kissed her.

"I wish I could come on the big aeroplane, too, Granny."

"Maybe one day you will Angeline and we can fly away into the blue sky together, just you and me . . . wouldn't that be wonderful?"

"Oh yes, Granny, it would," she said, her blue eyes shining with pleasure.

I get tremendous pleasure from my little grandchildren Angeline and Samuel. Like most grandmothers I spoil them like mad. When I get the opportunity that is!

My own daughter chipped in, "Why don't you get your own aeroplane, Mum?"

"Oh yes, Granny, that would be a good idea," said Angeline, who really thought that that was the answer and clapped her hands in delight. Her quaint old-fashioned manner never ceases to make me smile.

I turned to my seventeen-year-old daughter Ruthie who had asked the question, "That will be the day

143

Ruthie, will you be the pilot when I do?" We both laughed at the unlikely event.

"Well, you would certainly make a great *impact*, if you did," joked my husband and we all roared with laughter. Yes, there was no doubt about it I was home. We often say at our house, "You don't have to be crazy to live here but it certainly helps!"

My eldest daughter Julie lives in Cardiff and it really makes my day when she brings Angeline and Samuel to visit us. We have enormous fun together as a family and that's the way it should be.

While thinking over my trip to America I remembered that many people had been very superstitious and as such had had their eyes blinded to the truth. I had had to pray very hard for these people in order to break through the forces of evil that locked up their minds from receiving the truth. I had to tell them that all superstition was evil and should be avoided and shunned.

Several people told me weird and strange tales of how they had been affected by inexplicable happenings in their lives. These were mainly linked with superstitious beliefs and they wanted me to tell them why and how these things happened. I simply had to say, "I don't know." I found it very difficult to convince them that you do not have to know why or how these things happen, the fact remains, they happen and that is all that we ever need to know.

Some people seem to think that because I was once a witch and very deeply involved with the supernatural that I should know the answer to every mystery, evil or otherwise. They are astounded when I tell them that "I don't know."

The fact is God does not want us to know about every dark mystery. He does not want us to dwell upon evil because He knows that it would not be beneficial to us. The Bible says, "Whatsoever things are true, whatsoever things are honest, whatsoever things are just, whatsoever things are pure, whatsoever things are lovely, whatsoever things are of good report; if there be any virtue, if there be any praise, think on these things" (Phil. 4:8).

People have come to me after a meeting and asked, "Has the Lord told you, or shown you anything about me?" When I have answered "No", they have frequently been very disappointed. This happened to me several times and as a result I was very troubled in my spirit and asked the Lord to show me why some people think that I should have some special revelation about them. As I prayed, Jesus quietly showed me that those who asked this of me, thought of me as some kind of fortune-teller or seer and did not trust Jesus at all.

I do not have special revelations about people. Neither do I go around saying, "The Lord told me this and the Lord told me that". That is not my work at all. My job is to preach the Gospel in all its fullness and to lead men and women to the Lord Jesus Christ.

The Lord does not merely send out His servants to do His work. First of all He goes before them to prepare the way, then He goes with His servants to protect, lead, and guide them. This He has done for me. It has pleased the Lord to use his handmaiden in this way and He has sent me far and near to spread the Gospel. Christ has no lips but our lips, He has no hands but our hands, and He has no feet but our feet to do His work on the earth today. May we always be ready to obey His call.

I want to tell the world that I'm a Christian. I want to tell the world about the risen Christ and what He can do.

I had just returned from America, but I knew that there were many countries that I had not yet visited. I have a great burden for India and Africa. There is also New Zealand, Japan, Mexico, and many more countries where the Gospel needs to be preached.

I believe the doors will open for me to go to these and other lands and, when they do, I will go through them in faith, with Jesus by my side, telling the world that "Jesus Saves".

CHAPTER TWELVE

Accepted in the beloved

"To the praise of the glory of His grace, wherein He hath made us accepted in the beloved" (Ephesians 1:6).

THIS chapter is written especially for the many Christians who have written to me asking me to pray for them, because they cannot forget the sins and mistakes of their past lives. "Pray for me," they say, "pray that God will help me to forget my past sins and erase them from my memory forever more."

I understand these feelings. Indeed haven't we all experienced them at some time or another? But such feelings are to be avoided at all costs. They are self-condemning and self-defeating. The answer is simple. When we repent our sins, God forgives and forgets and they are then "as far removed as darkness is from dawn". It does no good to remember the sins and mistakes of the past. Paul says, "forgetting those things which are behind, and reaching forth unto those things which are before" (Phil. 3:13). Let the sins of the past go. Forget about the mistakes of the past and mark it all down to experience.

What about the future? What about your goals? The Christian life is purposeless without the setting of goals.

Your first goal should be complete faith in God's Word. Programme your heart and mind by practising faith and by recognizing His presence with you every hour of the day. When God says in His Word, "As far as the east is from the west, so far hath He removed our transgressions from us" (Ps. 103:12). He means it. We must accept God's Word as it stands. When God says "I, even I, am He that blotteth out thy transgressions for mine own sake, and will not remember thy sins" (Isa. 43:25), He means it. Why then should we dwell on our past sins. God's Word is true. He always means what He says.

You sinned before you became a believer, you have sinned since then, and you will sin again in the future. Our only hope is to acknowledge our sins to the Saviour in prayer daily, and to trust Him for forgiveness and mercy. The Bible says, "If we say that we have no sin, we deceive ourselves and the truth is not in us", also, "If we confess our sins, He is faithful and just to forgive us our sins, and to cleanse us from all unrighteousness" (1 John 8-9).

Many Christians have told me that they feel rejected by their fellow Christians, because of the sins of their past. The feel that they have not been accepted by the Christian community. I know exactly how they feel. I, too, have been rejected and often told that my testimony is far too dramatic and sensational. My answer has to be, that is how it happened! And was not the testimony of Paul and many others in the Bible dramatic? Was not the Resurrection of Our Lord dramatic? If Jesus had not been crucified and then raised from the dead, there would be no salvation for anyone, and no testimonies of any description!

It is true that not many Christians have had a past life like mine. They have not done what I have done or been where I have been, but just think how wonderful it is that God kept *them* from such evils as prostitution, drugs, and witchcraft, especially in the dark and troubled times that we live in today! My salvation and deliverance from sin is no more miraculous than anyone else's. *All* salvation is surely a miracle of love and grace!

It is often very difficult for me to speak about my past when giving my testimony, but I overcome my fears by the blood of the Lamb (Rev. 12:11). I overcame yesterday by giving my testimony, I overcame today by my testimony, and by His grace I will overcome every day by giving and living my testimony for the glory of God. It is not *my* story that I endeavour to tell out. It is the pure and undefiled love of Jesus, the story of Jesus and His love that reached out to one such as I. His love reached me and it can reach you, too. The love of Jesus can reach anyone, anywhere.

There are no degrees of sin with God. A sin is a sin in His sight, and the Bible plainly states that all have sinned and come short of the glory of God (Rom. 3:23). In verse 24 it continues "Being justified freely by His grace through the redemption that is in Christ Jesus". Jesus Christ died for the sins of the whole world. He died for your sin and for my sin. He shed His blood for everyone. When we accept Him as our personal Saviour, then we are truly accepted into the beloved. We are accepted and we are set free. We are all accounted a place among the redeemed. Isn't that just wonderful! So who can condemn us? "There is therefore now no condemnation to them which are in Christ Jesus, who walk not after the flesh, but after the Spirit" (Rom. 8:1), and also "Who is he that condemneth? It is Christ that died, yea rather, that is risen again, who is even at the right hand of God, who also maketh intercession for us" (Rom. 8:34).

God sees His Son, Jesus Christ, the one He sent down to dwell among *all* people. He sees His beloved Son crucified, risen, ascended, and glorious and then He sees us with all our faults and failings. And He still loves us! What a wonderful Saviour He is!

Remember that only people will ever make you feel unwanted and unaccepted. God will never do that. The unseen enemy, the Devil will do his best to make you feel rejected by your fellow Christians, but not Jesus. God does not reject you and make you feel unaccepted and degraded. You are very important to God and are very precious and unique in His sight. You are blood washed, God filled, and God owned. You are no longer the property of the Devil. You belong to God. Believe Jesus rather than the Devil. Satan is the father of lies.

Constantly remind yourself that you are a child of God and Satan will not be able to touch you.

You must never let these feelings of rejection eat into your soul and cause bitterness. No one likes unfair criticism and the only effective way to deal with it is to ignore it. Yes, it may be very difficult, but it is the Christian way. One Scripture that has helped me tremendously in this respect is, "No weapon that is formed against thee shall prosper" (Isa. 54:17). If your heart is right with God, no one can hurt or destroy you. If people criticize you, ask yourself, "Is what they say true?" If it is, then ask God for forgiveness. It only takes one prayer of repentance to put things right. If what they say is not true, then ignore it completely.

There is a wonderful story in the Bible. In the Gospel of John we read about a woman caught in the act of adultery. The self-righteous people of the community wanted to stone her to death but Jesus stopped them with these words: "He that is without sin among you, let him first cast a stone at her" (John 3:7). Of course when they heard this, being convicted by their own consciences, they went away one by one and the crowd dispersed.

Jesus was so full of love and compassion for this woman that He freely forgave her all. We can take this example of Jesus and freely forgive everyone, even those that seek to harm or criticize us. Do not get angry and build up a mountain of resentment and bitterness. We must forgive our fellows in order that our prayers can be answered and so that we can remain in the place of peace with God. Jesus taught us the model prayer: "For if ye forgive men their trespasses, your heavenly Father will also forgive you" (Matt. 6:14). This is the way of Christ. This is the way of love.

You must also confess that you have been wounded and hurt. Tell Jesus that you are discouraged. Confess your resentments and hurt pride then believe that God has forgiven you. You will then be able to forgive those that condemn you.

Are you discouraged? Are you cast down? Remember the prayer of David, "Why art thou cast down, O my

149

soul? and why art thou disquieted within me? hope thou in God" (Ps. 42:11). There is no reason to feel cast down and unwanted. God loves you so much He sent His only begotten Son down to this old world of sin to die for you. Jesus took the form of man, just for you and me and He knows exactly how you feel. He was the Son of God and the Son of man. He too was despised and rejected of men, a man of sorrows and acquainted with grief. "He came unto His own and His own received Him not" (John 1:11). But to those that did receive Him, He gave the power to become children of God. If you believe on His name and receive Him, then you are a child of God. You are accepted in the beloved. God understands how you feel, so hope Thou in Him. God has great plans for your tomorrows and has great things in store for you. He is not through with you yet, just as He is not through with me either. Think of tomorrow, not of the mistakes of yesterday. Aim for higher things. Look to Jesus who is able to keep you from falling. Remember that not all Christians will reject you and make you feel unacceptable. Many more will welcome you, just as you are. Just remember that God says that you *are* accepted in the beloved and you *are* free in Christ the risen Lord.

As I conclude this chapter I would like to thank personally all those who love and accept me and who make me welcome. People like Mr and Mrs D. Parker of Gamlingay, who poured out so much help and love on me and continue to do so. They are both fine Christians. Also Pastor Droz of Couvet and Pastor Morris of Berne who were so helpful to me in Switzerland. I would like to mention all the people who acted as interpreters for me on my European missions. They all did a wonderful job. I would also mention the Reverend Hanna, the Reverend Simpson, and the Reverend Ian R. K. Paisley all of whom helped me in Northern Ireland. There are many more, indeed too many to mention here, but to them all I wish to say "Thank you."

We are all accepted in the beloved. You are accepted, too. Hasn't the Lord been kind to us? Hasn't the Lord been good?

CHAPTER THIRTEEN

Watchman of the night

"Son of man, I have made thee a watchman . . . When I say unto the wicked, Thou shalt surely die; and thou givest him not warning, nor speakest to warn the wicked from his wicked way; to save his life, the same wicked man shall die in his iniquity; but his blood will I require at thine hand" (Ezekiel 3:17-18).

THE Apostle Paul has often been described as the greatest missionary that ever lived. He was certainly the greatest missionary of Bible days. What made him go "above and beyond the call" of Christian duty? What inner force possessed him? One imprisonment was not enough—he was willing to be imprisoned a second time. One shipwreck was not enough—he was willing to be shipwrecked again. One stoning was not enough—he was prepared to suffer another. When faced with all these hardships he did not draw back and say, "I cannot face this", or even "God does not expect me to go through this again." In effect he said, "I cannot stop. Something inside me makes me go on and on for the Lord." Paul states, "I am ready to preach the Gospel to you that are also at Rome. For I am not ashamed of the Gospel of Christ; for it is the power of God unto salvation" (Rom. 1:15-16).

Paul felt he owed the world the Gospel of Christ. What a tremendous driving force he had. He felt he had a debt to pay. He had vision and power and was on fire for the Lord Jesus Christ. But, of course, it was not always that way. Paul was once Saul, the persecutor of Christians and of Jesus Christ. He stood silent at the martyrdom of Stephen and watched as he was stoned to death for his faith. He wreaked havoc in the early Christian Church. He was well aware of the revival that was taking place in Samaria where Philip was preaching the Gospel. Sick bodies were being healed, the lame were made to walk, the blind were made to see, and many that were possessed with evil spirits were being set free from demonic bondage. It must have strengthened his resolve to crush the early Christian Church and to stamp out Christianity once and for all. Saul went to the Chief Priest and obtained written authority to bind all Christians wherever he found them and to bring them in chains to Jerusalem. But as Saul travelled along the Damascus road a bright light shone round him and the Lord spoke to him. Saul was never the same again. Henceforth he was called Paul and he belonged to Christ from that day forward.

The Lord said this of Paul: "he is a chosen vessel unto me . . . For I will shew him how great things he must suffer for My name's sake" (Acts 9:16). Paul was a different person and he had a new mission and purpose in life. He now had to preach Christ crucified and risen from the dead to every creature. He was possessed with a sense of divine obligation. He knew he had a great debt of love to pay.

Many Christians do not share this feeling. We live in a materialistic and affluent society and many are more concerned with themselves than they are about reaching the lost for Jesus. We rarely see the kind of all-consuming fire, zeal, and determination that was evident in the early Church. We can learn a lot from the early Christians. They all felt that they had a duty to preach about Christ, no matter what the consequences.

What a contrast exists between the Church in early times and the Church today. Many modern churches preach a social gospel and say, "God does not expect you to go that far" or "God does not expect you to sacrifice your time. Think of your friends and your loved ones." What a contrast! A handful of men in the early Christian Church swept the known world with the Gospel. They were on fire for the Lord and the Lord was their only priority. No risk was too great for them to take while doing the Lord's work. They were obeying God and remembering His words in Ezekiel, "If you do not give the wicked man warning and that same wicked man shall die in his iniquity; his blood will I require at thine hand" (Ezek. 4:18).

There was a power, a motivation that filled the early Christians and drove them on and on to turn the world of their day upside-down for Christ. They survived bitter and cruel persecution for their faith, being tortured, burned alive, or used as sport in Roman circuses. What faith they must have had to suffer so much!

The main problem facing the Christian Church today is apathy. People just do not seem to care enough for the lost. They have grown cold and disinterested in reaching the teeming masses that are outside a personal knowledge of Christ. There is only one way to reach the world for Christ today. We must "tell" them personally. Systems and rituals will not capture souls for God, neither will organization. We have over organized the Christian Church until it is a jigsaw puzzle of denominations and Church functions. Still, over half of the population of the world have never heard the name of Jesus, let alone had an opportunity to make a personal decision for the Saviour! Think of the teeming millions that inhabit our planet. Many of them are still enslaved in paganism or trapped behind the iron curtain of Communism where they are not free to learn about Jesus. And people still say, "It's a small world!" Watchman, what of the night?

The Devil would try to trick us by whispering, "There are thousands of trained evangelists and pastors. They are experts and they are educated. Look at all the colleges and training centres full of evangelists. Surely they are better equipped to preach the Word than you are? What can you do that they cannot do better? So slow down, take it easy. *Stop!*"

Satan is clever and he will try to discourage you in any way that he can. He wants you to give up and leave God's work to others. It does not matter to God what your standard of education happens to be. I am not saying that proper training is *not* important. I am saying rather, that it is not *all*-important.

If you love Jesus, you will read your Bible, so you will have Bible education. God needs every single one of His workers, every single Bible college, and every single training centre. God also needs *you* and God needs me. The most important thing is that we keep in touch with Jesus every day of our lives, so that we are strengthened to deliver the message of Salvation to the lost.

We must show that the power of the Resurrected Christ is far greater than the power of the Devil. We must also have real love for the lost as well as great zeal and enthusiasm to spead the word. Above all we need a sense of Divine obligation. We need what Paul and the members of the early Church had. And we need it badly. We need another Pentecost, a fresh outpouring of the Holy Ghost. We need a baptism of love and zeal.

We must throw off the apathy that we see around us and we should not be afraid to demonstrate the mighty power of God, for fear it might frighten people away. The early Christians did not hold back, and they carried the Word to the four corners of the known world. People were not frightened. On the contrary, when they saw God's miracles they believed.

In Chapter 3 of the Acts of the Apostles we read of a man over forty years of age who had been lame from birth and had to be carried daily to the gate of the temple to beg. When Peter and John saw him there, did they preach a long and involved sermon to him? No! They simply said, "Look on us." This poor cripple must have simply thought he was going to receive some money from them. He would not have known that anything spiritual was about to happen. Then Peter said, "Silver and gold have I none, but such as I have give I thee: In the name of Jesus of Nazareth rise up and walk." He then took him by the hand and lifted him up and immediately strength came to his feet and ankles and he leapt up and went with them to the temple, praising God. People who had known him all their lives saw this. Did it frighten them away? No! On the contrary, they were filled with wonder and amazement. Peter had proved the might of the God he served. The people had seen.

Being with Jesus makes a vast difference. Being constantly in touch with Him and filled with His power, will make a mighty impact on those around us. There are many ways to reach the lost. Great crusades with golden-voiced choirs, backed by massive organizational structures and led by the best preachers have a significant effect. But crusades alone are not enough. We have fallen into the trap of over-organizing Christianity, making it stiff and rule bound. The dynamic power of God has been hidden under a mountain of red tape.

If we cannot reach men and women by these "usual" methods, then how are we to reach them? The answer is, by the power and demonstration of the Holy Ghost. When men and women are wholly possessed with a sense of Divine obligation and are on fire for the Lord and burning with love, then they will be able to reach the millions that are perishing without light, without hope, and without Jesus Christ.

Satan cannot stop the process of Salvation, but he can and does prevent us from being more effective. He can keep us powerless and unfruitful and rock us to sleep in the church pews. He can steep us in apathy while countless millions are in need and do not know that Jesus is alive today, healing the sick, casting out demons, performing miracles, and offering power and Salvation to those that accept Him.

I know that if people saw miracles happening in ordinary Christian churches then they would flock in. If they saw the lame walking, the blind seeing, the insane made sane, and the possessed set free, even the toughest and hardest hearts would be changed overnight. They would be queuing up outside churches hoping to get in! And they would be in no great hurry to rush away after the service either. It always amazes me that most of our churches are locked and empty before ten o'clock at night. Surely this is just the time when they need to be open? The streets are filled with people "living it up" and our churches are locked and barred. Is this the way it should be?

Thank God there are a few churches where the Spirit is vital and active, where miracles are being done and God's power is being used to the full. But there should be so many more. Indeed every Christian church should be utilizing the power of the Holy Ghost. Would they be standing decaying and supported by tiny congregations if they were utilizing that power?

The time has come to do some straight talking. There is no time left to soft pedal the Gospel. It's time to wake up from the apathetic sleep that the Devil has lulled us into and meet the needs of those around us. We must reach people from all walks of life. They are not all drug addicts, wife-beaters, murderers, and prostitutes! They are just nice ordinary people, not perfect by any standards, but people who have not been forgiven and who do not know Jesus Christ as their own personal Saviour. Their very normality can make them the hardest people to reach as they do not realize that they are sinners and that they need Salvation. They lead decent lives and they think that that is enough.

We have a duty to tell them the truth of the Bible. That *all* have sinned and come short of the glory of God. No one is truly righteous and Jesus died for all sin, including theirs. There are no degrees of sin with God. A sin is a sin in His sight. There is no such thing as a white lie in the sight of God. A lie is a lie. We must tell them that the wages of sin is death and total separation from God forever. We must tell them that the gift of God is eternal life through Christ Jesus our Lord, and that that gift is freely offered.

The Gospel we preach is to all mankind, no matter who they are. No life is beyond repair. If that were so, I would have been a hopeless soul. The task of God's children is to bring beauty out of ugliness and to create peace where once was discord. God's children, *all of us*, should be busy creating beauty, peace, joy, love, and happier relationships wherever they go and we should be telling people about the most wonderful relationship of all, that of a personal relationship with the Lord Jesus

156

Christ. How then can we all help to bring this about?

Remember the story of Lazarus in the Gospel and how his two sisters Martha and Mary sent for Jesus? (And who better to send for than Jesus!) Remember that Jesus did not come straight away, but told His disciples that the sickness of Lazarus was not the sickness of death, but instead was "for the glory of God so that the Son might be glorified thereby" (John 11:4). Then Lazarus got worse and worse and finally died and was laid in the tomb. Jesus said, "Lazarus is dead." (John 11:14). Everything seemed lost. By the time Jesus came Lazarus had been dead for fully four days and was laid in a cold dark tomb, his body swathed in graveclothes. A great stone was set at the entrance of the tomb and to all intents and purposes that was that. Lazarus was indeed dead. Then Jesus came and raised him up from the sleep of death and commanded those standing near to roll away the stone. He could have moved the stone Himself without even lifting a finger, but He commanded those near, including some of the disciples, to move the great heavy rock. He said, "Take ye away the stone" (John 11:39).

There is a great hard stone of doubt, unbelief, and confusion set at the entrance to the hearts of men and women, and Christian, *you* can help roll that stone away. How? With a word of testimony, with the prayer of faith, with the authority given you by the power of the Holy Ghost, and by preaching the Gospel in that same power of the Holy Ghost. Then signs and wonders will follow the preaching of the word of God.

When the stone had been moved away, Jesus cried with a loud voice "Lazarus come forth" (John 11:43). Notice that Jesus called him by name. I imagine that if He had not, then perhaps the whole of the dead would have risen at His command. Such is the power and authority of Jesus Christ, the mighty Son of God. Jesus has given us that same power. He said, "greater works than these shall he do; because I go on to my Father" (John 14:12). Tremendous isn't it. Then Lazarus came forth from the tomb swathed in his graveclothes and Jesus said, "Loose him, and let him go" (John 11:44).

Jesus did not take off the graveclothes Himself, he told His disciples to do it. And it is our job as disciples of Jesus to take away the stones of doubt and unbelief, so that those that are dead can come forth out of the darkness into His light. It is our job to remove their gravecloths so that Jesus may surround them after they have left the darkness.

But if we ourselves are covered in doubt and unbelief and have grown cold and lack power, then we, too, need our graveclothes removed before we can help anyone else and before we can do the work that Jesus has commanded. Satan's primary objective is to stop men and women from receiving Christ as Saviour and what better way to achieve this than to render God's children powerless, defeated, and unable to reach the lost for Christ.

Many people today dismiss Satan as an outmoded, nonsensical figure from the Dark Ages. They just will not believe that he exists and, of course, Satan, the greatest saboteur of all, is very happy with this state of affairs. He would prefer people to think that he does not exist. What a disguise! Disbelief in his existence is the very best camouflage that Satan could ever wish for!

Imagine if you had a mortal enemy that was intent on destroying you, your family, and your home. If you were ignorant of the existence of such a foe, imagine how much danger you would be in and also how easy it would be for your foe to attack you! An unknown foe is infinitely more deadly than a known foe. Wouldn't you want someone to warn you? Watchman what of the night?

Not only is Satan deceiving people into thinking that he does not exist, he is even deceiving people into thinking that God does not exist! Take Communism for example. Youngsters are joining the party day by day and it is spreading throughout the world like a disease. People are tricked and brainwashed into believing that Communism is new, is fresh, is better, and will change the whole world.

In the face of such opposition from the enemy of souls,

we must be awake and alert. We must present men and women with the full truth of the Word of God and not be afraid to tell them that there are only two roads to travel. They must choose either the Devil and Hell, or Christ and Heaven.

Jesus wants us to live and walk in perfect freedom and light. Satan wants us to remain ignorant of his evil devices and ignorant of the truth. Jesus wants us to increase in wisdom, righteousness, and power. We can stand on the finished work of Calvary and command Satan to be gone. We can say, "Satan, you are a liar, you are a failure, you are defeated." Satan will have to flee from us.

We can and *must* proclaim the full Gospel in the power of the Holy Ghost and we must show lost and deluded souls that Jesus is alive today and that there is nothing that He cannot accomplish. *Nothing.*

The call to service is urgent. The world seems to be on the brink of total destruction and whatever we do it must be done *now!* We are rapidly approaching the time when God's day of grace will cease and those that have rejected Christ will be separated from God forever. Every time the clock ticks, hundreds all over the world die and go to a Christless eternity. "A true witness delivereth souls" (Prov. 14:25). Watchman, what of the night?

Let us be as watchmen for Christ, to warn and rebuke in love, and by His holy power, roll away the stones of doubt and fear. Let us do great things in His name. Love cannot be contained. It must be expressed. Love is measured by what it will do and does not count the cost of what it does or what it gives. Real love uplifts, inspires, gives, and leads others to higher ideals.

To love Him is to serve Him, and I have been set free from the power of the Devil to serve Him. I love Him very much and I will be His watchman forever. By His grace and strength I will go on loving, giving, and serving, until He comes, or until He calls.

And the end is still not yet—PRAISE HIS NAME!
Thank you Jesus. Thank you Lord.

Spiritual Warfare

DOREEN IRVINE

KINGSWAY PUBLICATIONS
EASTBOURNE

CONTENTS

FOREWORD

Over the years I have read all sorts of books and material on spiritual warfare, but it is rare to find one of this calibre. Some I have read with doubts creeping into my mind as to the validity of the contents and occasionally, complete sanity of the writers. Opinions vary from the very existence of a personal Satan through to the graphically detailed accounts of various exorcisms. Others seem to give more glory to the evil one than to God. "What I need" I thought, "to complete my study, is inside information." After reading Doreen Irvine's book I found it.

When any country is involved in a war the best person to capture from the enemy is a high ranking officer. If he can be convinced of the utter foolishness of his leaders, of their barbarism and inability to gain eventual victory, then he may be "turned". His information, should it prove to be accurate, will cause untold damage to those to whom he owed his previous allegiance.

Doreen Irvine is such a person. She has come out of the enemy's camp. Her conversion from witchcraft to Christianity is a true miracle of God's mercy and grace. Her intimate knowledge of Satan's ways make this book (in the right hands), a powerful weapon against him.

No-one knows better than Doreen the fact that there is most certainly a personal Satan, although our enemy of course, would do all he can to discourage any thought of him at all. He'd prefer us to think that he doesn't exist. No-one knows better his weaknesses than someone who has for many years moved in those most evil circles.

How easy it would be to blame the fall of man on God. How simple to make it all His fault. But Doreen will have none of it! We see Satan's fall through pride and arrogance and God and His angels victorious. We find out how Satan uses truth mixed with lies to lead Christians astray. We see the truth about him in sound scriptural teaching. Set down before us is a handbook and a signpost dotted with obvious personal experiences. Doreen pulls no punches either; the church of God needs to shape up and wake up if the kingdom of darkness is going to be pushed back.

Why is it when we read the Gospels we see Jesus dealing crippling blows to the evil one and his demons, yet in contemporary Christian circles little or nothing is known about the subject of spiritual warfare? Jesus knew the reality of Satan's temptations. Did you know that approximately one third of the Gospels are taken up with this subject? He implanted into His disciples the ability to recognise the enemy, and defeat him and pass on that same message of hope. The early church followed the apostles' teaching with great joy being seen as many were set free.

Take note of the chapter on the *"Four keys of authority"* and having read it and inwardly digested, *Fear not*. When we pray, Satan trembles. When we take the keys of authority and use them he turns tail and runs. Remember James 4:7, we can only resist Satan when we are humbly in submission to our God.

This book fills the gap in my reading, may it do so for you too. As I read it, and re-read it, I was reminded once again of how great a Saviour I have. I was thrilled to find that Satan has far less power than the God I choose to serve. My Father in heaven is establishing His Kingdom on earth, is equipping His army, and the gates of hell shall not prevail against us.

Revd Andy Titmarsh
Pastor—Brook Christian Fellowship

Feb 1992

Growing, glowing, going

"**B**UT grow in the grace and knowledge of our Lord and Saviour Jesus Christ" (2 Pe 3:18). "And the end is not yet, praise the Lord". It is with these words that I ended my first book *From Witchcraft to Christ* and my second one *Set Free to Serve Christ*. So what better words to use to introduce my third book? For the end is still not yet, so much is laid up in store for those who love and serve the Lord Jesus Christ. His blessings are new every morning.

In my first book I shared something of my former way of life, and its deep involvement in the occult. By the grace and mercy of God I was delivered from that life of sheer hell, darkness and despair through the power of the risen Christ. But what has happened since then? What am I doing today? It would take far too long to write about all that has happened, but I will share briefly some of the blessing of serving the risen Christ.

Growing

I am still growing in grace, as every true Christian should, still learning more of His wonderful ways. I am now nearly sixty years old, and I do not speak at as many meetings as I once did. I have not been in the best of health over the last few years, and I have learned from this experience that it is not all important to be seen as I once was, always on the move, always travelling from one place to another. It has not been easy; but what is easy? The Christian pathway is not an easy one, and as life is changing all the time, so is our walk with God.

At first, when I became ill, I found it difficult to adjust to a quieter way of life, I was so used to being active for the Lord. Slowly, very slowly, I was able to realize that the Lord wanted to show me very important things about my future ministry and work for the Lord. I also needed rest, and rest has never come easy to me. The Lord had to show me how important rest was, and how He could use me in other ways. He showed me how to come to terms with my illness, and this gave me so much more understanding and compassion for people who suffer with poor health.

My counselling ministry, helping those who were trapped in the web of occult practices, and those affected by the occult, and Christians who were oppressed, or depressed, suddenly had to come to an end; not that I refuse to counsel, but I have to be more careful. Counselling can become very stressful, if you are not careful.

God wants us to grow in our ministry for Him, and that means wisdom in what we do and how we do it, or our ministry will be fruitless. To be tired and ill, yet persist in what you are doing is not glorifying to the Lord. How can you glow for the Lord in this state?

There have been many openings on TV and radio to speak for the Lord, and warn against occult practices, where I have been able to help people who have phoned in to ask for help, and it has been a great blessing to help people who have been afraid and lonely. I have been able to help thousands more in my TV and radio ministry than I could ever have hoped to reach by travelling, and you can reach all classes of people. There are many people that no other method can reach, such as shut-ins, who cannot get to a church service.

In my role as a counsellor it is most important to be a

good listener. If you are not a good listener, you will not be able to do the work of a counsellor, because that is the reason people want to see you. They want to pour out their heart to you. There is nothing more off-putting to someone in need, than someone interrupting every five minutes. It is also very important to be *unshockable*. If you are going to look shocked when someone tells you something that you did not quite expect, it will frighten them, and they will draw away from you. Before you begin to counsel be prepared for anything people may say, show them that nothing they say will alarm you. They will then know that you do understand.

There is joy in serving Jesus, in His word we read, "In Thy presence there is fulness of joy, at Thy right hand there are pleasures for evermore". It is my earnest desire to continue to grow in grace, and mature in my ministry, whatever that ministry may be. I want to be in the centre of God's will, and do whatever He wants me to do, and go wherever He leads.

Glowing

If we are growing in grace, we will automatically glow for the Lord. The joy of the Lord in our hearts will be seen by others, and they will be attracted to us, and we can tell them about the Saviour. People will not listen to us if our lives, and our conduct contradicts it. A warm smile can warm the coldest heart, and as children of the living God, surely we have much to smile about. There is an inner glow that will shine out to all around, showing the beauty of His grace in our hearts and lives. In times of testing "the peace that passes all understanding" will rest upon us, and in us, and this is what people want. They want peace, they want love, they want joy. When people can see that even in times of difficulty and pain, that I still have peace and victory within; this will speak to them better than my words. I like these words from a hymn written by J. G. Whittier:

Drop Thy still dews of quietness,
Till all my strivings cease.
Take from our souls the strain and stress
And let our ordered lives confess,
The beauty of Thy peace.

Christ has put a blaze of love within my heart, and this fire will continue to burn until Jesus comes or calls.

Going

As we glow we will also go. Go where? Just wherever He wants us to go, not where we think we ought to go. He alone will open doors for us, the right doors. We must always remember that we have an enemy, and he will try to stop us in every way he can. So let us be mindful of this, and pray for the right discernment, and only go through the doors that He has opened for us. We all make mistakes, and it is so easy to believe that every door opened for us is the right one. We must not forget to make things a matter for prayer before we venture forth. When we are certain the door open before us is the right door, and we are in His perfect will, He will always bless us, and give us souls for our hire. He goes before us and will guide and protect us at all times. This has been my experience in the past, and I know that this will be my experience in the future days.

I have also learned a very valuable lesson: the devil is the greatest time-waster on this earth, and he can get you running here and there, doing this and that out of the will of God. Jesus said "Follow me, and I will make you fishers of men" (Mk 1:17). If we learn to follow where He leads, and not where men want us to go, when we listen to His voice, not the voice of man He will make us a blessing to many.

I have been able to write this book because I have already taught much of it in many churches, when I have been asked to speak about spiritual warfare.

There is a great need in our churches for the right teaching on this very important subject. There is a need for balance on the subject of the devil, and what he is doing. Many people today are looking for direction, in a world that's going nowhere. We know where we are going—and we can point them in the right direction. Jesus said "I am the way, the truth, and the life" (Jn 14:6). We can show them the way. We can show them the truth. We cannot show them the way if we ourselves are ignorant, or if we ourselves are afraid. So let us all go forward, in faith, with a message of hope, peace, and love; with the good news of salvation. He has given us a commission to go forth in His name. Let us march forward in victory, pulling down the strongholds of the devil. Let us tread all the powers of darkness down in the power of His might. Let us all go forward for the glory of God. Let us grow, glow, and go for Jesus now, while we have the time and the opportunity.

CHAPTER ONE

Is there a devil?

IN days of old, which are often described as the "dark ages" the devil was generally believed in, and seen as a real and present force of evil. So much so, that effigies of the devil were carved in wood or stone, and displayed outside, and sometimes inside church buildings, many of which can still be seen today. I suppose this was to remind worshippers that there was a devil, and to avoid him at all costs. The devil and his demons were believed capable of almost anything, like tormenting men and women and transforming them into sinister creatures. The devil was known as "Lord of the underworld". The mood of the times was a nightmarish mixture of truth and superstition, and the greatest fear of all was to be taken over by the devil. Many people wore on their person, or displayed on their premises, amulets and charms to ward off the devil and evil spirits, to protect themselves from the prowling devil and his evil agents.

They lived in fear of the devil who was held solely responsible for many diseases, such as epilepsy, asthma, and blindness. These were reckoned to be the hallmark of the devil on a person. Everything that could not be understood, or easily explained, was put down to the work of the devil. Witches were burned at the stake, and many who were completely innocent of witchcraft were also put to death, such was the fear and the superstition of the times.

Then gradually people became more knowledgeable, and therefore more analytical and critical of their past beliefs, more scientific, and less frightened by the unseen. In reaction against their former ideas and extravagant superstition and fear, enlightened people rejected the idea of the devil altogether. To them, Satan now became just a silly word, a superstition, a figment of the imagination, a bygone fear. There was no room for the devil in modern thinking. An actual devil had no part in the new world of psychology, test-tubes, and scientific discovery. Too much was now known about sickness of the body and the mind for it to be possible to take the devil seriously, and belief in a personal devil was swept away.

The devil was now depicted in a cynical way, with horns and a spear-like tail, with a pitchfork in his hand and a wicked grin on his face. No-one could actually believe or fear such a devil. Agents of the devil, such as witches, wizards, and demons were also discarded, or better still, transformed into comic figures. For the most part the idea of a devil became a great joke.

It is the same today. Many people today still dismiss Satan as an old-fashioned comic figure from the dark ages. They just do not believe that Satan exists. Some people today think of witches as hooked-nosed old hags, riding on broomsticks over the face of the moon, or as cackling old crones stirring up a wicked brew in a bubbling cauldron. All this unbelief in the devil's existence is one of his very best camouflages. The enemy you cannot see, or believe is there, is far more powerful and dangerous than the enemy you can see, and do believe is there.

Now the modern world is beginning to think again about the reality of the devil. People are beginning to wonder if they were wrong in discarding belief in a personal devil. They are being made aware of evil in this world today, and they are searching for answers; they are asking questions about the reality of evil, and where it comes from.

Faced by evil forces that are beyond their understanding, people are slowly coming to the realisation that behind the evil conditions of this world, there must be a power, not of this world—a supernatural evil power. For despite social improvement, educational advancement, and up-to-date technology the world is becoming worse, not better.

Furthermore, there is an unhealthy fascination with occult practices, such as have never been seen before. This has been emphasised in popular books and films about the devil such as *The Exorcist*, *Rosemary's Baby*, *The Omen*, and many others. Devil-related themes are big business in Hollywood, and the paperback trade. People are emerging from the cinema, having just seen a film about the devil and demon power with a mixture of excitement, fear, and apprehension, and people can now buy video tapes about the devil, and they sit and watch them in their homes. But there is no message of warning, no word of hope, and no understanding. They are being made aware of the devil and demons without knowing the way out of it all, and the effects are sometimes alarming. This is why, back in the sixties, Christians used to stand outside cinemas trying to help those who came out, and warning those going in, pointing them to the Lord Jesus Christ, whose power is greater than the power of the devil.

There is an increasing awareness of the devil's presence, but it is still beyond most people's understanding, and worse still, they have no assurance regarding the limitation of the devil's power. The realisation that the devil does exist, with power to control or influence people, is too much for the mind to cope with, so some still hold to the callous and rigid belief that the devil does not exist, while others are stricken with great fear of the reality of the devil, and what he is doing. Both reactions are wrong.

It is easy for people, faced with the fact of increasing evil in our world, to feel that the world is on the verge of collapse, and just as the Bible states "Men will faint from terror" (Lk 21:26). Sad to say, even Christians are frequently afraid of the subject of the devil, and avoid it as something negative and unhappy. By doing so, they add to man's historical fear of the devil, and they are not equipped to face and overcome the evil in this present world. They cannot help those who are in the clutches of the devil, and they cannot answer questions from those who are troubled and afraid, and are looking for a way out; they cannot help, because they themselves are afraid.

Christians should not be ignorant of the devil's devices; their eyes should be opened to the subtlety of the devil, so they are strong to fight the foe, and overcome the devil day by day. Their lives should be a shining example to those in darkness, and a testimony of victory over evil.

We can discover the cause of evil in these days from the Bible, and we can discern the pattern of demonic influence in the world today. There is no reason for Christians to be ignorant when we have an open book— the Bible, which shows us plainly the reality of a personal devil. The Bible shows us the way that the devil worked in days gone by, and the way he still works today, and it shows us how we can overcome and defeat the devil, because God is on our side. "The one who is in you [Jesus Christ] is greater than the one who is in the world" [the devil] (1 Jn 4:4).

Is there a devil? The question requires an honest and positive answer. What can we say to them? First of all let us consider some of the great and terrible evils that have happened in the world, and are still happening today. What, besides a personal devil, can explain how seemingly civilised, educated men, like the Nazis in World War Two could slaughter six million human beings, in a frenzied effort to wipe out the Jewish race? How, without satanic influence, can we explain the horrors of Belsen and Auschwitz, where many thousands were put to death in gas chambers? How, without a personal devil, can a man thought to be a loving father murder his children one by one, and say afterwards "I do not know what came over me"?

How can a man who dearly loved his little girl, drug her and then throw her off a high bridge into the waters below to a certain death, because he thought the world was too evil for her to live in, without a personal devil to motivate him?

One young man telephoned late one night and said, "Doreen, I have escaped from a mental hospital, because there are evil powers at work in that place, which are trying to destroy me. I have walked for hours in the rain, and I know they are still following me: I am thinking of taking my life. Can you help me?"

After talking to him for a long time on the phone, telling him of a greater power, of Jesus Christ, and how much He loved him, I tried to find out where he was. He was in such a confused state, he could not tell where he was. With the few vague clues he gave me, I, together with other Christians, tried to find him, but we failed to do so. Two days later, he was found dead at the bottom of Avon Gorge, Bristol. I had to attend the inquest at the Coroner's Court, because I was the last person he spoke to. The coroner brought in an open verdict. Was it merely mental illness that caused him to stumble, or jump off the rocks? If so, who was behind the mental torment? This is just one of the human tragedies that I have encountered, and there are hundreds of them every single day, all over the world.

When we open the newspapers today, we read sickening accounts of how low man has sunk; horrific accounts of rape, murder, cruelty, muggings, child abuse, pain and suffering, rioting, and senseless bombing, where innocent people are killed, or maimed for life, in a so-called just cause. Alcoholism and drug addiction has increased at such a rate the authorities are at a loss as to how to deal with it all. There are just not enough facilities to accommodate the growing numbers of young people who are hooked on drugs, and now we have the added problem of solvent abuse. Incest too, is apparently raising its ugly head in these very troubled times we live in, causing heartbreak and shame to many families.

So is there a devil? The answer must surely be—YES! Behind the terror and evil of our times, there must be a satanic force, stemming from a personal devil. The

19

devil's plan is to distort the truth about himself. He convinces many people that he does not exist, or he will try to give some logical explanation for it all, or contrariwise, he would have some people believe that he has more power than he actually has.

It pleases Satan to strike terror in the human heart, to have men and women cower before him in fear and trembling. Misunderstanding, fear, confusion, disbelief and ignorance, are the handiwork of the devil.

So who exactly is the devil? Where did he come from? What does he really want? How is he working to get it? What is our position as believers? We need to know! When the subject of the devil is clouded with mystery and ignorance, there will be fear and foreboding; but when there is enlightenment and knowledge, the fear is gone.

It is not my intention to glorify the devil in this book, but to make Christians aware of, without being afraid of, the reality of the devil and all his works.

When we explore the tangled scene in the light of God's word, we will find consolation and reassurance that God is still in perfect control of His universe, and His will shall prevail in the end.

If there is anyone who should know whether or not the devil is real, it is me, because I once served him as a satanist and witch, and have first-hand knowledge and experience of his power and how he works. Now I am a Christian, I belong to the Lord Jesus Christ, and have experienced His great power in my life, to save me, and deliver me from the power of the devil, and I know, without a shadow of doubt that God's power is far greater than the devil's power. I can speak plainly, and warn about the devil, without fear. I am not afraid of the devil, and neither should any Christian be. There is no need to fear because God's perfect love casts out all fear, and there is no power, no demon, that can harm me. In God's word we read these wonderful words, ''For I am convinced that neither death nor life, neither angels nor demons, neither the present nor the future, nor any powers, neither height nor depth, nor anything else in

20

all creation, will be able to separate us from the love of God that is in Christ Jesus our Lord'' (Ro 8:38–39). God's shadow is far greater than any fearful shadow of this day and age, and those who abide beneath the shadow of His almighty wings need fear no evil at all.

CHAPTER TWO

God's great mysteries revealed

THE word mystery suggests something obscure, hidden, something strange and unknown. The scriptural use of the word is somewhat different. It refers to some fact or knowledge that God shares with His people. A mystery, in this sense, is that which is not known intellectually, or generally understood, but is revealed by Christ to those who know Him, by the power of the Holy Spirit. This is one of the many benefits enjoyed by the child of God. God does not want us to be in the dark regarding His works or His plans, but He freely shares with us His wisdom and knowledge.

A mystery then, is a previously hidden truth, now revealed by the Spirit of God. God's great mysteries are only revealed to those who accept and believe the Scripture as the Word of God. Christians are able to understand great truths, which the non-believer can never understand or grasp, indeed it is foolishness to them. The apostle Paul says in 1 Corinthians 2:6–8, ''We speak a message of wisdom among the mature, but not the wisdom of this age or of the rulers of this age, who are coming to nothing. No, we speak of God's secret wisdom, a wisdom that has been hidden and that God destined for our glory before time began. None of the rulers of this age understood it, for if they had, they would not have crucified the Lord of glory.'' It goes on to say in verse 10, ''But God has revealed it to us by his Spirit.''

Jesus spoke to the multitude in parables: the parable of the sower and his seed; the tares among the wheat; the grain of mustard seed; the leaven in bread; the hidden treasure; the pearl of great price; the fisherman's net. The disciples asked the Lord why He spoke to them in parables, and He answered, that it was because it was given to them to know the mysteries of the Kingdom of heaven, but not to the multitudes, because although they had eyes and ears, they neither saw nor heard, nor understood (Mt 13:11–13). In other words they are blind to the truth. Jesus goes on to say in verse 17, ''Many of the prophets and righteous men longed to see what you see and did not see it, and to hear what you hear but did not hear it.'' Christians are privileged to be able to know and understand, by the Spirit of God, great truths which were hidden even from the prophets in the Old Testament.

Paul says in Romans 16:25–26, ''Now to him who is able to establish you by my gospel and the proclamation of Jesus Christ, according to the revelation of the mystery hidden for long ages past, but now revealed and made known through the prophetic writings by the command of the eternal God, so that all nations might believe and obey him.'' The prophets wrote down what God commanded them to write, although they themselves did not understand the hidden meaning, but it is revealed to those who love and serve the Lord Jesus Christ. Just think about that; it is very wonderful indeed. Everything that God wants us to know about is contained in the Scriptures. It is up to us to search them out and ask God to reveal them to us, and He will.

I have already mentioned one of God's mysteries, the ''mysteries of the Kingdom of heaven'' parables that Jesus taught. There are ten more mysteries, or revealed truths, I would like to point out. They are as follows:

The mystery of the translation of the living saints

Christians refer to this event as ''the rapture'': the time when Jesus will return to this earth to snatch away His waiting people, the body of Christ, His Church, also referred to as "the bride of Christ". These are those who have been washed in the blood of the Lamb, those who have accepted Him as their Lord and Saviour. I believe that Christ is coming back for a radiant church, a purified and victorious church, not a defeated one.

In Matthew 25:1-12 Jesus told the parable of the ten virgins, five of whom were wise, and five foolish. The foolish took their lamps, but they did not take any extra oil with them, but the wise did take extra oil along with their lamps. At midnight the cry went out, "Here's the bridegroom. Come out to meet him." Only the five wise virgins who took the extra oil were ready to meet Him. May we all be prepared, and filled with the oil of the Holy Spirit, when the Lord comes again.

In 1 Corinthians 15:51-52 we read, "Listen, I tell you a mystery: We will not all sleep, but we will all be changed—in a flash, in the twinkling of an eye, at the last trumpet. For the trumpet will sound, the dead will be raised imperishable, and we will be changed." When we speak of the second coming of the Lord to the unbeliever, it's all a mystery to them, they do not understand it at all, but to those who do know the Lord as Saviour, it is a revealed truth and our blessed hope.

The mystery of the body of Christ made up of Jews and Gentiles

Paul speaks in Ephesians 3:2-6 of the mystery made known to him by revelation. He says, "In reading this you will be able to understand my insight into the mystery of Christ, which was not made known to men in other generations as it has now been revealed by the Spirit to God's holy apostles and prophets." Then he goes on to say just what that mystery was, when he says, "This mystery is that through the gospel the Gentiles are heirs together with Israel, members together of one body, and sharers together in the promise in Christ Jesus."

24

The mystery of the living Christ dwelling in us

Paul was a servant of the Church by God's commission to him to preach the word of God in all its fullness, "the mystery that has been kept hidden for ages and generations, but now is disclosed to the saints" (Col 1:25–27). Then he speaks about the Gentiles again, when he writes in verse 27, "To them God has chosen to make known among the Gentiles the glorious riches of this mystery." He goes on to tell of another mystery, or revealed truth, which is "Christ in you, the hope of glory."

When we know Christ as our Saviour and Lord, He dwells within us. What a wonderful truth! His love reigns in our hearts, His power protects and keeps us, His presence is known to us, and He is precious to us, He is Lord of all.

Does the world at large understand this? To them it is all a great mystery, and many think that Christians are just plain crazy. But to us the living Christ is revealed, and is living in us.

The mystery of the Church as the bride of Christ

After Paul writes about how husbands should love their wives, even as they love themselves, so that the two will become one flesh, he goes on to say, "This is a profound mystery—but I am talking about Christ and the church" (Eph 5:25–32). The unity of husband and wife is compared with Christ and His church; we are members of His body. Christ loved the church and gave Himself up for her, to make her holy, cleansing her by washing with water through the word. Christ wants the church to be radiant, without stain or wrinkle or any other blemish, but holy and blameless. This is indeed a mystery to the unbeliever, but to those who love Christ it is beautiful, it is real.

The mystery of godliness

In 1 Timothy 3, Paul writes of how overseers and deacons should conduct themselves, and says, "If anyone does not know how to manage his own family, how can he take care of God's church?'' He lays down some very good guidelines for them to follow. They must have a good reputation with outsiders, so that they do not fall into disgrace; they must be ''men worthy of respect, sincere, not indulging in much wine, and not pursuing dishonest gain. They must keep hold of the deep truths of the faith with a clear conscience.''

Paul wrote these instructions so they would ''know how to conduct themselves in God's household, which is the church of the living God, the pillar and foundation of the truth.'' Then he says in verse 16, ''Beyond all question, the mystery of godliness is great.'' Man is restored to godliness through the sacrifice of the Lord Jesus Christ. It is His godliness, not our own, and it is very important that Christians conduct themselves in a godly manner both in, and outside, God's house. If outsiders come into God's house and see strife, disorder, confusion and disunity, what kind of testimony is it to them? None at all! It is important then to come into God's house with the right attitudes, displaying all the attributes of godliness. Satan's snare is to rob the children of God of true godliness, giving them a form of godliness, but denying its power (2 Ti 3:5). Some people think that godliness is a means to financial gain, but ''godliness with contentment is great gain'' (1 Ti 6:6). Paul tells us to ''pursue righteousness, godliness, faith, love, endurance and gentleness,'' and ''fight the good fight of faith'' (1 Ti 6:11–12).

Although many non-Christians admire true godliness, they still cannot understand it. Many think that God is a killjoy, and that godly people are miserable people. This again is a clever lie of Satan, because the opposite is true. Real godly people are very happy and contented, for they have the joy of the Lord in their hearts.

The mystery of the Godhead

This mystery reveals that the fullness of the Godhead dwells bodily in the Lord Jesus Christ (Col 2:9). The apostle Paul's purpose was that the saints should be encouraged in heart, and united in love, so they might have complete understanding, in order that they might know "the mysteries of God, namely, Christ, in whom are hidden all the treasures of wisdom and knowledge" (Col 2:2–3).

If Christ is dwelling in us, we too may know His fullness. Christ has all the treasures of wisdom and knowledge. We are *complete* in Him. Christ is head over all other powers and authorities, and as we abide in Him, we too can have power and authority over every opposing force that comes against us, for He has given us His power. We need never be afraid of anything, for God is with us. "We are more than conquerors through Him who loved us." Nothing can "separate us from the love of God that is in Christ Jesus our Lord" (Ro 8:37–38).

The mystery of Israel's blindness to the gospel of Jesus Christ

Paul writes in Romans 11:25, "I do not want you to be ignorant of this mystery, brothers, so that you may not be conceited: Israel has experienced a hardening in part until the full number of the Gentiles has come in. And so all Israel will be saved, as it is written: The deliverer will come from Zion; he will turn godlessness away from Jacob. And this is my covenant with them when I take away their sins."

In the first part of this chapter, Paul tells us that, because of Israel's sin of unbelief, the Gentiles were grafted into the olive tree. Some of the branches have been broken off, and the Gentiles, though a wild olive shoot, have been grafted in among the others, and now share in the nourishing sap from the olive root. If God did not spare the natural branches, the Jews, He will not spare the Gentiles either if they reject Christ. "Branches were broken off so that I could be grafted in" (verse 19). Paul asks, "Did they . . . fall beyond recovery? Not at all! Rather, because of their transgression, salvation has come to the Gentiles" (verse 11). "After all," says Paul in verse 24, "if you were cut out of an olive tree that is wild by nature, and contrary to nature were grafted into a cultivated olive tree, how much more readily will these, the natural branches, be grafted into their own olive tree!" Many of the Jews have returned, and many are still returning to their homeland, in preparation for the Lord's coming, and many are having their eyes opened to His salvation, through the preaching of the gospel in all nations.

The mystery of the seven stars

In John's revelation on the island of Patmos, he saw seven golden lampstands, and among the lampstands was someone "like a son of man, dressed in a robe reaching down to his feet and with a golden sash round his chest. His head and hair were white like wool, as white as snow, and his eyes were like blazing fire. His feet were like bronze glowing in a furnace, and his voice was like the sound of rushing waters. In his right hand he held seven stars, and out of his mouth came a sharp double-edged sword. His face was like the sun shining in all its brilliance" (Rev 1:12–16).

This was a beautiful vision of the living Christ. John was afraid and fell down at His feet, as if dead, but He placed His right hand upon John and said, "Do not be afraid; I am the First and the Last. I am the living one; I was dead, and behold I am alive for ever and ever." He told John to write down all he saw, and all that was about to happen. He told John the meaning of what he saw, and revealed the mystery of the seven stars and the seven lampstands. The seven stars were the angels of the seven churches, and the lampstands were the seven churches (Rev 1:17–20). The angels were not celestial angels, but messengers of God sent to the seven churches with the word of God, which in Scripture is likened to a sharp double-edged sword.

The mystery of Babylon

This mystery will be important to us as we continue to study the mystery of iniquity. The name Babylon is given to a system of apostate religion that is flourishing in our day and age, just as it did in Bible days. It is personified as a prostitute. "This title was written on her forehead: Mystery, Babylon the great, the mother of prostitutes and of the abominations of the earth" (Rev 17:5). John saw this when he was carried away in the Spirit into a desert. He "saw a woman sitting on a scarlet beast that was covered with blasphemous names and had seven heads and ten horns. The woman was dressed in purple and scarlet, and was glittering with gold, precious stones and pearls. She had a golden cup in her hand, filled with abominable things and the filth of her adulteries" (Rev 17:3–4). John was greatly astonished, and the angel said to him, "Why are you astonished? I will explain to you the mystery of the woman and of the beast she rides, which has seven heads and ten horns. The beast, which you saw, once was, now is not, and will come up out of the Abyss and go to his destruction. The inhabitants of the earth whose names have not been written in the book of life from the creation of the world will be astonished when they see the beast, because he once was, now is not, and yet will come" (Rev 17:7–8).

The beast is rearing its head more and more on this earth today, with false prophets bringing false doctrines, false cults and the practice of the occult, with all its abominations. This is Satan's last fling before the end of this age.

Apostate religion is an abandonment of true religion for the false. James says, "Religion that God our father accepts as pure and faultless is this: to look after orphans and widows in their distress and to keep oneself from being polluted by the world" (Jas 1:27).

The apostate religious system in these dark days, whatever form it takes, will be filled with such sin and iniquity that God Himself will bring the final judgment upon it. "For her sins are piled up to heaven, and God has remembered her crimes" (Rev 18:5).

I like what it says in Revelation 17:14, "They will

make war against the Lamb, but the Lamb will overcome them because he is Lord of lords and King of
kings—and with him will be his called, chosen and
faithful followers.''

The mystery of iniquity

In 2 Thessalonians 2:7 we read, ''For the mystery of
iniquity doth already work'' (AV). If God by His Holy
Spirit can reveal the mysteries I have named, why not
the mystery of iniquity? He does not want us to be
ignorant about the times we are living in, where Satan is
working overtime in a futile effort to overthrow Christianity, where there is chaos, disorder and fear. Paul
said it was already at work in his day, but is increasing
in our day, and it will increase and intensify as the days
get shorter and Christ's return nears. This will be a
revelation of truth, which can be traced in the Scriptures right from the very beginning up to this present
day and age. We need a fresh revelation today of God's
word. God's people are far too gullible, and sad to say,
it is our own fault. Are we truly examining everything
in the light of God's word? Are we truly examining
those who come into our midst, saying they have been
sent by the Lord? We should not be tossed about with
every wind of doctrine, for there are so many false
prophets today.

We must become more mature in our ability to discern
between that which is of Christ and that which is not.
Any teaching that is presented which is contrary to the
written word of God must be rejected by the church of
Jesus Christ. The Scriptures are not to be added to, or
subtracted from. The right hand of Christ, which John
saw holding the seven stars, represents Christ's absolute power and authority. When the word of Christ
comes forth from the mouth of Christ, through His servants who are God's appointed ministers, it is more
powerful than any other weapon in the whole universe.
''The word of God is living and active. Sharper than
any double-edged sword, it penetrates even to dividing

30

soul and spirit, joints and marrow; it judges the thoughts and attitudes of the heart. Nothing in all creation is hidden from God's sight. Everything is uncovered and laid bare before the eyes of him to whom we must give account'' (Heb 4:12–13). John saw Christ standing among the lampstands, which are the churches. Christ still stands in the midst of His church, and His eyes of fire search every single motive and deed. His voice was like the sound of many waters, and the voice of Jesus Christ is absolute power, absolute authority, absolute wisdom. That voice is multiplied today in the body of Christ's church, the people out of whom flow ''rivers of living water.''

If believers are to grow to maturity, they must also share in the ministries of the church. We cannot mature on our own, or be conquerors in Christ on our own. We need each other's fellowship and prayers. We need regular instruction and teaching from God's word in order for us to grow, and receive revelation from God's word. Believers must be willing to obey the leadership which God places in the church, men who are to be mature and steadfast, and filled with the Holy Spirit, fully yielded to Christ, keeping hold of the truths of God's word. Believers should take part in the corporate life-flow of Christ's church. There are too many who are doing their own thing, going their own way. It is dangerous to go your own way—you can fall into deception, which leads away from God's word. The revelation of the mystery of iniquity is not my own, it is not coming from my own mind; it has been revealed through careful reading and study of God's word. It is important to note that God will only reveal to us what he wants us to know about iniquity, because God does not want us to dwell upon dark and evil things to the extent that we lose all blessing and peace. God shows us in the Bible how Satan deceived our first parents, and how he worked against mankind in the beginning, and shows us how to overcome him today. The mystery of iniquity will be explained further in the following chapters, which cover a range of subjects.

John saw seven stars, and seven lampstands. Seven is the number of perfection, completeness, and wholeness. Christ is perfecting His church today, opening its eyes to deep hidden truths in His word, filling His people with His wisdom and knowledge. The mystery of iniquity need not remain a total mystery. There are some things we do not understand, let us not forget that God only wants the very best for the creation He has made, and will only show us what He wants us to know to make us aware of the devil's tactics, thus equipping us to conquer the foe, through Christ's power in our lives.

CHAPTER THREE

The origin and fall of Satan

TO many, the origin of sin and its continued existence, is a source of mystery, perplexity and confusion. They see the works of evil all around them, and its terrible results, and question how all this can exist under an eternal God of love. In their uncertainty and doubt they eventually come to believe that God does not exist. The belief in evolution is very widespread, but those who believe in the gradual development of the species from earlier forms of life will not find the answers to their questions, and can never be clear-cut about the power and presence of evil.

True Christians however, believe what the Bible says; "In the beginning God created the heavens and the earth" (Ge 1:1). Note, God created the heavens *before* He created the earth. In John 1:1 we read, "In the beginning was the Word, and the Word was with God, and the Word was God." Christ the Word was with God in the beginning, all things were created by Him. Christ, the only begotten of God, was one with the Father: one in nature, character and purpose, and the only one who could enter into all the counsel and purposes of God. Through Christ the eternal Father brought into being all the angels, cherubim, and seraphim. "For by him all things were created: things in heaven and on earth, visible and invisible, whether thrones or powers or rulers or authorities; all things were created by him and for him" (Col 1:16). Lucifer, now called Satan or the devil, was created as a beautiful guardian cherub.

Ezekiel 28:2–19 and Isaiah 14:12–17 give us a clear picture of Lucifer before sin entered his heart and he became Satan. Let us look at how he was created.

He was created by God alone and therefore dependant upon God for his existence. He was perfect when he was created (Eze 28:15) and perfect in his beauty, and full of wisdom (Eze 28:12). He was in Eden, the garden of God, and was decked with many precious stones, set in pure gold (Eze 28:13). He was a guardian cherub, placed by God to cover the throne of God (Eze 28:14–16). Compare this with the cherubim who covered the mercy seat, on the ark of the covenant in the tabernacle of Moses (Ex 37:9). He was also an anointed being, just as the Old Testament priests, prophets and kings. He was called "morning star, son of the dawn" (Isa 14:12). He was on the holy mountain of God (Eze 28:14). How very beautiful he must have been! He was made with music in his being, "The workmanship of thy tabrets and of thy pipes was prepared in thee in the day that thou wast created" (Eze 28:13 AV). He could have been the leader of the heavenly choirs.

It is important to note that Lucifer was created this way by God himself. He does not exist by or of himself. Neither did God create him as a mere force of evil but a very real heavenly being. There is a human tendency to think that the devil is just a force of evil, rather like a very strong wind. There is also a tendency to believe that two great powers exist, one good, the other evil, and the two are equal. Whilst it is true that two powers do exist; one good, the other evil, one from God, the other from Satan, it is by no means true that the two are equal. God is the creator, therefore His power is far greater.

Lucifer once held a very high position in heaven and had angels directly under his authority, who delighted to do his bidding. All heaven was his, all the heavenly beings reflected the glory of their creator, and worshipped God in adoration and praise. We read in the Bible, "The morning stars sang together and all the angels shouted for joy'' (Job 38:7). Sin then entered into the heart of Lucifer, we are not told how. There are many people today who get really confused about this; they cannot understand how sin entered the heart of this cherub, and why God allowed sin in heaven at all. If God wanted us to know this, He would have told us, but He did not tell us; all we are told is what is written in the Scriptures, and that is all we need to know. A note of discord must have marred the celestial harmonies when sin entered into the heart of Lucifer. Lucifer became full of pride because of his brightness and wisdom, and he said in his heart ''I will be like the most high.''

He became jealous of God's glory, and was discontented with his high office. He was ungrateful for the honours conferred upon him, and he aspired to be equal with God, his creator. It is noteworthy that it was in the heart that sin was first conceived. Isaiah 14:12–15 gives us details of Lucifer's iniquity and his fivefold plan of rebellion. Let us examine this fivefold plan of Satan's, taking our headings from the authorised version of the scriptures.

I will ascend into heaven

What does this mean, as Satan was already in heaven? Lucifer dared to aspire to a domain reserved for deity. There are levels, or stages in heaven as the apostle Paul intimated in his testimony that either in a vision or in his body, he had been caught up to the third heaven. It is accepted that the earth's atmosphere is the first heaven, the starry universe the second, and the abode of God the third. From an analysis of the further goals that Satan stated, we know that his ambition was to be like God. He who had been created by God now aspired to be like God and usurp His authority. He who had been created full of wisdom had now, by his iniquity, become filled with evil folly. He was jealous of all God had that he did not have, and conspired to enter into God's holy place, a place reserved for the Godhead alone.

35

I will exalt my throne above the stars of God

Lucifer's ambition included lordship and rulership over God's creation. At this point in Satan's rebellious plan there is an explicit reference to divine sovereignty and rulership from the very throne from which God rules creation. The hosts of heaven are sometimes referred to as the stars of God (Job 38:7). The word *star* is frequently used as a figurative reference to Christ and His church (Nu 24:17, Rev 1:16–20), also in Revelation 22:16 where we read "I, Jesus, have sent my angel to give you this testimony for the churches. I am the Root and the Offspring of David, and the bright Morning *Star*." The intention of Lucifer was to assert supremacy over all the celestial creation of God, by being like his creator in every way, including having his own throne.

I will sit also upon the mount of the congregation, in the sides of the north

Satan's ambition was to rule the universe, and gain its worship. This scheme of Satan's, emphasises his intention to control the world's religion. The word *mount* suggests rulership, and the word *congregation* suggests worship (see Isa 2:2 AV). In Psalm 48:2 we read, "Beautiful for situation, the joy of the whole earth, is mount Zion, on the sides of the north, the city of the great King." This psalm refers to Jerusalem, the spiritual centre of Jewish and Christian faith, and it is spoken of in a language similar to that Satan used. Now Lucifer's plan is made more clear. He would rule the universe, and all creation would worship him as well as God his creator, in the city of God, in Mount Zion on the sides of the north, the city of the great King.

I will ascend above the heights of the clouds

Clouds have always been associated in the Scripture with the glory of God. During the wilderness journeys of the Israelites, it was an accompanying cloud that represented the guiding presence of God, "Behold the glory of the Lord appeared in the cloud" (Ex 16:10 AV). God manifested Himself in clouds during the wilderness journeys, as when the tabernacle was completed, "Then the cloud covered the Tent of Meeting, and the glory of the Lord filled the tabernacle" (Ex 40:34). When Solomon completed his great temple of the Lord, "the cloud filled the temple of the Lord. And the priests could not perform their service because of the cloud, for the glory of the Lord filled his temple" (1 Ki 8:10–11).

Lucifer wanted to be equal with God and share God's glory, thus deflecting the glory from God alone. He wanted to sit where God sits. Whenever we see "glory" mentioned it speaks of the dwelling place of the Godhead, a place for God alone. What rebellion! What jealousy! At the second coming of Christ, He will be revealed, "on the clouds of the sky, with power and great glory" (Mt 24:30). Lucifer desired no other glory but his own, no other power or authority above his own. Such arrogance staggers the mind. It was insane, because there was no possibility of success, but he pursued it nevertheless, and he still pursues it today.

I will be like the most High

At last, Lucifer makes his evil plan complete by placing himself in direct comparison with God. He has mentioned heaven, the stars of God, His Holy Mount, the clouds of His glory, and now lastly he states his intention towards God Himself. He would be like Him. He, who had the highest place in God's creation now aspired to be higher still. He, who was the wisest and the most beautiful, now desired to be all-wise. He wanted to be omniscient: to know all things. He was powerful, but he wanted to be all-powerful. He wanted to be omnipotent. He was able to go anywhere his

37

creator willed him to go, but he wanted to be everywhere. He wanted to be omnipresent. What rebellion! What deception!

He did not hold to the truth, he became a liar and a murderer. He was self-deceived (Jn 8:44). He was the original sinner; iniquity was first found in him (Eze 28: 15–16). He is the original antichrist (2 Th 2:7 and Ge 3:1–6). He is a thief (Jn 10:10). He is a fowler, who traps and ensnares (Ps 91:3). He masquerades as an angel of light (2 Co 11:14). He is the source of all sin, and in him the mystery of iniquity is personified. Because of his iniquity Satan was cast out of heaven, and Jesus saw him fall, for we read in Luke 10:18, "I saw Satan fall like lightning from heaven."

Satan did not fall alone

Lucifer influenced a large part of the heavenly host. We get some idea of his authority from Revelation 12:9, "The great dragon was hurled down, that ancient serpent called the devil, or Satan, who leads the whole world astray. He was hurled to the earth, and his angels with him." It is very revealing to read that the angels who fell with him are referred to as *his* angels. It shows you what power and authority he once had in heaven. No, Satan did not fall alone, and it is my belief that he was not cast out immediately sin was conceived in his heart. I am convinced that he had to work over a period of time, in order to influence the angels under him.

I believe he worked with great and mysterious secrecy, and concealed his real purpose under a pretence of reverence to God, although it is certain that God was not fooled by this. He was greatly loved and respected by the heavenly hosts; and as someone as high as he was, an anointed cherub, he was highly exalted, and his influence was very strong. I believe he sought to create sympathy for himself, and his cause, by stirring up discontent among the other angels, and trying to influence them, as well as those who were directly under him.

I can imagine this lofty cherub questioning "Why should Christ have the supremacy? Why is Christ honoured above me?" The angels had no knowledge of sin, they could not discern the consequences that would result from this rebellion. I believe that Satan lied to the angels under him, telling them that they too could gain a higher place in the heavenly sphere if they followed him. We are told in the Bible, "And there was war in heaven. Michael and his angels fought against the dragon, and the dragon and his angels fought back. But he was not strong enough, and they lost their place in heaven" (Rev 12:7-8).

It is difficult to imagine a war in heaven, but that is what the Bible says happened. The angels were deceived by Satan, whose power to deceive is very great, and I believe he disguised himself in a cloak of falsehood and gained an advantage and his high position gave greater force to his lies, and many were induced to rebel with him. Rebellion is a grave sin against God, and in God's word we are told that it is like the sin of witchcraft.

We read in Revelation 12:4 that a third of the host of heaven rebelled, and fell with Satan. That might seem like a lot of angels, but there are billions and billions left, which make up a far greater army than that of the devil; so there is no need to fear.

God's angels protect the children of God. There are instances recorded in the Bible where angels protected and aided God's servants. We have a guardian angel who watches over us, and protects us, if we obey the Lord and walk in His ways.

Satan's plans for supremacy came to nothing, because Michael and his angels fought against him, and Satan and his angels were cast out of heaven (Rev 12:7-9). Now united with Satan, they have through all succeeding ages co-operated with him in his warfare against divine authority. We are told in the Scriptures of their confederacy and subtlety, and their malicious designs against the peace and happiness of man.

Under Satan's control there are a vast number of demons, who obey his every command. They make up a very strong, and highly organised army, and represent him and his evil cause all over the world. But the very fact that Satan has to rely on them to do much of his work, proves how limited he is. Because although he lusted for omnipresence, he did not get it. The demons who represent him, however, are capable of travelling in a split second to any given place at any given time.

Only God our creator is omnipresent. Even I, when I was a Satanist, knew that Satan was not omnipresent. When he appeared in one of the temples of Satan (and he did appear), we all knew it was Satan, and not one of his demon spirits. We knew that while Satan was there, he was nowhere else in the whole universe.

Many Christians do not realise this truth, they seem to think that the devil is everywhere at the same time. I wish Christians would grasp the truth that the devil is not omnipresent, and therefore limited in where he can go.

The vast army of demon spirits under Satan's control are referred to in various ways in the Bible. They are called deceiving spirits, principalities, powers, rulers of darkness, wicked spirits and demons. These different titles suggest different stages, or levels of authority in Satan's kingdom. Although many believe that these names refer to the same beings, there is a difference. For instance, deceiving spirits deceive the world in many ways, and wicked spirits incite great wickedness, and so on; and there is a difference between demons and fallen angels. This is another study, so I am just touching briefly on this subject. It has been made clear that when Satan fell, a third of the heavenly host fell with him, preferring to do his bidding than God's.

There are two scriptures however, that have caused confusion to some Christians; namely 2 Peter 2:4, "For if God did not spare angels when they sinned, but sent them to hell, putting them into gloomy dungeons to be held for judgment" ... And Jude 6, "And the angels who did not keep their positions of authority but abandoned their own home—these he has kept in darkness, bound with everlasting chains for judgment on the great Day.'' So how, Christians ask, can demons be responsible for evil on the earth, if they have been bound in chains, and cast down to hell to await judgment?

Here I would like to expose the teaching of modern-day satanism, which should throw some light on the subject. As a one-time satanist and witch, I can tell you that the following facts are true. This teaching was first presented to the ancient priests, when Satan himself appeared in the first satanist temple many thousands of years ago; at least this is what I was taught, and what is written in the satanist bible, and other ancient manuscripts.

Satanists do not teach that God does not exist, and Satan exists alone. On the contrary, they teach that God does indeed exist, but they teach that Satan is also a God in his own right. What is more they teach that Satan had a part in creating the heaven and the earth. It is important for Christians to know the teaching of the satanists, because it will open their eyes to the audacity of Satan. Satan is saying he is a god, and always was a god, he is saying he and our true God were dual gods working together, and they made the world together; that Lucifer was not created, but was like God. This is what Satan lusted for, but did not get, so he then started teaching people on the earth that he was equal with God, teaching that Jehovah God was unjust to Lucifer, and did not give to Lucifer equal power and authority in heaven.

Moreover, they teach that because of God's unjust treatment, Satan's rebellion was justified. When Satan stood up for his rights for equal power, God ordered the Archangel Michael and his angels, who were stronger than Satan's angels, to overpower Satan's strongest angels, and bind them in chains and cast Satan and the rest of his angels out of heaven. Furthermore, they go on to teach that one day Satan will gain strength to regain his place in heaven, by recruiting people on this earth who will be, in fact, ''the devil's angels'' who will assist his angels, and he will rescue the angels that God bound in chains, overthrow the hosts of heaven (including God himself), and Satan will then rule the whole universe. Satan creates sympathy for himself from his followers with this false and evil teaching. So, the more people who follow Satan and do his will on this earth, the more wickedness that is done, the sooner Satan will rule, they say. Satan is a liar and the father of lies, and this lie really shows how he goes on from one lie to another, thus confirming that he is indeed the father of lies.

You may wonder why Satan reveals that more wickedness must be done, in order to do what he says he will do; surely this in itself gives the game away; surely this reveals that he is evil and people will not want to serve him. Satan always oversteps his mark, and shows himself as he really is, but still people are willing to be deluded by him. Satan has to go along with all his teachings, which also contradict each other. One of the teachings of the satanists is that evil is good and good is evil, darkness is light and light is darkness. When we read Isaiah 5:20 we see clearly that people did this then, and are still doing it today. Everything the devil does is twisted, just as he himself is twisted. All the teachings of Satan are false, and a perversion of the truth. Satan does not deal with whole lies, they would be too easily discerned. He takes half-truths, and turns them into lies. It is far easier to deceive when the truth is mixed with lies, and made to appear wholly true. It is important that Christians know how he twists things; this makes Satan the greatest twister of all time.

It also reveals to us how desperate Satan is, because he knows his end is drawing near. He oversteps his mark by revealing how limited he is without the angels of God bound in chains, who rebelled with him. We should at least rejoice to know how limited he is. What God has bound is bound, Satan cannot loose anything. All evil spirits that are now working on this earth will be joining those whom God has bound in chains, and they will all be cast into the lake of fire.

Satan is always ready to supply the desires of the human heart, and palms off his deception in the place of the truth, and he spreads his net where least expected. If people would only read and study the word of truth with earnest prayer, that they would understand the deep truths of God's word, they would not be left in any doubt regarding it, and less open to receiving false doctrine. Some people do not want to receive the truth, and the apostle Paul speaks about those who refuse to love the truth, that they may be saved. He declares, "For this reason God sends them a powerful delusion so that they will believe the lie and so that all will be condemned who have not believed the truth but have delighted in wickedness." (2 Th 2:11-12).

Later on in this book I will reveal further evil teachings and works of Satan, and open people's eyes to his subtlety. When Jesus walked this earth, He cast out many demons that possessed people, and set those people free from Satan's power. If every single angel that rebelled with Satan, and was cast out of heaven, were bound in chains, they could not possess, oppress, depress or distress anyone, and there would have been no demons for Jesus to cast out. So it is plain to me that only a certain number of the angels who rebelled with Satan were bound in chains, and the rest assist Satan today in his work upon the earth. But it is very important to remember that Satan cannot do all the evil on his own, and has to rely on the demons to do it, and this should be an encouragement to every Christian. God has many more angels, who do the perfect will of God, and make up a far greater and more powerful army than that of the devil, and these angels are on our side.

When Satan lost his place in heaven, he also lost his heavenly body and his heavenly name, Lucifer. In the satanist movement, however, he is always referred to as Lucifer, not the devil, or Satan, or any other name, just Lucifer. He still wants to be known by his original name. That does not alter the fact that he lost all he had before he fell from heaven. He is now known in the Scriptures by many names. In Scripture the name of a person usually depicts the nature, experience, or function of the person named. This is true of the many names of God. This is also true of Satan. His name shows who he is, and how he works. Here are some names by which Satan is known, or recognised, today:

Satan: Adversary, Hater, Opponent, Enemy—1 Pe 5:8, Job 1:6–12, 2:1–7.
Serpent: Enchanter, Beguiler—Ge 3:1–14, Rev 12:9, 20:2.
Prince of this world: Jn 12:31, 14:30, 16:11.
Man of lawlessness: 2 Th 2:3–4.
Ruler of the kingdom of the air: Eph 2:2.
Fowler: One who traps and ensnares—Ps 91:3.
Accuser of the brethren: Rev 12:10.
Angel of light: 2 Co 11:13–15.
Wolf, Thief, Robber: Jn 10:10.

So now we see Satan has lost his place in heaven, his heavenly body, and his name. But did he then give up? No! He still plots and plans. He did not give up his plans, he simply revised his strategy, but not his aims, as we shall see as we continue to trace the pattern of apostasy and rebellion.

The origin and fall of man

A LMOST every known villain recorded in history did not set out to become a villain; they were first of all filled with evil pride, just as Satan was in the beginning. Satan did not intend to fall, or lose his place, but to rise up, and gain a much higher one.

One such villain readily springs to mind—Adolf Hitler. He did not intend to become a monster, to be loathed; he had far more splendid ideas than that. He viewed himself as a great champion, a powerful leader, one to be admired and adored. He was self-deceived, believing that the master race, as he called it, would rule the world, and he would be their leader. He would stop at nothing to achieve this, going as far as trying to wipe out the Jewish race completely.

The Jews have always been known as God's chosen people. Hitler was an atheist, so the Jews posed a threat to him and his evil plans, so he told his leaders that the Jews were an inferior race, and he intended to get rid of them. The fact was, they were a very superior people, a powerful people, and there were too many of them for Hitler's comfort. His twisted mind was so perverted, he saw his cause to be proper and good. Those like him, before and after him, who lusted for power, yet brought about horror, destruction and death, were inspired by nothing else but demon power. It all goes back to the beginning, in the garden of Eden.

When God made man, which was after Satan was ejected from heaven, Satan was intensely jealous, just as he was when he was in heaven. Satan was created,

God created him, and Satan himself could not create anything so he was jealous of God's creative powers. Now God had made Adam and Eve, and God created them with some of His own attributes. Man and woman were made in the image of God, and everything that God made was good (Ge 1:31). Satan's envy was so fierce, so strong, as he gazed at the beautiful couple, the beautiful home God had made for them, and the sweet fellowship God had with them, that he was determined to cause their fall. Not satisfied with bringing about the fall of some of the angels, he now sought the downfall of human beings. Satan turned his attention towards man, and he has been doing so ever since.

Satan employed for his medium the serpent, who was then a creature of fascination and beautiful appearance. The serpent in his Edenic form is not to be thought of as a writhing reptile; that was the effect of the curse. The serpent that lent himself to Satan may well have been the most beautiful of creatures. Traces of that beauty still remain despite the curse. Every movement of the serpent is graceful, and many species are beautifully coloured. Had Satan appeared in his own form, which was ugly and dark, Adam and Eve may well have been repelled at once, so he took on a form that was beautiful, concealing his real purpose so that he might more effectually accomplish his aim. He still does the same thing today. He makes sin appear lovely, inviting, and even good, to attract us and cause us to sin.

The very first thing the serpent said to Eve was, "Did God really say, 'You must not eat from any tree in the garden'?" (Ge 3:1), sowing a seed of doubt in the mind of Eve as to what God had really said. Had Eve refused to enter into conversation with the serpent, she would have been safe, but she chose to parley with him, and fell a victim to his wiles. God made Adam and Eve with a free will; Eve did not have to listen to the serpent, she could have walked away.

It is the same today. People choose to doubt and argue about the commandments of God; instead of accepting His divine commands, they accept human theories, which are just a disguise of Satan's wiles.

"The woman said to the serpent, 'We may eat fruit from the trees in the garden, but God did say, "You must not eat fruit from the tree that is in the middle of the garden, and you must not touch it, or you will die"'" (Ge 3:2–3). "'You will not surely die,'" said the serpent (suggesting God was untruthful), "'your eyes will be opened, and you will be like God, knowing good and evil.'" Being like God, remember, is what Satan himself desired before he fell. Eve was deceived by the serpent, and yielded to temptation, and through her influence, Adam was also led into sin.

Satan lead Adam and Eve to distrust their creator, and to believe God had restricted them by withholding wisdom and knowledge from them. It is the same today. Satan suggests to mankind that God restricts people, taking away their freedom and liberty, and that Christianity is oppressive and cruel. Adam and Eve's disobedience was a great triumph for Satan, for with it sin passed into the human race (Ro 5:12).

Their sin had separated them from God, so they could no longer enjoy direct fellowship with God. It would now mean that man would need a mediator to reconcile him to God. The first promise of a Redeemer is given in Genesis 3:15, "'And I will put enmity between you and the woman, and between your offspring and hers; he will crush your head, and you will strike his heel.'"

We read in Isaiah 53:5, "But he was pierced for our transgressions, He was crushed for our iniquities." When Satan heard God's curse on him, he must have trembled, for he knew that his efforts to deprave the human race would one day be interrupted by means of a Saviour, who would reconcile man to God.

The enemy of Christ and His followers is Satan, and the enemy of Satan is Christ and His followers. Jesus once said to those who were against Him, "You belong to your father, the devil, and you want to carry out your father's desire" (Jn 8:44).

Jesus also called the devil a liar, and the father of lies.

It is only the grace of Christ implanted in our hearts which creates in us enmity against Satan. Satan's enmity against the human race is kindled by the knowledge that believers are, through Christ's death on Calvary, objects of God's mercy and grace.

The words of Satan to Eve, 'Your eyes will be opened' proved true only in this sense, their eyes were opened to discern their folly; they knew evil, and they tasted the bitter fruit of transgression. Until fully developed, sin does not appear the evil thing it really is.

Let us look at the consequences of Adam and Eve's sin, a condition which must remain until the Kingdom age, when Christ rules the earth.

1. The serpent, Satan's tool is cursed (Ge 3:14, Ro 16:20) and becomes God's graphic warning in nature of the effects of sin—the most beautiful and subtle of creatures becomes a loathsome reptile. The deepest mystery of the cross of Christ is strikingly pictured by a serpent of bronze, a type of Christ made sin for us; bearing punishment we deserved (Nu 21:6–9, Jn 3:14–15, 2 Co 5:21).

2. The light occupation of Eden is changed to burdensome labour (Ge 3:17–19).

3. The woman's state is changed, in respect of her increased pain in childbirth, and in the headship of the man (Ge 3:16). Sin's disorder makes necessary a headship, which is vested in man (Eph 5:23, 1 Ti 2:11–14).

4. The brevity of life and the tragic certainty of physical death to Adam and his descendants (Ge 3:19).

In the middle of the garden grew the tree of life whose fruit had the power of perpetuating life. Had Adam and Eve remained obedient to God, they would have had continued access to this tree, and lived forever. By partaking of the tree of knowledge of good and evil, they became subject to death. God banished them from the garden and placed the cherubim, and a flaming sword to guard the way to the tree of life. God had to banish them from the garden, or they would have eaten from the tree of life in their sinful state, thus condemning man to everlasting life with a sinful nature.

The wages of sin is death, both physical and spiritual; the gift of eternal life can only come from Christ, who shed His blood at Calvary that we might live.

From the days of Adam to our own time, our great enemy, the devil, has been exercising his power to destroy and oppress. All who know Christ will in one way or another be brought into conflict with this relentless foe. All who actively engage in the cause against Satan and sin, seeking to expose his deceptions and present Christ to the world, will be the target of Satan, but Christ will give power and strength to overcome him day by day. No-one can be overcome unwillingly, the tempter has no power to control the will or force the soul to sin. The very fact that Christ conquered death at Calvary should inspire His followers to fight the good fight of faith, with courage in their hearts. Satan may distress us, but he can't contaminate; he can cause agony, but not defilement. Let us think of that lovely scripture in Romans 8:35–37, ''Who shall separate us from the love of Christ? Shall trouble or hardship or persecution or famine or nakedness or danger or sword? As it is written: 'For your sake we face death all day long; we are considered as sheep to be slaughtered.' No, in all these things we are more than conquerors through Him who loved us.'' In the following chapter we will be looking at how Satan worked until Christ came into the world, to make a way back to God for mankind.

CHAPTER FIVE

A religious devil

SATAN is consistently, emphatically religious. Religious but not Christian, and not holy. Although he declared his intention to attain God's throne, he nowhere mentioned any desire for the holiness of God.

As long as people enjoyed creator fellowship with God, there was no place for the devil. It was therefore essential for Satan to drive a greater wedge between God and man. We have seen his vile footsteps in the garden of Eden, in his first encounter with Adam and Eve and his success in disrupting the simple fellowship and communion they had with God. This disruption became even more pronounced as time passed, for even after the great flood God sent upon the earth because of man's wickedness, people continued to break God's laws.

Satan is basically religious, and wants to be worshipped. Under his deceitful influences, the inherent need to worship was perverted, leading people to worship false gods. In fact, their devotion was turned to the devil, who hid behind many guises and names. People forgot God and became entangled in perverted and horrible practices of worship. Except for the true faith of God held by the children of Abraham, the world became filled with apostasy.

We read in the Scriptures "Certain men, the children of Belial, are gone out from among you, and have withdrawn the inhabitants of their city, saying, 'Let us go and serve other gods, which ye have not known.'" (Dt 13:13 AV).

In the Old Testament, Satan was frequently referred to as Belial, a profane and worthless one. The devil does not discourage worship, he perverts it with lies and deception, and turns it towards himself.

People came to worship many things under the deception of Satan; the sun, the moon, the stars, fire, water, and almost every natural feature of the earth. To these were added earth's creatures, such as the bull, the monkey, the cat, the cow, the jackal, the wolf, the eagle, and above all—the serpent. We read in Romans 1:21–25 exact details of how, and what, people worshipped. "Although they claimed to be wise, they became fools and exchanged the glory of the immortal God for images made to look like mortal man and birds and animals and reptiles. . . . They exchanged the truth of God for a lie, and worshipped and served created things rather than the Creator" (Ro 1:22–23, 25). People still do the same thing today. Some really believe that the planetary system affects their lives. Some worship the moon, others the stars, some the power of fire. Although it all sounds stupid, it is a fact.

Among the deities mentioned in the Scriptures are the human leaders of the nations: the pharaohs of Egypt, the kings of Babylon, Assyria and others. In addition to these deities which could be seen with human eyes, people, through the influence of Satan, invented a multitude of invisible gods.

Egypt had literally hundreds of gods: Horus, Osiris, Amon, Ptah, and many more. In the midst of all the religious confusion was Israel, where the worship of Jehovah was preserved, which made the Israelites a very special people. Yet the devil repeatedly, and persistently, introduced other forms of worship into the land, to contaminate the pure worship of God.

Although the Israelites were led out of slavery in the land of Egypt, by the divine hand of God, they still inclined to worship the gods of Egypt. The people demanded of Aaron, "Come, make us gods who will go before us. As for this fellow Moses who brought us up out of Egypt, we don't know what has happened to him.'' (Ex 32:1).

The bull god Apis, sacred to the Egyptians, was the model of a calf of gold which the newly freed Hebrew slaves worshipped. They decided they wanted to worship, and worship they did.

They wanted an object they could see and touch, something to excite the imagination. Satan took advantage of their confused emotions, and reminded them of their past life in Egypt, and the gods of Egypt. They demanded that Aaron make a golden calf for them and gladly gave up their gold for its construction.

The bull god Apis represented a sexual imagery, in its association with the procreative energies of the bull, which inspires sensual worship. Under the influence of Satan its worshippers could experience awe, excitement and release in an orgy of worship.

This bull god, Apis, which modern-day satanists call a demon god, is still worshipped in satanist temples and black witches' covens. When I first became a Christian and started to read my Bible, I was so surprised to find that many of the gods worshipped and called upon by satanists were mentioned in both the Old and New Testaments. I could hardly believe it at first, but it helped me to understand spiritual warfare, and opened my eyes to the reality of deception. It proved to me how very methodical Satan is, and proved beyond a shadow of a doubt that devil worship is as ancient as the world itself.

In the end, it was Israel's worship of the gods of Canaan that caused their exile from their homeland. We read in 2 Kings 17 just how wicked they had become. They just did not take heed of the warnings, so the Lord rejected them and gave them into the hands of the plunderers (verse 20). We read a long list of their evil acts in this chapter. I will quote a few of them:

''[They] secretly did things against the Lord their God that were not right. From watchtower to fortified city they built themselves high places in all their towns" (verse 9).

"They set up sacred stones and Asherah poles on every high hill and under every spreading tree" (verse 10).

"At every high place they burned incense" (verse 11).

"They worshipped idols, though the Lord had said, 'You shall not do this'" (verse 12).

"They followed worthless idols and themselves became worthless" (verse 15).

"They forsook all the commands of the Lord their God and made for themselves two idols cast in the shape of calves" (verse 16).

"They sacrificed their sons and daughters in the fire. They practised divination and sorcery and sold themselves to do evil in the eyes of the Lord, provoking Him to anger" (verse 17).

This is what the Lord said would happen, and it happened: "The Lord will scatter you among the peoples, and only a few of you will survive among the nations to which the Lord will drive you. There you will worship man-made gods of wood and stone, which cannot see or hear or eat or smell" (Dt 4:27-28).

Let us take a closer look at these gods. Baal (plural Baalim) was a god of the Canaanites. The Baalim were worshipped in nature, outdoors on high hills in forest groves (Dt 12:2-3, Jdg 6:25, 1 Ki 16:31-33). The worship of Baal was deep-rooted in the land and proved a lasting confusion to Israel.

Although various godly men tried to stamp it out, the worship of Baal lasted for years. What most people do not know is that Baal is still called upon in many black witches' covens today. Mother earth is regarded as a great goddess—forests and hills are still the favourite place for witches, and Baal is still worshipped today. The Baal (sun or lord) was the supreme divinity of the Phoenician and Canaanite nations. Ashtoreth was their supreme female divinity. We find her worship well established among the Moabites, and their allies the Midianites, in the time of Moses. Through these nations the Israelites were seduced to worship this god, under the form of Baal Peor (Nu 25:3).

The worship of Baal among the Jews appeared to be appointed with much pomp and ceremony, for temples were erected to him (2 Ki 11:18). The worshippers appear to have been arrayed in appropriate robes (2 Ki 10:22) and worshipped by burning incense (Jer 11:13). The worship of Baal in the satanist temples today is almost identical, with pomp and ceremony, robes and incense. Satan worship is not new, it was with us before the flood.

The goddess Ashtoreth was worshipped widely along the coasts of Palestine. She was a goddess of fertility, and was worshipped with lewd sexual rites. The Hebrews forsook the Lord and served Baal and Ashtoreth (Jdg 2:12–13). They were both worshipped with licentious sexual acts in groves and high places.

During the lifetime of Samuel he influenced the people to return to God and abandon the worship of Baal and Ashtoreth (1 Sa 7:3–4). Ashtoreth is still worshipped today and held in great esteem among witches, black and white. The very same things go on today in covens as in Old Testament times.

Dagon was the chief deity of the Philistines. Although the Jews did not widely serve him, his cult was well established, and a huge temple was erected for it. It was in this temple of Dagon that Saul's head was displayed after his defeat by the Philistines. When the ark of God was captured it was put in Dagon's vile temple, but the image collapsed in the presence of the ark, which represented the true God. Even when they put his images back, the next morning, its hands and its head were broken off, and only his body remained (1 Sa 5:1–6). It was the temple of Dagon that Samson destroyed (Jdg 16:23–30).

When Satan introduced the vile god Molech, it plainly showed the basest side of his evil nature. Molech was worshipped by means of human sacrifice, especially the sacrifice of children.

The Jews allegiance to God had really sunk low, when they were willing to sacrifice their own children to this false and cruel god. Before they entered Canaan God had warned them against this terrible practice (Lev 20:2–5). The warning went unheeded. They still went ahead and did things which can only be described as barbarous. Huge images of Molech (Malcam or Milcam as the god was variously called), were erected in Israel. His arms were used as fiery altars, where children were burned in sacrifice to satisfy the hunger of this cruel god. The Jews even tried to blend their devotion to God and Molech by going from one place of worship to another. This is plainly described in Ezekiel 23:37–39 which reads: "They committed adultery with their idols; they even sacrificed their children, whom they bore to me, as food for them. They have also done this to me: At that same time they defiled my sanctuary and desecrated my Sabbaths. On the very day they sacrificed their children to their idols, they entered my sanctuary and desecrated it. That is what they did in my house."

One can hardly take it in. The Jews, who once served God, who had brought them into a better land out of slavery in Egypt, and provided for them in many wonderful ways, could now resort to this. They could only have been taken over by demon power. Satan was always nearby, chuckling with glee. The Jews were so confused, so perverted, that they hardly knew whom they worshipped, or how, or why.

A popular place of pagan sacrifice was the valley of Hinnom, from which comes the word "Gehenna" which is the root word for hell (Jer 19:6). What a horrible array of gods!

People really feared these gods. They were so blinded that they really believed these gods were true gods, and many thought that if they did not please these gods they would be destroyed.

It is the same today. Many who are caught up in devil worship in one way or another, are fearful of displeasing the devil and his followers, and this is why many are afraid of giving it all up. It was, and still is, a religion of fear. No, the devil does not discourage religion, he promotes it, and twists it into something horrible and ugly.

The most bewildering case of apostasy in Israel's dark history is that of Solomon. He began well, with a humble prayer for wisdom to enable him to lead the people in truth and love, but in the end he fell victim to Satan's wiles.

Solomon had overwhelming success as king, as long as he served the Lord God with his whole heart. He accumulated 1400 chariots and 12,000 horses. He had riches beyond comprehension; he was greater in riches and wisdom than all the kings in the earth. The whole world sought audience with Solomon, to hear the wisdom that God had put in his heart.

Year by year everyone who came to see him brought a gift: silver and gold, robes, weapons, and spices, horses and mules. Solomon however had one weakness, he loved many foreign women. The Lord had said, " 'You must not intermarry with them, because they will surely turn your heart after their gods.' " But Solomon held fast to them, he had 700 wives and 300 concubines, and his wives led Solomon astray. He made provision for his wives to worship their gods, and as he grew older he himself went after them; he followed Ashtoreth, the goddess of the Sidonians, and Molech the detestable god of the Ammonites (1 Ki 11:1–5).

Satan always plays on the weaknesses of people. As soon as you let your guard down he is there to tempt and entice you and cause you to sin. Had Solomon cried to God for help in the hour of temptation, the Lord would have helped him to overcome, but we do not read that Solomon did this. Instead, he listened to the devil, just as Eve had done and was deceived. Solomon's position as king, his wealth, and his wisdom, did not make him immune to temptation—these are no safeguards at all. The only safeguard is obedience to God's word, and earnest prayer for strength, courage and power to overcome. Solomon did not repent as David his father had done when he sinned with Bathsheba. If he had repented of his sin, God would have forgiven him, just as he forgave David before him. We read in Psalm 51, the prayer of David, "Wash away all my iniquity and cleanse me from my sin" (verse 2), and "Create in me a pure heart, O God, and renew a steadfast spirit within me" (verse 10).

There are many Psalms in which David testifies to the mercy of God, when he cried to Him for help and strength in the hour of need. There is no temptation put upon us that is more than we can bear, for when we are tempted, God will provide a way out so that we can stand up under it (1 Co 10:13).

It is always sad to see someone who once loved the Lord, now serving the devil, and unrepentant of their sin, with a heart that is cold and hard. We should take heed of the words of Jesus, "'Watch and pray so that you will not fall into temptation. The spirit is willing, but the body is weak'" (Mt 26:41).

Although Satan set up many gods so that the people would worship them instead of God, he could not and never will, overcome those who worship the one true God. Time and time again God gave His people victory in battle against their enemies. The Lord declared by the prophet Isaiah, "Tell the righteous it will be well with them, for they will enjoy the fruit of their deeds. Woe unto the wicked! Disaster is upon them! They will be paid back for what their hands have done" (Isa 3:10–11). We read again in Ecclesiastes 8:12–13, "Although a wicked man commits a hundred crimes and still lives a long time, I know that it will go better with God-fearing men ... because the wicked do not fear God, it will not go well with them, and their days will not lengthen like a shadow." God always rewards those who love Him, and He will give them the victory over all their enemies if they obey Him, and walk in his ways.

Under the influence of Jezebel, the worship of Baal had taken the place of the worship of Jehovah—but Elijah, a prophet of God, challenged 850 prophets of Baal, and got the victory. This is a true story of one man's courage and faith in God, and is a great testimony of victory over evil. But even when Satan sees he has lost, he still persists. What a lesson we can learn from this! If only Christians could be as persistent as this, even when we fail. He doesn't give up so why do we? Satan doesn't age, but his tactics change as we change as a generation of people. He will not give up his plans until the final day when he will be cast into the lake of fire, and all who follow him will go with him.

Satan did his evil work very successfully in Old Testament times. He brought about the downfall of man and the apostasy of a people, not by denying religion, but by perverting it. He did not oppose God's temple in Jerusalem, he merely added to it—a temple of vice for Ashtoreth, a temple of rioting for the Moabite god Chemosh (2 Ki 23:13), and altars of sacrifice for Molech. This was, and still is, the pattern of apostasy, the strategy of Satan. Now there is apostasy in today's religions: Islam, Hinduism, Mormonism, the Jehovah Witnesses and other cults, but also in the established churches such as the Church of England, Catholic, and yes, even in the modern Charismatic churches.

Satan is seeking to overcome people today, as he overcame our first parents, by shaking their confidence in God and leading them to doubt His wisdom, His government, His laws.

Those who have chosen Satan as their leader are not prepared to enter into God's presence. Pride, rebellion, cruelty, deception, disobedience, and other evil diversions are works of Satan to stop men and women from having pure, sweet fellowship with God, through our Lord Jesus Christ.

We carefully secure our homes with locks and keys from those who may seek to harm us, but do we think of the evil one, who is seeking to destroy our soul, who is constantly seeking access to our lives, and against whose attacks we in our own strength, have no method of defence? Those who yield to the claims of

Christ, are always safe under His care, the wicked one cannot break through as long as we are obedient and faithful to Him.

CHAPTER SIX

A way back to God

THE devil, as we have seen, enjoyed a long period of
success; he seemed to hold the whole world in his
sway. In the duration of time between the Old and New
Testaments, Satan was not asleep or inactive, neither
was God asleep, for we read in God's word, that He
never slumbers or sleeps. It was a very pagan world
(except for the Jews' worship of God). There were
witches, sorcerers, and gods of every description, and
every perverted practice imaginable. Far from being
non-religious, seldom had the world been more completely religious. Typified by Athens, the world was
wholly given over to idolatry (Ac 17:16). In New Testament times the Old Testament gods were largely exchanged for new ones, although the old gods were still
there somewhere. The Hellenic culture for example, was
full of deities like Zeus, the supreme god, and Hera, his
wife; Poseidon, god of the sea; Athena, goddess of wisdom and many more. Rome, which occupied Israel in the
lifetime of Jesus, had its assortment of gods, which the
Romans worshipped throughout the whole empire:
Mars, god of war; Apollo, god of literature and healing
(and still very highly regarded by modern-day spiritists);
Quirinus, the state god; Mercury, the messenger of the
gods; Jupiter, the prime god, and many others. Among
the array of gods were an elaborate assortment of goddesses, who seemed to have attributes applicable to
every human circumstance: Juno, wife of Jupiter and
protector of marriage; Ceres, goddess of grain and
plenty; and rising above them all, Cybel, the mother of

gods. Gods of love, still popular today, like the Greek Eros and Roman Cupid, represent the deep longing in the heart of men and women for real love. Goddesses of love, like Venus, Isis, and Aphrodite are still very much esteemed among those who are involved in occult practices.

The devil did his work very thoroughly, he spread his false gods all over the known world. It was into such a world that the promised Messiah was born.

Satan had been warned by God of this event in the garden of Eden, after he successfully deceived Eve, and caused man's fall. The devil was also reminded of it through the prophets of the Old Testament, and I have no doubt he dreaded the dawning of that day.

We read many prophetic promises concerning the birth of Christ in Scripture, ''For to us a child is born, to us a son is given, and the government will be on his shoulders. And he will be called Wonderful Counsellor, Mighty God, Everlasting Father, Prince of Peace'' (Isa 9:6). Other great promises concerning the coming of the Christ to this earth are in Isaiah 53 and 63:1–6, Psalm 22, 68:18, 110 and Jeremiah 23:5–6. These and others shone like stars in the dark night of Hebrew history.

Satan really trembled when the birth of Christ was announced; he knew a way back to God was made for mankind. There was absolutely *nothing* Satan could do about the birth of Christ, for in the fullness of time Christ was born of a virgin in Bethlehem, Judea. Satan then set about trying to kill the Christ child using Herod, the king of Judea as his medium. He filled his heart with anger, and conspired to use the Magi to find the child. But the Magi, who brought gifts and worshipped the child, were warned in a dream not to return to Herod.

When Herod heard that he had been outwitted by the Magi, Satan stirred up even more hatred in his heart, and ordered the slaying of all male children of two years of age and under. This shows yet again the savage side of Satan's already evil nature. Satan delights to cause sorrow, grief and pain.

We do not read much about the childhood of Jesus, apart from the visit to Jerusalem with His earthly parents, when at the age of twelve Christ amazed the teachers in the temple by His understanding. There is no doubt God protected the child, for we read, "Jesus grew in wisdom and stature, and in favour with God and men" (Lk 2:52). This did not please the devil very much, who then planned to oppose Jesus, trick Him, trap Him, and even tried to kill Him before He could complete the work His father sent Him to do, namely, to destroy the works of the devil (1 Jn 3:8).

Christ came to a very pagan world, a world of great evil, a world very much like our world today. Everywhere Christ went, in everything He did and said there was a direct challenge to the devil. He set an example for us to follow, and established for us victory over the forces of darkness. In a world of darkness, Christ was the light. In a world of deceit, Christ was the truth. In a world of great evil, Christ was righteous. In a world of demonic power, Christ was the power of God. Christ's coming to earth signalled a time of direct confrontation with the devil. Satan tempted Christ to forsake His divine purpose, and end the long hard struggle between them. Yet this confrontation was necessary to establish Christ's divine and eternal supremacy over the devil, on earth, as well as in heaven.

Let us look at the first direct confrontation between Christ and the devil. In Mark's Gospel we read, "The Spirit sent him out into the desert" (Mk 1:12), which speaks of Christ's absolute necessity for direct confrontation with the devil, in order to establish and gain mastery over him, once and for all.

They met in the wilderness of Judea, a place so wild, so forbidding, that only the wild beasts lived there. It was a place searing with heat in the daytime and miserably cold at night. Christ had no opportunity to eat; it was only after the forty days had ended, that he was hungry (Lk 4:2).

When the forty days of fasting were ended, the devil took advantage of Christ's physical weakness and hunger to attack His ministry with three subtle temptations.

This is how the devil still works today. When God's children are physically weak, he sees an opportunity to attack them, vex them, and discourage them in every way he can. This is especially true with God's appointed ministers: Satan attacks their ministry for the Lord when circumstances are difficult. The devil tried to lure the Lord into an abuse of His ministry, an abuse of His power and authority and a perversion of His allegiance to His Father.

The first temptation

In the first temptation, Satan struck at a basic human need, suggesting the Lord should turn stones into bread. Listen to what Satan says: " 'If you are the Son of God, tell these stones to become bread'" (Mt 4:3). Satan tried to plant seeds of doubt into the Lord's mind, concerning His Sonship, just as he planted doubts into Eve's mind in the garden of Eden. Christ answered Satan, "'Man does not live on bread alone, but on every word that comes from the mouth of God'" (Mt 4:4). Christ used the same word of God, found in Deuteronomy 8:3. This is our weapon, Jesus set us an example, by using God's word, for His word is sharper than any double-edged sword (Heb 4:12).

Satan hates the word of God, he knows how powerful it is, and how much damage it can do to him and his satanic hosts; so this should encourage us to believe God's word, and use God's word at all times. Hide God's word in your heart, meditate upon it, and you will always get the victory.

The second temptation

The devil then tempted the Lord to leap from the pinnacle of the temple in Jersualem, making an irrelevant use of Scripture to assure Christ he would be safe. Once again the devil tempted Jesus to resort to sensationalism as a means of demonstrating His power over all other powers. The devil is very clever; he can use Scripture to try and confuse the child of God. He can make them take Scripture out of its context. Notice here that Christ said "It is written" in answer to the devil's first temptation, and the devil comes back with the same words that Christ used: " 'If you are the Son of God, throw yourself down. *For it is written*: "He will command his angels concerning you, and they will lift you up in their hands, so that you will not strike your foot against a stone." ' Jesus answered him, '*It is also written*: "Do not put the Lord your God to the test" ' " (Mt 4:6–7). Christ teaches us that even while He was tempted, tired and hungry, one scripture does not contradict another.

The third temptation

Satan's last assault on the divinity of Christ was so blatant, so overt, so specific in its aim it almost defies belief. The devil actually suggested that Christ should bow down and worship him (Mt 4:9). Satan showed Christ all the kingdoms of the world and their splendour, and said, " 'All this I will give you, if you will bow down and worship me.' " There was a particularly subtle side to this temptation: by yielding to it, the devil implied that Jesus could have dominion over the whole world without going through the agony of Gethsemane, the humiliation of the judgment hall, and the suffering of Calvary. Satan tried to tempt Jesus to take a short cut to His dominion, to bypass His death by crucifixion.

The deep implication of this temptation is too terrible to consider. If Christ had failed the test it would have eliminated the only way back to God, the only way by which we can be saved. It is the blood of Christ, shed on Calvary's cross, that provides a way back to God, and salvation for the whole human race. If Christ had failed the test, He would have abandoned mankind to certain death. But let us rejoice that Christ did not abandon mankind, He overcame temptation, and made a way back to God for us.

When we look at the last temptation alongside the devil's desire to usurp God, we see again that the original ambition of Satan has never been abandoned: he still seeks worship. In the last days we shall see him increasingly seeking worship for himself by perverting the true worship of God.

After the wilderness ordeal, we read that the devil departed from Jesus until an opportune time (Lk 4:13). Although we do not read of any further face-to-face encounters there are numerous descriptions of other confrontations. For example, Jesus came upon many demoniacs and cast demons out of them. The gospels are full of accounts of Christ's liberation or healing of the demon-possessed, some of which are worth mentioning, because they provide proof of Christ's spiritual authority. In Mark 5:1-20 we read how Christ and His disciples encountered a man in the regions of Gadara whose demon-possession was very severe; he wore no clothes, he lived among the tombs and no-one could tame him. Night and day he cut himself with stones, and it seemed that everyone was afraid of him. He saw Jesus coming from a distance and fell on his knees in front of Him, and shouted at the top of his voice, ''What do you want with me, Jesus, Son of the Most High God? Swear to God that you won't torture me.'' Jesus asked his name, and the man replied, ''My name is Legion, for we are many.'' Jesus commanded the demons to come out of the man. In the Roman militia a legion was a force of three to six thousand soldiers. As the term was used to refer to the demoniac, it meant that this man was possessed by multiple demons. When Jesus cast them out they begged Him to be sent into a herd of pigs; Jesus gave permission, and the demons entered the pigs, which ran down a steep slope into the sea and were drowned. The man who had been possessed then sat at the feet of Jesus, clothed, and in his right mind. I do not doubt that Satan, who had this poor man bound for so long, was absolutely furious.

Christ's authority over the spirit world was further demonstrated in other cases, as when Peter, James and John met a demoniac on their way down from the Mount of Transfiguration (Mk 9:14–27). Just like the man who was possessed with multiple demons, this boy had numerous maladies as a result of demon-possession, and his father said that the evil spirit threw the boy into convulsions, he foamed at the mouth, gnashed his teeth, and became rigid. The father was very distressed, and brought the boy to Jesus' disciples. They could not cast the evil spirit out, but Jesus cast the demon out and the boy rose up from the ground where the demon had thrown him. He was cured, delivered, free, and the people were amazed at the mighty power of God (Lk 9:43).

Neither the number nor the nature of the demons mattered to Jesus; He was master of every enemy power. Jesus exercised authority over them. Frequently the demons recognised Jesus, with such words as these: '''You are the Son of God''' (Mk 3:11). Jesus ordered the demons to be silent. He would not allow demons to announce His deity.

Jesus went about doing good. He healed the sick, gave sight to the blind, cleansed the leper and set free the demon-possessed. Satan was just a bystander; he could not do a thing about it. Everyone was attracted to Jesus. His compassion accepted people, His power healed people, and Satan's power was to put to flight.

Christ had authority over death—the greatest and the most dreaded power of all. Death is the final truth that we all must face, death is the consequence of sin, the fruit of rebellion that reaches back to Satan's deception of Eve in the garden of Eden. Now Jesus Christ manifested His power over death by restoring the dead to life. He raised at least three people from the dead: the widow's son in Nain (Lk 7:11–15),

Lazarus in Bethany (Jn 11:11–44), and the daughter of Jairus (Mt 9:18–26).

Christ had authority over sin. Christ's forgiveness of sin was the rescue of souls from the bondage of the devil, an action so bold that even the religious leaders were astonished by it. They questioned His authority, or rather Satan through them dared to question it: "Why does this fellow talk like that? He's blaspheming! Who can forgive sins but God alone?" (Mk 2:7).

Christ demonstrated His authority to forgive sins when he forgave the woman caught in the act of adultery (Jn 8:3–11). The religious leaders of that day laid a trap for Jesus by bringing the woman to him (supposedly for advice and judgment). This was a direct challenge to Christ's authority, another of Satan's attacks on the Lord's Sonship, working through these so-called religious leaders, who were nothing but hypocrites themselves. Jesus resolved this confrontation by writing on the ground, which exposed the sins of these hypocritical leaders, who were the woman's accusers. They left one by one, and the woman was left alone with Jesus, who said, "Woman, where are your accusers? Has anyone condemned you?" "No-one sir," she said. "Then neither do I condemn you. Go now and leave your life of sin." Satan was defeated yet again.

Christ had authority over the elements. Jesus and the Father were one. Christ was with God in the beginning, and the world was made by Him, therefore He had authority over that which He had made. Jesus said to Philip, " 'Don't you believe that I am in the Father, and that the Father is in me? The words I say to you are not just my own. Rather, it is the Father living in me, who is doing His work' " (Jn 14:10).

On one occasion Jesus was in a small boat on the lake of Galilee, and a sudden very fierce storm arose. The disciples were with Him in the boat. They were experienced fishermen, and knew the moods of the sea but they were unable to cope, and cried to the Lord who was asleep, "Teacher, don't you care if we drown?" He arose, and rebuked the wind and waves, and there was a great calm (Mk 4:35-39).

I believe this was yet another time the devil tried unsuccessfully to get rid of the Lord before He could die on the cross. What better opportunity than when the Lord was asleep in a boat, in the middle of the sea? But even the wind and waves obeyed Him (Mk 4:41).

On another occasion Jesus walked on water (Jn 6:16-21). The disciples were afraid when they saw Jesus walking on the water towards them, but the Lord said, "'It is I, don't be afraid'" (Jn 6:20).

Jesus invested His disciples with His own power and authority. In Luke 9:1 we read, "When Jesus had called the Twelve together, he gave them power and authority to drive out all demons and to cure diseases." Satan not only attacked the Lord, he attacked the disciples, and he still does today.

The greatest opposition Christ encountered came from the religious leaders: the Scribes, Pharisees and Sadducees. The Pharisees had once been an honourable body of men, whose name means "the separated ones". They who had once been worthy, who for so long awaited the coming of the Messiah, they who had once kept Judaism fit for His coming, were now not fit themselves when He did come. They followed the pattern of apostasy by ministering error mixed with truth, by substituting self-righteousness for true righteousness and by crushing the spirit of the law with the letter of the law. The devil had so successfully infiltrated this proud sect, that even the harlots, drunkards, tax collectors and thieves were more sympathetic to Jesus than they were (Mt 21:31). This proud sect committed the ultimate blasphemy when they accused the Lord of casting out devils through Beelzebub the chief of devils (Lk 11:15).

Jesus asserted truth without hesitation, and was very strong in His opposition to these pretentious religious leaders, criticising them with boldness (Mt 5:20). Christ asserted truth because error must always be silenced with truth, and the power of wrong must be overcome with the power of righteousness. Christ overcame the devil in every situation, and by doing so he staked a position for His children, and showed us the way to attain it.

When the seventy-two returned, whom the Lord had sent before him to every place He himself would go later, they said, "'Lord, even the demons submit to us in your name.'" Jesus replied, "'I saw Satan fall like lightning from heaven'" (Lk 10:17–18). Jesus saw Satan cast out of heaven long before these men, or anyone else, encountered him, so Jesus knew just what He was up against here on the earth.

Jesus said these wonderful words to His disciples, "'I have given you authority to trample on snakes and scorpions and to overcome all the power of the enemy; nothing will harm you. However, do not rejoice that the spirits submit to you, but rejoice that your names are written in heaven'" (Lk 10:19).

Just as Jesus recognised the devil, so can we. By the power of the Holy Spirit, we can discern what is of the devil, and what is of the Lord; between right and wrong, true and false. It is entirely up to us to use the power He has given us, and resist the devil, and then he will flee from us (Jas 4:7).

The Lord preached good news to the poor, He proclaimed freedom for the prisoners, and the recovery of sight to the blind, release for those who are oppressed, and proclaimed the year of the Lord's favour (Lk 4:18–19).

Everywhere He went He was a blessing: the sick were healed, the blind received their sight, the lame walked, the deaf heard, and those who were bound by Satan were released. But Jesus also came to die for the sins of the whole world. When Jesus tried to teach the disciples that the Son of Man must suffer many things, to be rejected by the elders, the chief priests and teachers of the law, they did not understand—especially Peter, who took Jesus aside and rebuked Him. Jesus knew instantly that Satan was speaking through Peter, and He rebuked Satan, saying, "'Get behind me,

Satan! . . . you do not have in mind the things of God, but the things of men'" (Mt 16:23).

The time was approaching for Jesus to be brought before Pilate to be tried, and the disciples forsook Him and fled. They could not even stay awake and pray in the Lord's darkest hour in the garden of Gethsemane, where He prayed and agonised and sweat great drops of blood (Lk 22:44). The battle was fought and won right there in the garden of Gethsemane, where Christ prayed to His Father and asked His Father if it was possible for that hour to pass from Him. He prayed, "'Father, if you are willing, take this cup from me; yet not my will, but yours be done.'" Christ was willing to pay the debt of sin; He was willing to be crucified for us, that we might go free.

Satan then filled Peter's heart with great fear and he denied the Lord he loved three times with curses, saying, "'I don't know him'" (Lk 22:54–62). Satan must have gloated over this at the time, but later Peter repented and wept bitterly, and that silenced Satan for a while.

This was the time that Satan dreaded the most, and if he trembled when Jesus was born, he trembled even more when Christ, the Son of God, was made sin for us at the cross of Calvary, because Satan was defeated at the cross where Jesus shed His blood, so that men and women could be saved. Satan suffered a massive blow when the veil of the temple was torn in two, from top to bottom, for it meant that a way back to God was made for sinners. Yes! Satan knew that the prophecies concerning the Messiah were fulfilled, and the supreme and perfect sacrifice for sin was made and now mankind could come again and have pure and sweet fellowship with God. This little chorus that I learned in Sunday school many years ago puts it very simply and plainly:

There's a way back to God from the dark paths of sin,
There's a door that is open, and you may go in.
At Calvary's cross is where you begin,
When you come as a sinner to Jesus.

We read with reverence and awe how Jesus suffered all the agony in the garden of Gethsemane, all the humiliation of the judgment hall, and the terrible suffering of the cross. All that Satan tried to tempt Him to bypass, Jesus willingly endured so that mankind could be reconciled to God. The scene of Calvary was a powerful sight, a heart-rending sight. How anyone can read the accounts leading up to His crucifixion, and the crucifixion itself without being deeply moved is beyond comprehension. We read in Matthew 27:51-53, ''At that moment the curtain of the temple was torn in two from top to bottom. The earth shook and the rocks split. The tombs broke open and the bodies of many holy people who had died were raised to life. They came out of the tombs, and after Jesus' resurrection they went into the holy city and appeared to many people.''

When Christ rose from the dead he triumphed over the grave, he triumphed over death, showing plainly that He was victorious over the devil. The devil must have been really shaken, because he knew that those who had been in his dreadful grip for so long could be freed, and receive the gift of everlasting life.

How the disciples rejoiced to see their beloved Master alive! He appeared first to Mary Magdalene, one of Satan's former slaves, whom Christ set free from seven evil spirits (and that was before He went to the cross). Now Christ had conquered death so that men and women who trust Him as Saviour will never die. At one time Christ spoke these words to Martha, the sister of Mary and Lazarus whom Christ raised from the dead, '''I am the resurrection and the life. He who believes in me will live, even though he dies; and whoever lives and believes in me will never die''' (Jn 11:25-26). How those words thrill us today!

When Christ died and rose again, He took the keys of death away from Satan, He descended into the lowest parts of the earth, He led captives with Him, and ascended on high (Eph 4:8-10). Can you imagine how Satan felt when Jesus did this? Not only did Satan fail to stop Christ dying on the cross for lost and sinful man,

Christ released captives; the dead saints arose from their graves and Jesus took the keys of death and hell away from Satan. What a massive defeat all this was for the devil! In Revelation 1:18 we read, "I am the Living One; I was dead, and behold I am alive for ever and ever! And I hold the keys of death and Hades." I can just imagine the look on Satan's face when Jesus Christ, the Son of God, took the keys of death straight out of his ugly blood-stained hands. This scene really excites me. My Jesus, so mighty, so powerful, looks Satan straight in the eyes and pronounces his power over death, and takes away the devil's authority over death, in the devil's domain. What a sight that must have been!

Satan, powerful as he may seem, is not *all powerful*. Satan does not hold the keys of death, Christ does, and no-one can die, neither saint nor sinner, unless Christ permits it to happen. What a revelation! What an eternal truth! How very wonderful it is!

What Satan had robbed man of in the garden of Eden, Christ, the second Adam, through His death and resurrection, had restored, to those who own Him as Lord and Saviour. For since death came through a man (Adam), the resurrection of the dead comes also through a man (Jesus). For as in Adam all die, so in Christ all will be made alive.

When Christ arose from the dead, Satan re-organised his army of demons to devise another plan in order to divert men and women from accepting Christ, who said, " 'I am the way and the truth and the life. No-one comes to the Father except through me.' " (Jn 14:6).

One of Satan's first diversions was to tell people that Christ did not rise from the dead, that Jesus Christ was still in the tomb. The chief priests and elders were alarmed when they heard the news that Christ had risen from the dead and had been seen by many. They bribed the soldiers with a large sum of money to tell the people that the disciples had come and stolen the body of Jesus by night, and this story circulated among the Jews (Mt 28:11–15).

This lie has been passed on into even our generation. There are a great many people who do not believe in the resurrection of Christ, and sad to say, even some in the church who have said the same thing. This is just a clever trick of the devil, who knows his time is short, and still desires to destroy men and women and take them to hell with him. It is very convenient for the devil because he knows that by telling this lie, men would say, "Jesus Christ is dead, so He cannot change me." Some people just do not want any changes in their lives, it is easier for them to hold on to their sin. A great many people know that Jesus is alive, because they also know that a dead Christ could not change them, only a risen glorified Saviour can do this, and He is still changing lives today. He changed me!

It matters not how Satan diverts people today, as long as they are diverted from the foot of the cross. The devil caters for every class of society, and all modern trends. We will be looking at some of these diversions in the following chapters.

CHAPTER SEVEN

Devilish diversions

SATAN is always ready to supply the heart's desires, and to palm off deception in the place of truth. Not everyone would believe the lie that Christ had not risen from the dead, there was too much evidence to the contrary, "The Lord added to their number daily those who were being saved" (Ac 2:47). Very often though, people who throw up their hands in horror at one deception will readily believe another, so what better for Satan than to raise up false doctrines, and cause confusion and division?

In Revelation the devil is repeatedly referred to as a deceiver: "Satan, which deceiveth the whole world" (Rev 12:9 AV). "He deceived the inhabitants of the earth" (Rev 13:14). The truth is, that Satan has been a deceiver from the beginning, is now, and will be till the end.

Satan panders to the heart's desires, inclinations and weaknesses of his prey. The world is full of people who are willing to be deceived, as long as the deception is pleasant and fulfilling, if only for a short time. Satan's scheme is to conquer the cause of Christ by means of division, duplication, and diversion.

Satan knows that when there is division in the Church of God, the whole body of believers are weak and defenceless. Satan can then say to the outsider, "Christians are always quarrelling among themselves." Paul speaks of this in 1 Corinthians 3:3-4: "You are still worldly. For since there is jealousy and quarrelling among you, are you not worldly? . . . For when one says, 'I follow Paul,' and another, 'I follow Apollos,' are you not mere men?'' Paul speaks of this again in Romans 16:17–18, ''I urge you, brothers, to watch out for those who cause divisions and put obstacles in your way that are contrary to the teaching you have learned. Keep away from them. For such people are not serving our Lord Christ, but their own appetites. By smooth talk and flattery they deceive the minds of naive people.''

Who is behind all divisions in the house of the Lord? No-one else but the devil himself! Much is said in the world today about divisions in the church, and much is said about the breakdown of morals, and this is appropriate for these should be guarded lest Christian integrity be lost altogether. But there are other breakdowns which are just as important and threaten the cause of Christ in our world: the breakdown of fellowship, faith, confidence and love. When there are breakdowns of personal relationships within the church, the body of believers are weak, and nothing invites the attacks of Satan more than schism and division. When Christians devour each other with suspicion, jealousy and backbiting, they are doing the devil's work for him. In 1 Peter 5:8 we read, ''Be self-controlled and alert. Your enemy the devil prowls around like a roaring lion looking for someone to devour.'' When we on the other hand, love one another and build one another up, the whole world will know that we are genuine; we read this in God's word, ''All men will know that you are my disciples, if you love one another'' (Jn 13:35).

Divisions are nothing but clever diversions of the devil to stop Christians from doing what we should be doing: loving the Lord with all our hearts, minds, and spirits, and reaching out to the lost with a message of hope, love, and salvation through the shed blood of Christ, God's Son.

Diversion is another clever tactic of the devil in his warfare against the church of Jesus Christ. Diversion is the focussing of attention on one matter whilst another of greater importance passes unnoticed. There are many hundreds of diversions today that negate important issues, that lead away from Christ and His plan of salvation, and we are going to focus on just a few of them.

Duplication is probably the worst of Satan's diversionary tactics. It is certainly the most confusing to many people, and the surest way to victory for the devil. What Satan cannot deny, he imitates, and obtains the same result as with a successful denial. The adverse effect of duplication is clearly illustrated by the metaphor of a sudden influx of bogus money. The flood of counterfeit notes creates suspicion of the genuine article. It works the same way with Christianity. The counterfeit version causes suspicion and confusion, which in the end leads to an outright rejection. The devil is very busy supplying false Christs and false religion, which is just what he did in the Old Testament, only now it is centred around Christ, rather than God.

Jesus warned the disciples that false Christs would appear. Mark 13:21–22: "At that time if anyone says to you, 'Look, here is the Christ!' or, 'Look, there he is!' do not believe it. For false Christs and false prophets will appear and perform signs and miracles to deceive the elect—if that were possible." Let us take a look at some of the false Christs, and false doctrines that Satan has raised up. Some of these false Christs have claimed they were Christ reincarnated, and others have said they were Christ himself returned to the earth.

Father Divine

This was the assumed name of the leader of an American Messianic movement that was strong in the 1930s to the 1960s. He lived in a New York mansion, which his devoted followers gave him, in the lap of luxury, until he died in 1965. He claimed he was Christ, and many hundreds believed him.

Children of God

In 1968, a Christian and Missionary Alliance minister, named David Berg, began an outreach among the hippies. He recruited many hundreds who assisted him. They gave up possessions, they left family and friends, schools and jobs to live in communes, and shared all things in common. Things went very wrong when Berg started to teach false doctrine, and things got too hot for him, so he kept moving around. The movement soon spread to England, bringing yet more error and deceit. Berg assumed the identities of Moses and David, king of Israel. His vulgar letters, which he called MO letters, MO being short for Moses, were, according to him, God's word for today, as compared with the Bible, which now became God's word for yesterday. In addition to having all things in common, Berg and his followers began to share wives and husbands, and began to offer free sex for new converts, calling it "flirty fishing." This is so tragic, because it all got even worse. Those who started out with a genuine desire to serve the Lord, were deceived into following this man, Berg, who led them far away from the truth, into almost unbelievable perversions. They started out with the name "Children of God", but were in fact far from doing God's work, and are now doing the work of the devil. Later on they changed their name to "the family of love"—but what kind of love? They were diverted from the right path, and trod the path of wickedness.

Hare Krishna Society

When members of this cult first began their recruiting activities in this country, it was looked upon as a huge joke. Surely we send missionaries to the Orient to convert people from paganism, not them to us! Wearing Oriental garb and with shaven heads, they peddle their literature and articles to finance their movement. They can be seen at airports, bus-stations, and sometimes the main shopping centres, dancing around and chanting some mumbo-jumbo, which is often a source of amusement to passers-by. The main teaching of this cult is that Krishna is a personal god and present in any form he chooses: in wood, stone, marble, and in the things made by his followers. Krishna is also present in people, and has been for 5000 years or more. Although Krishna is the official god, Swami Prabhupada the guru of the cult, is also given god-like devotion by his followers. Here we see that Satan uses the element of mystery. People are drawn to something that looks, or seems mysterious or spooky, something different, which attracts people, especially young people, who go through a stage of being generally bored and discontented with their lives. Satan, the greatest deceiver of all time has certainly deceived many people by this awful cult.

The Unification Church

This is yet another cult that came from the Far East, and its adherents are widely known as "The Moonies". Sun Myung Moon is of Presbyterian background, but has strayed far away from his Christian roots. The Moonies follow a creed that is a pot-pourri of Biblical teaching, Oriental philosophy, and the personal views of Sun Myung Moon. New converts are won through an aggressive recruitment programme. The Moonies operate under numerous related organisations and raise funds by selling flowers they have grown on their land, and making candles, and they call their methods "heavenly deception". Deception it is, but heavenly it is *not*. They practise communal living, in common with most cults, but they have the added flourish of mass marriages of couples, who have been personally paired off by Moon himself. The Moonies have attracted much attention from the international press because of their rigid rules which, when investigated amount to nothing else but brain-washing. Followers are compelled to forsake all to follow Moon: family, friends and jobs. Many have given their property, houses and cars to the movement, and many distressed parents have tried to win their teenage children back. Some have been successful, others have not. Altogether, it is a heart-breaking fact that the Moonies have been responsible for causing the break-up of families, who have never been the same since.

Moon speaks of a trinity of religions: Judaism, Christianity, and the Unification Church, and believes that there should be a religious-political movement, with him as the leader, of course. His followers believe that he is the Messiah, a belief that Moon does not discourage. He often speaks of the so-called mistakes of Jesus, such as His failure to use political power to build a material empire. Moon in the late 80s had a worldwide following of 60,000 members, and well over 10,000 workers, with a total following (as distinct from membership) of more than three million in the United States alone; although there has been a break away from the movement since the exposure of the financial swindle it was mixed up in some years ago.

The Moonies and Hare Krishna are just the tip of the iceberg of false religions; there are many more major and minor cults in our world today. They include such movements as Divine Light Mission, The Church of Scientology, Eckankar, the faith of Total Awareness, and a host of others. Most of the cults are fairly obvious to most mature Christians, but let us not forget those others which, because of the fact that they are well-known to the general public, are often overlooked, and therefore often escape exposure. We are going to have a fresh look at the more well-known cults.

Jehovah's Witnesses

The operations and the literature of the "Jehovah's Witnesses" have spread into 160 countries, and they are still expanding. That there is a huge and efficient organisation behind the movement is evidenced by the vast coverage of its literature. The founder was Charles Taze Russell, of Pittsburg USA. Finding no existing religion to his liking, he assumed the title "Pastor" and founded one of his own, the most attractive feature of which was the non-existence of hell. He became increasingly popular in his denunciation of organised religion and the clergy.

Mr Russell prophesied that our churches, schools, banks and governments would be completely destroyed by October 1914. Later, when it did not happen as he said, the destruction was promised in instalments ending in 1925. Here are some of their errors: denial of the Trinity; Christ was created and not Divine until His resurrection; He was merely a human atonement and His body was not raised from the dead; His second advent took place in 1874, and the saints were raised in 1878; there is no personal Holy Spirit; the Lord is now a purely spirit being; the Christian church was rejected by God in 1878; there is a second probation for the wicked.

Christians are told that their way, and their church is wrong, and only the Witnesses are right. The door-to-door workers are very highly trained and know just what Scriptures to refer to, which are cleverly twisted to confound the unwary. It is wise to know just how they do twist the Scriptures and take them out of context. They will not stay with you long if they think they are in danger of being caught out themselves.

They try very hard to get inside your home for a Bible study—which is always taken from their own version of the Bible. Here Satan takes advantage of lonely people who have let these people enter their homes, confusing their minds regarding Christianity by telling them their way is the only way of truth. Often they get their converts through (what they call) Bible study in their homes. Christians who have been let down and hurt by the church in one way or another are also the people they pursue, and the Jehovah's Witnesses have been known to call back time and time again in order to win them over. Here we see the devil at work among those who have left the church, playing upon their emotions. We see the craftiness of the enemy telling people that all churches are wrong, and all churches have failed. Some Christians have not received the right counsel, or none at all, and some have been rejected by the church, which again is the work of the devil.

People just cannot understand that some of our churches have grown cold and are not preaching the truth, but the fact is, this is just the place where the devil seeks entry to drive people away from God and lead them into error. It is vital therefore that the Christian church should hold fast to the truth, in preaching the truth, caring for the flock, and always being watchful and alert, with prayer, and loving counsel for those who are troubled, giving the devil no opportunity to gain a foothold.

The Mormons

Mormonism, or the church of Jesus Christ of the Latter Day Saints, is yet another false cult that specialises in door-to-door work, with a membership in 1960 of 1,650,000 in all its branches. Magnificent and costly Mormon temples have been erected in places as widely separate as Los Angeles and New Zealand. Their story is that Joseph Smith, an illiterate young man, who was hardly able to read until manhood and knew practically nothing of the Bible, had an angelic visitor in 1823. This angelic visitor, Moroni by name, revealed to Smith that, in 420 AD, there had been secreted in the hill Cumorah, near Palmra, New York, several golden plates on which were inscribed the history of the Nephites, who came to America from Jerusalem in 600 BC. Joseph Smith went to the spot, and there were the golden plates and a large pair of spectacles, which he called "Urim and Thummin", and by the aid of which he was able to decipher and translate into English the mystic hieroglyphics, which he claimed were "reformed Egyptian".

All this so-called new revelation resulted in the *Book of Mormon*. The degree of credulity required to accept the Mormon version of the origin of their supposedly holy book seems inexplicable, unless it be that "because they refused to love the truth and so be saved . . . God sends them a powerful delusion so that they will believe the lie'' (2 Th 2:10–11).

If it is asked why Mormonism should be classed as a heresy, the answer is three-fold. Firstly it is anti-Christian. While concealing its errors under the terminology of Christianity, it either perverts or denies all fundamental truths of Christianity, for instance

1. Christ's atonement has only to do with the sins of Adam.
2. Christ is the Son of Adam, God, and Mary, not born of a Virgin.
3. The Holy Spirit is a divine fluid.

All these points are substantiated in their teaching (*Cults and Isms*, J.O. Saunders, Lakeland (1984), p. 109).

Secondly, polygamy was practised among Mormons, at least from the time of the first public announcement of the doctrine in Utah in 1852. It is true that, after a legal battle, the practice was officially abandoned in 1889, but it has been sporadically indulged in until a date as recent as 1944, when law enforcement officers arrested 46 members of the fundamental sect of Mormons in Utah, Idaho and Arizona. It was reported in an interview, ''Of course we believe in what we are doing; this is far bigger than the individual, for it will encompass much more than the man-made laws by which the world lives, and will become a fundamental component in the lives of all righteous living people.'' Here are Joseph Smith's words, from the 1944 edition of *Doctrines and Covenants*: ''If any man espouse a virgin, and desire to espouse another, and the first give her consent, and if he espouse the second, and they are virgins, and have bowed to no man, then he is justified, he cannot commit adultery, for they are given to him.'' All this in spite of such scriptures as, ''The overseer must be above reproach, the husband of but one wife'' and ''A deacon must be the husband of but one wife'' (1 Ti 3:2,12).

While the reorganised Mormon church repudiates polygamy, even they cannot deny that it was practised by all their original twelve apostles. The very fact that polygamy was tolerated at any stage amongst Mormons is sufficient to condemn the whole Mormon system.

Thirdly, Mormons have a counterfeit Bible, the *Book of Mormon*, the origin of which is doubtful and suspicious. They believe the Bible to be the word of God, so far as it is correctly translated, but they say they also believe the *Book of Mormon* to be the word of God. To the Mormons the Bible is not the sole and infallible word of God, it is just a tool to further their subtle teachings. This is what they say concerning the Bible: "If it be that the Apostles and the Evangelists wrote the books of the New Testament, that does not mean they were divinely inspired at the time they were written." Furthermore, "Wilford Woodruff is a prophet, and he can make more scriptures as good as those in the Bible" (Apostle J. W. Taylor Conference, Salt Lake City, April 1897). And about the writings of Joseph Smith, "His literary labours must not be forgotten, he produced more scriptures than any other man we have on record."

We are clearly warned in Revelation 22:18 about adding to God's word: "I warn everyone who hears the words of the prophecy of this book: If anyone adds anything to them, God will add to him the plagues described in this book." The same applies to those who take away words from the Bible: "If anyone takes words away from this book of prophecy, God will take away from him his share in the tree of life and in the holy city, which are described in this book" (Rev 22:19).

The whole of the teachings of the Mormons are blasphemous, yet the outward appearance of those who knock at the doors is clean and upright, which proves the devil does indeed appear as "an angel of light" and deceives many today. The command of the Scriptures is clear, "From such turn aside". We are warned about deceitful workers in 2 Corinthians 11:13, "For such men are false apostles, deceitful workmen, masquerading as apostles of Christ."

This collective confusion of cults is Satan's handiwork.

It provides a fertile field for him, and imposes great difficulty for the true church of God. One thing is very clear, the devil is not anti-religious, only anti-Christian. The devil has provided a massive supermarket of false religions for the last days, and people who are lonely and hungry for love and acceptance are buying. It's all part and parcel of the clever diversion away from the foot of the old rugged cross and the simple way of salvation through Jesus Christ, and the diversions are varied and many.

Let it be emphasised again that the devil, choosing duplication from among his deceitful works, has flooded the world with every conceivable religion, in order to confuse the followers of Christ, and those who are earnestly seeking the truth. He has mixed true with lies, and it is often difficult to know what is true and what is false. The only safeguard is the written word of God. Stray from it, or put your own interpretation upon it, and you are heading for danger, deceit and error.

This also goes for diversions which are already in the Christian churches. Although many would not believe me, or agree with me, I have to speak the truth, without fear of what men think or say. I have seen great error creeping into our churches. The subtle part about it all is that it creeps in very *slowly*, and no-one sees it at first. Let me state emphatically that I believe every word of the Bible is truth, but I have seen the truths of God's word exaggerated beyond truth, until the precious truth of His word is lost. For example, I believe in the gifts of the spirit, and believe these gifts are for the church today, but the devil has even tried to distort these with false manifestations. I have heard false tongues, and false prophecy in the church, but these are not easily discerned even by the true child of God, so it is vital that we discern aright, and deal with this in a proper way.

Let me give you an example of the false gift of discernment of spirits. This has happened on several occasions, and if I did not myself have the true gift of discernment of spirits, it could have greatly upset me or discouraged me, which is just what the devil planned. I was speaking in several churches, giving my testimony, and teaching on spiritual warfare when someone came to me and said, "I discern sister that you are still in bondage to witchcraft." Knowing this was a lie, I replied, "What makes you say such a thing?" "Because I have the gift of discernment," she said. "There is no such gift," I answered her, "I am not in bondage to witchcraft at all, or what would I be doing here warning about it? I also have the gift you say you have, but it is not called the gift of discernment, it is called the gift of *discernment of spirits*. This lady, and others who have tried through the enemy of souls, to stop my ministry, have sadly been deceived by the great deceiver himself. Let me also share with you something else that happened to me not very long ago.

For some time I have not been in the best of health, and although I have been prayed for, I have not been fully healed. This has not worried me as much as it has worried other people, who have tried in their own strength to do something about it. Some have said to me, "I discern that you are bitter, and that is why you are not healed." Others have said to me, "You are resisting the Holy Spirit." And again others have stated, "There is unconfessed sin in your life." All this can be very upsetting to someone who is ill, and knows full-well that the things they are saying are not true. The so-called revelation from God these people gave to me are always the answers that are given when they themselves have run out of answers. When Christian people do not receive healing the way they think they should, they blame the person who needs healing. When I did not fall down on the floor, as many others did, and get up healed, it seemed to offend them. How very careful we should be! The devil seeks to pull down, to discourage, to harm, to damage the Christian's faith, to make the word of God, and the gifts of the spirit look suspicious, and even stupid.

Another trick of the devil concerning the Christian church is to bring into the church false prophets who are readily accepted as true prophets of God by the leaders of the church.

This is because the leaders are ignorant of the Scriptures as to how the devil is working today. Many dear children of God have been in deep despair because of false prophecies. When someone prophesies over you and brings condemnation upon you in front of a congregation, that is not from God, because God does not work like that. The devil is an accuser of the children of God, and will do all in his power to bring condemnation upon them. We read in God's word, "Therefore, there is now no condemnation for those who are in Christ Jesus . . . who do not live according to the sinful nature but according to the Spirit" (Ro 8:1,4).

There is also a spirit of entertainment creeping into the church where the word of God takes second place to music. Music has a very important place in the worship of God, so it is to be expected that the devil will try to pervert this, and put in its place music to entertain, rather than edify, the church of God. When prayer and worship, and the preaching of the word of God takes second place to music, singing, and dancing, then something is very wrong. When singing and dancing and other forms of entertainment take up most of the service, and the preaching of the word of God and prayer takes only 20 minutes at the most, then something must be wrong somewhere. When so-called men of God take more time begging for money than they do preaching the word of God, and praying for those in need, then something is wrong. Although it seems that God is blessing them when the money flows in, the devil is laughing his head off, because he sees how easy it is to deceive many people, even in the church.

There are precious people sitting in our congregations, in great need of healing, those in need of deliverance from bondage, and indeed, who are unconverted, and those in need of counselling in many areas—the list is endless; and there is not even an invitation to go forward for prayer in order to get their needs met, or to talk to someone about their needs. It seems tragic to me. There seems to be a lack of compassion for a lost and dying world, and God will judge His people for this.

What is needed today more than ever before, is the repentance of God's people: for the absence of real compassion, the lack of conviction of sin, and the lack of the power and presence of the Holy Spirit. Coldness, apathy, disregard for the truth, worldliness, loss of vision, lack of power, loss of courage, teaching and instruction from God's word—all this, and much more, is an opening for bringing in further diversions of the devil into the church of Jesus Christ. We must be watchful and alert, prayerful and wise, powerful in the Holy Spirit, humble and true, always abounding in the work of the Lord, seeking to do His will, and building His church, as Christ has commanded us to do. Jesus is building His church today, despite the devil's attempts to tear down and destroy, but this does not excuse us from playing our part, to prevent this from happening.

There is no time to waste. Christ is coming soon. It is time to wake up from the sleep of carelessness, and repent, so that the Lord can pour out His Spirit upon His people, and to hasten the times of refreshing and growth. To meet the needs of this and other lands, there is a need for Holy Ghost revival, and it starts in the house of God. The devil will do his utmost to stop revival and keep God's people in darkness and bondage. The preaching of the word of God under the anointing of the Holy Spirit, is the only way that the conviction of sin will fall upon the hearers, and the devil will be overcome and defeated in his intentions towards the church of Christ today.

This is God's promise to His people, "If my people, who are called by my name, will humble themselves and pray and seek my face and turn from their wicked ways, then will I hear from heaven and will forgive their sin and will heal their land" (2 Ch 7:14).

Keep two things in mind. First, behind every scheme of Satan there is a determination to pervert true worship, and replace it with his own; this is the intention behind all apostasy. Second, the deceptive traps of Satan pose no danger to those who keep their place in Christ and shun evil whenever or however it appears.

When we know who we are in Christ and we are not ignorant of the devil's devices, we will be safe—for the loving Saviour knows how to keep His own. But those who nibble at the traps of Satan, as a mouse nibbles at the cheese in the trap, will be caught in that trap. Those who play with fire will be burned; but those who keep their eyes on Jesus, and walk in His ways, He will keep them in perfect peace until He comes or calls.

CHAPTER EIGHT

The sanctuaries of Satan

ALONG with false Christs and false prophets, there is now an added dimension of deceit: the revival of the practice and belief in occult practices. Judging by the way Satan is wheeling out all his big guns to use against the church, he is apparently getting really desperate. In the book of Revelation we read just what his intensity will be like in the last days: "Woe to the inhabiters of the earth and of the sea! For the devil is come down unto you, having great wrath, because he knoweth that he hath but a short time" (Rev 12:12 AV).

Witchcraft, satanism, spiritism and other black arts were with us long before the flood and were forbidden, first to the Jews, and then to the Christians. As the children of Israel drew near to Canaan, where evil spirits were prominent in idolatrous worship, God commanded them not to be contaminated with such worship. All occult practices are very definitely forbidden by God, and are the sole work of the devil, and as such they are condemned by Scripture: "Let no-one be found among you who sacrifices his son or daughter in the fire, who practises divination or sorcery, interprets omens, engages in witchcraft, or casts spells, or who is a medium or spiritist or who consults the dead. Anyone who does these things is detestable to the Lord" (Dt 18:10–12). Again, in Leviticus 19:31, "Do not turn to mediums or seek out spiritists, for you will be defiled by them. I am the Lord your God."

As we have seen in the previous chapters, the devil

had many who worshipped him in the form of false gods, and he works in the same way today. Until the middle of our century, witchcraft and devil worship seemed to have taken a back seat. Although it was still going on behind the scenes, more attention and interest was given to new scientific discoveries. In 1951 however, the English courts repealed the country's witchcraft act, a law almost forgotten since 1735. Although to most people this seemed insignificant, it proved a major breakthrough to those who practised witchcraft. What had previously been done in secret now became more open, apart from the activities of the black witches, who for the most part prefer to remain secret.

There are many thousands involved in some form of occultism. In 1980 there were an estimated twenty million people in Europe alone. Judging from the increased interest in these things, the number may well have doubled by now.

In my first book *From Witchcraft to Christ* (Concordia 1973), I described much of what went on in the satanist temples, but much was omitted, which I now feel should be exposed. The temples of Satan were mostly situated in large houses which belonged to the richer members of the movement. Walls were torn down inside the houses to provide space for at least 400 worshippers. The temples were never left unattended; some satanists were always in residence to guard the temple from outsiders, and to care for the upkeep of the temple and its contents.

The walls were covered with effigies of Satan, half man, half beast, with cloven hoofs and horns, protruding tongue and ears. Satan can take on any form satanists wish. There are no seats for worshippers. Satanists were there an hour before any ceremony began, no-one was late. If you were late and did not give a very good reason, you were punished by whipping. When you worshipped the devil you stood for hours with arms upraised, or you prostrated yourself on the floor, which was usually made of marble, and engraved with snakes, dragons and flames of fire. On the high altar were cups, knives, bowls, snuffers and candlesticks all made from solid gold and silver. At the side of the altar was a throne-like seat, where the chief satanist sat. The throne itself was carved with expert skill and cunning, with snakes, dragons and flames of fire. The chief satanist's robes were made from the very best black velvet, and embroidered in gold threads with the same snakes, dragons and flames. All this work must have taken a great deal of time and money, but satanists spare no time or expense. There is nothing cheap or imitative in the satanist temples, but in fact, it is all an imitation of what God has. Take the satanist bible for instance. Because God has a book, the Bible, the devil has to have one. They call it the satanist's bible; I prefer to call it an evil book. It is a very poor imitation indeed, since it is filled with evil revelations from former chief priests, which date back over centuries. Here again, no expense was spared for the upkeep of these ancient manuscripts; each one was beautifully bound with gold. No-one could remove them from the temples, except for the chief satanist. Their main teaching, regarding the origin and fall of Satan, has already been described. They also teach that black is white and white is black; that good is evil and evil is good; and that light is darkness and darkness light. Everything is twisted round the opposite way. No matter how stupid this teaching sounds, many believe it; I did once. When you are repeatedly told the same thing, over and over again, you begin to believe it; it is just like a massive brain-washing. We get a very clear picture of witchcraft and satanism from Isaiah 5:20: "Woe to those who call evil good and good evil, who put darkness for light and light for darkness, who put bitter for sweet and sweet for bitter." When I first saw this in the Bible, I was surprised, and showed it to other Christians who were most enlightened by it; it exposes witchcraft and satanism very well indeed.

The satanist book is six times thicker than the average Bible, yet I was able to learn it by heart in a very short time. I did not understand this fully myself at the time, but now I realise how I did it—Satan educated me. Satan does not care two hoots what kind of educational background you have. You can be as thick as two planks, he does not worry about that; all he asks, demands in fact, is allegiance to him and his cause. He will do the rest. When I left school at the age of fourteen, I could barely read and write, yet when I became a prostitute, drug addict and witch, I learned very quickly the ways of evil. When I became queen of black witches and travelled to France, Holland, Germany and South Africa, I was able to converse with people, and teach them the evil art of witchcraft, having never learned their languages. This was a surprise even to the chief satanist, who was unable to achieve this himself.

Satan is educating people today. How do very young children pick up so quickly the bad things, while they are often slow in picking up that which is right and good? Satan is poisoning young minds today by many different means. Video nasties are one of them, depicting dreadful acts of violence, murder, rape, pornography, horror and the occult. Although there has been a clampdown on video nasties, they are still around. Filthy magazines are still being published and sold, and some are on open display for all to see. Sex shops are still open to the public, and some of these sell books on the occult. There are magazines which publish advertisements inviting inquiries about the occult world, and many are falling into the evil web of witchcraft. It is all part of the devil's educational and recruitment programme. I thank my lovely Saviour that when I received him into my life, He uneducated me, and then he re-educated me in the things of God.

People are ignorant of the dangers of even the slightest involvement in occult practices. Little did I realise what I was getting bound up with when I first got involved. No-one warned me of the dangers, because no-one knew about it but the satanists themselves, and they were not going to warn me of what to expect. It is far easier to get into however, than to get out of, as I and others later found out. This is the very reason why I warn people, and expose the occult, no matter what form it takes, and tell them the way out of it all. There is only one way out, and that is through the salvation and deliverance of Christ, who said, "I am the way and the truth and the life" (Jn 14:6).

I have actually burned Bibles and other Christian books in satanist temples; it is all part of the ceremony in every temple. In each temple there are two huge torches crossing each other at either side of the high altar which, when lit, provide light for the temple and fire on which Christian books are burned. I have held Bible after Bible for a full half hour in the white hot flames, until they have disintegrated in ashes, and my hands have remained unburned. This shows how real Satan is, but it proves a far more important point than that—it proves how much Satan hates and fears the word of God, and anything Christian. All the more reason then, for Christians to read and study God's word, and believe God's word, and act upon it. God's word can put the devil to flight. The Bible I once hated and despised, burned and ridiculed, I now love with all my heart, and believe that it is the sole and infallible word of God, inspired by the Holy Spirit from cover to cover. It is our only safeguard from evil and deceit: it is full of God's promises, which never fail; it is a source of inspiration, encouragement and blessing.

One young satanist I know actually gave her whole hand to Satan as a sacrifice in the satanist temple. They took one of the swords from the high altar, kissed it, and raised it high in the air, then cut off her hand and offered it to the devil on a silver platter. Everyone was in a trance-like state, and thought it was a wonderful miracle, because the girl felt no pain. Her arm was then cauterised in the flames of the torch. That girl, and others who at various times gave fingers and toes to the devil, were maimed for life—and what for? Absolutely nothing! What did Satan do for them? Nothing but bring them misery and pain! Jesus said this of the devil and how true it is, "The thief comes only to steal and kill and destroy." Thank God He went on to say, "I have come that they may have life, and have it to the full" (Jn 10:10). I am so glad that I did not sacrifice any part of my body to Satan. I believe that the Lord kept me from that, because He knew that one day He would save me, deliver me from the power of the devil, and use me for His glory, to lead others to Himself and warn of the terrible dangers and the evil of occult practices.

Satan desired a throne while he was in heaven, God's throne, but what he could not get while he was in heaven, he gets right down here on earth. Although the devil has set up many elaborate thrones and altars on the earth in temples of Satan and witches' covens, the greatest throne he has is the throne-room of men's and women's hearts. He sits on the throne of their hearts and minds, ruling over them and influencing human decisions over the affairs of nations. He is "the ruler of the kingdom of the air, the spirit who is now at work in those who are disobedient" (Eph 2:2).

Satan knows full well that he cannot possibly persuade everyone to worship him directly in satanist temples or witches' covens, so he blinds people's minds to the truth some other way, and gets the same result: a denial of God. He tells people that there is no heaven and no hell, no God and no devil. He tells thousands that there is no life beyond the grave, and that the Bible is just an old-fashioned book, written by old-fashioned superstitious men; OK for small children maybe, but not for grown-up educated men and women. Satan is the god of this world: "The god of this age has blinded the minds of unbelievers, so that they cannot see the light of the gospel of the glory of Christ, who is the image of God" (2 Co 4:4). The world loves pleasures and riches more than God. Jesus said this in John 3:19-20: "This is the verdict: Light has come into the world, but men loved darkness instead of light because their deeds were evil. Everyone who does evil hates the light, and will not come into the light for fear that his deeds will be exposed." Some people do not realise just how dark some darkness is, and this can certainly be said of those who are caught in the trap of occultism.

In Revelation 3:9 we read of those who say they are Jews but are of "the synagogue of Satan." This is so very true of all those who practise witchcraft and satanism. Their evil temples are indeed sanctuaries of Satan, the synagogues of Satan. In my first book, *From Witchcraft to Christ*, I described the difference between witches' covens and satanists' temples, but for the benefit of those who still do not know, it is worth repeating. Satanists need a temple and always worship the devil through the chief satanist or a high priest or priestess. Different orders have slightly different rules. Witches, black and white, always gather together in covens, made up of thirteen people, six male and six female if possible, and one being the head, who is called the high priest or priestess. They need no temple; they worship anywhere they can but prefer a secluded place such as a clearing in the woods or a lonely beach, or if indoors, again they prefer a place that is isolated. Their numbers are smaller, but only when they are counted in groups or covens. Altogether the numbers go into many thousands, all over the world.

In God's sight there is absolutely no difference between black and white witchcraft; it is all evil and forbidden by God in Scripture. Because of confusion in people's minds regarding white and black witchcraft, some people think that white witchcraft is all right because they claim they do no harm. This is a gross lie; white witches do a lot of harm. Their religion is as pagan as black witchcraft, their god is Mother Earth, and they call upon and believe in mythological spirits and gods. They chant and dance in their ceremonies, and their sexual rites are disgusting, to say the least. They claim they do no harm yet they do not hesitate to put curses on those who are their enemies, using voodoo methods to do so. They claim they bring rain for the farmers, find lost objects or lost loved ones, heal people and charge no fee for doing it. This is again a total lie. They manage to extract huge sums of money for their favours, by deceiving people with smooth talk. The increased interest in witchcraft is alarming, but it proves the fact that Satan is waging an all-out war against the church of God. God's people are going to come into contact with it one way or another, so it is wise to know just what we are up against.

Jesus spoke of the things that would happen upon the earth in the last days: "And many false prophets will appear and deceive many people. Because of the increase of wickedness, the love of most will grow cold" (Mt 24:11–12). Again in verse 24: "For false Christs and false prophets will appear and perform great signs and miracles to deceive even the elect." Christians should not be afraid about these things, but should instead rejoice, for the coming of the Lord draws near. If we are ignorant and fearful, we cannot fight the good fight of faith with full assurance of victory. Those who are members of the family of God need not fear the evil one, and no witch's curse can affect the child of God. We are instructed in God's word to be alert and watchful and to be clad in the armour which God supplies through His eternal Son. With Christ as our Captain we can face the evil one and his dark angels day by day, hour by hour, fearlessly, knowing that He goes before us. As we abide in Christ, and Christ abides in us, and as we claim His promises in prayer, we stand invincible.

Another sanctuary of Satan is the spiritist movement. One baneful symptom of today's spiritual warfare is a recrudescence of spiritism, the attempt to hold communication with the spirits of the dead through the agency of mediums. The revival of spiritism should not surprise or alarm us as we heed the prophecy of Paul, "The Spirit clearly says that in later times some will abandon the faith and follow deceiving spirits and things taught by demons" (1 Ti 4:1).

There are many who delight in dabbling in the mysterious, and the occult offers something spooky, which has the attraction of a candle for the moth. The movement has gained its greatest numbers from among the bereaved, who are seeking comfort and consolation regarding their lost loved ones. Our sympathy goes out to them, but the tragedy is when the bereaved resort to what is forbidden by God. The church is partly to blame for not sounding a clear warning note, and for not providing healing and comfort for a sufficient length of time after bereavement.

Two of the early founders of the movement were Margaret and Kate Fox. Both died from alcoholism, but not before they had both openly renounced the spiritist cult. In 1888 Margaret Fox said in front of her sister, "I am here tonight as one of the founders of spiritism, to denounce it as absolute falsehood, the most wicked blasphemy the world has ever known." If ever the devil manifests himself as "an angel of light" it is at the spiritist seance. Christ spoke an eternal truth when He said "By their fruit you will recognise them" (Mt 7:20). Judged by its fruit, spiritism has very little to offer the seeker. On the contrary, the effects of spiritism on those who have been involved has been disastrous. The physical effects on the mediums is startling and frightening. They frequently fall to the floor, roll around, and have been known to froth at the mouth; just as those who were demon-possessed in Christ's day. Often they go into spasms but this is supposed to be OK because they are "getting through" to the spirit world; which is quite true, they are getting through to the spirit world, but what they do not know or accept, is that they are getting through to evil spirits. They of course think they are getting through to good spirits or departed spirits. There is only one good Spirit, and that is the Holy Spirit, which comes from God. Their workers are often rendered more and more nervous, more and more excitable, and many have gone completely insane. The effects on the ignorant followers is worse still; many thousands have been confined to mental hospitals through having tampered with the supernatural. Is this the mark of spirituality, the possession of "a sound mind"? (2 Ti 1:7 AV).

A passage of Scripture that forms part of the foundation of the spiritist movement is 1 Samuel 28, but wrongly interpreted, this incident becomes a liability rather than an asset. The passage records a solitary instance in which someone who had died reappeared. Disregarding the explicit command of God, Saul resorted to the witch of Endor for comfort, for he was now out of touch with God. He asked for Samuel to be brought up. To the utter astonishment of both Saul and the medium, God interrupted the seance by causing Samuel himself to appear. Note that in this scriptural record it plainly states, "Samuel said to Saul," (verse 15) thus ruling out any possibility of an impersonating evil spirit. It would seem that God (who had every right to do so) allowed Samuel to appear in order to deliver to Saul the last terrible message of God's rejection.

It is clear from the scriptural record that Samuel did not appear at the call of the witch, or else why should she be so astonished, and cry out with a loud voice? In any case, this solitary instance would be slender evidence on which to base the whole supernatural structure of the spiritist system.

The main reason for rejecting the spiritist movement is its attitude to the written word of God. They have said themselves, "To assert that it is a holy and divine book, that God inspired the writers to make known the will of God, is a gross outrage, and misleading to the public" (*Cults and Isms*, J. O. Saunders, Lakeland (1984) p. 13). "The miraculous conception of Christ is merely a fabulous tale" (*Spiritual Telegraph*, number 37). "Advanced spirits do not teach the atonement of Christ. It is an absurd idea that Jesus was more divine that any other man. Christ was a medium and a reformer in Judea. He is now an advanced spirit in the sixth sphere. Tom Paine is in the seventh sphere, one above the Lord" (Dr Weisse, noted spiritist). "Man is his own saviour" (Rev. W. Stainton Moses).

It would be strange indeed, if God left us with no infallible test of the nature of this pseudo-religion. "Do not believe every spirit, but test the spirits to see whether they are from God." How do we test them? Do they speak according to, and in harmony with the word of God? To ask this question is to answer it. Do they confess that Jesus Christ is come in the flesh? If they do not, they are not of God, but are the spirit of the anti-christ (1 Jn 4:1–3).

I think I have given sufficient evidence to make anyone seeking after truth shun any connection with spiritism, whatever form it takes. To those who are already ensnared by it, God's word is "Come out from among them and be separate ... touch no unclean thing" (2 Co 6:17).

It is absolutely amazing to me how many people are so gullible, and take for granted what is told them without first testing it, and proving it to be of God. Multitudes eagerly accept teachings that leave them at liberty to please themselves, and obey the promptings of the carnal mind. Satan beguiles people now, as he beguiled Eve in the Garden of Eden, by flattery, and by kindling a desire to obtain knowledge by encouraging ambition for self-exaltation. We read in Isaiah 8:19: "When men tell you to consult mediums and spiritists, who whisper and mutter, should not a people enquire of their God?" If only men and women sought the Lord on every point of their lives, and did not stray from the word of God, He would show them the pathway, and He alone would guide them into all truth. Thousands reject the word of God as unworthy of belief, but in eager confidence accept the deceptions of Satan. Satan has been long preparing for his final effort to deceive the world. The foundation of his work was laid by the false assurance given to Eve in the Garden of Eden "you will not surely die ... For God knows that when you eat of it your eyes will be opened, and you will be like God, knowing good and evil" (Ge 3:4). People think they are going to live and die knowing all things, and some live as if they are never going to die at all.

Little by little, Satan has prepared the way for his masterpiece of deception in the development of the occult in its various forms. He has not yet reached the full accomplishment of his designs, but they will be reached in the last remnant of time. We read in Revelation 16:13–14, ''Then I saw three evil spirits that looked like frogs; they came out of the mouth of the dragon, out of the mouth of the beast and out of the mouth of the false prophet. They are spirits of demons performing miraculous signs, and they go out to the kings of the whole world, to gather them for the battle on the great day of God Almighty.'' Except for those who are kept by the power of God, through faith in his word, the whole world would be swept into the ranks of this delusion. People are fast being lulled into a sense of false security, to be awakened only by the outpouring of the wrath of God.

It is imperative that soldiers of Christ stand up and be counted. We are needed more than ever before to fight the good fight of faith, to spread the good news of salvation to the lost, to warn, rebuke and shun evil. Be assured that God is stronger than His foes. The wicked one cannot break through the guard which God has stationed about His people. There is no limit to the power and authority Christ has given to those who watch and wait for his appearing.

There are a great many more evil places that can be classed as ''the sanctuaries of Satan'' like the cinema clubs that show x-rated films, strip clubs, and other clubs, some of which are for members only, not to mention the secret society of the ''freemasons'' whose activities are as devilish as any witchcraft coven. Whenever there is a club whose activities are questionable, and secret, you can be sure that the adversary is behind it. Many of our young people, who have left school, and are unable to find employment often set up their own clubs to keep themselves amused, as they cannot afford to pay to get into the expensive clubs and entertainment centres, and who knows what they get up to? Gangs of young people, with nothing to do, and nowhere to go, who roam our streets at night, are easy pickings for evil men and women, who lure them away with promises of fame and easy money, and often they end up on the streets as prostitutes, and involved in other evil activities.

The devil roams around like a roaring lion, looking for those he can devour. It is up to us to warn them, and point them to the Saviour, who alone is able to break the bondage of sin and darkness that fills their hearts and lives. We as Christians can break down the strongholds of Satan. With Christ as our leader, our Captain, and our King, there is *nothing* we cannot do, for we know that our Jesus will go before us. He will prepare the way for us to reach out to those who are bound in spiritual darkness, in "the synagogues of Satan" and bring them into the light.

CHAPTER NINE

Signposts to Jesus' coming

JESUS was asked by His disciples what would be the sign of His coming, and the sign of the end of the age. Jesus gave them His reply in the form of a parable; the parable of the fig-tree sprouting the first leaves to indicate the nearness of the Summer (Mt 24:32–35). An accumulation of events on the earth and in the sky, would signal the arrival of God's judgments upon those who would witness these things, yet take no notice.

The events which would accumulate are plainly described in Matthew 24, "Many will come in my name claiming, 'I am the Christ,' and will deceive many" (verse 5). Many have already been deceived in the past by claiming that they were the Christ: many are still being deceived today by false prophets bringing false doctrines, false security, and false peace. The devil, as I have mentioned before, is the arch deceiver, the greatest deceiver of all time.

"You will hear of wars and rumours of wars" (verse 6). War is being waged in Northern Ireland and in the Middle East, for despite the fact that the Gulf War has been declared over, war is still being waged there; the Kurdish people are still suffering untold misery and pain. The war is not over for them. Many thousands have died and been injured and maimed in what is regarded in some places as a holy war. Nothing could be further from the truth. The devil is the author of wars and bloodshed, and he has stretched his bloody hand and stained the heart of our own nation. "Nation will rise against nation, and kingdom against kingdom" (verse 7). There is much unrest, suspicion and distrust among nations today; the fear of the atom bomb is real. Men have the capability of wiping out complete nations with the press of a button.

"Many will turn away from the faith and will betray and hate each other" (verse 10). The devil is using his own devices to blame God; he is using trials, pain, sorrow, persecution, fear and disappointments as tools to turn men and women away from God. "Because of the increase of wickedness, the love of most will grow cold" (verse 12). Because of these things, people, even Christians, have become cold and indifferent towards the things of God.

To further illustrate His coming, Christ gave an historical allegory about the great flood in the days of Noah (verses 36–39). He said that people were going about their business as usual—eating and drinking, marrying and giving in marriage, but paid no attention to the warnings of Noah about impending judgment. Their ears were deafened and their eyes were blinded to the truth by Satan, and they had no idea that God's prophetic time of judgment had come until the flood came and destroyed them all.

We are told that the coming of Christ will be similar to the destruction of Sodom. Two angels told Lot that God was going to punish the wicked residents of that city, and they escorted Lot and his family to safety. The people of Sodom went about their daily business, eating and drinking, buying and selling, planting and building, but the day Lot left that city God rained down fire and brimstone, and Sodom was destroyed (Lk 17: 28–29). Jesus said that His coming would be exactly like that. There is a pattern! First there is a prophetic warning, then God removes His people, and then lastly judgment falls upon the unbelievers.

The days immediately prior to this will reveal to the world Satan's capacity for evil, but they will even more reveal the triumphant power of God. *There will exist side by side, a steadfast faith in some, and spiritual apostasy in others*—a situation clearly foretold in the Scriptures. Peter, on the day of Pentecost, spoke of a last-day outpouring of the Holy Spirit (Ac 2:17). Paul on the other hand, wrote about a latter-day departure from the faith (1 Ti 4:1). It has been the spiritual outpouring that has induced the counteracting surge of iniquity. Now it has become necessary for the Holy Spirit to restrain the works of Satan, for it is only the power of the Holy Spirit that can check the power of evil in the last days. Except for the presence of the Holy Spirit, this world today would be overrun with evil people like Idi Amin, Father Divine, Hitler, Stalin, Saddam Hussein, and worse. Much worse! Worse men than these shall soon rise up, as part of an attempted takeover by the anti-Christian influences. Iniquity and spiritual deception would be unchecked were it not for the restraining power of the Holy Spirit.

The Scriptures teach us that men and women must repent and turn to God so that their sins may be blotted out, and that times of refreshing may come from the Lord, and that he may send the Christ who must remain in heaven until the time comes for God to restore everything, as promised long ago through the prophets (Ac 3:19-21). That time has almost come! God's word is basically a book of restoration. After the fall of man into sin in the Garden of Eden, God promised to restore to man fellowship with Himself. The succeeding generations of mankind were alienated from God because of imputed sin. They too were in need of restoration. The process God chose to bring this about was that of redemption through the shed blood of His Son, Jesus Christ.

The final instrument for the accomplishment of God's purposes of restoration, is the church. Yet the New Testament church failed and lapsed into the dark ages. The church itself needed to be restored to its former glory, so that He might accomplish the ultimate restoration of believers to perfection. The New Testament Greek word for restoration is *apokatastasis*. It means to set something back into its former state.

Through the restored church the gospel, in all its fullness, is being preached all over the world. Jesus Himself said this would happen before he came back; "And this gospel of the kingdom will be preached in the whole world as a testimony to all nations, and then the end will come" (Mt 24:14).

During the dark ages the church declined and lost its strength. Who, and what, caused that decline? No-one but Satan himself. It is the devil that causes the church of God to grow cold and indifferent towards the things of God. The arch-enemy of souls robbed the church of the truth: the truth of salvation through faith (Ac 16: 30–31); of water baptism by immersion (Ac 8:38–39); the truth regarding holiness and sanctification (2 Co 6:17, 7:1); the truth regarding healing which was practised by the early church (Ac 5:16, Mk 16:18); the truth regarding praise and worship (Ac 16:25); the truth of laying on of hands and prophecy (Ac 13:3, 1 Ti 4:14); and the truth of the baptism of the Holy Spirit (Ac 2:1–6).

The early believers submitted to the Lordship of Christ (Ac 2:36–40) and led lives of holiness (Ac 6:3, 11:24, 20:32). They were led by the Spirit (Ac 11:12). They had great joy (Ac 13:52). They experienced supernatural signs and wonders (Ac 2:43, 5:12, 8:13). There was church growth (Ac 2:41). There was long-suffering in times of persecution (Ac 4:1–41, 5:17–42). There was edification of one another (Ac 9:31). The word of God was spread (Ac 6:7). They were founded on the word of God (Ac 1:15–20). They had spiritual authority over evil powers (Ac 8:7, 16:16–18).

What happened to this triumphant church? As Christianity spread throughout the known world, there evolved a gradual mix with the practice of pagan religions. Impurity and compromise with worldly views began to be tolerated. Total commitment to the local church was no longer emphasised. False teaching crept into the church, bringing decline, spiritual blindness, loss of vision and loss of power. The New Testament prophets confirm this. They said it would happen (2 Pe 2:1–3, Ac 20:28–31). False ministries went unhindered (2 Pe 2:1–9). There was loss of spiritual hunger for the truth (1 Ti 4:1–2). There were self-willed believers (2 Pe 2:10). There was carnal indulgence (Eph 2:3). There was spiritual lukewarmness (Rev 3:15–16). There was worldliness (1 Jn 2:15–17). There was loss of vision (2 Pe 1:9, 1 Jn 2:11). The early church witnessed the apostolic ministry, but after the death of the last apostle John, the apostolic ministry disappeared. There was no evidence of the apostolic ministry continuing after John.

In 140 AD, the ministry of the prophet vanished. In 150 AD, the gifts of the Holy Spirit began to disappear. Bit by bit the church was stripped of its truths, its strength, its power, its glory, its vision.

In 225 AD, church membership became a matter of agreeing with a creed, and was no longer based on conversion.

By 240 AD, holiness had disappeared as worldliness infiltrated the church. The church continued its decline, reaching its lowest ebb in the dark ages.

God has been restoring truth in the same order as it was lost. In 1517, God began to restore the most fundamental of all doctrines—justification by faith. Martin Luther was used by God in restoring this doctrine as opposed to a system of justification by works.

In the seventeenth century, a dynamic spiritual life with Christ, based upon correctness of life as well as doctrine, began to be restored.

In 1750, sanctification and holiness began to be restored to the church under the ministry of John Wesley.

In 1900, the baptism in the Holy Spirit began to be restored to the church, under the ministry of A. B. Simpson, and others.

In 1906, the gifts of the Holy Spirit, and the five-fold ministry of Ephesians 4:4–11 began to be restored in the Azusa revival.

In 1948, the doctrine of laying on of hands of the Presbytery began to be restored and spontaneous praise and worship was restored, with the singing of spiritual songs, in the Canadian revival.

Today there is a great movement of God among His people. What the devil robbed the church of, is being restored. There is a great spiritual awakening in our churches. The devil does not like it one bit, and he is fighting to keep the church of God bound, blind, cold and indifferent. There are still those who will not respond to what the Lord is doing, and are content to stay where they are. We should learn an important lesson. God is still moving His people on, and we must be willing and ready to move forward with Him.

The restoration of the church to its former glory, power and strength, with joy and praise, vision and faith, victory over evil, holiness and truth, is one of the major signposts pointing to the near return of Christ for His radiant, spotless church. Elijah prepared the way for Elisha. John the Baptist prepared the way for the Lord. The Lord prepared the way for the church. The restored church is preparing the way for the second coming of Christ for His bride, the church.

We are rapidly approaching the time when God's day of grace will cease and Christ will return to snatch away His waiting bride (the true church)—those who are waiting and watching for His coming. The warning sound is being heard again as Christ's near return is being heralded in the four corners of this globe. There can be no excuse from the people of the earth that no warning was given to them. The people of God need not fear the fast-moving events leading up to the return of Christ. Their tremendous significance should gladden the heart of every believer, for the coming of the Lord draws nearer and nearer, the time when the dead in Christ will be raised, and those who are alive and remain will be caught up to meet Him in the air (1 Th 4:16–17).

Let us take a look at some of the other major signposts pointing to the coming of Christ. One is the return of the dispersed Jews to become a nation again in 1948, and the Jews recapture of the Old City of Jerusalem in the 1967 Arab-Israeli War. In spite of 2000 years of being scattered, the Jewish people have preserved a distinct national identity. During all the years of dispersion, these people have suffered the most cruel persecution ever endured by any other nation of people, and yet, Jewish history with all its tragedies and triumphs has been foretold in the Bible. Moses predicted they would be chastened or disciplined for not believing their God, and rejecting his ways. Moses predicted that a mighty nation would invade and destroy Israel and the prophet Isaiah added details to his prophetic warning about 150 years before it occurred: "The time will surely come when everything in your palace, and all that your fathers have stored up until this day, will be carried off to Babylon. Nothing will be left, says the Lord" (Isa 39:6). It all happened exactly as it was predicted. The Babylonians swept into the Southern kingdom of Israel and Jerusalem and it was destroyed. Moses, who predicted the first stage of discipline, also predicted the second stage. As the time of enslavement (which was 70 years) came to an end, the Persian king Cyrus released some of the Jews who had survived the horror and destruction to return and rebuild the temple in Jerusalem, and yet they continued in their disbelief and rejection of God.

Moses said that Israel would once again be destroyed as a nation. The survivors would then be scattered throughout the world in every nation. In Deuteronomy 28:64-68, Moses gave a clear and accurate description of what it would be like: "Then the Lord will scatter you among all nations, from one end of the earth to the other . . . There the Lord will give you an anxious mind, eyes weary with longing, and a despairing heart. You will live in constant suspense, filled with dread both night and day, never sure of your life . . . There you will offer yourselves for sale to your enemies as male and female slaves, but no-one will buy you." Other prophets like Isaiah, Jeremiah, Ezekiel and Amos, foretold the worldwide exile of the Jewish nation and its destruction. Jesus said it would happen, and used these words: "When you see Jerusalem being surrounded by armies, you will know that its desolation is near" (Lk 21: 20). He said they would "fall by the sword and will be taken as prisoners to all the nations. Jerusalem will be trampled on by the Gentiles until the times of the Gentiles are fulfilled" (Lk 21:24). It all happened! Less than forty years after the death of Christ, Titus and the Roman armies destroyed Jerusalem, slaying thousands. Those who survived were shipped off to the slave markets of Egypt. For almost 2000 years the Jews wandered around the earth with no country of their own, in constant fear of their lives. Christians have watched in utter amazement and compassion, as the suffering of the Jewish nation became a worldwide phenomenon. Israel's history of heartache, misery, sorrow and pain, exactly matched and fulfilled prophetic warnings from God, which should teach us all a lesson: when God says He will do something, He will do it. God means what He says.

The same prophets who foretold the massive exile of the Jews, also foretold their final restoration as a nation before countdown to the coming of Christ to this world. Many things have happened since the recapture of the old city of Jersualem in 1967. We heard how thousands of Ethiopian Jews were airlifted from their famine-stricken land to Israel. The secret airlift of thousands of starving people required superb efficiency, the exact details of this rescue were a closely guarded secret. The Ethiopians stumbled barefoot from the planes clutching cans of water, because they believed Israel had no water. Some kissed the ground and asked, "Are we really in Zion?" That flight into the twentieth century must have been a frightening experience for the thousands of bewildered black Jews who had never been inside a plane before. The Israeli government, despite their own problems of growing unemployment, put these Ethiopians before any other consideration. It was a leap forward for the Ethiopian Jews, it was also a leap forward in the fulfilment of Biblical prophecy. Every month more and more Jews are returning to

Israel, and no opposition will stop the Jews returning to their homeland. *The stage has been set, the players are in place, and no-one can stop the great plan of God. The devil cannot stop the plan of God.* Not only has the actual State of Israel been restored, through the efforts of the Jews, but spiritual Israel is being restored; the true church of Jesus Christ. Jesus is building His church, and the gates of hell shall not prevail against it (Mt 16:18).

The devil does not like it when Biblical prophecy is being fulfilled, because he knows it signifies the beginning of the end for him, and he knows that there is absolutely nothing he can do about it. As might be expected, the mightiest of recorders, Martin Luther, seems to have been a special target of the devil. Luther's biographers made much of his conflicts with Satan. These included a story that once, while translating the New Testament in Warburg Castle, he became so aware of the presence of the devil that he threw an inkwell at the apparition. In his excellent biography *Luther* Rudolf Thiel says that the devil attacked Luther with his utmost power and craftiness and thought to bring him down. Much earlier, Thomas Carlyle recorded that Luther on one occasion wrote, ''I have seen and defied innumerable devils.'' The devil always attacks the truth of Christ's return, so much so that even those who say they are Christians are ignoring the signs of the times recorded in Scripture.

The rapid decline of sexual morality is another sign of the times we are living in today. The devil is twisting the real meaning of love into something ugly, mean and hurtful. The divorce rate has shot up alarmingly, and it is now easier to get a divorce. Abortion and VD rates have soared. Illegitimacy has risen, despite contraception, so much so in fact, that in the past fifteen years legitimate births have only risen by twenty per cent compared to illegitimate births which have risen by a hundred per cent.

The Bible tells us that God is love, and shows us what His love is like. ''But God demonstrates his own love

110

for us in this: While we were still sinners, Christ died for us'' (Ro 5:8). And again in John 3:16, ''For God so loved the world that he gave his one and only Son, that whoever believes in him shall not perish but have eternal life.'' God's love is unselfish. In the name of so-called love today (what some people call ''free love''), many a heart and home has been broken and darkened. There is much that passes for real love, but in fact it is just lust masquerading as love. For lust says, ''I want, so I must have,'' while real love says, ''I must give.'' God is not against real love. Real love is a pure and wonderful gift from God. It is the devil who has tainted human love, for it is often mixed with jealousy and vanity, and it can be selfish and thoughtless. The Bible tells us that ''God is love.'' It does not say, ''As long as love is present, love rules, and you can do as you please.'' God's love never degrades, it is not selfish; the love which God gives is personal, and lasting, satisfying and ennobling and sacrificial. Does God's love stop? Of course not! But affairs do. There is much talk about endless devotion and self-sacrifice, but afterwards all that is left is a tangled web of disillusionment, depression, self reproach, and broken empty hearts. The devil tells many that this kind of love will last forever, but all it brings is loneliness, fear and guilt. Does real love hurt? If you really love someone, would you expose them to hurt and pain? Yet there is plenty of hurt and pain where sex outside of marriage is concerned. There is plenty of pain when adultery is committed. What about abortion? Who gets hurt then? The young woman herself, her family, and everyone concerned. The devil is behind the collapse of families; it is him who is the author of misery, depriving parents of children, and children of parents, he is robbing children of love and protection, joy and happiness, and warmth and security.

The Bible tells us that, ''Perfect love casteth out fear'' (1 Jn 4:18 AV) and this is true. For those who know Him and trust Him, God gives peace of mind and binds up the wounds that transgression has made. The same

Bible passage states that "fear hath torment." Think of the torment of a young woman who fears that she is doing wrong, but cannot get out of the situation she finds herself in: the torment that she may be pregnant; the fear of her parents finding out that she is having an affair with a married man, and the fear that the relationship will not last.

What about homosexuality which is rampant today? Who hurts? Who fears? Who feels trapped? What about the misery, shame and guilt this brings? Does love do that? No, but the devil does! The evil part about it all, is that it is accepted by society as normal. Smutty jokes are made all the time about homosexuality, and many are afraid to use the word *gay* because of its association. It has now become a dirty word.

Who gets hurt when rape is committed? Everyone involved! Many of our lovely young women have been scarred for life in their minds; others face a long hard journey back to self-respect, although the offence was not their fault. Rape today is not confined to the dark streets, homes are being broken into and often violence is used to a terrible degree. It has become unsafe to walk the streets after dark for fear of being raped, mugged, or both. No, it's not just the dark streets, it's the light streets as well; it's done in the daytime. It is frightening, but it's true, and the devil, the one who manages to convince people he does not exist, is behind every dark and evil deed.

Lies and deceit accompany promiscuous sex, and who is the author of lies and deceit? No-one else but the devil who is the father of lies. All lovers think their love will last forever, but it does not always turn out that way—hearts get broken. It's a horrible thing to be jilted. It brings a fear of trusting people, even those you love. Real love is very challenging in a wonderful way. Love does not go around demanding responses, that is why real love is so liberating. It's a wonderful thing to be able to trust someone and to know you are trusted in return. At one time you could trust people's word, but today being let down is an everyday occurrence. That old saying that, "a gentleman's word is his bond," seems almost obsolete, and sad to say, even Christians break their word and let people down. Many today have trusted someone entirely, only to be let down badly and as a result of which they find it very hard to trust again.

In this world there are many who are not accepted by society. They are in fact, rejects, cast aside by those who are considered to be more attractive or intelligent. These are the ones who are the most gullible and grasp at anything that looks like love, only to find out that it was false and unreal. God's love is a faithful love, He never lets anyone down, He is faithful and true, and His love never ends.

God loves us, not because we are lovable, but because of His grace; not because we deserve it, but because He is love. His name is love. God's love accepts us just as we are, crooked nose, warts and all. God's love challenges us to love the unloveable, to love our enemies, and those who have treated us wrongly. God, because He loves us, does not cover up our sins and pretend they are not there. God's love shows up our failures, and shortcomings. He wants us to see sin for what it is. He came to die for our sins, in the person of His Son, Jesus Christ. Jesus gave His life so that our sins can be forgiven, and to barricade the way to hell. God's love is honest. The devil's work today is to blind people to the pure, unfailing love of God, to deceive them about real love and what it really means, and to give them a false love. This should challenge us to reflect the love of God wherever we go, and talk to people about the love of God.

There is widespread drug addiction today. It's now easier to obtain drugs than ever before, and young people everywhere are in danger from the dealers in drugs. The authorities are more and more concerned; there has been much talk, and much written about drugs and the damage they cause, but still drug addiction is increasing at an alarming rate. Drug addiction is a kind of chemical enslavement—and who is the enslaver? The devil, the enemy of souls, and the hardest task-master ever known. That old saying, "the devil looks after his own," is complete nonsense, and a gross lie. When the devil has finished with you, he throws you on the rubbish dump and makes you into a reject. The devil tells the vulnerable, the lonely, the depressed, and those with deep-rooted problems, that drugs will not harm them if they just take a little now and then to ease the tension. A baby rattlesnake has just as much poison as a fully grown one and just as much venom—just enough to kill. Many start out by experimenting with so-called soft drugs, and end up as hopeless hard drug addicts.

Addiction brings out all the worst characteristics of a personality, and due to the progression of psychological and spiritual decay, it becomes increasingly difficult for a non-addict to form a relationship with the addict, who then feels more and more of an outcast. Education and prevention are important in the battle against drug addiction and alcoholism. These are two conditions with similar causes, and in many respects, similar results.

But these measures of prevention are not sufficient if we have nothing to offer in return to fill the void and the emptiness of life, and remedy the insecurity which crushes the personality of the addict. The way Christ offers is not easy—in fact, initially, it may appear much harder than the quick answer of a bottle, a pill, or a needle. The devil will make it look harder than it really is for the hopeless addict. This is another one of the clever tricks of Satan. He will try and make them give up, before they even get started.

There is one ray of light in the seemingly hopeless plight of the addict. Christians are no longer afraid of addicts, and are reaching out to them. There are now centres opening up for those caught in the web of drugs, if they are willing to be helped. They can receive understanding, counsel and guidance, and some are being set free from the awful bondage of drugs. The devil is not having all his own way. Many have received

114

the Saviour into their lives, and are completely changed. Many former addicts are now working for the Lord and reaching out to those who are in the same state as they once were. They will testify to the fact that Christ is the answer to drug addiction, and indeed, to every other problem in life.

There are important signposts pointing to the near return of Christ, and I will list some of them:

1. The increase of international revolution.
2. The increase of wars and rumours of war.
3. The increase of famines.
4. The increase of knowledge.
5. The increase of earthquakes.
6. The flood of occultism and false cults.
7. The move towards a one-world religion.
8. The departure of some of the churches from the historic truths of Christianity.
9. The increase of lawlessness.
10. The increase of suicides.
11. Men's hearts failing them for fear because of the increase of wickedness.
12. The apathy of people because of hardship; unemployment being just one example.

It is not my intention to go into great detail about the events following the rapture of the church. This is another study of its own, and many books have been written on the second coming of Christ, and what follows it. Sad to say, there has also been a lot of controversy and even heated arguments as to whether the rapture will take place before the great tribulation or half-way through, or whether we are in fact in the tribulation right now. While there are debates and arguments and speculation about this and about the anti-christ, the most important point is being missed. God will fulfil all that is written in the Scriptures. Everything will take place precisely as God has planned it. In His exact time, and in His exact order.

Every Christian knows that these things will happen. We know in advance what Satan's end will be, so it's pointless to speculate and argue. This is just what the devil wants people to do. Instead, we should be busy proclaiming the gospel story, warning of the near coming of the Lord Jesus Christ, and pointing lost souls to Christ who is the only escape from the things that are going to happen upon the earth. Our task is to keep our eyes on Jesus and to be obedient to His word, and walk in His ways.

There is evidence that Satan knows his is a lost cause, but this does not mean he will slacken his efforts to wrest victory from his approaching doom. Indeed, he will pour more and more wickedness, more and more deception into our generation. We must keep courage and faith as the distress increases, knowing that one thing is certain—God and His righteousness shall triumph; the devil cannot win. To bring this chapter to a close, I would like to share with you a poem I wrote some time ago which puts what I have been saying into a nutshell.

The day of his appearing

When we read the daily papers and listen to the
  news,
Then we read what the Bible has to say,
Events we see and hear about are foretold in God's
  word,
They are signposts to the coming judgment day,
We are living in the latter days, there is trouble
  everywhere,
With earthquakes, false prophets, division and
  war,
Men's hearts are failing them for fear on every
  hand,
As wickedness increases more and more.

Evil signs and lying wonders, and scoffers all
  around,
Blasphemers, who God's Holy word deny,

Dark powers will soon be shaken, sun and moon
    will cease to shine,
All the stars will be falling from the sky,
Then a far greater light will be seen in this dark
    world,
When the Son of Man in power and glory comes,
With a host of holy angels, in a radiancy so bright,
It will outshine a thousand billion suns.

There is no condemnation for the blood-bought
    child of God,
No fear of punishment, no death, no pain,
We are looking for that blessed hope when Jesus
    we shall see,
Then forever with our Saviour we shall reign,
For we shall be changed in a twinkling of an eye,
When we rise up to meet Him in the air,
Receive a crown of glory that fadeth not away,
In the City of our God bright and fair.

As in the days of Noah just before the mighty flood,
Men continue in rebellion just the same,
All those outside the ark of salvation will be lost,
Very soon the Lord will shut the door again.
So let us be as watchmen, and warn them of the
    night,
Let us raise up our banner—hold it high,
Lift up our voice like a trumpet—shout aloud,
The coming of the Lord is drawing nigh.

CHAPTER TEN

The four keys of authority

WHEN we look at the life of Christ, there can be no doubt that He knew who He was. He knew He was the Son of God. He knew he was King. He knew why He had come to earth. He knew he had power and authority. He was never stumped for an answer, and He was in perfect harmony with His Father's timetable; "Father, the time has come. Glorify your Son, that your Son may glorify you" (Jn 17:1).

There are two kingdoms, one of darkness, the other of light; one is ruled by Satan, the other by God. The kingdom of God is far more powerful than the kingdom of darkness. Christ manifested kingdom living while He was dwelling on this earth. He was constantly in communion with His Father, and speaking about His Father's kingdom.

Kingdom living is only possible through the cross. The kingdom of God is born in us through the cross when we repent and turn from our sin. When Jesus started His ministry, Satan knew that the kingdom of God was advancing and his dark kingdom was in jeopardy. Our work today is to extend the kingdom of God. What Jesus accomplished on Calvary, we can carry on doing through the power of the Holy Spirit within us. The life of Christ was repeated by His disciples and the early church. The power of the Holy Spirit enabled them to do what Jesus did.

Where there is a kingdom, there is a king who rules and reigns. Jesus Christ is the King of Kings and Lord of Lords. He is reigning in our hearts, and we can experience kingdom rule and reign with Him: "The kingdom of God is within you" (Lk 17:21). It is a spiritual kingdom. God gives us grace to live as sons and daughters, to rule and reign in life. All the fullness of God dwelt in Jesus Christ, and we can know the fullness of God in our lives, just as Jesus did, for we read in Ephesians 3:19, "That you may be filled to the measure of all the fullness of God."

We have authority to reign with Him, for He has given us the keys of the kingdom. We belong to the household of God and we reign as kings and priests, right now! 1 Peter 2:9 tells us, "But you are a chosen people, a royal priesthood, a holy nation, a people belonging to God, that you may declare the praises of him who called you out of darkness into his wonderful light." The question is, as children of His wonderful kingdom and wonderful light and as children of a King, are we living as kings and priests, as He wants us to? Are we claiming our inheritance? We can reign with Him in every situation, conquer every foe, have victory in trouble and temptation, and power over all the power of the devil. Jesus reigned in life, meeting every need, and we can do the same. The laws of the kingdom are written in our hearts. The laws of the kingdom are found in God's word. "I will put my laws in their minds and write them on their hearts. I will be their God, and they will be my people" (Heb 8:10).

Jesus said this, "In my Father's house there are many rooms; if it were not so, I would have told you. I am going there to prepare a *place* for you" (Jn 14:2). Many people picture this as a place where angels sing and play harps, and where we will all go sometime in the future. Jesus went to prepare a *place* for us now, as well as in the future: a *place* of blessing for us, a *place* of victory and authority, and power over all the power of the devil, day by day. I have seen this even more as I have come across the demons who have opposed me, and the ministry the Lord has given me, and when I have been used in casting out demons from those who have been demon possessed and oppressed. He gave

119

me a place of victory to do what was needed in the hour of need.

This is what we read in Ephesians 2:6, "And God raised us up with Christ and seated us with him in the heavenly realms in Christ Jesus." We can experience blessing and victory now, because we are seated with Him in the heavenly realm, in the place of authority, and the devil is under our feet. When the devil knows that I recognise who I am in Christ, he does not bother with me, in fact, he is afraid of me. Many people I have met have told me plainly, "I am afraid of the devil," others do not actually state they are afraid of him, but I know they are, and cannot understand why I am not fearful of him. In fact, I have been asked, "Doreen, how is it that you are not afraid of the devil?" My answer was, "Why should I be?" "Well, you were in his grasp for so long" they replied. "Yes, that is true, but I am not now, am I? I belong to the Lord Jesus Christ, and He has given me authority over him, in His name. The devil is afraid of me now, because Jesus in me is greater than him, and all the hosts of hell put together."

Christians have not recognised their place as conquerors in Christ. This is sad, and I wondered why at first, but now I realise that many do not receive the right teaching, and some have not grown in the Lord or read and believed His word.

The authority of His name

Jesus has a name higher than any other name. It is higher than Gabriel, it is higher than the name of any earthly potentate. "Therefore God exalted him to the highest place and gave him the name that is above every name, that at the name of Jesus every knee should bow, in heaven and on earth and under the earth, and every tongue confess that Jesus Christ is Lord, to the glory of God the Father" (Php 2:9–11).

In this spiritual kingdom where we are reigning with Christ, He has given us keys, and the name of Jesus is one of them. He has placed this key in our hands and He wants us to use it. In Exodus 4:1-4, the Lord tells Moses to throw his staff upon the ground; he did so, and it became a snake. The Lord then told him to reach out his hand and take it by the tail. Moses reached out, took hold of the snake, and it turned back into a staff in his hand. He later used the staff to part the Red Sea. A staff represents a rod of authority. What the staff was to Moses, the name of Jesus was to the apostles.

In 1 Samuel 17:45 we read that David said to the Philistine, "You come against me with sword and spear and javelin, but I come against you in the name of the Lord Almighty." David triumphed over the Philistine with a sling and a small stone—without a sword, but with the authority of God. God has given us the authority of the name of Jesus, to come against giants: giants of fear, giants of rebellion, giants of sin and giants of evil. David learned as a lad to trust God. He faced the giant in the name of the Lord, and we can do the same.

Many Christians mumble, "in the name of Jesus" at the end of a prayer, sometimes as an afterthought, but mostly because they have been taught to do so; which is right and good, but using the name of Jesus is an introduction into a personal life in Jesus, not a matter of form and ceremony. The name of Jesus otherwise becomes formal, technical, and of a functional importance only rather than a personal and powerful name. The name of Jesus should not be used parrot-fashion, nor in a flippant way, because His name is precious, so let us use it wisely and with reverence. It would be better still, and be more specific, to give Jesus his full title "The Lord Jesus Christ" because Christ means "the anointed one" as there are many people, even today, named Jesus.

Elijah had a cloak which he used to strike the water and it divided to the right and left, and he crossed over the Jordan (2 Ki 2:8). He used what he had in his hands. In Acts 3:1-10 we read of a man who was crippled from birth. Peter said to him, "Silver or gold I do not have, but what I have I give you. In the name of Jesus Christ

121

of Nazareth, walk'' (verse 6). And he did so. Peter took him by the right hand and he helped him up.

Jesus said in Matthew 28:18–19, ''All authority in heaven and on earth has been given to me. Therefore go and make disciples of all nations, baptising them in the name of the Father and of the Son and of the Holy Spirit.'' Every born-again Christian has the power and authority to tell Satan to go in the name of Jesus. When the seventy-two returned with joy they said, ''Lord, even the demons submit to us in your name.'' Jesus replied, ''I have given you authority to trample on snakes and scorpions and to overcome all the power of the enemy; nothing will harm you'' (Lk 10:17–19).

There are Christians who try to fight the devil blindfolded. If you were a prize boxer, and entered the ring with a blindfold on, you would be beaten to a pulp. The bell rings, your opponent starts punching you, but you can't punch back because you can't see who he is and where he is. You are not fighting your husband, your wife, your children, your pastor or any person of flesh and blood, but a very real foe—Satan. ''For our struggle is not against flesh and blood, but against the rulers, against the authorities, against the powers of this dark world and against the spiritual forces of evil in the heavenly realms'' (Eph 6:12). The trouble with Christians today, and I say this kindly, is that they have too much fear of the devil. Fear is the opposite of faith. The moment you start to fear, the devil has gained a foothold. The door is open for more fears to creep in, and before you know where you are, you are in bondage to fear. The Bible tells us, ''There is no fear in love. But perfect love drives out fear'' (1 Jn 4:18).

The realm of demonic activity is not confined to worldly places. It may be hard to accept the idea of demonic manifestations in a church, but this is the very place where demons are likely to manifest themselves. There is a scriptural precedent for this in Mark 1:23–26: ''Just then a man in their synagogue who was possessed by an evil spirit cried out, 'What do you want with us, Jesus of Nazareth? Have you come to destroy us? I know who you are—the Holy One of God.' 'Be quiet!' said Jesus sternly. 'Come out of him!' The evil spirit shook the man violently and came out of him with a shriek.'' When someone interrupts a service in the house of God, it is more often than not, a demon. The Holy Spirit does not interrupt someone who is preaching under the Holy Spirit's anointing.

One night I was preaching in a tent in Liverpool, when suddenly a man cried out with a loud voice. The whole congregation was silent. They all knew it was a demon by the way he cried out and by his appearance. I silenced the evil spirit in the name of Jesus, and carried on preaching. The evil spirit was quiet until I invited people to come forward for salvation, healing and deliverance. The man came forward, shrieking at the top of his voice. I then commanded the evil spirit to leave in the name of Jesus. The man fell to the floor, the evil spirit came out, and I then led the man to the Lord; he was completely delivered. There was no long dialogue with the demon. There is no need for that. Jesus cast out demons with one word: ''Go''—and the demons left at once. We can cast out demons with six words today: ''Go, in the name of Jesus.'' If demon-possessed people are willing to be freed and are repentant of their sins, demons have to go at once.

The devil is highly delighted with eight-hour deliverance meetings, which last until three in the morning, while demons play hide and seek, wear out the Christians, confound them with knowledge, and frighten them by their strength. It was not like that in the New Testament. Jesus spoke the word and demons came out immediately. The devil has made some Christians believe that casting out demons is a long, hard struggle. This is not true. In fact, it is easier to cast out demons than many people think. The Lord has shown me that his rest enters into the realm of deliverance. It is true that demons come out in various ways. Sometimes they do scream and throw people to the ground. We must not be afraid or astonished should this occur. This should only be a momentary manifestation as the demons leave, not a long, drawn-out process. Prolonged manifestations indicate the need for counselling, repentance and the reading of God's word.

There is a great need for balanced teaching regarding deliverance today, and how to keep it within the body of Christ. Because of unbalanced teaching, which leads to excessive and fanatical demonstrations in the house of God, many have come to the wrong conclusion that demons do not exist. This is a great pity because demon possession, oppression and obsession is increasing as more and more people are involved in the occult and other unclean practices, and many more need deliverance today.

I have been present at a meeting where bowls were provided, into which people could cough up demons; people were going forward and coughing and spitting and there was a lot of shouting and screaming, which caused much confusion. Many got up and left, including me. It is part of the devil's work to make Christians look stupid and bring the gospel of salvation and deliverance from the power of the devil into disrepute. I am not saying that no-one is delivered by such methods, or that they were at fault in any way, but I am saying there is no need and no room for fanatical measures, because they result in the devil getting a lot of glory that is not due to him.

There is not one of us who is exempt from any demonic thought flowing towards us. Many of our temptations are very much the same, for the Scriptures tell us, "No temptation has seized you except what is common to man. And God is faithful; he will not let you be tempted beyond what you can bear. But when you are tempted, he will also provide a way out so that you can stand up under it" (1 Co 10:13). There are some people who almost tempt themselves. They begin the day by saying, "It's not going to be a very good day for me today. I feel depressed. I'm going to have a rotten headache,"—and they are always depressed, and lo and behold, the headache appears. Some people have been in bondage for years over certain areas in their lives. They are always looking on the black side of things and are never positive about anything at all. They have never learned the secret of calling upon the name of Jesus. They have never claimed their inheritance as a child of God. They have never experienced God's power and authority in their lives.

There is a wonderful chorus that was sung frequently at the Billy Graham crusades here in England, called *Majesty*. Some of the lines go like this:

> Majesty, worship His Majesty
> Unto Jesus be glory, honour and praise.
> Majesty, kingdom authority,
> Flow from His throne unto His own,
> His anthem raise.
> So exalt, lift up on high the name of Jesus . . .

If we fail to use the key of the name of Jesus, we will be powerless and suffer defeat. The devil does not have to pull out any new tricks for some Christians, because they have fallen for the same trick of the devil for years, and all the devil has to do is to keep it up.

There are four good ways to resist the devil: the first is to quote Scripture, like Jesus did during his forty days and nights in the wilderness. The devil hates the word of God when quoted with authority. It is no use saying in a meek and fearful voice, ''Please, Satan, go away,'' because he won't. If you came home and found someone in your house who was up to no good, you would tell him to leave in no uncertain terms. You must do the same with the devil. You must tell him to go in the name of Jesus, as if you mean it. Using Scripture with power and authority is a sure way to victory over the devil.

A second way is to start praying in the Spirit, namely in the supernatural prayer language of tongues. The devil cannot understand a word of Holy Spirit prayer, so it is impossible for him to eavesdrop for very long, and he will soon leave.

The third way is to learn to be rebellious— rebellious

to Satan. The only time rebellion is accepted by God is when it is rebellion towards Satan. Do exactly the opposite of what he is tempting you to do. For instance, if you are being tempted to say an unkind word, say a kind word instead. If Satan tells you to be bad-tempered, irritable, unhappy and miserable, start singing the praises of the Lord at the top of your voice, if possible. Satan cannot stand to hear God's children singing His praises.

The fourth way to resist the devil is by simply ignoring him and the thoughts that he brings to your mind. I do not believe the Lord went about rebuking the devil all day long. He simply went about His Father's business, listening to His voice and doing His will. "My Father is always at his work to this very day, and I, too, am working" (Jn 5:17). When we learn to ignore the devil we will live in victory in our thought lives.

When the devil can say of us, "I can't even get to talk to him. He just won't listen"—that is victory. That is power and authority over the devil. Many times the devil has tried to tell me something, but as soon as I am aware of it, I simply ignore him. Nothing is more final than silence. We don't have to accept every demonic thought that comes to our minds. Our bodies are temples of the Holy Spirit. I like this Scripture in 2 Corinthians 10:5 which says, "We demolish arguments and every pretension that sets itself up against the knowledge of God, and we take captive every thought to make it obedient to Christ." When we are ruling and reigning in kingdom authority, the effects of sin, seen and manifested all around, cannot possibly affect us, for we are living above these things, seated with Christ in heavenly places.

In John 14:12–13 Jesus tells us, "I tell you the truth, anyone who has faith in me will do what I have been doing. He will do even greater things than these, because I am going to the Father. And I will do whatever you ask in my name, so that the Son may bring glory to the Father."

Behind the name of Jesus is the Godhead. Psalm

138:2 says, "For you have exalted above all things your name and your word." His name represents His will. He wants us to rule and reign. He wants us to use His name. He wants us to learn His secrets. We must ask in faith, speak out in faith, use His name in faith. It is a lovely name, a precious name, a glorious name, a powerful name. "Salvation is found in no-one else, for there is no other name under heaven given to men by which we must be saved" (Ac 4:12).

The key of prayer

The spiritual kingdom that is within us only comes through new birth. We have been born into the kingdom of God through Christ's shed blood on Calvary. There are two kingdoms, one of darkness and one of light: one of Satan and one of God. Light exposes darkness. Light penetrates darkness. Darkness cannot penetrate light. The kingdom of God opposes the kingdom of darkness, and vice versa. The work of Christ's church today is to enforce the victory of Calvary and to continue Christ's mission, which was to destroy the works of the devil (1 Jn 3:8). How? By preaching the gospel, healing the sick, raising the dead and casting out demons, and by taking back the ground that Satan has stolen. Christ conquered the devil at Calvary: "He forgave us all our sins, having cancelled the written code, with its regulations, that was against us and that stood opposed to us; he took it away, nailing it to the cross. And having disarmed the powers and authorities, he made a public spectacle of them, triumphing over them by the cross" (Col 2:13–15).

Satan is violently opposed to those who would come into the kingdom through the cross of Christ. Jesus said we should pray like this: "Your kingdom come." We all know that we will reign on the earth one day in the Millenium, but His kingdom has come now, within our hearts. Jesus went on to say, "Your will be done on earth." It is His will that His kingdom be increased on the earth, and we can put to flight the powers of darkness that would hinder us. It is His will that prisoners should be released; this is why He came. It says in Isaiah 61:1, "The Spirit of the Sovereign Lord is on me, because the Lord has anointed me to preach good news to the poor. He has sent me to bind up the brokenhearted, to proclaim freedom for the captives and release from darkness for the prisoners."

Satan has to be bound, and we can do this in prayer. Satan is doing his utmost to stop people from coming to the cross of Christ. The prayers of the blood-washed saints of God can release those whom God is preparing to come into His kingdom. Satan has to yield to the greater power of Jesus Christ. Christ's resurrection shows the extent of His stronger power. His resurrection was victory over death. Christ conquered hell's worst. He took the keys of death and hell away from Satan, and Satan was powerless to stop Him. In James 5:17–18 we read how Elijah prayed earnestly that it would not rain, and it did not rain on the land for three and a half years. He prayed again and the heavens gave rain, and the earth produced its crops. Placed in our hands, prayer is the key to unlock the storehouse of God's provision. It is the key to unlock prison doors for those in darkness and bondage. Prayer opens doors for the impossible. It opens up the way for God to move in and do His work. Prayer prepares the way for the Lord. This key is in our hands, and we can use it. Authority in prayer gives us the ability to communicate with God, to know His mind in matters of utmost importance, and in times of great need in our lives and in the lives of others. We use our voices naturally to communicate and we can use our voices spiritually, our voices can be elevated to speak the things of God. Neglecting to use this key renders us powerless and defeated, and an easy target for the devil to oppress us.

Mark 1:35 tells us that Jesus rose up early in the morning, while it was still dark, to pray. We should begin the day with God in prayer. The ministry of prayer is a very powerful ministry. Revival begins with

128

prayer. Prayer opened up the way of ministry for Jesus to reach out His hand to heal the leper (Mk 1:40–45). The leper recognised the Lordship of Christ. He recognised the authority of Christ. He willingly believed, and submitted to the Lordship of Christ. Submitting to the Lordship of Christ made a way of healing and cleansing.

Prayer does not have to be complicated, long and drawn out, full of complicated, and well thought out sentences. Prayer should be simple, not childish, but asking in childlike faith believing He will hear and answer your prayer. The key of authority is also a key of faith, a simple childlike faith. Jesus gives us the authority to ask: "I tell you the truth, my Father will give you whatever you ask in my name" (Jn 16:23). God wants us to be successful, and to get the job done. He is not reluctant to give, or to answer prayer, in fact, I believe it thrills Him to answer our prayers, when we ask according to His will. The barrier is hesitancy, fear, and a reluctance on our part to pray. We must co-operate with God in order to bring His plans and purposes about. God is not so overloaded with requests that He cannot cope with them all. His storehouse is full, we only have to ask. Some Christians do not receive, because they have not asked, or they ask for selfish reasons, which is clearly out of God's will.

Intercessory prayer brings about revelation and illumination of God's plan and purpose. It lights up God's word to us in new ways, and brings revelation in matters of urgency and utmost importance when we engage in it. Yet intercessory prayer is often painful, and it's sacrificial. It means that we have to give of our time to pray, to devote ourselves to prayer, mostly over things of great importance, where we need to know what we must do, and what we should say, and how best to help someone with great difficulty. Words of God's wisdom will be given to us in this kind of praying, not from our own mind, but from the mind of God. God gives us His wisdom, and makes known to

129

us His purposes in prayer. Prayer and fasting is needed when we are going to deliver people from demons, and God will show us His will in this matter. We touch God's throne in intercessory prayer, and this endues us with His strength and power to do what is needed. Are we willing to be taught how to pray? Many are the plans in the heart of man, but it is the Lord's purposes that must prevail. It is no longer what I want, or think I need, it is Him that must increase, and I must decrease. The only way we can know the plan of God for our lives is through prayer, He will show us His plan only when it is His will to do so. If we knew every single thing that He has for our lives, we could well be overwhelmed, for our future is in His hands. It is only when we are going to work for Him, that we need to know His direction. His will for us all is that we should be conformed to the image of His Son (Ro 8:29). As we give ourselves to prayer and His word we will grow to maturity so that we can minister to a lost and dying world. As we give ourselves in full commitment, and make ourselves available to Him, the life of Christ within our hearts will be released to reach out to others who are bound by the devil. This is our spiritual warfare.

The authority of his word

Revelation 1:2 tells us the word of God is the testimony of Jesus Christ. It is also the word of prophecy, and it says in verse 3, "Blessed is the one who reads the words of this prophecy, and blessed are those who hear it and take to heart what is written in it, because the time is near." The disciples were taught by Christ through Old Testament Scriptures. Jesus Christ is the very breath of the testimony of the prophets, for the Old Testament Scriptures were fulfilled in Him. We are a kingdom. "To him who loves us and has freed us from our sins by his blood, and has made us to be a kingdom and priests to serve his God and Father" (Rev 1:5-6). Details of how we should serve Him are found in God's word. In Revelation 1:19 John was told to write what he had seen, and what was taking place then, and what would happen in the future—which is now. We can understand what is taking place now by the revelation of the Holy Spirit, and by the written word of God.

If we want Christ to rule in our lives, if we want to experience kingdom rule and reign with Him, we must play our part and obey His word. Jesus said in John 14:21, ''Whoever has my commands and obeys them, he is the one who loves me. He who loves me will be loved by my Father, and I too will love him and show myself to him.'' Jesus will reveal Himself to us as we obey His commands. If we do not obey His commands our victory will be lost. We must put into practice what God is saying. If we want to hear what God is saying, and be blessed by it, we must do as He says. What is the use of hearing His voice, if we do not obey it? How can he bless us if we do not obey His word? There must be a desire in our hearts to hear His voice and obey His word.

There is a restoration today of the teaching ministry, revealing the deep truths of God to us. God speaks to His children through His word, and the gifts of the Holy Spirit.

The prophetic voice is also being heard again today, and we must have open hearts to receive what God is saying to us. When God speaks through prophecy, people with open hearts will understand clearly what God is saying to them. It will give them insight, wisdom and knowledge of the deep truths of God's word, and they will know how to apply it to their lives. The preaching of God's word under the anointing of the Holy Spirit brings about transformation in people's lives. It brings about conversion, healing and release from the grip of Satan. There are many false doctrines going around today, and when we have knowledge of God's word, we can recognise them, and it is important that we do recognise them, or we could be led into error and bondage. If what we hear is not found in God's word, or is twisted in any way, we should shun it completely.

His word is eternally settled in heaven, it cannot be altered.

Throughout this book, God's word is being quoted, for without it, this and everything I endeavour to do for God will be of no avail. I love His word, I have come to lean on it more and more. There are many treasures found in His word, many words of comfort, and guidance to steer me through this world. God does not leave us without a light to guide us; how much we need the truth of God's word in a world that is darker than ever before. God's word is a firm foundation to build upon, to go astray from it will lead to the complete collapse of our house, our building. When we build on His word He will bring forth fruit in our lives for the glory of God, which will build up our faith, and bring comfort in times of difficulty and hardship.

The key of the Holy Spirit

In John 2:1–11 we read about the first miracle that Jesus performed, when he turned water into wine at a wedding in Cana in Galilee. They had run out of wine, and nearby stood six stone water jars. Jesus said to the servants, ''Fill the jars with water'' so they filled them to the brim. Then He told them to pour the water, and it turned into wine. The best wine was left to the last.

We are living in the last days today, and God is pouring out the wine of the Holy Spirit upon all flesh. The best wine of the Holy Spirit is kept for this day of visitation. The vessels need to be filled to the brim, not half full, and we, the children of God are the vessels that God wants to fill with the fullness of the Holy Spirit. Holy Spirit prayer, praise and worship will transform us. Holy Spirit praying, preaching, praise and worship in His house prepares the way for the Lord to move in people's hearts. Holy Spirit prayer, praise and worship will create an atmosphere where God can move in and do His work. We must have open hearts to receive what God is doing today. God has difficulty with those who have an independent spirit, because their hearts are closed to what He is doing, and what He wants to do in this world. It is very sad when Christians think they know it all and are unteachable, because they cannot receive what God wants them to receive, a fresh in-filling of His Spirit in their lives, anointing upon their ministry for the Lord. 1 Corinthians 3:9 says, "For we are God's fellow-workers; you are God's field, God's building." He is pouring out the rain of the Holy Spirit upon His people, His field, His building, in order for it to produce fruit.

Our lives are made richer and softer when we allow the Holy Spirit to work in our lives. God wants us to experience a greater outpouring of the Holy Spirit in our lives today. Satan's onslaught on the world is real and very strong, and the Holy Spirit is the only answer, the only way through which we will have power to reach out into the darkness, and pull out of the strong-holds of Satan. Holy Spirit-filled people are the only ones who can be used mightily of God to release the prisoners of darkness. The Holy Spirit will also enable us to rule and reign over circumstances which are against us.

When Paul was in Ephesus, he found some disciples, and asked them if they had received the Holy Spirit when they believed; they answered they had not even heard that there was a Holy Spirit. So Paul asked what baptism they had received, and they replied, "John's baptism." Paul said that John's baptism was a baptism of repentance, and John had told the people to believe in the one coming after him, who was Jesus. When they heard this they were baptised in the name of the Lord Jesus. Paul placed his hands on them, and the Holy Spirit came upon them, and they spoke in tongues and prophesied (Ac 19:1-7). There are still people today who have never heard of the baptism of the Holy Spirit, or the gifts of the Holy Spirit, because in some places it has not been preached. Perhaps some of them have been put off the baptism of the Holy Spirit, because of some of the excesses they have seen, or have heard about. Some do not believe that the baptism of the Holy Spirit is for us today, but just for the birth of the New Testament church. The Bible, however, tells us this, ''Repent and be baptised, every one of you, in the name of Jesus Christ for the forgiveness of your sins. And you will receive the gift of the Holy Spirit. The promise is for you and your children and for all who are far off—for all whom the Lord our God will call'' (Ac 2:38–39).

We can experience the baptism of the Holy Spirit today, and God is pouring out His Holy Spirit in a mighty way. Miracles are happening today, sick bodies are being healed, the demon possessed are being set free. Those who have been caught up in occult practices, those on drugs, those whose lives have been broken and ruined, are being marvellously delivered and restored.

Preparation for kingdom living was given to us through Christ and the apostles. Kingdom living itself, is just a preparation for the time when we will be living in His presence continually. So it is wise, and also a source of great blessing to get some practice in now. Kingdom living should come naturally, because the kingdom of God dwells within us now. So let us live in victory, confident and joyful, free from fear, worry or stress and strain, so that others will be attracted to us, and we can then talk to them about our Saviour and Lord.

The keys of authority I have mentioned in this chapter are all found in operation in Acts 4:29–31. This was the prayer of the believers: '' 'Now, Lord, consider their threats and enable your servants to speak *your word* with great boldness. Stretch our your hand to heal and perform miraculous signs and wonders through the *name* of your holy servant Jesus.' After they had *prayed*, the place where they were meeting was shaken. And they were all filled with *the Holy Spirit* and spoke the word of God boldly.'' All these keys belong together, although each key has a different function unique in itself. They all work in harmony together, and they are all essential in building up the kingdom of God.

Some time ago I was reading through the book of Nehemiah, that man who had a vision, a burden and a commission from God to rebuild the walls of Jerusalem. The walls of Jerusalem were broken down and the gates were burned with fire. When Nehemiah heard this he mourned and wept, and fasted and prayed before God in heaven. Nehemiah was so sad that it showed on his face, and even the king noticed it asking, "Why does your face look so sad when you are not ill?" Nehemiah answered "Why should my face not look sad when the city where my fathers are buried lies in ruins, and its gates have been destroyed by fire?" (Ne 2:2–3). In other words, Nehemiah said, "I've every right to look sad when my heart is heavy with grief."

Today, when I see the waste places the devil is making in this and other lands: the misery, the pain, the wars, the consequences of sin and godlessness all around me, I can understand how Nehemiah felt. But Nehemiah did not just leave it like that, he did something about it. He had a great burden, and a great vision, and in the end the king himself commissioned him to go and rebuild the broken walls of Jerusalem. While his enemies scoffed, Nehemiah prayed to God and continued with the work God had given him to do. It was no easy task, but he never wavered; he just kept on building up the broken walls and gates. He did not do it alone. The vision of Nehemiah was caught by others, and they helped him in the task God had given him. Everyone involved had a different, important part to play. The high priest rose early in the morning with his brethren to work, and women worked too. There was much to do, and much rubbish had to be cleared away so that the building could begin.

They were well-equipped against the enemy who conspired to hinder the work right from the very beginning. While one half worked, the other half held spears, bows and shields. Some even worked with one hand, and held a weapon in the other, while others blew trumpets to warn of the approaching enemy—these were the watchmen. Every worker held a shield, and they all worked in harmony and unity. How they laboured! From the rising of the sun until the stars appeared at night. How zealous they were in building up the broken walls and gates of Jerusalem!

What we need today are men and women like Nehemiah, with a vision, with a burden, and courage to get on with building up the waste places the devil has made, and is still making in the sin-sick world we live in. We need to rise up in unity and strength, and power to pull down the strongholds of Satan. We need to be men and women with courage, calling and zeal to do what God wants us to do, and to go where He wants us to go.

Oh yes, there will be scoffers, but you will find that the people who scoff do nothing themselves for the Lord. All these people want to do is tear down—but these are the enemies of the Lord, and we should be well equipped against them, just as the watchmen were in Nehemiah's day. The devil is working overtime in diverting, destroying and laying waste precious souls for whom Christ died. We must warn them, we must rescue them before it is too late. We need watchmen who can see with the eyes of faith what is needed to build up the kingdom of God.

We need more men and women of prayer, who can blow away the rubbish that the devil blows in at us, like apathy, unbelief, scoffers, and everyone else who would discourage us from doing the work.

The task of God's children, all of us everywhere, is to create beauty out of the ugliness of this world, and create peace where there is discord and strife. God's children, all of us, should be busy creating love, joy and happier relationships wherever we go. We should be telling people everywhere about the most important and sweetest relationship of all, a personal relationship with the Lord Jesus Christ.

I am glad I read through Nehemiah; because it has helped me. It has enlarged my vision, and encouraged me to go on building up the kingdom of my God. It has helped me to be a better watchman for Him. The hour is getting late. The midnight cry goes out today—will you meet the call? The Lord has given to us, to you and me, the keys of the kingdom, and has given us the authority to bind and loose (Mt 16:19). Will you use those keys?

CHAPTER ELEVEN

The power of love and praise

THE power of love is one of the greatest powers known to men and women. Even those who have never received Jesus as their personal Saviour, know, and have known at some time in their lives, the power of love. The love of a mother for her child is as strong as death, she would willingly lay down her life to save her child. There are all kinds of true stories that have told of the power of human love, where men, women and even children have risked their lives to save another, and have laid down their lives to save people who they have dearly loved. Millions of tears have been shed because of love. Tears of joy, tears of anguish, tears of heart-break and pain have been shed, and still will be, because of love: love of a man for his wife, a wife for her husband, love for parents, love for children, love for brothers and sisters, love for a just cause, love for a country, love for an animal, love for a friend; so powerful is the force of love.

We read in God's word, "God is love." His very nature is love. Love stems from God. Love is a free gift to mankind from God. We read in His word, "How great is the love the father has lavished on us, that we should be called children of God" (1 Jn 3:1). What love can be more merciful, more pure and more kind than the love of Jesus? He loved us even in our sin and shame, and when we cried to Him for mercy, forgiveness, and cleansing, He freely forgave us all. He died that we might be forgiven, restored and healed and free. He never turns anyone away who comes to

Him. Anyone can come to Jesus just as they are, in all their sin and unworthiness, and He takes them into His kingdom of light. What a wonderful Saviour! His love is like a never-ending river that knows no bounds and flows on and on, giving joy and blessing to everyone.

Human love, marvellous though it may be, pales into insignificance compared with His divine love. Human love can be restricted. Its ability to express itself can be limited but the love of God which comes from above is immeasurable. Human love can be debased by lust and deteriorate, or be degraded by jealousy and envy. Many a heart and home has been broken in pursuit of human love, but in God's great love there is no darkness at all. There is no forgetfulness, no unfaithfulness, and no disappointment in God's great love. His love is unfailing. Human love, through disappointments and disloyalty, can turn to hate and bitterness. Some types of love have no vigour or height; they are weak and sickly, they have no power to uplift. The purer love is, the higher it is, and such love always uplifts and never degrades. Restricted love is like a stagnant pool, confined and limited, it cannot flow out.

God's love is liberal and generous. Have you stood beside a waterfall and watched the sunlight play upon the face of the waters as they cascade down? A beautiful sight isn't it! The beauty is the result of the height of its fall. It comes a long way down. That's exactly like the love of Jesus. He came all the way from heaven to earth to show us His love. He came a long way down to pick men and women up. If we want our love to inspire anyone, it must have height and be able to reach down to the deepest depths to lift up, and bring hope to the hopeless, and light in the darkest situation. The love of the Saviour has depth. Jesus stooped low to wash the disciples feet. He sat with publicans and sinners. We read in the Bible that He "made himself nothing, taking the very nature of a servant, being made in human likeness" (Php 2:7). God's love can, and does, reach down to the darkest sinner and lifts them up to sit in heavenly places with Christ Jesus. This is what He did for me and you. What a wonderful Saviour!

What has all this got to do with spiritual warfare, you may ask. Plenty, because only the love of Jesus dwelling in us can warn in love those who are in the evil grasp of the devil, and point them to the Saviour. This needs grace, courage, and a great love for lost and sinful mankind. Satan does not want God's children to have compassion for the lost; no! he would frighten us off for fear of what might happen to us if we dare to even try to reach them with the message of God's love.

I well remember how frightened Christians were of me—and I was a Christian! I had received Jesus as my Saviour but they knew about my past and they just could not believe that I was a true Christian. They were also afraid of what they thought was the evil in me; afraid I would somehow contaminate them if they came too near me. It really upset me. I felt rejected by Christians. I used to go away and cry my eyes out and sometimes this rejection frightened me and it really discouraged me. Not for some time did I realise it was the devil, who was by now my enemy as well as theirs, that brought such fear upon them. Christians seemed to be completely devoid of courage, faith and love, and were really frightened of the devil.

Jesus recognised the need for blending opposites. He knew His disciples would face a difficult and hostile world where they would confront evil at its worst. He knew they would meet cold and arrogant men whose hearts had been hardened by the long winter of traditionalism, so he said to them, "I am sending you out like sheep among wolves." He gave to them a formula for action, "Therefore be as shrewd as snakes and as innocent as doves" (Mt 10:16).

It is difficult to imagine a single person having, simultaneously, the characteristics of a serpent and a dove, but this is what Jesus expects of us. We must, by His grace, combine the toughness of a serpent and the softness of a dove: a tough mind and a tender heart.

Let us consider the need for a tough mind. The tough individual has a strong warrior spirit which makes him able to make decisive judgments and discern truth from falsehood. He is able to make the right decisions at times of utmost importance. He is not chained to conformity, the ''we have always done things this way, so why change now?'' attitude.

Soft-minded people are afraid to step out in faith for fear of failure and upsetting the crowd. Soft-minded people swallow up everything that looks interesting, from an orange to a tennis ball. The tendency for soft-mindedness is found in man's unbelievable gullibility. Take TV adverts for instance; advertisers have long since learned that most people are soft-minded and they capitalize on this susceptibility with skilful and effective slogans. Few people have the toughness of mind to judge critically and discern the true from the false, fact from fiction. Our minds are constantly invaded by half truths and false information. We must be more mature and strong in our discernment, strong in our decisions in this world of deceit. Soft-minded individuals are prone to embrace all kinds of superstitions. Their minds are constantly invaded by irrational fears, which range from fear of Friday the 13th, to the fear of a black cat crossing their path. The soft-minded man always fears change. He feels security in the status-quo and has a morbid fear of the new. For him the greatest pain is the pain of new ideas, because new ideas involve thinking, and thinking is a pain to him. He wants to freeze the moment, and hold life in the gripping yoke of sameness. Change is too hard; it's a pain for him to have to think things through, it's safer and easier for him to do things on the spur of the moment without thinking of the possible consequences. In the days we are living in there seems to be a universal quest for quick answers and half-baked solutions.

Now let us consider the hard-hearted person. The hard-hearted individual never truly loves. He never experiences the beauty of friendship because he is too cold to feel affection for another and is too self-centred to share another's joy and sorrow. He or she is an isolated island. No outpouring of love links him or her to the mainland of humanity. People can stay on an island of isolation for years, never seeking to reach out, or cry for help, to those who pass by. The hard-hearted person never sees people as people, but rather more like objects or cogs in a wheel. The hard-hearted man depersonalizes life itself. Often these people have had little or no love shown to them. They have never experienced real love so they are unable to show love or express love. The fear of rejection holds many back. Rejection is tragic; it leaves a wound so deep that nothing can cleanse or heal it, except the loving, healing hand of God.

The greatness of our God lies in the fact that He is both tough-minded and tender-hearted. He has qualities of sternness and gentleness. He expresses His toughness in His justice and wrath against wickedness, and His tender-heartedness in His grace, mercy, and compassion. On the one hand God is a God of justice who punished Israel for her waywardness, and on the other hand He is a forgiving Father, whose heart is filled with unspeakable joy when He sees sinners repenting and prodigals returning home. If God were only tough-minded He would be a cold, passionless despot, sitting in some far-off heaven disdaining the human race. If God on the other hand were only soft-hearted, He would be too soft and sentimental to function when things go wrong and would be incapable of controlling what He had made. God is tough enough to transcend the world, and He is tender-hearted enough to live in it. He put on the form of a servant and dwelt among men.

There are times when we need to know that our God is a God of justice. When the lumbering giants of injustice emerge on the earth and cause suffering and pain to untold millions, we need to know that there is a God of swift wrath, who can cut them down and leave them to wither like grass in the sun. When our efforts fail to stop the surging sweep of oppression, we need to know that in this universe there is a God whose matchless strength is a solid contrast to the sordid weaknesses of men.

There are also times when we desperately need to know that our God is a God who possesses compassion and mercy. When we are shattered by the stormy blast that rages around us, when the storms of disappointment threaten to overcome us, we can call upon a tender-hearted God for courage and strength. When our courage fails it is good to know we serve a God who is able to sustain us with His power and might. It is good to know that our God can refill us and refresh us with His tender loving care.

We need the strength to love with a love like God's. Strength to be tough when the situation calls for it, and strength to be humble enough to love the unlovely. God hates sin, but He loves the sinner. He can and He will give us the courage to stand up and be counted among those who stand for righteousness and justice. When we can love with a love like God's, the devil and all his agents will flee from us in fear. My desire is to have the strength to love like Jesus loves, to have the courage to be tough, and to know the gentleness of heart that Jesus has, because: ''You stoop down to make me great'' (2 Sa 22:36).

I have known His tenderness, I have felt His gentleness for me and I have felt with wonder, thrills of holy grace. God's love is as wide as the ocean, deeper than the deepest sea, higher than the highest heaven, and broad enough to encompass the whole human race. God loves witches and satanists! He does not love the sin of witchcraft, He hates it, but all sin is sin and there is no such thing as white lies with God: all lies are lies. God does not put sins into categories labelling one sin worse than another. Rejection of Christ and the way of salvation He offers us, is just as sinful as hatred, pride and jealousy. It is easy to condemn occult practices, but let us be careful not to condemn people. We must remember that God sent His son to die for the whole human race. Let us ask God to fill our hearts with His love for *all* lost and sinful mankind. He came to die for the sins of the whole world. I want to be able to see with the eyes of Christ, love with the heart of Christ, listen with the ears of Christ, lift up with the tender hand of Christ, and be tough with everything that is anti-Christ.

While I have been writing this chapter about the power of love, I have felt the blessing and the love of God welling up within me. Having just read through what I have written, I got so excited I just wanted to go on writing about the love of God because it thrills me so much. I realised that I could never come to an end of speaking about His great and wondrous love. When you begin to meditate on the love of God, speak about the love of God, write about the love of God, a great joy floods your very being, and this leads me naturally and easily into the next section of this chapter.

The power of praise

The purest, sweetest, praise must surely come from a heart that is filled with a tremendous love for God. At these times of blessing, being alone with God, or gathered together with others for prayer, it is easier to praise the Lord. But what about the times when it is not so easy to praise the Lord? I have often been in situations where I have felt far removed from praising God and it is just at these times we should praise the Lord. In the Book of Psalms we read how David praised God in every circumstance. By the very act of praising God his faith was strengthened. He never doubted God had the battle won, even before it commenced. Praise brings faith and faith brings hope; therefore praise, faith and hope will always be intertwined. Faith helps us to accept the divine promises of God in their divine reality; hope goes on to embrace the promises which have already been accepted, and faith is the substance of things hoped for, the evidence of things unseen. When we start to praise the Lord He will honour us, and give us the victory.

David the psalmist shouted the victory against overwhelming odds. He knew God was on his side; he said in Psalm 34:1, "I will extol the Lord at all times; his praise will always be on my lips." When everything and everyone seems to be against us we should start to praise the Lord for the challenge, praise Him for the answers, praise Him for the wisdom he will give us, and He will do the rest. He will not let us down when we honour Him in this way. Remember the disciples of Jesus? They were so discouraged and so fearful because their beloved Master had been crucified and buried. They were gathered behind locked doors for fear of the Jews. At that time they were living on the dark side of the cross, the defeat side of the cross. Many church-goers who have never come to a saving knowledge of His grace are doing just that today—they do not see the Saviour risen, alive, powerful and real. They are dragging around a dead Saviour, and have still got the Lord Jesus nailed to the cross.

Discouragement knocks people flat, and Satan knows it. It is the most powerful tool the enemy has and he uses it to the full. Satan hates to see the child of God on his knees and he hates to see him praising God, so he soon turns tail and runs. I myself was very nearly flattened by discouragement shortly after becoming a Christian, when my fellow Christians avoided me and were afraid of me and could not believe I was a true Christian. "See that," said Satan, "they don't believe you are a Christian, so you may as well give up being one." Satan tried to tell me that I was unwanted by the Christians, therefore God did not want me either. This was a clever trick of the devil, but even though you do not know all the secrets, because you are just a babe in Christ, the Lord knows how to encourage His children and Satan will be put down. No matter how the devil tried to stop me from going on with the Lord, I somehow knew that the Lord did want me and I was indeed a child of God.

Paul must have felt discouraged at times because his past was too fresh in the minds of the Christians of his day, and they did not accept him at first. Through it all Paul went on preaching the gospel and the Lord honoured him with souls. I well remember when I first started to preach the grand-old gospel story: it was in a public house, not a church, and I got more converts than the Christians who went to the church I used to attend. I asked some Christians once, "How many souls have been converted recently?" They looked at me as if I was quite mad. "We do not get many people coming to the church to be saved," they said. "Why?" I wanted to know. "Well, it is not easy to get people saved" they replied. "I preach to people where they are, I go to them, and they do listen, and some do get saved" I replied. I asked the Christians to come with me, and help me, but they were too afraid to come.

So I started to praise the Lord for all the people who would get saved through my ministry on the streets and in the public houses, and the outcome was absolutely amazing—I was leading them to the Lord every single time I went out. I might not have had much encouragement from Christians but the Lord honoured me by giving me souls and it seemed worth all the rejection from my fellow Christians. Praise to God drowns out discouragement and the victory is sure. Listen to what it says in the good news for modern man; these are the words of Jesus Himself: "Blessed are you when people insult you, persecute you and falsely say all kinds of evil against you because of me. Rejoice and be glad because great is your reward in heaven, for in the same way they persecuted the prophets who were before you" (Mt 5:11–12).

If I was able to lead people to the Lord in the public houses and on the streets of Bristol in the early sixties, surely Christians can do the same in the nineties because the Lord has not changed. I believe there will come a time when the gospel will *have* to be preached more on the streets than anywhere else, because this is the place where those who Jesus wants to save will be. Do you realise that more people walk the streets today? More are homeless today, more are roaming the streets as prostitutes today, more young people are unemployed and just drifting around, bored and lonely, with nothing to do and nowhere to go. So what better place to meet them and tell them about the Saviour?

Young Christians, the Lord is looking for you. He knows you can reach people for Himself. He knows they will listen to what you say. Do not let the devil drag them down to hell—go out there and compel them to come into the kingdom of light. Go out there to them, praising the Lord, despite the setbacks. The devil will try to make it look too hard for you; take no notice of him, he is a liar anyway, he cannot tell the truth. Go out in joy and prove for yourselves how faithful and powerful love and praise is. Prove the power of love and praise.

I wish I was still young and strong in health to be able to do street evangelism. I would be out there as often as I could, having the joy of seeing Satan fleeing down the street defeated. Do not be afraid of those who are involved in occult practices, the devil cannot harm you if you belong to Jesus Christ. Jesus is stronger than Satan and sin. The devil is far more afraid of you, so do what the Lord commands: "Preach the gospel to every creature." Do it in the power of the Holy Spirit; do it in great and tender compassion; do it in great joy; do it in boldness.

Do not fear demons, demons cannot harm you either. Remember: "Greater is He who is in you, than he that is in the world." In the name of Jesus, devils fear and fly. The curse of a witch cannot harm you, nothing can harm you. Read, and believe the word of God, and claim the promises of God. Read what the Bible has to say regarding your protection from the power of demons and the authority Jesus has given you over them. Try to memorise these Scriptures as this will be a powerful and effective tool against the lies of the enemy. I have quoted many of these Scriptures throughout this book, see if you can remember them. Fear of demons is only one of the devil's tricks to stop people from reaching out to those who are involved in occult practices, because the devil just does not want them to be delivered and neither does he want you to get powerful in the Holy Spirit for fear he may lose even more of his slaves. When those who have been bound by the devil in occult practices receive the Lord as their Saviour, encourage them in every way. Let them know they are accepted by you, and love them with the love of the Lord. Treat them no differently to anyone else who comes to the Lord because they are no different. God is not a respecter of persons (Ac 10:34).

So young people, go forth in the name of Jesus and meet the needs of the people who are lonely, lost in sin, and bound by the devil. Ask the Lord to fill your heart with compassion for those who are in the darkness. Be filled with the Spirit, go out and slay the giants in the name of Jesus for the Lord is with you and will greatly bless you and give you even more power, even more courage, even more love, even more authority over the devil. Deplete the kingdom of darkness and swell the ranks of the army of the Lord.

CHAPTER TWELVE

The army of the Lord

"**F**INALLY, be strong in the Lord and in his mighty power. Put on the full armour of God so that you can take your stand against the devil's schemes" (Eph 6:10–11).

Does Satan give up on us after we become Christians? Does he leave us alone? No! Satan never gives up; as long as we inhabit these mortal bodies he opposes us. Satan cannot undo our salvation, but he will do his utmost to render us powerless and ineffective as far as spreading the good news of salvation is concerned. He can cause us to grow cold and indifferent toward the things of God, and apathetic about the lost. He can rob us of vision, faith, power and love, if we allow him to.

As Paul concludes his letter to the Ephesians, he depicts the Christian pathway as a struggle, an active fight against Satan and the powers of darkness. As Christians we are called to warfare. Our repentance and faith in Jesus Christ is not the end, it is essentially a struggle against Satan and sin, and the works of evil, some of which you have been reading about in this book. In this fight we are not left to fend for ourselves. The full armour of God is at our disposal, and with this defence we can stand against the wiles of the devil, and anyone and anything the devil uses to oppose us. We are faced with forces of evil today such as have never been known before. We are not in civvy street, we cannot take our boots off, and rest on our laurels: we are in the army, God's army, and the Lord wants us to work together with Him, so that the army will grow, both in numbers and in His strength and power.

We are instructed to be strong in God's mighty power by putting on the full armour of God (not just part of it). The devil has weapons which he uses against the children of God, and we too need weapons, and we have them, and the authority to use them. We are soldiers of the cross, soldiers of Christ the King, we belong to the army of the Lord. And the Lord's army is far greater and stronger than the army of Satan. Jesus, who is the author of our salvation, is also our Captain, and He goes before us. The battle is the Lord's, He fights for us and with us, and we must keep our eyes on Him (Heb 12:2).

Paul was often in prison, often in chains (2 Co 11:23) which gave him time to take in every part of the Roman soldier's dress. He would have been able to give an accurate description of the armour, and this probably inspired him to write Ephesians 6:10–18, giving us a spiritual picture of the armour of God, and how to fight the good fight of faith which he mentions in 1 Timothy 6:12 and 2 Timothy 4:7.

In an army every soldier is properly equipped for battle, and trained for warfare, or they would be cut down on the battlefield. They are taught how to use their weapons, and are expected to be well-disciplined and obedient to their superiors. As soldiers of Christ we should be the same. It is only those who are obedient to Him, and walk in His ways, who will be victorious. We must obey Him in every area of our lives: "Whoever has my commands and obeys them, he is the one who loves me" (Jn 14:21). God has set His leaders in His army and we must submit to their authority, for it comes from God (Heb 13:17). There are many today who will not submit to the leadership which God has placed in His house: they would rather do their own thing, and go their own way. Is it any wonder that so many are so easily led astray, and fall into deception and error?

We are instructed to endure hardship as good soldiers

of Christ Jesus, and not be influenced by the opinions of those who are not in the army of the Lord. "It is better to trust in the Lord than to put confidence in man" (Ps 118:8 AV). A good example is set us in 2 Timothy 2:3–5 and in Hebrews 12:7–12. It may seem hard, but it produces results, it produces fruit, and it is for our good.

As true soldiers of Christ we are instructed to put on the full armour—literally the panoply of God. Paul urges us to an awareness of the nature of the fight, he warns us against the wiles of the devil (Eph 6:11) and urges us to know his strategy. Satan is a very subtle foe and works and plots, not openly, but by stealth and cunning behind the scenes. It is not a fight against flesh and blood, but against the rulers, against the authorities, against the powers of this dark world, and against the spiritual forces of evil in the heavenly realms. The principalities and powers of which Paul speaks in Ephesians 6:12 appear to be beings and forces that originated in creation (Col 1:16), but now stand against God. These are coupled with the world rulers of darkness who, according to the book of Daniel, appear to be demonic forces who control the evil ambitions of nations and rulers in an attempt to undermine the will of God. Great wickedness is not the result of a badly adjusted society, or the petty failings of a few individuals at the top. There is a mighty force of evil trying to govern a world system against the will of God.

If we minimise the power of the devil or of evil, we do so at our own risk. The enemy is spiritual, the foe we face today attacks minds, bodies and spirits. His sphere of operation is described as being in "high places" literally, "heavenly places". He attacks the place to which the sinner has been raised by the quickening effects of salvation. Ephesians 2:6 says: "God raised us up with Christ and seated us with him in the heavenly realms in Christ Jesus." Satan wants to bring us down, to seek to poison our sanctification, to damage our faith, to block the process of holiness, to penetrate the realm of our thoughts, and to pervert the very high calling of

God. This is the enemy, and this is spiritual wickedness in high places.

The enemy is very real, and the effects of his activities are very real and often devastating. He seeks to enter each day to insinuate his purpose into our very thoughts and actions. Never underestimate him, for to do so would mean that we lack awareness both of the nature of the fight against Satan, and the forces of darkness with which we contend.

The first, and perhaps the most important part of the armour of God is the helmet of salvation. First of all you must be born again by the Spirit of God: "Clothe yourselves with the Lord Jesus Christ" (Ro 13:14); "Put on the new self" (Eph 4:24). The "new self" is the regenerated person as distinguished from the "old self" (Ro 6:6), and is a new person in having become a partaker of Christ's divine nature and life (Col 3:3–4). In no sense is the "old self" improved in any way. "Therefore, if anyone is in Christ, he is a new creation; the old has gone, the new has come!" (2 Co 5:17). The "new self" is Christ, "formed" in the Christian. "For it is by grace you have been saved, through faith—and this is not from yourselves, it is the gift of God—not by works, so that no-one can boast" (Eph 2:8–9). Christ is our salvation.

We must understand what wearing the helmet of salvation means. We know salvation, or deliverance from the *penalty* of sin, as we accept Christ as our personal Saviour. We can know salvation, or deliverance from the *power* of sin, as we continue to follow Him and obey His commands. I like what it says in John 1:12 (AV): "But as many as received him, to them gave he *power* to become the sons of God, even to them that believe on his name." As we wear this helmet daily, we shall know salvation from the *presence* of sin in the future, when the Church Militant becomes the Church Triumphant at the second coming of Christ—the hope of our salvation. Exciting, isn't it?

Furthermore, the constant wearing of the helmet of salvation is a protection from the onslaughts of Satan to the mind. God's word tells us to, "Be transformed by the renewing of your mind" (Ro 12:2). How do we do this? By reading God's word, by believing God's word, and by putting it into practice. In Isaiah 26:3 we read, "You will keep in perfect peace him whose mind is steadfast, because he trusts in you." God also gives us a sound mind (2 Ti 1:7 AV). There is often a battle in the mind. Satan is clever, he knows the mind is the greatest battlefield, and he can have a field day if you let him. Christians have said to me while I have been counselling them, "I can't help it; sinful thoughts keep coming to my mind." I have replied, "We may not be able to stop wrong thoughts coming to our minds, but we can choose what to do with them after they get there." There is an old saying which is so true, "You can't stop the birds flying over your head, but you can stop them from building a nest in your hair." If we harbour wrong thoughts instead of taking authority over them in the name of Jesus, it will cause much spiritual bondage. We do not have to allow our minds to be used like an open field, so that the devil can trample across it, and use it as a dustbin. We do not have to be governed by sinful thoughts. In God's word we read, "We demolish arguments and every pretension that sets itself up against the knowledge of God, and we take captive every thought to make it obedient to Christ" (2 Co 10:5).

Wearing the helmet of salvation we enjoy spiritual blessing in Christ: "Praise be to the God and Father of our Lord Jesus Christ, who has blessed us in the heavenly realms with every spiritual blessing in Christ" (Eph 1:3). So let us enjoy our salvation, live out our salvation to the full, sing about our salvation, talk about our salvation! Then we will experience the reality of Philippians 4:6–7: "Do not be anxious about anything, but in everything, by prayer and petition with thanksgiving, present your requests to God. And the peace of God, which transcends all understanding, will guard your hearts and your minds in Christ Jesus."

Working from the head downwards, the next piece of

the armour of God is the breastplate of righteousness. When we experience salvation, we start to walk a new pathway. Jesus, our Captain, is also the Good Shepherd, and guides us in the paths of righteousness (Ps 23:3). Christ is our righteousness. We have no righteousness of our own, but He gives us His righteousness. As we are obedient to Him and follow Him, this righteousness will increase in us. The righteousness which Paul speaks of in Ephesians 6:14 is not the righteousness that Christ imputes to us, but the practice of righteousness, the character of the believer, which springs up from the righteousness that Christ imputes to us as believers. We must put on righteousness, as a deliberate act, in obedience to God's word. Doing what is right and pleasing to God, and avoiding that which is not righteous, will give us sure victory over the devil, and it will be a testimony to those who are lost. Righteousness is another part of the protective armour of God.

The next part of the armour is the belt of truth. In Paul's day the belt was the symbol of the Roman soldier. The girding up of the loins, the gathering up of the garment under the belt, was a prelude to marching, and indeed fighting. The soldier was made more mobile, and naturally more effective. We, as Christ's soldiers, must don the belt of truth as an act of obedience. We must always speak the truth, and hate all lies and deceit, cast away all that is false and untrue, which would cause us to fall on the battlefield. We cannot be hindered by dishonesty, disloyalty, or deceit as true soldiers of the cross. Jesus is all truth; He is the way, the *truth* and the life, and He will lead us into all truth. It gives God great joy to see His children walking in the truth, because this means we are being conformed to the likeness of His Son. The devil is a liar and the father of lies. He is delighted when God's children resort to lies and deceit, and will entice them into further falsehoods and keep them defeated. So it is of vital importance for Christian soldiers to surround themselves with the truth at all times. Truth is found in

God's word; His word is true from the beginning, so let us please His great heart of love and walk in the light of truth, and put Satan to flight.

Paul speaks of our feet being shod "with the preparation of the gospel of peace" (Eph 6:15 AV). In Paul's time, gall traps, or sharp sticks, were set into the ground to impede the progress of approaching armies, so the feet of the Roman soldier needed to be well shod to surmount these obstacles. We too, by constant renewal in the gospel of Jesus Christ, must be ready and alert. There must be preparation of the heart and mind in order to bring the good news of the gospel to those who are lost. We must be prepared to go where He wants us to go, and do what He wants us to do. Let us also be aware of the obstacles that Satan would place in our pathway to try to stop us from doing this, and then we can march forward sure-footed to victory.

The Christian soldier is now clothed from head to foot in the full armour of God, but three other vital elements are needed: the shield of faith, the sword of the Spirit, which is the word of God, and prayer in the Spirit. The Roman shield, which was made of wood and then covered in leather, was large enough to protect the whole body. In ancient warfare, missiles, first dipped in tar and then ignited, were hurled through the air at the advancing army, which was why Paul used the expression "flaming arrows". The shield not only protected the Roman soldier by stopping the flaming arrows, but actually extinguished their flames, making them totally harmless.

The shield of faith performs the same function for the Christian soldier. With faith as our protection we can render all the flaming arrows of opposition, fear, doubt and anything else the enemy would hurl at us, completely harmless and useless. Satan will endeavour to shake our faith and confidence in our God, in His love for us, in His word, His protection, His power, His faithfulness, His mercy and grace. He often uses human circumstances in order to do this, and we must be aware of his sinister schemes. We must hold up the shield of faith, by putting our complete trust in our God, for He is faithful. He is mighty and strong; He never fails us even though we at times may fail Him. He remains faithful and true forever; he cannot break His word. The Bible gives numerous accounts of how God rewarded His servants who put their complete trust in Him. Even though everything else was against them, God never let them down once, and neither will He let us down. In Hebrews 11:6 we read: "Without faith it is impossible to please God." But with God nothing is impossible. Faith in God is a mighty weapon against the enemy of our souls, so let us use it. Let us put it into operation so that God will reward us, and Satan will flee.

No soldier is properly equipped without his sword. The shield protected the Roman soldier, but his sword slew the enemy and eliminated him altogether. We can do the same with the sword of the Spirit, which is the word of God. We can slay the enemy of our souls with the word of God. Satan hates God's word, because God's word is infallible. The integrity of the word is the basis of faith, so faith and God's word always go together. The reason for unbelief and a faltering faith is a lack of assurance of the integrity of the promises in the word of God. In Romans 10:8 it is called, "the word of faith." God's word gives birth to faith; it is God's faith expressed. Hebrews 11:3 states: "By faith we understand that the universe was formed at God's command, so that what is seen was not made out of what was visible." All God did to create was to say, "Let there be," and there leapt into being the things that are. God and His word are one. He named Jesus "the Word": "In the beginning was the Word, and the Word was with God, and the Word was God. He was with God in the beginning. Through him all things were made; without him nothing was made that has been made" (Jn 1:1–3). God linked Himself with His word. He made Himself part of it, and you cannot separate Him from His word.

In Genesis 22:16–17 we read this: "I swear by myself . . .

I will surely bless you and make your descendants as numerous as the stars in the sky and as the sand on the seashore.'' This was God's promise that backed the Abrahamic Covenant. Abraham believed just what was spoken to him. He did not waver through unbelief regarding the promise of God, but was strengthened in his faith, being fully persuaded that God had power to do what He had promised.

All heaven is behind God's word and backs up God's word. The very throne of God is behind God's word and Jesus and the Father are behind the throne. They are all a part of this word, and he watches over His word to fulfil its promises for, ''He cannot deny himself'' (2 Ti 2:13 AV).

In 1 Thessalonians 2:13 Paul thanked God that the people received his words as the word of God: ''And we also thank God continually because, when you received the word of God, which you heard from us, you accepted it not as the word of men, but as it actually is, the word of God, which is at work in you who believe.'' The word of God is active; it is always for now, it is never old, it is always fresh and new. The word of God is like its author: eternal, unchanging, living. ''The word of God is living and active. Sharper than any double-edged sword, it penetrates even to dividing soul and spirit, joints and marrow; it judges the thoughts and attitudes of the heart'' (Heb 4:12). Now notice the next verse: ''Nothing in all creation is hidden from God's sight. Everything is uncovered and laid bare before the eyes of him to whom we must give account.'' Of what is he speaking? He is speaking of the living Word, Jesus, who is the Word!

The Father's word in the mouth of Jesus accomplished things. It stilled the storm; it quietened the wind; it healed the sick, cast out demons, raised the dead and fed the multitudes. His living word on our lips today can do the same thing. When you know, without a shadow of doubt that the Word of God is speaking, you will speak the word with authority. Remember, that faith in God is faith in His word. The senses war against the recreated spirit holding it in bondage, refusing to act on the word, and until the mind is renewed, the word will never have its proper place in the believer's life. Reason must give place to the word of God, for reason often robs the word of God of its authority. When you know that His word is as authoritative today as it was when it fell from the lips of Jesus, then the word will be a living reality in you.

Let the word of God dwell in you richly. Start to confess the word. Hide God's word in your heart. Meditate upon His word and let it grow in you. Stand upon His word. Act upon His word. His word is a living message to us now. The reality of His word flowing through us, throbbing in us, is real; it is the foundation for faith, and faith gives substance to prayer, and makes prayer a reality. It gives us boldness to enter the holy place. What a mighty sword! What a deadly weapon it is to Satan! Soldiers of Christ, use your swords, come against the enemy with it, cut down the forces of evil in His name.

We are surrounded by demonic forces that are dominating the earth, and if the church hasn't authority over these, then no-one has. But the church has, and prayer is its method of dominating these forces. Everyone has a place in the prayer life; God has no inferior sons and daughters. There is no useless member in the physical body and neither is there in the spiritual body. God has planned the body of Christ with infinite wisdom, and the moment you are born again by the Spirit of God you have a place in which to function. So take your place, give yourself to prayer and meditation, and the study of God's word. Don't allow anything to stand in the way of finding your place.

No-one can say that they have no responsibility in the prayer life. To see a need, whatever it is, is a call to prayer. There is much need, in our homes, in our schools, in our places of business, in our church, in our nation. There is breakdown in homes, in business, and in spiritual life, because of the absence of intercessory prayer. If you are a wife, a mother, or a husband, there are certain duties which you perform every day for your family. The greatest duty that you can perform will be prayer duty. Paul says, "Pray in the Spirit on all occasions with all kinds of prayers and requests. With this in mind, be alert and always keep on praying for all the saints (Eph 6:18).

Prayer has several elements. It brings you into contact with the Father, and with the Holy Spirit, and with Jesus. All three members of the Godhead are brought into the prayer life. You are praying *to the Father*. You are praying *in the name of Jesus*. You are praying *through the power of the Holy Spirit*. It brings our hearts into contact with the heavenly centre of all divine power. It is possible to spend any length of time in prayer without being affected by it.

In the very beginning the first man, Adam, lived in the presence of the Creator, his Father. He had no sense of inferiority, no sense of fear or guilt, for he belonged, and because he belonged he took his place as a child of God. Then in one foolish moment he sold out all his vast privileges and rights to the enemy, Satan, and was driven away from the presence of God. God then made a covenant with Abraham, giving him a promise of the Messiah to come through his seed. His descendants were also given a Law and a priesthood; the covenant was made with Jehovah through the priest. God dwelt in their midst in the Holy of Holies. No-one could approach Him unless he was covered by a cloud of incense, and had a basin of blood in his hand to sprinkle on the mercy seat, and that could only be done once a year by the appointed priest.

Down through all history, people's hearts have hungered for true worship and true fellowship with the true God. Satan sets up all kinds of diversions, all kinds of perverted worship. The incarnation of Jesus, the birth of Christ into this dark world of sin, was God's master-stroke of love for lost, fallen, deluded mankind. In His life on earth, Jesus talked with God His Father, the God of the Jews, with an intimacy that they could not understand. He called their God His Father. They took up stones to stone Him for it. They accused Him of blasphemy for it. They crucified Him for it. Jesus paid the price of confessing that God was His Father.

Before Jesus died He said, "I am the way and the truth and the life. No-one comes to the Father except through me" (Jn 14:6). Later on, Paul, who was then Saul, was sent to Damascus with authority to arrest any that he found who were of "the Way" (Ac 9:2). There are several other references in Acts to Christianity as "the Way". In his trial, Paul, defending himself, said, "I admit that I worship the God of our fathers as a follower of the Way" (Ac 24:14). Why did he call it "the Way" and preach that Christ was the "Way" into God's presence? Hebrews 10:19–22 makes it clearer: "We have confidence to enter the Most Holy Place by the blood of Jesus, by a new and living way." Jesus, our great High Priest, was the way into the presence of the Father. We can now draw near with sincere hearts in full assurance of faith. We can now understand Mark 15:38, "The curtain of the temple was torn in two from top to bottom."

The sin problem has been settled because Christ was made sin for us, that we might be brought into full fellowship with the Father. God can be approached, he can be met. Why do His children neglect to meet Him in prayer? Adam lost the way, but what Adam lost has now been restored through Christ's death upon the cross, and there is now a restored righteousness, a restored fellowship. When you grasp what this means, you will grasp the meaning of prayer. It means we can stand in the Father's presence without a sense of guilt, condemnation, or inferiority. The last barrier between the Father and His children has been removed for us by Christ, and we can come into His presence with the same freedom that Jesus had. Prayer is not the old idea of pleading, begging, and crying. We can come to the throne of grace with boldness, with confidence, so we may "find grace to help us in our time of need" (Heb 4:16). We stand in God's presence with fullness of joy, fullness of fellowship, fullness of love.

Relationship means nothing without fellowship. Fellowship means "drinking out of the same cup." The Father has called us into communion with His Son; we drink together. We come with the fruit of our lips, our praise and worship. Our prayers are the fruit of the vine. Jesus said of Himself, "I am the vine; you are the branches. If a man remains in me and I in him, he will bear much fruit" (Jn 15:5).

We come into God's presence with thanksgiving. We come with our praise, we come with our love, we come with our heartaches and burdens, and we come with our petitions. Jesus wants us to come, and He also wants us to ask. These are the words of Jesus: "Until now you have not asked for anything in my name. Ask and you will receive," and note his next words, "and your joy will be complete" (Jn 16:24). It says in James 4:2–3 that we do not have because we do not ask, or we ask with the wrong motives. I like what it says in Ephesians 3:20–21; "Now to him who is able to do immeasurably more than all we ask or imagine, according to his power that is at work within us, to him be glory in the church and in Christ Jesus throughout all generations, for ever and ever! Amen." Nothing can take the place of prayer. How desperately we need it! How desperately the church needs it! No wonder Paul said, "Pray in the Spirit on all occasions" (Eph 6:18).

The armour of God is held together with prayer. It is an armour of light. "The night is nearly over; the day is almost here. So let us put aside the deeds of darkness and put on the armour of light" (Ro 13:12). We are children of the light: "You are all sons of the light and sons of the day. We do not belong to the night or to the darkness" (1 Th 5:5). Now notice verse eight, "But since we belong to the day, let us be self-controlled, putting on faith and love as a breastplate, and the hope of salvation as a helmet."

If you can just catch a glimpse, a vision, of the army of the Lord, all marching forward to victory, all clad in the full armour of God, which is an armour of light, picture how great that light would be! Now place yourself in that army, and hear the mighty sound of it. It is the sound of praise, the sound of war, the sound of victory. What an army! When you put yourself in that army there will be no place for the devil, no place for fear, for you will live in victory over all the power of the devil. You will be assured that the devil is a defeated foe—he cannot win. Furthermore, not only is the army of blood-washed saints bigger and greater than the devil's host, but God has a vast army of angels too, and they are on our side. Listen to what it says in Psalm 68:17 AV: ''The chariots of God are twenty thousand, even thousands of angels: the Lord is among them, as in Sinai, in the holy place.'' Tremendous, isn't it? We also read in Hebrews 12:22: ''But you have come to Mount Zion, to the heavenly Jerusalem, the city of the living God. You have come to thousands upon thousands of angels in joyful assembly.'' What a great and might army! What a privilege it is to belong to it, to be part of it! Praise the Lord!

There is a shout of victory in the camp because, ''The angel of the Lord encamps around those who fear him, and he delivers them'' (Ps 34:7). Whatever the devil is doing today, there is still much he cannot do, much he cannot stop. He cannot stop the kingdom of God from increasing and advancing. ''From the days of John the Baptist until now, the kingdom of heaven has been forcefully advancing, and forceful men lay hold of it'' (Mt 11:12). Satan cannot stop the building of Christ's church, His army, and Jesus Himself said, ''I will build my church, and the gates of Hades will not overcome it'' (Mt 16:18).

Jesus has equipped His church with keys and with weapons to use against the devil. ''The weapons we fight with are not the weapons of the world. On the contrary, they have divine power to demolish strongholds'' (2 Co 10:4). Christ is returning for a victorious church, not a defeated one. Christ is returning for a radiant church: ''Christ loved the church and gave himself up for her to make her holy, cleansing her by the washing with water through the word, and to present her to himself as a radiant church, without stain or wrinkle or any other blemish, but holy and blameless" (Eph 5:25–27). To Him be all the praise and glory for evermore!

I have come to the end of this book. The mystery of iniquity has been revealed, but more important still, so has the way of deliverance; so has the way of restoration; so has the way of victory; so has the way of overcoming iniquity through Christ the risen Lord, so:

> Soldiers of Christ arise,
> And put your armour on,
> Strong in the strength which God supplies
> Through his eternal Son.
>
> From strength to strength go on,
> Wrestle and fight, and pray;
> Tread all the powers of darkness down,
> And win the well fought day.

Classics from KINGSWAY

The Kingsway Classics series presents favourite best-selling titles by well-known authors in special omnibus editions, for the same price as a single-volume paperback.

Classics from Jamie Buckingham
Risky Living, Where Eagles Soar and *A Way Through the Wilderness.*

Classics from Arthur Wallis
Living God's Way, Going On God's Way and *Into Battle.*

Classics from Watchman Nee Vol 1
The Normal Christian Life, Sit Walk Stand and *Changed Into His Likeness.*

Classics from Watchman Nee Vol 2
A Table in the Wilderness, Love Not the World and *What Shall This Man Do?*

Classics on Prayer
Learning the Joy of Prayer by Larry Lea, *Pray in the Spirit* by Arthur Wallis and *Praying Together* by Mike and Katey Morris.

Classics on Worship
Worship by Graham Kendrick, *The Believer's Guide to Worship* by Chris Bowater and *To the Praise of His Glory* by Dave Fellingham.

Classic Real-Life Stories
Vanya by Myrna Grant, *Blood Brothers* by Elias Chacour and *Streetwise* by John Goodfellow.

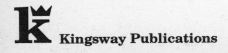

Kingsway Publications

Classics from KINGSWAY

Don't miss the following new titles in the series published in 2001:

Classics on Revival
containing the text of *Revival* by Selwyn Hughes, *Why Revival Tarries* by Leonard Ravenhill and *In the Day of Thy Power* by Arthur Wallis.

Classic Stories: Women of Faith
includes *No Greater Love* by Joy Bath, *Living Under the Volcano* by Christine Perillo and *I Dared to Call Him Father* by Bilquis Sheikh.

Classics from Merlin Carothers
with *Power in Praise*, *Bringing Heaven into Hell* and *What's On Your Mind*.

For further information contact Kingsway Publications at Lottbridge Drove, Eastbourne, East Sussex BN23 6NT (tel: 01323 437700) or email books@kingsway.co.uk